LEANDA DE LISLE

Leanda de Lisle is the highly acclaimed author of three books on the Tudors and Stuarts, including the bestselling *The Sisters Who Would be Queen* and *Tudor: The Family Story*. She regularly writes and speaks on historical matters for TV, radio and a number of publications including *The Times*, the *Spectator* and *Daily Express*. She lives in Leicestershire.

LEANDA DE LISLE

WHITE KING

The Tragedy of Charles I

VINTAGE

1 3 5 7 9 10 8 6 4 2

Vintage
20 Vauxhall Bridge Road,
London SW1V 2SA

Vintage is part of the Penguin Random House group of companies
whose addresses can be found at global.penguinrandomhouse.com.

Penguin
Random House
UK

First published by Chatto & Windus in 2018
First published by Vintage in 2019

penguin.co.uk/vintage

A CIP catalogue record for this book is available from the British Library

ISBN 9780099555278

Printed and bound in Great Britain by Clays Ltd, Elcograf S.p.A.

Penguin Random House is committed to a sustainable future
for our business, our readers and our planet. This book is
made from Forest Stewardship Council® certified paper.

For Peter

Contents

Part Three
HIS TURNCOAT SERVANT

Part Four
NEMESIS

List of Illustrations

Henry Rich, 1st Earl of Holland, studio of Daniel Mytens, *c.* 1632–33 © National Portrait Gallery, London

Henrietta Maria as St Catherine, Anthony Van Dyck, *c.* 1630s © Philip Mould & Company

Lucy Hay, Countess of Carlisle, Adriaen Hanneman, *c.* 1660–65 © Minneapolis Institute of Arts / Bridgeman Images

John Pym, by or after Edward Bower, *c.* 1640 © National Portrait Gallery, London

Louis XIII at the Siege of La Rochelle, French School, *c.* 17th century © La Sorbonne, Paris / Bridgeman Images

Charles I, Anthony Van Dyck, *c.* 1635 (Photo: Royal Collection Trust / © Her Majesty Queen Elizabeth II 2017)

Marie de Rohan, Duchesse de Chevreuse, as Diana the Huntress, attributed to Claure Deruet, 1627 © Castle Museum, Versailles (Photo: Leemage/Corbis via Getty Images)

Charles I, Henrietta Maria and Charles II when Prince of Wales dining in public, Gerrit Houckgeest, 1635 (Photo: Royal Collection Trust / © Her Majesty Queen Elizabeth II 2017)

An Allegory of Marriage, Tiziano Vecellio (Titian), 1576 (Photo © RMN-Grand Palais, Musée du Louvre / Stéphane Maréchalle)

The Five Eldest Children of Charles I, Anthony Van Dyck, 1637 (Photo: Royal Collection Trust / © Her Majesty Queen Elizabeth II 2017)

Second Plate Section

Charles I, studio Anthony Van Dyck, *c.* 1636 © The Weiss Gallery, London

William II, Prince of Orange, and his bride, Mary Stuart, Anthony Van Dyck, 1641. Photo courtesy of Rijksmuseum, Amsterdam

Atrocities in Ireland, from 'The Teares of Ireland' by James Cranford', Wenceslaus Hollar, *c.* 1642–46. Photo © Courtesy of National Library of Ireland, Dublin [PD 2133 TX]

The Chair organ, Robert Dallam, Tewkesbury Abbey © Martin Goetze and Dominic Gwynn Ltd

The execution of Strafford, Wenceslaus Hollar, c. 1641–77. Photo ©
The Thomas Fisher Rare Book Library, University of Toronto, Canada

The death of Boy at Marston Moor, 1644. Photo © Chronicle / Alamy
Stock Photo

Prince Rupert of the Rhine, Gerrit Van Honthorst, c. 1630s–56
© National Trust Images / John Gibbons

The fingernail of Thomas Holland © Courtesy of Tyburn Convent

The saddle used by the King at the Battle to Naseby, Private Collection.
Photo courtesy of Graeme Rimer

The battlefield at Naseby, Robert Streeter, c. 1645

James II & VII, Princess Elizabeth and Henry, Duke of Gloucester,
John Hoskins, c. 1640s © The Fitzwilliam Museum Cambridge

Anne of Austria, queen consort of France, with Louis XIV as a child,
French school, 17th century. Photo: Christophel Fine Art / UIG
via Getty Images

Mary, Princess Royal, studio of Gerrit van Honthorst, c. 1655 © Philip
Mould & Company

Oliver Cromwell, Samuel Cooper, c. 1653 © Philip Mould & Company

Thomas Fairfax, circle of Robert Walker, 17th century. Photo: Lebrecht
Music and Arts Photo Library / Alamy Stock Photo

Charles I at the time of his trial, after Edward Bower, 17th century ©
Philip Mould & Company

Charles I, miniature portrait with mica overlays, artist unknown, c.
1650–1700 © Carisbrooke Castle Museum Trust

Pearl earring owned by King Charles I, removed from the King's ear
after his execution, 1600–10 © The Portland Collection, Harley
Gallery, Welbeck Estate, Nottinghamshire / Bridgeman Images

Portrait of Queen Henrietta Maria as a Widow, artist unknown, c.
1650s. Courtesy of The Walters Art Museum (CC0 1.0)

St George's chapel, Windsor Castle, Josep Renalias, 2008 © Josep
Renalias (CC BY-SA 3.0)

Frontispiece of the *Eikon Basilike*, Wenceslaus Hollar, 1649. Photo ©
The Thomas Fisher Rare Book Library, University of Toronto, Canada

Religious divisions in Europe in 1600

NORWAY
Oslo
SWEDEN

North Sea

DENMARK
Copenhagen

SCOTLAND
Edinburgh

York

Dublin
IRELAND
ENGLAND
London
Calais
English Channel

Amsterdam
Cologne

HOLY
Wittenberg

ROMAN

Prague

EMPIRE
Vienna

Atlantic Ocean

Paris

FRANCE
Basel
Munich
AUSTRIA

Bay of Biscay

La Rochelle
Geneva
Milan
Lyon
Venice

Toulouse
Genoa

SPAIN
Madrid

Rome

PORTUGAL

Lisbon

Mediterranean Sea

Algiers
Tunis

| 0 | 100 | 200 | 300 mi |
| 0 | 100 200 300 400 | 500 km |

Key Catholic — Lutheran — Orthodox

Reformed/Calvinist — Hussite — Muslim

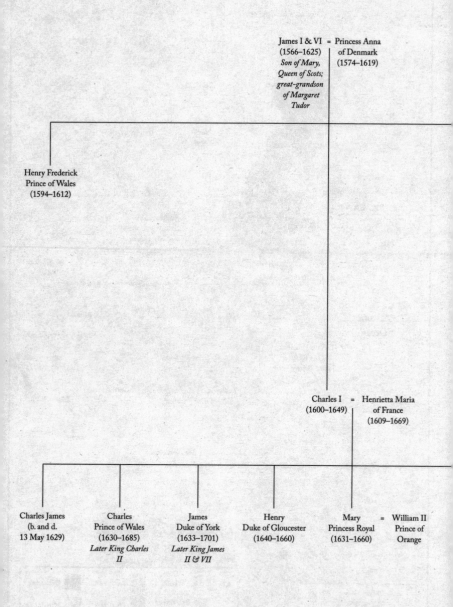

House of Stuart (simplified)

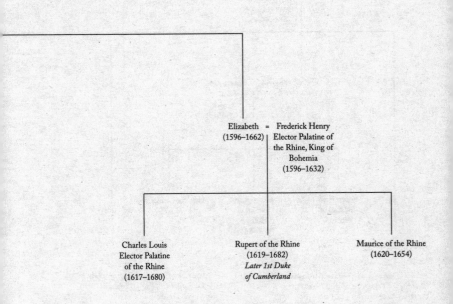

Elizabeth = Frederick Henry
(1596–1662) | Elector Palatine of
the Rhine, King of
Bohemia
(1596–1632)

Charles Louis
Elector Palatine
of the Rhine
(1617–1680)

Rupert of the Rhine
(1619–1682)
*Later 1st Duke
of Cumberland*

Maurice of the Rhine
(1620–1654)

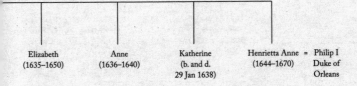

Elizabeth
(1635–1650)

Anne
(1636–1640)

Katherine
(b. and d.
29 Jan 1638)

Henrietta Anne = Philip I
(1644–1670)   Duke of
Orleans

House of Devereux (simplified)

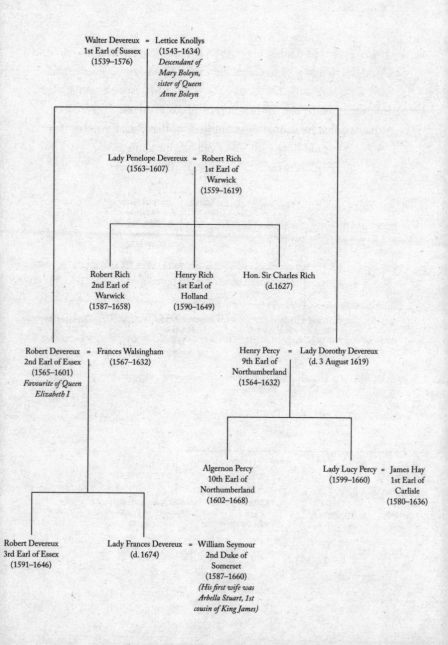

It was observed ... that his majesty on that [coronation] day was clothed in white ... and this some looked on as an ill presage that the king laying aside his purple, the robe of Majesty, should clothe himself in white, the robe of innocence, as if thereby it were fore-ordained that he should divest himself of that Regal majesty that would have kept him from affront and scorn.

Peter Heylyn, *The Life of William Laud*

This Dreadful Deadman, intends nothing I tell thee, but confusion to thy long continued happiness, thy laws and liberties ... The White King and the Dreadful Deadman are all one.

William Lilly, A *Prophecy of the White King and Dreadful Dead Man Explained*

As the King's Body was brought out of St George's Hall, the sky was serene and clear, but presently it began to snow, and fell so fast as by the time they came to the west end of the Royal Chapel the black velvet pall was all white (the colour of innocency) being covered over with snow. So went the white king to his grave, in the 48th year of his age.

Sir Thomas Herbert, *Memoirs*

Author's Note

The title of this book – *White King* – is drawn from a sobriquet used by Charles's contemporaries. To supporters he was the saintly White King crowned in robes the colour of innocence. To opponents he was the White King of the prophecies of Merlin, a tyrant destined for a violent end. It is a sobriquet that is unfamiliar today. I hope it inspires curiosity: that people wonder what other unexpected things they might discover about the extraordinary Charles I.

This portrait, informed by new manuscripts, depicts a king of high ideals, who inspired great loyalty: but who was also a man of flesh and blood. Charles the Martyr and Charles the Murderer, lauded by friends, condemned by enemies, is largely forgotten, but in popular memory something just as extreme remains. Charles has been pinned to the pages of history as a failed king, executed at the hands of his own subjects, and now preserved like some exotic, but desiccated, insect. In many accounts it seems that Charles was doomed to fail almost from birth, his character immutable.

We like to believe we have turned our back on old prejudices but the way we remember Charles shows how they lie just below the surface, still influencing the way we think. In the past disabilities were seen as marks of man's fallen nature. The twisted spine of Shakespeare's Richard III was an outward sign of a twisted soul. It has been surprisingly common for Charles's fate to be read back into the physical difficulties of his childhood, as if his weak legs were physical manifestations of weakness of character. The determination and resilience he showed in overcoming his disability, emerging as an athletic adult, is surely more interesting.

Meanwhile the misconceived traditional view of Charles achieves two things. The first is that it inspires indifference to one of the greatest stories and most significant reigns in royal history. Despite the wealth of exciting new scholarship, and the fascinating women who surrounded Charles, the well trodden ground of the Tudors continues to produce more books for the general reader. Publishers and authors shy away from a riskier subject. The second consequence is that in conveniently blaming Charles for the horrors of the civil wars, it covers the tracks of those others who shared responsibility for the conflicts – and popular memory of the parliamentary heroes of the past could also stand some revision.

Many viewed Charles as a martyr after his execution but *White King* does not attempt to restore him to this position, rather to give him life, to show him grow and change, to place him properly in the context of his times and amongst his contemporaries. Where Charles's story has in the past been given a very masculine focus, here, the leading female political figures of the age, so often forgotten or dismissed, are part of the action.

The lost royal letters, quoted here for the first time, give a voice not only to Charles, but also to his maligned Catholic queen, Henrietta Maria. Her reputation remains lost in the eye of a storm of sexist tropes. Women have always been judged to be creatures of emotion, not of reason, and too often she has been depicted as an hysterical girl who, even as a mature woman, has all the wit and political grasp of a child. It is women who brought evil into the world and Henrietta Maria (despite her supposed stupidity) is still depicted as a seductive Eve to Charles's Adam, leading the king astray.

In *White King* Henrietta Maria is revealed in a new light, as every inch the daughter of the great warrior king, Henri IV of France, and as remarkable a queen as any of the wives of Henry VIII.

The early chapters of *White King* take us into Europe and its empires. This is the world of Charles's sister, the Winter Queen of Bohemia, of Protestant churches in flames and the advance of the Counter-Reformation, of the France of Dumas' *The Three Musketeers* and the Puritan colonies of New England, of a London buzzing with a fast-moving new media reporting on politics from parliament.

Events are underpinned by ideas about power and faith that have a very modern resonance: one where populism meets religious justifications for violence, and where the theory of divine-right kingship is part of a royal war on terror.

Among the key figures is the court beauty Lucy Hay, Countess of Carlisle, a descendant of Henry VIII's mistress Mary Boleyn and the would-be lover of the king. This last Boleyn girl is a significant political player in her own right, but also important as a member of what historian John Adamson coined the 'Essex cousinage'.

They are the heirs to a Tudor past: the son, nephews and nieces of Elizabeth I's last favourite, Robert Devereux, 2nd Earl of Essex. They help carry and explain the story from the beginning of Charles's reign to its end.

Lucy's cousin Robert Rich, Earl of Warwick, is the greatest privateer of the age and deeply involved in the Puritan colonies. This 'American' connection is a significant one – it links Warwick to other totemic civil-war figures and to the radical opposition in London. Warwick's younger brother Henry Rich, Earl of Holland, is, by contrast, close to Charles, he is the reputed lover of the subversive French courtier Marie de Chevreuse and a favourite of Henrietta Maria. Like Lucy Carlisle, Henry Holland will prove both friend and enemy to the royal couple. Seemingly faithless, he and Lucy will turn and turn again, their fates linked to those of their master and mistress.

The trigger event in Part One of the book is Charles's decision to take his kingdoms into the Thirty Years War, fighting for the dynastic interests of the Stuarts and the Protestant cause in Europe. The title of this part, 'His Father's "Wife"', refers to the royal favourite, George Villiers, Duke of Buckingham. The shooting star of the Jacobean age, judged beautiful and damned, he damages the young king's relationship with his parliaments and supports controversial religious reforms, while his military failures heighten the sense of Counter-Reformation threat. One of the royal letters now revealed in *White King*, gives Henrietta Maria's personal account of Buckingham's assassination.

Part Two, 'His Wife's Friend', opens with Charles's own Brexit as he takes his kingdoms out of the Thirty Years War. Charles's court enjoys the 'halcyon days' of peace, with exquisitely beautiful court masques depicting an idealised world of deference and social harmony. This period at court is immortalised in the paintings of Anthony Van Dyck, and his images of the king's growing family in their sensual silks and lace. It ends in 1642 in a very different world, in the aftermath of an invasion from Scotland, rebellion in Ireland, mobs on the streets and Charles and his family fleeing London. The royal favourites, Lucy Carlisle and Henry Holland, are now with the opposition, which they believe will be the winning side in the coming conflict between the king and the English Parliament.

Part Three, 'His Turncoat Servant', covers the English civil war and its title refers to Henry Holland. An extravagant peacock, rather than a dour Puritan, Holland is a reminder of how close sections of the opposing sides are to each other – and how fluid those sides will become. The propaganda of Charles's enemies, with its narrative of popish threat and trolling of Henrietta Maria, remains influential today, with a secular post-Protestant mistrust of Catholicism still lingering.

In fact this is to be a war of Protestant against Protestant over the nature of the Church of England and where exactly the balance of power between king and Parliament lies. Many MPs will fight for the king's cause. And many MPs who begin by fighting against him, end up fighting against their former comrades – Holland amongst them.

The tragedy ahead embraces not only Charles, but also his subjects, the civil war reducing England to the misery of a failed state. The intense violence and battle scenes are an important part of the narrative of *White King*. Charles is an extraordinary survivor, but at the conclusion of this section he is in captivity. A new rebellion, this time against the iron rule of Parliament, has begun and a new invasion is coming from Scotland.

The final part of the book, 'Nemesis', introduces another little-remembered woman to Charles's biography: Jane Whorwood, a Royalist spy whom Charles desires as his mistress. The real Charles was neither a saint, nor his wife's puppet, but a man of strengths and failings. He resembles the tragic heroes of classical Greek literature: a courageous king, of high ideals, whose flaws and misjudgements lead to his ruin. We feel horror and pity as the endgame approaches. For all the hate he engendered, he dies loved in a way his son, the cynical, merry Charles II, would never be.

The final chapter of *White King* opens with Charles's burial. The belief that Charles was the only king ever to have been crowned in white, the basis for his sobriquet, turns out to be untrue, while the famous description of him being buried in a snowstorm also melts into myth. But the intensely moving drama of Charles's life and reign remains. The tales of his vilified queen, of crowd-pleasing politicians and religious terror, of foreign engagements and civil wars, of the suffering of ordinary people, the hopes vested in a different future and the shadow of a coming genocide, make this an epic story for our times.

VENTUROUS KNIGHT

MONSIEUR DE PREUX CONSIDERED THE REQUEST OF THE TWO Englishmen standing at the old eastern gate of the Louvre. It was Saturday 22 February 1623, and Paris was labouring under a third winter of exceptional cold. De Preux, a former tutor to the French king, was no longer young and perhaps his eyesight was not what it had been. In any event, he decided to overlook the Englishmen's wigs and false beards. Nor did it seem to trouble him they appeared remarkably unalike for men whose names – John and Tom Smith – suggested they were related. One was still boyish, small and slight, his wig covering a high forehead; the taller man, well built and strikingly handsome. De Preux simply treated them as two gentlemen of fashion travelling Europe as part of their education. As such, he was happy to introduce them to the spectacle of the Bourbon court and, at its heart, his master, Louis XIII.

The men walked past the musketeer guards in their feathered hats and livery of blue and red to enter the palace. The buildings of the Louvre were strung along the Seine like a mismatched necklace, ancient medieval towers with arrow-slit windows alongside new light-filled Renaissance galleries. It seemed you never knew what you might find around the next corner. Yet little could have been as surprising as the true identities of the Louvre's latest visitors. De Preux surely knew, however, or had heard rumours of the shocking truth. The older man was no less than the thirty-year-old George Villiers, Marquess of Buckingham, Lord High Admiral of England and royal favourite to King James of Britain. Still more extraordinary, however, was the presence of the second man: James's heir, the twenty-two-year-old Charles Stuart, Prince of Wales.

Although by some measure the smaller of the two men, Charles was an attractive youth, his long hair swept back from a fine face and large eyes that turned down at the outer corners. His paternal grandmother, Mary, Queen of Scots, was well remembered here in Paris. She had inherited her Scottish throne as an infant, and been the child bride of a King of France, loved for her beauty and charm. Widowed when aged only eighteen, she had returned to Scotland from France, the Catholic queen of a newly Protestant Scotland. As the senior descendant of Henry VIII's elder sister, Margaret Tudor, she had expected one day also to be queen of Protestant England. To help secure this inheritance she had married a junior Stuart who, like Mary herself, had English royal blood. But by the time Charles's father, James, was born in 1566, Mary's marriage had turned sour. Months later her husband was murdered. The Protestant lords and their allies in the Scottish 'kirk', or church, accused Mary and overthrew her. Her baby, James, was made king in her place and raised in the Protestant religion. Mary sought refuge with Elizabeth I in England but the Tudor queen instead imprisoned her Stuart cousin. Those who feared a Catholic heir to the English throne wanted Mary dead. Nearly twenty years later, in 1587, they got their way. After Mary's desperate plots to escape she was tried for treason (although no subject of Elizabeth) and executed with a woodsman's axe. There had been angry riots when the news reached Paris, but in London bonfires were lit in celebration.

Charles's grandmother had not been the last monarch to fall victim to Europe's religious divisions. The fault line in Western civilisation begun at the Reformation had sent seismic shocks across the Continent, triggering rebellions, civil wars and assassinations. Even now, the aftershocks continued. Beyond Paris's Champs-Élysées, named after the heavenly Elysian Fields of Greek myth, the political and religious map of Europe was shifting, churches were in flames and thousands were dying.

The Reformation, launched in Germany in 1517, had been born in hell – or rather, in the question of how to avoid it. The Catholic Church taught that to gain salvation you needed to live a life of good works, such as giving to charity. Martin Luther, the great prophet of the Reformation, called for liberty from what he judged as spiritually burdensome rules, and railed against the corruption that had become part of them. The good work of giving to charity did not seem so good when you were being blackmailed with the prospect of hell, and the charities in question were the prestige projects and foundations of the mighty. Luther preached that God offered heaven to an elect few in return for faith alone, that nothing people did could gain them salvation. Scripture, furthermore, was the sole basis of religious truth: the ancient traditions of the Catholic Church and the teachings of its councils had no share in such a role.[1]

People had, however, soon begun to draw opposing truths from their reading of scripture. What became known as Protestantism split into faiths united only by their rejection of Catholicism. Lutheranism's greatest rival within Protestantism were the so-called 'Reform' churches that had begun in Switzerland and came to be labelled 'Calvinist' after the theologian John Calvin.[2] Reform Protestantism had swept away what Calvinists judged the obfuscations and half-measures of Lutheranism. They emphasised that God's total power over salvation meant that while He had predestined an elect to heaven, He had also predestined everyone else to hell, whatever good deeds they did. The most significant departure from Luther's teaching was, though, their rejection of any belief in the physical presence of Christ in consecrated bread and wine.* Rituals and altars were rendered superfluous and even judged idolatrous, while in place of a caste of priests they had ministers, who had no special status beyond academic credentials, reflected in their black gowns. The religious life of Calvinists centred on reading scripture, listening to sermons, spiritual self-examination and prayer.

This was the Protestantism of Britain.

The Scottish kirk was the purer Calvinist church of the Stuart kingdoms, for the Church of England remained only partially reformed, retaining its pre-Reformation structure of priests, deacons and bishops. English Protestants nevertheless saw themselves as leading members of the international Calvinist community. This embraced parts of eastern Europe, particularly Poland, the Electoral Palatinate in the Rhineland, the northern provinces of the Netherlands which formed the Calvinist Dutch Republic, and in Catholic France, where the sixteenth-century Wars of Religion had left a substantial minority of Calvinists known as the Huguenots who had been granted the right to practise their Protestant religion.[3]

There was no certainty of survival, however, for these Calvinist communities. Protestantism in Europe and in Britain had survived only when it had been imposed by rulers, or was permitted by them.[4] To protect themselves British Protestants had, therefore, developed 'resistance' theories, which argued that rulers took their authority from the people who therefore had the right to overthrow, or kill, any monarch of the 'wrong' religion. These theories had justified

---

* For Catholics, Christ's death on Calvary is an event of such cosmic significance that it is not bound by time. The Mass, the central act of Catholic worship, tears away the veil between the present and the past, to the moment of Christ's sacrifice. As it is a sacrifice, the Mass is carried out on an altar. There, when the priest says the mystical words at the moment of consecration, the bread and wine become Christ's body and blood – a miracle known as 'transubstantiation'. Luther's moderated view was that, while the bread and wine did not entirely transform, there was a 'Real Presence' of God in the Eucharist. For Reform Protestants the Communion service was an act of remembrance called 'the Lord's Supper'.

the Scottish Protestant overthrow of Mary, Queen of Scots. But Catholics – especially those associated with the Jesuits – had also developed resistance theories. There had been several attempts to overthrow or kill their persecutor Elizabeth I. Indeed, she had only reluctantly permitted the execution of her fellow monarch, Mary, Queen of Scots, when she could no longer afford the risk of keeping her Catholic rival alive.

Resistance theories had thus cost James his mother but he believed they were also the source of much of the disorder of his early reign, and the sedition he had faced from fellow Calvinists in Scotland. James's famous advocacy of the 'divine right' of kings was his answer to such theories, launched in a verbal war on religiously justified terror.[5] His 1598 tract 'The True Laws of Free Monarchy' argued that kings drew their authority from God, not the people, and so had a 'divine right' to rule. A good king would choose to rule by the law, but in the last resort he was above the law – a 'free' monarch. Whether a king ruled tyrannically, or failed the 'true' religion, only God could punish him: there could be no religious justification for sedition or regicide. To the modern mind divine-right kingship appears like megalomania but its acceptance was intended to ensure stability, which was a basic function of monarchy.

By the time Elizabeth had died on 24 March 1603 James was ready to publish his religious and political works for an international audience. It was later said that her Privy Council had debated whether or not James should be invited to become King of England with conditions – in other words he would have to accept that his kingship was limited by English law and he would not be 'free' to do as he wished. This was voted down.[6]

With James's ambition to inherit the English throne achieved, he had united the crowns of Britain for the first time, though not the kingdoms. To James's frustration the English saw no advantage in a political union with their 'old beggarly enemy', the Scots.[7] And even though many accepted James's theories on divine right in principle, in practical terms England was a 'mixed monarchy'. Sovereignty lay with the king, mixed with that of Parliament, which gave his actions the force of law. There could be no British union without Parliament's agreement and English MPs would not agree to one. Consequently, while James had given himself the title King of Britain, there was no such political entity.

Charles was heir to the kingdom of England, together with its colony, Ireland (which had its own Parliament), and the entirely independent kingdom of Scotland (which retained its own system of law, its own Parliament and kirk). Nevertheless James's achievement in 1603 had raised the Stuarts to the ranks of Europe's greatest ruling dynasties. As the Stuart heir Charles should have been greeted in Paris with fanfare. He was, however, on a secret mission and wanted to pass through France undetected.

Charles was well rewarded by his visit to the Louvre, where he saw Louis XIII walking in a gallery among his courtiers: a young man, with black curly hair, a pursed mouth, and dark, guarded eyes.[8] Aged twenty-one, Louis was Charles's almost exact contemporary, but had become king of the most populous kingdom in Europe aged only eight.[9] This had followed the assassination in Paris of his father, the great warrior Henri IV, at the hands of a Catholic fanatic: a reminder that kings, and the stability of their kingdoms, faced dangers even from zealots of their own religion.[10] Marie de' Medici had acted as regent for her son, until Louis overthrew her aged fifteen, in a coup that had begun with her unpopular favourite being cut down by swordsmen at the eastern gate of the Louvre. Louis now faced continued problems of religious division in France between Huguenots and Catholics and of a powerful nobility obsessed with matters of 'honour'. Deaths in duels were commonplace and reflected the same contempt for the rule of law as modern gangland murders. The fact the killers came from the top of society, rather than the bottom, just made them more dangerous, with the nobility's willingness to resort to violence leading to large-scale revolts. The strain on young Louis was evident in his frequent illnesses and bursts of temper. He was also said to be 'so extreme a stutterer that he would sometimes hold his tongue out of his mouth a good while before he could speak as much as one word'.[11]

It would be untrue to say all was now forgiven and forgotten between Louis and his mother – who had even joined a noble revolt in 1619 – but there had been an official reconciliation. Charles and Buckingham saw Marie de' Medici treated with honour at the Louvre, dining in state, her voluminous golden coiffure framing a sensual face immortalised many times in fleshy extravagance by the Flemish artist Peter Paul Rubens.[12]

Charles and Buckingham arranged with de Preux to return to the Louvre in the evening hoping also to see Louis' Habsburg wife, Anne of Austria – a marriage that Marie had arranged during her regency. Anne was performing in a rehearsal for a form of allegorical dramatics called a masque and was reputed to be a green-eyed beauty.

While the Stuarts ruled the kingdoms of Britain and the Bourbons ruled France, the Habsburgs ruled seemingly almost everywhere else. Their origins lay in Austria and Switzerland, hence their sobriquet, the House of Austria. There were, however, two branches. At the head of the junior branch was Ferdinand II, the Holy Roman Emperor, a title associated with the crowns of Hungary and Bohemia, and the overlordship of over 200 independent territories in central Europe, both Protestant and Catholic. They extended to borders as far west as France, as far east as Poland, north to Denmark and south to Italy. Marie de' Medici's mother had come from this branch. Anne of Austria, despite her confusing appellation, came from the still more powerful senior branch, headed by her brother, the seventeen-year-old Philip IV of Spain. His empire, known simply as 'La Monarchia' – 'the Monarchy' – included Naples, Sicily, Lombardy and the southern Netherlands (present-day Belgium), as well as Spain, Portugal and their colonies. It was an empire upon which the sun could never set, spanning the globe from the Americas to Africa, to Asia and the Philippines.

That night de Preux's son duly escorted Charles and Buckingham to Anne of Austria's masque, where Louis' youngest sister, Henriette-Marie, was also performing. The princess had been named after her parents Henri (IV) and Marie (de' Medici). It was how she would always sign herself, although it is as the Italianate 'Henrietta Maria' that the future Queen of England, Scotland and Ireland is remembered.[13] Her reputation remains tainted today by misogyny, religious prejudice and the propaganda of her enemies, but she was to prove every inch worthy of the names of her remarkable parents.

Aged thirteen, Henrietta Maria was a pretty, 'black-eyed, brown-haired' girl with a beautiful voice. She had been cast in the masque as the goddess Iris: in Greek myth the personification of the rainbow. The part was usually given to a young girl dressed with wings and in all the colours of the spectrum. Henrietta Maria was perfect for the role. Charles, however, barely noticed her. When he wrote to his father that night he didn't mention her name, just noting there had been 'nineteen fair dancing ladies', of whom Anne of Austria was 'the handsomest'.[14] But then it was Anne of Austria's sister, the infanta Maria, whom he was planning to marry, not the child Henrietta Maria, and, as he told his father, watching Anne dance gave him an even 'greater desire' to see the infanta.[15]

The next day Charles left Paris with Buckingham riding south-west for Madrid.[16] He was ready for marriage and eager for a wife, but this journey was less about seeking a bride than about his resolve to settle a matter of family honour. 'At bottom', Charles said of his mission, 'this concerns my sister.'[17] For the first time Charles was striking out independently of his father in a foreign-policy endeavour of his own. Over 700 miles lay ahead of him before he would reach the capital of La Monarchia. He faced many possible dangers on the road, and to his father's Calvinist subjects his destination marked the heart of an evil empire. English Protestant identity had been forged in the fires of the Elizabethan war with Catholic Spain, when their homeland and faith were threatened by the invasion attempt of the Armada. Today the threat to that identity appeared even greater.

In the 1590s Protestantism had held half of Europe, but it was now being rolled back. The Catholic Church had reformed since Luther and had emerged stronger than ever, with a well-educated, confident clergy, led by popes known for their personal austerity. Assaulted by the vitality of this Catholic Revival, also called the Counter-Reformation, and weakened by inter-Protestant quarrels, Calvinists once again faced the military might of the Catholic Habsburgs. The armies of both the Spanish and Austrian branches of the dynasty were on the march in Europe and they were re-Catholicising Protestants by force.[18]

James sent a message after his son and his favourite, praising them as 'Venturous knights, worthy to be put in a new romance'. In truth, however, James too feared where Charles's adventure in Spain would lead.

Part One

HIS FATHER'S 'WIFE'

1

'DEAREST SON'

CHARLES WAS FOURTEEN WHEN BUCKINGHAM ENTERED HIS LIFE AS James's new favourite. The then plain Mr George Villiers was twenty-two, an ordinary gentleman, blessed with extraordinary good looks: 'From the nails of his fingers – nay from the sole of his foot – to the crown of his head, there was no blemish in him. The setting of his looks, every motion, every bending of his body was admirable.'[1] James, who had always been attracted to handsome men, gave his favourite the Scottish diminutive 'Steenie', after the angelic-faced St Stephen. Charles hated him with all the usual passion of a teenager towards an interloper in their relationship with a parent. The two young men often fought, Charles once spraying the favourite with water, and he in turn telling the prince to 'kiss his arse' – and getting away with it. The king was plying his favourite with wealth and office, making him a 'Gentleman of the Bedchamber and Knight of the Order of the Garter; and in a short time (a very short time for so prodigious an assent) he was made a baron, a viscount, an earl and a marquess, and [in 1619] became Lord High Admiral of England.'[2] Buckingham was still only twenty-six.

The new Lord Admiral had, however, come to realise that he couldn't depend on an aging king to secure his future. Buckingham needed the goodwill of James's teenage heir – and he had begun to take a serious look at the prince who would one day be king.

* * *

Charles was born in Scotland on 19 November 1600, a day of Gothic horror and of royal triumph. It began with the decomposing bodies of two Scottish noblemen being gibbeted and quartered at the Mercat – or Market – Cross near the High Kirk of St Giles in Edinburgh. The traitors' heads were then stuck on poles and their quarters were packed in salt and sent for public display in Dundee, Stirling and Perth.

It was early the following morning that a messenger arrived from Fife at Holyrood Palace and gave King James the news that his wife, Anna of Denmark, had delivered a son at 11 p.m. A delighted James tipped the messenger £16 and when the sun came up James left Edinburgh for Dunfermline Palace to see his 'Annie' along with their newborn child.[3]

The heads of the twenty-two-year-old John Ruthven, 3rd Earl of Gowrie, and his twenty-year-old brother, Alexander, would remain on view in Edinburgh through the lifetime of James's new son. The noble brothers had been killed in August 1600, during what James believed was a kidnap attempt against him made in league with ministers of the kirk. Their motive was the fear that James was poised to impose Crown-appointed bishops over the kirk's Calvinist councils – known as presbyteries – and so place it under tight royal control. The brothers never had an opportunity to answer the kidnap charges, but their rotting bodies had been propped up in court, tried and found guilty of treason. This had left James free to advertise his vengeance for insults to the Stuart crown dating back to the overthrow of his mother Mary, Queen of Scots, and he would now crush all remaining opposition to his rule.

By the time James's cousin Elizabeth I of England died on 24 March 1603, his notoriously violent kingdom was at peace. Nevertheless, it was said that James was as delighted to leave Scotland as if he had spent forty years in the wilderness and was now to enter a land of milk and honey: England was known to be as rich as Scotland was poor. His wife and children were to follow him south – save for Charles, who had to be left behind.

The kirk disapproved of the Scandinavian Anna for her 'night waking and balling' as well as her Lutheran beliefs. But this dancing queen, the sister of King Christian of Denmark, had done her royal duty in producing heirs. Charles had an elder sister, Elizabeth, who was four years his senior, born on 19 August 1596, and a brother, Henry, born on 19 February 1594, who was a full six years older. But a younger brother had died only months earlier and Charles's health was also fragile. He had been born with a lingual deformity, possibly ankyloglossia or 'tongue tie'. This would have made feeding difficult, and the two-year-old Charles was undersized. It was only the following year, in 1604, and after James had sent a physician back to Scotland along with £100 for drugs and other medical necessities, that Charles was brought to his father's new kingdom.[4]

A year later, Charles faced a threat to his life of a different kind. On 1 November 1605 one of his servants, Agnes Fortun, was questioned by a member of the royal ceremonial guard about Charles's daily life, 'the way into his chamber, when he rode abroad, how attended etc'.[5] Four days later it emerged that this man, Thomas Percy, was part of an extremist conspiracy. A group of Catholics had planned to blow up the Palace of Westminster during the opening of Parliament, killing King James, the eleven-year-old Prince Henry, England's peers and members of the House of Commons. They had then intended to kidnap the surviving royal children, but feared it would be particularly difficult to smuggle Charles out of London. One plan was to inflict a superficial stab wound, so that the four-year-old could not be moved before the Catholic takeover was complete. Happily the Gunpowder Plot was foiled, and the would-be bombers were either killed or executed. It was Charles's first direct experience of the murderous consequences of resistance theory.

Charles, meanwhile, had continued to struggle with his disabilities. Some of his earliest memories must have been of trying to talk and communicate. His garrulous father once threatened to have the tendons under Charles's tongue cut to help him articulate. Besides the problems with his speech, Charles's legs lacked strength and he had trouble walking. But with courage and determination he came 'through temperance and exercise to have as firm and strong a body as any'.[6] By 1609 he was able to dance at the celebrations for his brother Henry's installation as Prince of Wales, and he soon walked so quickly it was said he almost ran. Charles also found singing lessons helped him control his stutter and he later advised other sufferers that 'the best and surest way is to take good deliberation first, and not to be too sudden in speech'.[7] It enabled him to express himself far more eloquently than the stammering Louis XIII.

Being a second son, in a hereditary monarchy, Charles had to grow used to being treated as second best. When James spent £800 on a 'chain of stone' and an insignia of the Order of the Garter for Henry, he gave Charles a jewel worth only £130. In letters James wrote to Henry as 'our dearest son' and to Charles as merely his 'dear son'.[8] But Henry's treatment reflected respect for rank as much as any emotional bond. Charles enjoyed security and family love such as his father had never known. He would remember his parents' affection all his life and there were no signs of jealousy towards Henry who bore the heavier responsibilities. On the contrary, Charles admired and emulated his cleft-chinned and martial brother. He played with soldiers and read enough about war to be complimented on his knowledge of military affairs. He also shared Henry's passion for art.

Britain had become something of an artistic backwater following the Reformation. For Calvinists all religious images, even crucifixes, were idolatrous, and in England and Scotland over 90 per cent of religious art – which was most art – had been destroyed since the Reformation. Henry embodied the aspirations of a new era, collecting mannerist painting from Italy and the Netherlands, as well as Florentine bronzes.

Charles was overseeing the preparations for a masque to celebrate Elizabeth's forthcoming marriage when he was told that Prince Henry was ill. It was October 1612 and Elizabeth had matured into a golden-haired sixteen-year-old, admired for a tenacious memory and discerning judgement.[9] Her groom was a contemporary, the Calvinist Frederick V, Prince-Elector of the Palatinate and, as such, already leader of a German military alliance known as the Protestant Union. Plans were being laid for Prince Henry to be married as well, possibly as early as the following year. Catholic brides from France or Savoy were mooted. This, James hoped, would boost the role he aspired to of peacemaker in Europe with his family acting as a bridge between religions. Henry, however, was now in the last stages of typhoid fever. Charles dashed to see him and stayed at his brother's bedside while doctors treated Henry by tying a dead pigeon to his head.[10] Charles was thirteen days short of his twelfth birthday when, on 6 November 1612, he watched Henry die.[11]

The following spring of 1613 Charles had to say farewell to his last sibling, Elizabeth, on board the ship that was bound for her new German homeland. Her leaving, she recalled, left her heart 'pressed and astounded'.[12] It was painful also for Charles who alone now bore the weight of national expectations as James's 'dearest and only son', the sole male heir on whom the Stuart crown in England depended.[13]

The Spanish ambassador the Conde de Gondomar thought the twelve-year-old Charles a 'sweet, gentle child'.[14] In a cruel age Charles detested cruelty. 'None but cowards are cruel,' he later observed.[15] He found people difficult to read and preferred his books to the competitive world of the court. He proved a better scholar than Henry had been in his studies. These included theology, French and Latin, while he particularly enjoyed history, music and mathematics. He liked having the time study gave him to weigh up arguments, and distrusted the instant judgements that come with instinct, marking his autograph books with a favourite Neostoic motto, 'If you would conquer all things submit yourself to reason.'[16] The static nature of the past, the precision of rules and logic, made them less disconcerting than courtiers with hidden agendas.

There was another less cautious side to Charles: a physical restlessness and a 'nature inclined to adventures'. This made him 'apt to take extreme resolutions', if encouraged by those he trusted.[17] For now, however, his energy was directed in line with his strong sense of the responsibility of his position, and he pursued a new physical regime to further improve his health. By April 1613, only five months after Henry had died, the Venetian ambassador had noticed an improvement in Charles's physique. Nine months later Charles added running to his programme, taking a group of servants on a long circuit past the handsome houses around his residence, the 'pleasant and splendid' St James's Palace. They soon found they were unable to keep up with him or even to finish the course.[18]

As Charles continued to grow stronger, and he began to perform successfully at the joust, his mother, Anna, encouraged his interest in the ancient chivalric Order of the Garter. Charles showed no trace of his father's contempt for women and had a warm relationship with his mother, teasing her when she was ill that he missed not only her company, but also her 'good dinners'. They shared an appreciation of beauty and courtly ceremony, and he found the chivalric and spiritual values of the Order of the Garter appealing. The knights were called on to defend the church and the weak, especially women, to be loyal to each other and to obey their king. The Garter insignia of St George killing the dragon represented the conquering of sin and of rebellion – the first sin having been an act of rebellion against God that brought disorder into the world.[19]* Almost two-thirds of fifty volumes found in Charles's personal library at Whitehall at the end of his life would be connected to the Order, many of them gifts from Anna.

---

* People believed God had created peace and order from chaos when the cosmos was born. He created a perfect hierarchy – the Chain of Being. This placed mankind above animals on earth and above angels in heaven. The devil rebelled against this and sought to return the universe to chaos. He tempted the first woman, Eve, to rebel against God and she brought suffering and disharmony into the world.

Charles's closest childhood companion at this time was a boy called Will Morray, or in modern spelling, 'Murray', whose uncle Thomas was Charles's tutor. The family was Scottish, a reflection of James's decision to favour his native-born subjects amongst his family's closest servants. Charles, in consequence, spoke English with a slight Scottish inflection, detectable in his spelling of 'hes' for 'has'.[20] William is also said to have been his whipping boy: legend has it that if Charles was badly behaved, it was Murray who was beaten. Yet there was no vogue for whipping boys in the early modern period. Louis XIII was beaten when he was a child king, as James had been. The tale is a literary phantom. Its origins lie in fiction, conjured in the aftermath to the English publication of James's tracts on divine right, with their assertion that you could not legitimately raise your hand against God's anointed. It has gained acceptance simply by repetition and because it appeals to our modern dismissal of divine-right theory as ridiculous and perverse.[21]

As James's heir Charles accompanied the king on his progresses and attended all major state occasions. James did not think it necessary for Charles to visit Scotland or, indeed, Ireland. England was by far his greatest kingdom and James boasted, with some justice, that he could rule Scotland from London, at the stroke of his pen. He did, however, expect Charles to study his Scottish writings, while he also acted as his son's spiritual instructor.[22] James's most significant tract in this regard was a 'how to rule' handbook that had been written for Prince Henry and was entitled the *Basilikon Doron* or 'Royal Gift'. It was the contents of this 'gift' that had so disturbed the Ruthven brothers and their kirk allies in 1600.

In the *Basilikon Doron* James traced the sedition and instability that he had faced in Scotland to the beginning of the Scottish Reformation. In England, Henry VIII had claimed a 'Royal Supremacy' over the church, giving England's monarchs the power to direct religious change. In Scotland, by contrast, the kirk was founded in defiance of royal authority and, James recalled, 'many things were inordinately done by a popular tumult and rebellion'. For this James blamed the 'fiery ministers' of the kirk who had sought to take advantage of his period as a child king, seeking to create a 'popular' government, in which they would 'lead the people by the nose and bear the sway of all rule'. The *Basilikon Doron* hammered home the dangers of 'popularity' – by which James meant demagogy which led to violent disorder – and its antidote, which was hierarchy, in church and state. James saw no clash between his Calvinist beliefs and his support for an episcopate (that is, church government by bishops). Episcopacy dated back to the earliest Christian times and he saw it as a pillar of monarchy, imposing control on those fiery ministers who, like the Pope, sought to usurp royal authority.

James had not yet felt able to bring the Scottish kirk into full align-ment with the Episcopalian Church of England, as he would have liked, but there were now bishops – who dressed like ordinary minis-ters – working alongside the kirk's presbyteries.

James's lessons left Charles convinced that the Church of England was 'the best in the world', keeping 'the middle way' between the 'pomp of superstitious tyranny' of a Catholic Church led by the Pope, and 'the meanness of fantastic anarchy', represented by Protestants who rejected an episcopate.[23] For others, however, the Church of England's combination of Calvinist theology and Catholic structure was not so much a golden mean as a 'leaden mediocrity': a dangerous 'mingle mangle of the popish government with pure doctrine'.[24]

The word 'popish' did not mean merely Catholic. It referred to a form of spiritual and political tyranny that challenged the scriptural authority of 'true' Protestantism, while also threatening its political security at home and abroad. It was associated with the Catholic Counter-Reformation, but could be applied to Lutheranism or any reversal of Calvinism. For it to be used about long-established aspects of the Church of England was indicative of the depth of divisions between English Protestants. Indeed some would later judge it was here, in the half-reformed Church of England 'he had received from his fathers', that the source of Charles's future troubles lay.[25]

English Protestantism is usually dated from Henry VIII's break with Rome in 1533. In fact Henry had ushered in little more than a nationalised form of Catholicism. It was under his son, the boy king Edward VI, that the Reform Protestantism of Switzerland and Strasbourg was first introduced to England. Edward VI had died aged only fifteen in 1553, leaving the process incomplete. A five-year hiatus under the Protestant-burning Catholic Mary I had followed. Then in 1558 the Protestant Elizabeth I had succeeded to the throne and it was assumed that she would continue to push the Reformation in England forward. Elizabeth, however, had proved to be a protestant of a very conservative kind.[26]

The Church of England owed its Catholic structure to the religious settlement established at the beginning of Elizabeth's reign, when other 'popish' elements in the church were also retained. The term 'Puritan' was coined in the 1560s to describe those 'hot' Protestants who wished to abolish the use of a white clerical overgarment called a surplice. For Puritans the surplice was a remnant of the vestments Catholic priests wore for the Mass. It was therefore valid for mainstream Calvinists to complain about their use. Yet they were damned as fanatics, or 'Puritans'. For Elizabeth surplices were simply part of the ceremonial style she preferred in her religious services and which she maintained in her royal chapels, along with a Catholic tradition of choral music abhorred by Calvinists as a distraction from prayer. By the 1590s Elizabeth's example had encouraged a new religious movement within the Church of England whose members shared her tastes. But neglect of other aspects of her religious leadership had left many of her subjects ignorant of the basic tenets of their Protestant faith.[27] It was the Puritans, as the most evangelical members of the church, who had done most to address this problem.

Puritans were distinctive from other Calvinists in their attention to moral detail and their shunning of the impious, often forming 'godly' communities to encourage each other.* The sermons heard from their pulpits were full of showmanship, similar to the evangelical revivalism of later centuries. With Protestantism facing the challenges of the Counter-Reformation, they had attracted 'the most ardent, quick, bold, resolute' recruits, and had 'a great part of the best soldiers and captains on their side'.[28]

In 1585 England had gone to war with Spain on the side of the Calvinist Dutch rebels against Habsburg rule in the Netherlands. Although Elizabeth is rightly remembered for her inspiring defiance of the Spanish Armada in 1588, what little enthusiasm she had ever had for the war had soon waned. She had disliked aiding rebels against a fellow monarch, and resented the huge financial burden of the war. This helped to turn her own favourite, the glamorous soldier-scholar Robert Devereux, 2nd Earl of Essex, against her. Essex had belonged to a generation who believed it was the duty of the nobility not to simply obey royal orders, but to work for the commonwealth – a term that came from 'commonweal', meaning the public good. That meant showing dedication to great causes. For Essex, England's war with Spain was such a cause: one necessary to the very survival of Protestantism in Europe.[29]

---

* The teachings the Puritans were most anxious to drum home began with the Calvinist teaching on predestination: that God has chosen 'elect' individuals for heaven, in return for faith, while everyone else goes to hell. Puritans referred to themselves as the 'Godly', by which they meant the 'elect'. Although no good you did on earth could make you one of the elect, Puritans followed a 'pilgrim's progress' that brought them some reassurance that they were amongst the chosen. This involved shunning the society of the impious, being fastidious in attention to moral detail, and spending hours in prayer and listening to sermons. This gained access to God's grace, and through grace you gained faith and could be 'born again' as a Christian to live a holier life. Eventually your journey would reach the final stage of 'glorification', when you 'knew' you were one of the saved.

By the time Charles was born in 1600 the English Crown had been impoverished by inflation and by generations of land sales. Elizabeth was £400,000 in debt and desperate to make peace. On 3 February 1601 Essex attempted to raise London against the queen, hoping to invite James to London as her successor. His efforts failed and he was executed as a traitor.[30] Yet Elizabeth went to her grave with ballads still being sung at court in praise of Essex.[31]

As soon as James had become king he had immediately set about healing the wounds left by Elizabeth's reign. At the beginning of 1604 he had addressed the urgent need for reform of the Church of England at the Hampton Court Conference. He was extremely knowledgeable on issues of theology and had proved largely successful in splitting moderate Puritans (who wished to get rid of popish surplices and set prayers) from those he judged radical (which included any who wished to abolish episcopacy). James had since built a well-trained and effective clergy, commissioned the superlative translation of the Bible into English known today at the 'Authorised Version', or the King James, and he allowed a broad range of opinion to flourish.

James had named Essex his 'martyr' and leading members of Essex's old war party had been placed in Prince Henry's household. James had, however, shared Elizabeth's fears concerning the expense of war.[32] The Crown's sources of income were still shrinking, and James was by nature extravagant. His experiences of violence and disorder in Scotland had, furthermore, shaped a determined conciliator. After James had signed a peace treaty with Spain in the summer of 1604, Prince Henry had become the focus of the war party's hopes for the future. He had been a passionate advocate of a seaborne empire that would rival that of Spain. With Henry dead the old Elizabethan war party needed a new prince to look to.

When Charles's mother Anna died in 1619, she left her son aged eighteen, a still awkward teenager, as isolated at his father's rumbustious court 'as a planet in its sphere'.[33] But the new Lord Admiral

Buckingham stepped in to offer him a helping hand into the adult world. Intelligent and charming, the twenty-six-year-old favourite 'understood the arts and artifices of a court, and all the learning that is professed there'.[34] He was also able to mediate Charles's relationship with James. The prince responded with gratitude and growing affection.

In a letter of that year, Charles thanked Buckingham for smoothing out a quarrel with his father, and told him about an assignation he had with a woman 'that must not be named'. With the physical energy that was characteristic of the Stuarts came a strong sex drive. James, however, took a strict line against mistresses, fearful that royal bastards could pose a threat to legitimate heirs. Charles's unnamed woman had to be kept secret and Charles, with typical wit, asked Buckingham to leave his letter, once he had read it, in the 'custody of Mr Vulcan' – in other words to burn it. He signed the letter simply 'Your constant, loving friend, Charles'. Buckingham was the only non-royal person to whom he would ever sign himself with his Christian name alone.[35]

James was delighted by the improvement in the relationship between his son and the man James would later call his 'wife'. He told Charles his new friendship with Buckingham demonstrated 'what reverent love you have towards me in your heart'. He also suggested it would be politically astute for Charles to keep Buckingham at his side as king, observing that those who had been loyal to his mother and predecessor Mary, Queen of Scots, had also proved to be amongst those most loyal to him.[36]

James used Buckingham as his amanuensis as he wrote his last political tract, which he dedicated to Charles. 'A pattern for a King's Inauguration' looked at the last days before Christ's crucifixion and examined the rites of the coronation ceremony in light of this. James compared Charles's future role to that of Christ the King. He told Charles he would be God's image on earth and that his subjects would owe him a duty of obedience as to God. James warned, however, that 'he must not expect a soft and easy crown, but a crown full of thorny cares'.[37] It was a heartfelt comment. James's thorny cares included debts of £900,000.

Royal finances remained in urgent need of reform, but James's profligacy with gifts and pensions – not least for Buckingham – had convinced his parliaments that his financial woes were of his own making. James responded by cultivating independent means of raising money. In particular he extended the raising of customs duties under his prerogative powers – that is, those powers exclusive to him as a monarch. But the money the duties raised only allowed James's financial survival in peacetime. He could not afford to go to war without Parliament's financial backing – and there would be a political cost to James for any money they raised for him.

It was with trepidation therefore that James saw that the Anglo-Spanish peace was being threatened by a new conflict in Europe. A war had begun in 1618 when the Holy Roman Emperor had curtailed the religious freedoms of Protestants in Bohemia and they, in turn, had appealed to other Protestants for help. The sighting of a 'star with a tail' would be remembered as a warning of what was coming: 'lament-able wastings, barbarous destructions of countries and cities'.[38] By the time the war was over, thirty years later, parts of the Continent would have lost three-quarters of their population to battle, expulsions, hunger and disease. The Stuart kingdoms could not be immune from the passions it generated, and the fate of Charles's sister lay at the heart of Europe's tragedy.

BECOMING KING

ON 7 NOVEMBER 1619, A PREGNANT ELIZABETH STUART WAS PROCESSED to the high altar at St Vitus Cathedral in Prague. She was attended for her coronation by blue- and violet-clothed Bohemian clergy and was bestowed with the crown of St Elizabeth, a circlet of double arches surmounted by a cross. Anna of Denmark had been disappointed when her daughter had been married to a mere Elector of the Palatinate. Now, eight months after Anna's death, Elizabeth's husband Frederick was King of Bohemia and she was his crowned consort. For how long his reign would continue remained to be seen. Frederick had accepted the throne at the hands of Calvinist rebels against the Habsburg Holy Roman Emperor, despite his father-in-law King James's strong advice. Frederick's enemies had warned that his reign would vanish with the snows of winter. The following September, 1620, Habsburg armies made ready to fulfil that promise and advanced on Prague.

Elizabeth sent her 'only dear brother' Charles a desperate plea to 'move his majesty [King James] that now he would assist us'.[1] Charles responded as his martial brother Prince Henry would surely have done. He promised her £10,000 of his own revenue, and offered to lead a military expedition in person. James forbad it. In November 1620 Habsburg forces defeated Frederick at the Battle of White Mountain and Elizabeth fled Prague with Cossack horsemen at her heels. Legend has it her new baby, Prince Rupert of the Rhine, was almost left behind, tossed into her carriage at the last minute, the swaddling unravelling at her feet. The lower Palatine territories of the Rhineland were also soon lost, overrun by Spanish Habsburg forces in alliance with their Austrian cousins. Elizabeth and Frederick were forced into exile in The Hague, the capital of the rebel Calvinist Dutch Republic. The Habsburg prophecy had come to pass. Frederick's short reign had earned Charles's sister no more than the bitter sobriquet 'the Winter Queen'.

Thousands were now being killed in Bohemia. Protestant worship was banned, while the Palatinate had been given to the Catholic Maximilian of Bavaria for services to the Habsburg cause. With the Protestant states of Germany and the Netherlands still at war with both the Habsburgs and the 'Catholic League', under Maximilian, it seemed only a matter of time before the Lutheran kingdoms of Scandinavia and Calvinist Britain were drawn into the conflict. James persisted, however, in seeking a diplomatic solution to the crisis.

James believed he could persuade the Habsburgs to withdraw from the Palatinate as part of a marriage alliance between Charles and the infanta Maria of Spain. An additional benefit would be a huge dowry that would help free James from financial dependence on Parliament. In return, James would offer the Habsburgs an alliance against their Continental rivals the French. But first James had to convince the Habsburgs that, if they refused his offer, he would fight a war against them. To this end he called a parliament in 1621 and asked for the subsidies he would need.

James's MPs instead demanded that Charles marry a Protestant. James was outraged that the Commons saw fit to encroach on a decision that fell under the royal prerogative. Indeed, when they also attacked his raising of customs duties outside parliamentary control, it seemed to him they had left no aspect of royal sovereignty 'unattempted but the striking of coin'.[2] He dissolved Parliament, but Puritans in particular continued to attack the Spanish match as an alliance with forces of Satan.

Elizabeth I was portrayed as having been a paragon of warlike intent against Spain and the myth was used as a means of criticising the peace-loving James. The martial Prince Henry, meanwhile, was remembered as her true heir. There were posthumous advantages to Henry's reputation in having lived long enough to embody great hopes, and not so long as to have had the opportunity to disappoint them. With Charles seen as James's dutiful son, the old war party even sought a legal basis for an alternative dynasty to the Stuarts from amongst junior descendants of the Tudors.[3]

In the face of this Puritan opposition to peace, James began to actively favour anti-Puritan clergy within the Church of England.[*] To his dismay, however, the Spanish were slow to respond to his overtures. As the marriage negotiations dragged on, and anxious to help his sister, Charles decided the answer was to cross Europe incognito and break the deadlock by winning the infanta in person. There was a proverb Charles quoted, 'Few great talkers are good doers'.[4] His father was a good talker, but Charles wanted to take action. Buckingham encouraged Charles in his project, although others feared the prince could be kidnapped in Spain, or even killed.

Charles was of an age when he wished to develop an identity separate from his father. The danger for Buckingham in this was that when Charles became king he might signal his independence by swiftly retiring his father's favourite. There would certainly be pressure on Charles to do so.

---

[*] To Puritans the war in Europe was evidence that the End of Days was approaching. As the pre-eminent Calvinist kingdom England had a divinely ordained role to lead the final battle against the Antichrist – a demonic entity that they believed was embodied in the papacy. This ruled out any peace or compromise with the Habsburgs who were seen as the military arm of the Counter-Reformation. For more moderate Protestants the Pope was not a demon but merely the invalid leader of a Catholic Church in need of Protestant reform. This allowed them to be open to the possibility of peace in the way the Puritans were not.

The 1621 parliament had seen the revival of the medieval practice of 'impeachment', whereby royal officials accused of criminal behaviour were tried and punished by Parliament. It had been used successfully against James's Lord Chancellor, Francis Bacon, and Buckingham feared he could be next. He was deeply resented for his monopoly of power, 'managing his glory to the eclipse of other great men'.* There was also anxiety about the nature of his relationship with the king. It was said that in Europe 'men talked familiarly' of James's unnatural love for Buckingham, that 'the sin of sodomy' was now frequent in London, where 'boys grown to the height of wickedness' painted their faces like women, and that the whole realm was at risk of divine punishment.[5] Buckingham needed royal protection in the next reign, and so made himself integral to Charles's first solo political venture, backing it to the hilt with the king. Buckingham told James that Charles's plan would put the Spanish on the spot, and that James had 'once for all to know what satisfaction they were like to have in the business of the Palatinate'.[6]

It was with James's extremely reluctant agreement that the venturous knights left for Paris, where they had their adventures at the Louvre and Charles saw Henrietta Maria for the first time, before riding on to Spain. Avoiding wolves and (with more difficulty) duels, they arrived in Madrid on 7 March 1623.

Charles and Buckingham passed suburban palaces with beautiful gardens and rode on down streets of great houses with plain brick facades embellished only with granite doorways and iron balconies. A travel book of the period observed that while Parisians walked 'so quickly and actively that they look as though the law were after them', here in Madrid the 'calm and repose' of the Spanish was such that 'any

---

* Buckingham could hardly forget that one of Henry VIII's first actions on inheriting the throne had been to arrest two of his father's loyal and effective, but most hated, servants. They were later executed.

who saw them, will think that they have just recovered from a serious illness'.[7] There was rather less repose in Madrid, however, when the astonishing news broke of Charles's arrival.

Their Habsburg king, the seventeen-year-old Philip IV, was treated as a living icon. Tall and fair-haired, with the undershot jaw that was a feature of the family's inbreeding, he was rarely seen in public.[8] Most of the time he was kept screened from the world by a barrier of protocol, jealously guarded by an elect group of nobles and officials. Diplomats who were invited to see him in the gloomy Moorish fortress of the Alcazar were escorted through a succession of dark but richly furnished rooms to an audience chamber where they would find the young king standing alone by a small console table. He would raise his hat in greeting, then remain still and silent while the diplomat spoke.[9] A few polite words from the king would then conclude the audience. Any visiting princes had to be greeted with even greater formality to protect the divine image of monarchy. They weren't expected to bound into town, hoping to throw themselves at the feet of Philip's carefully chaperoned sister.

The teenage Philip was shocked, but also excited, to discover he was to entertain a Prince of Wales. When Philip had become king two years earlier, he confessed he had found himself quite unprepared for his duties, adrift in a 'sea of confusions and ocean of difficulties'.[10] He knew Charles was highly educated, an accomplished horseman, and a young man of taste. He wanted to both learn from him and impress him.

Philip had recently introduced an entirely black court dress, worn unadorned save for a small white standing collar. He decided to relax this code. He would not go so far as to wear colour but, in honour of Charles's visit, his suits were sewn with gold thread and rich jewels. The personal encounters Charles had wanted with the infanta Maria were not permitted, but he was given a suite of rooms in the Alcazar. A household was also appointed for him and he was waited on in a manner unknown at the English court since the days of the Tudors.

James had introduced to England the relaxed style of the Scottish court where he would chat to those around him while he ate. In Madrid noblemen served Charles on their knees, and watched him take his food almost as if they were witnessing Holy Communion. Charles saw in image and ritual what his father had written on the theory and nature of divine kingship. He was impressed, and, as the summer heat fell on Madrid like a weighty blanket, days turned to weeks and weeks to months.

Philip's court, despite its formalities, was also one of glitter and liveliness. There were fireworks, bullfights, torchlit processions and chivalric games, in which Philip appeared splendidly arrayed, commanding squadrons of horses. There were balls too, ballets and plays, which incorporated elaborate theatrical machines that allowed quick and dramatic changes of scenery. Above all, however, there was art. This was Spain's golden age and Charles wanted to grab all it had to offer. He purchased Renaissance works by Titian, Raphael and many others. He had an exceptional eye as a collector, investing in the cutting edge of modern art as well as old masters. Only eighteen months later Peter Paul Rubens would call Charles 'the greatest student of art among the princes of the world'.[11] Buckingham – whom James made a duke in May – shared Charles's tastes and was the perfect companion in this regard.

The Spanish were shocked, nevertheless, to see how Buckingham would sit while the prince stood, and even leave his hat on, the two men calling each other 'ridiculous names'. It was as if they were ordinary brothers rather than prince and servant. James had, perhaps unintentionally, encouraged this – they were his 'babies', although of them Buckingham was 'my bastard brat'.[12] Philip's leading minister, the Count of Olivarez, expressed concern that if the infanta married Charles and did not immediately put a stop to this 'unsuitable licence' then 'she would herself experience its mischievous consequences'.[13] It was not to come to that, however, as it became evident that the religious differences between Charles and Maria were too great for any marriage to take place. The Habsburg infanta, as pink-cheeked and full-lipped as a German doll, believed that marrying a Protestant would imperil her soul, while Charles angrily rejected the efforts Philip made to convert him to Catholicism.

In October 1623 Charles and Buckingham returned to England. The nation was relieved that Charles was safe and remained Protestant. Church bells rang and cheering crowds lined the roads from Portsmouth to London to greet the prince's return. But he had been left angered by the failure of the trip to Madrid. It appeared to Charles that Buckingham had been correct in suggesting that the Spanish had all the while been stringing his father – and himself – along, and taken them for fools.

Buckingham, meanwhile, wrote to James to tell him how he was looking forward to their reunion, and promised never to part from him again. He was 'only bent', he said, on having James's 'leg soon in my arms'.[14] The collapse of the Spanish match would, nevertheless, now open up a rift with the peace-seeking king. Buckingham's months with Charles, and the stress of the marriage negotiations, had forged a deep loyalty in the prince for his friend, and Buckingham continued to groom his affections. Charles had given up on his father's dream of a Spanish match, but he had not given up his intention to help his sister. If the Palatinate were not to be regained by peace, then, Charles believed, it must be regained by war.

The Winter Queen and her children were Charles's heirs. If her eldest son ever inherited the Stuart kingdoms, then the Palatinate would belong to the English and Scottish crowns. For Charles, its restoration to Elizabeth's husband was a dynastic imperative and a national duty. While Charles pressed his father to plan for military conflict with the Habsburgs, Buckingham, once again, backed his policy and piled further pressure on the king.

Charles's anti-Habsburg policy stood to win over some of Buckingham's fiercest critics, many of whom came from the old war party, now often called the 'patriots'. But were their hopes of the possible gains of a war with the Habsburgs in any way realistic? The Stuart Crown was 'in a miserable state', one Frenchman observed, 'without money, without friends and without reputation'.[15] The royal income of Castile alone was six times that of England.[16] The Habsburgs had secured Bohemia by armed force. James had no armed force. After James had made peace in 1604 the English army had virtually ceased to exist, and the logistic supply systems for food, clothing and weapons had all gone.[17]

With no standing army and little money, Charles needed an alliance that would bring him both. The obvious place to look was France. The Bourbons had a history of backing Protestants when it suited their dynastic interests. A marriage to Louis XIII's sister, the pretty young Henrietta Maria, would provide the Stuart Crown with the support of Louis' great army, and money from a dowry with which to raise an army of their own. Charles also sought tax support from his father's subjects, asking the king to call a parliament where he would seek to ask for the necessary subsidies. In 1624, he duly sat in the House of Lords as Prince of Wales and proved to be an effective leader of the 'patriot' party.[18] There were concerns that a French marriage would oblige James to 'take off or slacken the execution' of the penal laws against English Catholics. These laws forced Catholics to attend Protestant services or face ruinous fines and denied them the freedom to attend Catholic worship. Although there was only a small Catholic minority in England, the threats in Europe meant that rooting out all popery was seen as vital for Protestant survival in Britain. After James had signed a House of Commons petition promising to continue to enforce these laws, MPs voted tax subsidies of £200,000. The money paid for an army of mercenaries and pressed men under the German general Ernst von Mansfeld, with the intention they be sent to fight the Habsburgs in the Netherlands on the side of the Dutch rebels.

Some of the English poor drafted into the army rubbed salt into their eyes to escape being sent across the Channel. James was scarcely more enthusiastic and in mid February 1625, he called a halt to the war. Countermanding Buckingham's orders to relieve the besieged Dutch garrison at Breda, James forbad Mansfield from engaging with Spanish forces. Mansfield's army was already succumbing to disease in the cold and wet weather as they awaited orders, and their supplies were dwindling. If the army did not have their orders to march soon, Parliament's money would be wasted – and the war policy Buckingham had advocated with Charles would fail. To add to Buckingham's worries the former Spanish ambassador, the Conde de Gondomar, was proposing to return to England and help James gather support for a revived Anglo-Spanish peace.

In England too, meanwhile, the weather was bad. There were floods in London, where Westminster Hall was under two feet of water. This was particularly dangerous to the old, and at the beginning of March 1625 James developed a 'tertian ague' while at the Elizabethan palace of Theobalds in Hertfordshire. The fifty-eight-year-old king was over-weight and heavy drinking had further weakened his health. Nevertheless, he had survived such fevers many times before. Indeed he was reported as recovering well when, on 21 March, he became 'extremely sick'. The cause appeared to be a poultice and a cordial brought by Buckingham.[19] With the king suffering violent fits of diar-rhoea, his Scottish attendants began to quarrel. Some feared Buckingham had unintentionally poisoned the king. James refused to have the cordial again.[20] On 25 March a Habsburg agent in the palace reported his suspicion that Buckingham had tried to murder King James. Out of Mansfield's force of 12,000 only 5,000 were now fit for service. James was still awaiting Gondomar, but the agent reported that Buckingham had used the king's stamp to sign a warrant to stop the Spaniard from coming.[21]

Two days later Charles was sitting at the side of his dying father. James tried to speak to his son, but found he had 'no strength to express his intentions'.[22] James VI of Scots and I of England died at noon on 27 March 1625, with Buckingham holding his hand.

James was perhaps the greatest ever King of Scots, but he was an outsider in England and it showed. He had left a difficult legacy for his son. His incontinence with money, his quarrels with his English parliaments, and the anger provoked by negotiations for the defunct Spanish match had generated mistrust, while royal finances remained in a parlous state with the Crown dependent on the diminished revenue of a medieval monarch. There were problems stored up for the future also in his other kingdoms. James had failed to unite their divergent religions. The Irish remained predominately Catholic, while the Scots kept their distinctive kirk. Subjects who differed from their king in matters of religion were judged unlikely to be fully obedient or loyal. Charles had bridges to mend everywhere, and needed to do so urgently if he was to have his people behind him for the conflict ahead.

In the following days England continued to be wracked by storms. As the words of the proclamation declaring Charles king were read in Cambridge, the townsfolk were unsettled by a blast of thunder like a cannon's roar.[23] After over twenty years of Jacobean peace it heralded the new king's war.

A MARRIAGE ALLIANCE

IT WAS DUSK WHEN THE PROCESSION ACCOMPANYING JAMES'S coffin arrived in London. Black smoke from thousands of coal fires curled up from tall chimneys into the gloom. A quarter of a million subjects and immigrant workers lived in Charles's capital. Usually the streets were jammed with people and carts as well as the newly licensed hackney carriages.[1] But that night, 4 April 1625, the roads on the processional route were cleared. Crowds gathered behind rails to watch the mayor and aldermen greet their new king, who rode before his father's bier, accompanied by a guard of foot soldiers and horsemen. Behind, a long line of coaches carried 'many great lords'.[2] Haloed in torchlight the procession continued to Denmark House, the classical palace on the Strand James had built for his wife, and where James's coffin was to lie in state.

Just over a week later Charles lifted James's orders refusing General Mansfield permission to fight. With the army now heading for the besieged Dutch garrison at Breda, Charles pushed ahead with the marriage to Henrietta Maria to seal the French alliance. Unfortunately his bride was already proving an unpopular choice. Women had been key to the survival of Catholicism in England. Catholic men could be – and were – stripped of their property if they refused to attend Protestant services. Wives owned no property and were more defiant. They harboured priests and raised their children as Catholic. Henrietta

Maria was, furthermore, no ordinary Catholic. Her brother boasted he was the 'first Catholic among all kings'.[3]

Rumours had also surfaced that the French marriage treaty had stipulated an end to the persecution of Charles's Catholic subjects: rumours that were based on fact. Secret promises had been made that Catholics would not be punished for worshipping in their own homes. It was a necessary concession and reluctantly made. Charles now acted to allay Protestant fears. He refused leading Catholics the funeral blacks required to attend his father's funeral, due to take place on 7 May. This snub signalled that Catholics would remain second class. Anxieties about the French marriage remained, nevertheless, as a proxy wedding took place in Paris on 1 May while Charles remained in England for the funeral preparations.

Henrietta Maria was now fifteen, but small for her age and only 'on the very skirts of womanhood'.[4] In other words she was a barely pubescent child. For much of her life it had been expected that she would marry into a cadet branch of the French royal family and her education had been limited to religious and courtly matters. With this she had acquired a 'spirituality' and 'delicacy', but to one French courtier, 'above all there was something about her person that was noble and grand. Amongst all the princesses she had the great likeness to her father', Henri IV; 'Like him she had a noble heart, a magnanimous intrepid heart full of tenderness and pity'.[5]

An elevated walkway hung with violet satin had been built at the archbishop's palace, giving the crowds a perfect view of the bride as she was accompanied the short distance to the Cathedral of Notre Dame. 'The princes, marshals, dukes and peers of France' stepped out first, each dressed 'in robes of inestimable value': a brilliant moving tableau. Henrietta Maria followed in a shimmering bridal gown of silver tissue and gold fleur-de-lys, and a diamond-studded crown. Her figure was 'finely proportioned', she had 'a perfect complexion', her 'large, black eyes' were 'soft, vivacious and shining', her hair dark, her 'teeth pretty' and 'big mouth … nicely made'.[6] King Louis walked on his sister's right in his velvet and ermine robes. The princesses of France bore her velvet mantle, embroidered with another large fleur-de-lys, and behind them was her mother, Marie de' Medici: the former Regent of France a living reminder that, beyond their roles as wives and mothers, queen consorts could wield significant political power.

At the west entrance to the cathedral, Louis handed Henrietta Maria to Charles's proxy. The role had been given to a kinsman, the French Duc de Chevreuse. He was a member of the Guise family of Charles's great-grandmother, Mary of Guise, the French wife of James V of Scots. As Charles was in mourning for his father, the duke had dressed in black, but his cloak was so thickly embroidered with gold and diamonds that 'he seemed to burn and bear a living flame about him'.[7] The wedding vows were taken on the platform at the doorway under a golden canopy. Since Charles would not attend a Catholic service the duke – although himself Catholic – would not enter the cathedral for the nuptial Mass. Charles's young bride walked alone through such a profusion of candles the church resembled 'the Palace of the Sun, described by Ovid in his Second Book of the transmutations of shapes'. Against a backdrop of cloth of silver, gold and rich tapestries she then took Communion alone beneath the soaring Gothic arches.[8] That night, however, the Duc de Chevreuse played Charles one last time, lying in bed alongside Henrietta Maria, one leg touching, in a symbolic consummation of the marriage.[9]

Charles longed to see his wife for himself and spent much of his spare time gazing at her picture bemoaning the fact 'he could not have the happiness to behold her person'.[10] She, in turn, was surely curious about her groom. Before they could meet, however, James's funeral had to take place.

James's embalmed body was still lying in state at Denmark House, his coffin covered with a velvet cloth and mounted with a lifelike effigy dressed in royal robes. It was a statement of the undying nature of monarchical authority. This was something the funeral would express even more dramatically. Charles had borrowed the unprecedented sum of £50,000 for a funeral judged 'the greatest ever known in England'.[11] A cavalcade of several thousand plain-black-clad mourners escorted James's body a little over a mile to the medieval splendour of Westminster Abbey. Each mourner was precisely ranked according to his status, while heraldic banners – symbols of chivalric virtue and dynastic greatness – shone in brilliant colour against this river of black. Buckingham rode one place behind the coffin, in his role as Master of the Horse. But 'the greatest glory', it was said, 'was Charles's own presence'. Dressed in a long black robe and hood he walked immediately behind the chariot bearing James's body – it was only the third time an English king had ever done so and it was judged a striking mark of his love for his father.

In the abbey the congregation heard a two-hour sermon recalling James's survival of dangers, his success in achieving the union of the crowns and his strong support of episcopacy. James had argued that bishops, like kings, drew their authority from God and to deny their divinely sanctioned status was also to deny divine-right kingship: 'no bishop, no king', as he had once said. The sermon concluded with the statement that James's kingly body now lived on in his son. At this, Charles stepped forward to accept his father's hatchment, receiving James's heraldic arms in a ritual enactment of the succession and an advertisement of the stable transfer of power.

With the funeral over, Charles now dispatched Buckingham to Paris to collect his bride and firm up the French alliance. A revolt had just broken out in La Rochelle, a key port in south-west France and a Huguenot stronghold. Charles feared that Louis was poised to make peace with Philip of Spain in order to free him to focus on crushing this Calvinist rebellion at home. Charles relied on Buckingham to keep Louis on track for war.

Buckingham was more than ready to impress the Bourbon court. He had ordered three coaches lined with velvet and gold lace to convey him around Paris. For travel by river, he took twenty-two boatmen with him, each of whom would be dressed in sky-coloured taffeta embroidered with gold. Even they, however, could not compete with his own appearance. Buckingham had packed twenty-seven rich suits in which to represent Charles. One alone, in white velvet spangled with diamonds, was said to be worth 'fourscore thousand pounds' – more than a rich knight would earn in over a decade.[12]

When Buckingham then appeared in Paris, he was judged 'the best-looking and best-built man in the world'. Dressed in his 'splendour he filled the populace with admiration, the ladies with delight – and something more; the gallants with jealousy, and the husbands, with something worse.'[13]

He discovered that Marie de' Medici had hurried Rubens to finish a cycle of twenty-one full-length portraits celebrating her achievements in time for the wedding celebrations. The paintings had just been installed at the newly completed Luxembourg Palace and she took Buckingham to see them. It was impossible not to be impressed, both by the great palace, with its windows of rock crystal framed in silver, and also by Rubens' masterpieces, which today are kept in the Louvre. He was a profoundly original and powerful Counter-Reformation artist, and one whose dynamic and plump nudes would give the term 'Rubenesque' to the English language. Marie's blank face and sexualised body overwhelm any images of her husband and her son. They include one of her giving birth to Louis, a scene reimagined in a vast outside space with Marie seated on a throne-like birthing chair. Marie gazes with her hazel eyes at the infant Louis, in the arms of a nurse, but he no more outshines her than does the pug that sits at her feet.[14]

Buckingham immediately commissioned Rubens to begin a ceiling painting for his own house in London. It was to depict him being carried up out of the reach of the forces of Envy towards a temple of Virtue and Abundance: a theme close to his heart. The forces of envy against Buckingham were stronger than ever, with it disappointing many 'that he should be found favourite to both father and son'.[15]

Meanwhile Paris glittered with welcome for Buckingham. Suppers, musical evenings and masked balls were thrown for the duke and his train of English and Scottish courtiers. Louis XIII's new chief minister, Cardinal-Duc de Richelieu, gave one such party in the gardens of his small country palace of Ruel.[16] Richelieu's wiry frame, dressed in the flashes of scarlet that denoted his cardinal's rank, exuded nervous energy. It was said you either liked Richelieu or hated him. He was not a man who inspired neutral opinions. He had served Marie de' Medici as her Secretary of State during the Regency. After her fall, when she had plotted with Louis' enemies, he had effected the reconciliation between son and mother. Louis had made him his chief minister the previous year and Richelieu was now set on making France the greatest power in Europe. Cardinal or not, his loyalties in all secular matters lay with the king, not the papacy; if he thought it was in France's interest to ally with Protestant heretics against Catholic Spain, he would.

Richelieu's gardens were his place of relaxation.[17] There were evergreen trees and avenues with elaborate fountains. One, in the form of a serpent, shot out plumes of water sixty feet into the air that would sharply twist to catch the unwary passer-by. Buckingham had still more disconcerting experiences, however, at Richelieu's hands. In their private meetings the cardinal refused to align France more openly against the Habsburgs, arguing that a formal military alliance would only antagonise neutral countries. When Buckingham requested that Charles at least be given a written promise that Louis not make a separate peace with Spain, Richelieu dismissed it as unnecessary. It seemed that his focus would indeed be on crushing the Huguenot rebellion. And even Rubens took the liberty of lecturing Buckingham on the virtues of peace with Spain, as the duke sat for his portrait.

Buckingham was not the only Englishman in Paris to be troubled by Richelieu's slipperiness concerning the alliance. So was the diplomat Henry Rich, Earl of Holland, who had led the marriage negotiations. The thirty-four-year-old Holland was a 'very handsome man, of a lovely and winning presence'. By nature easy-going, and generous with his money, he also relished intrigue and Richelieu was now in his sights.

The French alliance had a personal dimension for Holland, one that was linked to his family's legacy of hatred for Spain and support for the Calvinist cause in Europe. His mother, Penelope Devereux, was the 2nd Earl of Essex's favourite sister. When Holland was ten he had seen her go to prison, reportedly for urging his uncle on in his revolt against Elizabeth I in 1601. Holland's elder brother, Robert Rich, Earl of Warwick, had continued in the family tradition. He was the greatest anti-Spanish privateer of the day, and deeply involved in colonial and trading enterprises in the Spanish-dominated Americas.[18] Warwick had acted, for example, as a signatory of the famous Pierce Patent, which confirmed the rights of the Puritans who had sailed on the *Mayflower* to plant and govern land in the Plymouth area of New England.[19]

Holland had had to be more circumspect than Warwick in defying James's peace with Spain. As a younger son he did not have his brother's vast landed inheritance. He needed a successful court career to pay for the magnificence he enjoyed, and his achievements had recently earned him his earldom. Nevertheless, Holland shared the family's anti-Spanish values, as well as having a taste for women in his mother's image: clever, alluring and dangerous. His current lover was reputed to be no less a figure than the wife of Charles's proxy, the twenty-four-year-old Marie de Rohan, Duchesse de Chevreuse – or Mme de Chevreuse as she was known. She was due to travel with Henrietta Maria to England as *dame de la chaise percée*, the queen's closest body servant.[20] Meanwhile, she was happy to join Holland in his intrigues.

A fair-skinned, petite woman, Mme de Chevreuse looked innocent enough. She had a round, almost baby face, framed with long tawny curls called 'serpents' and an expression that was both 'majestic and sweet'. This belied a ruthless political animal, recalled in Richelieu's memoirs with grudging respect: 'She had a fine mind, a potent beauty, which she knew how to use to her advantage, was never disheartened by any misfortune and always retained her evenness of temper.'[21] Mme de Chevreuse, in return, viewed the cardinal only with contempt for his social origins in merely minor nobility.* The higher nobility believed they had a right to dominate the king's councils and she saw the power given to Richelieu as an insult. As for Louis, she thought him 'an idiot'.[22] With Richelieu out of the way, she believed the French king would be easy to manipulate – and she advised Holland and Buckingham that the most effective tool to weaken the cardinal's power was Louis' queen, the green-eyed Anne of Austria.

Mme de Chevreuse and Queen Anne were close friends, their intimacy sealed by a tragic event three years earlier. A boisterous game the young women had been playing in the corridors of the Louvre had ended in the queen miscarrying her first child. Louis had sent Chevreuse into exile, which she had bitterly resented, while his angry treatment of his wife had damaged his marriage. Mme de Chevreuse was now back at court and closer than ever to Anne. No one was better placed to help Buckingham ingratiate himself with Louis' wife and the French would never forget his efforts. Buckingham's extravagant glamour, his flirtatious behaviour with the Queen of France and his enmity with Richelieu later inspired Alexandre Dumas' nineteenth-century novel *The Three Musketeers*.[23]

Henrietta Maria spent the eve of her departure from Paris in a Carmelite convent. It was a peaceful and spiritual retreat, offering the new Queen of England a simple diet and time to reflect.[24] In the far future, when Henrietta Maria had all the more reason to appreciate its serenity, she would ask for her heart to be buried here.

---

* Her sense of her own status is reflected in her family motto: '*Roi ne puis, Prince ne daigne, Rohan suis*': 'King I cannot be, Prince deign not to be, Rohan I am.'

On 23 May she was carried out of Paris in a litter lined with red velvet, amidst 'shouts of applause' and 'a countless throng of people'.[25] In her train were an estimated 4,000 courtiers, 'all the flowers of France', servants, diplomats and members of her family, as well as Buckingham and his British train. Scarlet coaches rolled along the bumpy roads on gilded wheels, the footmen dressed in the red of the Stuart livery, the horses trapped to match, with white plumes of feathers nodding from their heads. Behind, carts carried the trousseau. There were beds of estate, furniture for her chapels and a vast wardrobe of clothes: embroidered shoes, red velvet boots lined with marten fur, perfumed gloves, cutwork handkerchiefs, a royal mantle of crimson violet, a petticoat in the fawn colour 'Isabella', embellished in gold, a silver dress embroidered with brilliant coloured flowers, and much, much more.[26]

To one Englishman in the train the young Henrietta Maria was 'a sweet, lovely creature', and a 'brave lady' who was 'full of wit'.[27] Holland had also found her intelligent, observing that her conversation showed 'extraordinary discretion and quickness'. Although Buckingham's focus remained on Anne of Austria, and Venetian diplomats reported growing gossip about the pair, this was largely forgotten in the great spectacle of Henrietta Maria's formal entry to Amiens.[28] The gates of the city had been hung with the arms of England, and seven triumphal arches, built at enormous expense, led her in procession to the cathedral. The last was fifteen metres high and depicted five virtuous former queens of England.[29] The strain on Buckingham of a potential collapse of the French alliance against Spain was beginning to tell – and it prompted a row with Charles's young wife.

The anger felt by Protestants in England at the impending lifting of the anti-Catholic penal laws was mirrored in France by the hope that, indeed, English Catholics would now be allowed some religious freedom. In 1622, Pope Gregory XV had founded a new department – Propaganda Fide – for the evangelising of the faith. It would prove a powerful force across the globe. There were now twenty-eight priests in Henrietta Maria's train, each of them ready to serve as a

Counter-Reformation missionary. The sight of such men, dressed in Catholic religious clothes, was bound to cause deep unease in England, and Buckingham knew that as the man judged responsible for the treaty that permitted this, he would be blamed. His concerns were brought into even sharper focus with the arrival at Amiens of a papal legate.

Henrietta Maria had written to Pope Urban VIII promising to remain faithful to the church after her marriage and to work for 'the liberty of the Catholics' in England – that is, for their freedom from persecution.[30] Without this the Pope might not have granted the dispensation necessary to permit her marriage to a heretic king. The Pope's representative now expressed the Pope's delight in her promises, bestowing on Henrietta Maria the honour of the Golden Rose, an ancient Catholic symbol of joy following sorrow. In an accompanying text the Pope further urged her to become like a rose, 'a flower of the root of Jesse among the spines of Hebrew iniquity', who would spread the true Catholic faith amongst the heathen in England.[31]

When the ceremony was over, Buckingham berated Henrietta Maria for the warm welcome she had given the legate. It must have been intimidating for a young girl to be lectured by a strapping man like Buckingham, who was also the representative of an as yet unmet husband. Nevertheless, Henrietta Maria defended herself, reminding him 'that it behoved her to treat with respect the representative of the head of her religion'.[32] It was an unfortunate start to their relationship, and on this unhappy note, the stay in Amiens concluded.

Marie de' Medici had been unwell for days and remained too ill to travel, so she said farewell to Henrietta Maria outside the town. Marie had enjoyed a strong influence over her fatherless daughter and she now gave Henrietta Maria a final letter of instruction, written in her own hand 'so that it will be dearer to you'. It reminded the queen to be grateful for the privileges God had given her and to remember that she had been placed on earth for His glory. A longer version, which also still survives, encouraged her to love her husband and to be kind to all his subjects, but also to remember she had a duty to her perse-cuted co-religionists: 'God has sent you into this country for them ... who have suffered for so many years'.[33] It was a role the young queen accepted with the utmost seriousness. It was traditional for a queen consort to intercede on behalf of the condemned. Who would she wish to intercede for more than those punished for sharing her religious faith? Two days later Henrietta Maria was on the coast at Boulogne, 'in good health and very merry'.

The last of the French queens of England, Margaret of Anjou, had also left her homeland aged fifteen. It was 1445 and England, under the Lancastrian Henry VI, was losing the Hundred Years War with France. Margaret of Anjou was seen as the child of the enemy. When that war was lost and civil war came to England, she had fought bravely for her husband's cause, but this negative view of her never changed. Shakespeare condemned her as the 'she wolf of France' and a 'tiger's heart wrapped in a woman's hide'. Now, 180 years later, English Protestants judged Henrietta Maria a child of the powerful Catholic enemy. But hers was 'a nature inclined to gaiety' and she was excited to be taking the boat from France.[34] Henrietta Maria was watched that evening dashing to the water's edge, letting the waves lap over her shoes: a haunting image of carefree childhood before the wind caught the sails of an English ship and brought her to a new shore.[35]

4

'UNDER THE EYES OF CHRISTENDOM'

HENRIETTA MARIA SPENT HER FIRST NIGHT IN ENGLAND AT DOVER Castle. Buckingham had had it dressed with goods from various royal palaces, but many of these furnishings were old. Her servants expressed their disappointment. Charles was also unable to afford, either politically or financially, to fund such lavish greetings as had been seen on Henrietta Maria's route from Paris to Boulogne. From the castle, if she now looked out across the sea and it was clear, she could see France and mourn what was past. 'Goodbye, sweet banks of the Seine where I have enjoyed a thousand pleasurable entertainments ... Fountains, goodbye, I will no longer look into the mirror of your crystal waves.'[1] If she turned inland, there was, however, also the kingdom of her future, with its beautiful 'up and down' countryside, 'many good woods and pretty houses with rows of trees'.[2]

The young queen was due to meet Charles the following day at Canterbury, seventeen miles away. Instead, he arrived without ceremony at ten the following morning. Henrietta Maria was having breakfast. 'Nimble and quick', she dashed down the stairs to greet him, falling to her knees as she saw her husband for the first time. Charles had grown a moustache and a short 'royale' beard, and although he was dressed casually in his riding clothes and tall boots there was 'a majesty in his appearance'. Henrietta Maria was nervous: she did not yet speak English and, after giving a rehearsed speech in French about her love and duty, she burst into tears. Charles raised her from her knees, took her in his arms and kissed her.

Charles had been warned that his wife was small and was surprised to discover she reached his shoulder.[3] He glanced down to check if she was wearing high shoes. She noticed immediately and, raising the hem of her dress, assured him, 'Sire, I stand upon mine own feet. I have no help by art. This high am I, and neither higher nor lower.'[4] Charles's father had advised that with a wife you must 'rule her as your pupil'.[5] If so, it was evident Henrietta Maria was not going to be a slow-witted or unobservant pupil.

That night, Charles's first with his wife, was spent at Canterbury in the archbishop's palace. There, Mme de Chevreuse handed Henrietta Maria her night attire in a formal ceremony and prepared her for her bridal *coucher*. When Charles arrived in her bedchamber, he asked their servants to leave. He then bolted all seven doors to her rooms. This was to be a private night, without courtiers joking around the bedside, as they had at court weddings under James. Henrietta Maria had been told something of what to expect in her first sexual experience. Her tutor in this matter, Mme de Chevreuse, had done her job well and would return to France that summer having earned Henrietta Maria's affection and Charles's gratitude.[6]

The next day Charles emerged from the queen's rooms 'very jocund'. Henrietta Maria appeared more subdued. She was concerned for her friends. The crumbling Anglo-French military alliance was already having an impact. Nationalist tensions had emerged on the way to Canterbury, when a row had broken out over which women could travel in her carriage.[7] The English had taken the side of their ladies, with their French rivals described dismissively as 'poor, pitiful sort of women'. Only Mme de Chevreuse was judged worth looking at and it was said 'though she be fair', she 'paints foully'.[8]

Henrietta Maria retreated amongst her familiar friends, but that evening, in her rooms, she invited Charles to watch from behind a screen as she danced a slow sarabande by candlelight.[9] Dance was 'a

kind of mute rhetoric', a teacher of the art had once said, the movements suggesting the dancer was worthy to be 'acclaimed, admired
and loved'.[10] Charles looked on discreetly, as he had when he saw her
perform in the masque in Paris in 1623, but as she danced her French
adaption of this old and erotic Spanish dance, he had the opportunity
see how beautiful his wife was growing. Buckingham boasted in a
letter written to Louis that night, it would not be long before Charles
sired a child with the queen.[11] Charles's happiness was still evident
on 16 June when, with Henrietta Maria at his side, they approached
London by barge.

The king and queen were dressed in matching green costumes,
the colour chosen as a symbol of their love and youthful fertility. The
London skyline, with its myriad church spires and tall chimneys, was
veiled in rain. This had not, however, put off the crowds. James had
told Charles that his people's love would be his 'chiefest' security, yet
had also warned that such love was best earned by ruling a well-ordered
society: that meant subduing the rabble, not exciting it by playing to
the gallery.[12] Taking his father's advice, Charles had instructed his
subjects 'to dispense with public shows of their zeal, cheerfulness and
alacrity'.[13] Yet still they cheered along the riverbanks and a courtier
reported he had 'never beheld the king to look so merrily'.[14] One ship
by the shore was leaning dangerously in the water, with over a hundred
people piled on the side with the best view of the royal couple. As
they bunched closer the ship tipped, then capsized, spilling the occu-
pants into the river. Numerous small boats dashed to fish them out.[15]

That night, as Londoners toasted the royal couple and lit bonfires,
Henrietta Maria was introduced to Whitehall. Charles's principal residence in London was described by one Frenchman as 'the largest and
ugliest palace in Europe'; 'a heap of houses, erected at divers times',
observed another.[16] Charles was keen to replace its 2,000 musty Tudor
rooms with a palace in the clean, modern lines of Inigo Jones's
Banqueting House, which had been built next door by his father.
Unfortunately, such a project would soak up the money he needed

for the war with Spain. Instead, Charles was doing what he could do to transform life in the palace: the life of the court.

Not only power but also virtue was supposed to flow from a king, through his court, to the people. At James's coronation, the Archbishop of Canterbury had prayed that 'the glorious dignity of his royal court' would 'brightly shine as a most clear lightning'.[17] The reality had proved rather different. James's court had become notorious for its drunkenness and immorality. Charles had announced early his determination to 'establish government and order in our court from which thence may spread with more order through all parts of our kingdom'.[18] The informality and hard drinking habits of James's court were brought to an end and the strict 'rules and maxims of the late Queen Elizabeth' were reintroduced. Charles asked that the nobles not 'enter his apartments in confusion as heretofore'.[19] Each rank was to have its appointed place, as they had at James's funeral. This emphasised the importance of hierarchy outlined in James's *Basilikon Doron*. For Charles, however, rank did not exist to encourage a sense of entitlement, but rather service, and not only to those above you but also those below you to whom you had a duty of care and to foster talent. More elaborate ceremonies were planned as Charles began to craft a kingly figure as impressive as any of his contemporaries in Europe. Foreign observers were impressed and judged him 'well, active, resolute'.

Now Charles was ready also to assert the honour of the Stuarts against Habsburg power. He needed £1 million a year for his war. To get it he had reconvened Parliament: the first of his reign.

For weeks Westminster had been a hive of activity as the palace was prepared for the coming influx of 600 MPs and 150 peers. Workers had mended windows, delivered furniture from the king's other palaces, hung curtains and sewed seats of wool and canvas in preparation for what was the largest representative assembly in Europe.

The daily business of ruling England was centred on the monarch. At his right hand were his councillors, all of whom were courtiers since they had to be where the king was. Parliament was only called periodically – sometimes not for years – but it was England's highest legislature and an effective tax-raising body which had grown enormously in importance since the Reformation. Parliamentary legislation had rubber-stamped the legitimacy of monarchs, and, time and again, had been used by monarchs to alter religion. The Elizabethan theory that the king's authority resided not in the physical person of the monarch alone, but was 'mixed' with that of Parliament, had further empowered it – although not, necessarily, to the disadvantage of the monarch.[*]

'The truth is,' a future Royalist observed, 'the Kings of England are never in their glory, in their splendour, in their Majestic Sovereignty, but in Parliaments. Where is the power of imposing Taxes? ... Where is the legislative Authority? ... The King out of Parliament hath a limited, a circumscribed Jurisdiction. But waited on by his Parliament, no Monarch of the East is so absolute.'[20]

Charles appreciated the potential value of king and subjects working together through Parliament. It would take national will, as well as money, to face the military challenges ahead.

The most powerful figures in Parliament were the peers who sat in the Chamber of the House of Lords. They included the Lords spiritual – the Church of England's bishops – and the Lords temporal, the hereditary nobles. Their great houses were centres of local political authority and they influenced who were chosen as the House of Commons MPs. These MPs were also mostly from landed families (if not landed themselves). Some had trained as lawyers, which was a common profession for a younger son in the gentry. They often

---

[*] In the 1550s Protestants had argued there were biblical injunctions against female rule. To get round this issue when the Protestant Elizabeth became queen it was explained that royal sovereignty was 'mixed' with that of Parliament and so it was not 'she that rules, but the laws'.

acted as agents for the peers, but they still had to engage the backing of their electorate.

Every freeman with property valued at over £2 had the right to vote – as much as 40 per cent of the adult male population.[21] For many Parliament had come almost to define what it was to be English, Protestant and free. But there was no certainty where exactly the balance of power should lie between a king and his MPs in a 'mixed' monarchy. And here the language of both monarch and Parliament had become increasingly defensive during James's reign. MPs had felt threatened not only by James's words – his insistence that a monarch's authority was drawn from God and 'free' of legal restraint – but also by what he did.

James's extension of customs duties, raised under the royal prerogative, had freed him from the financial necessity of calling regular parliaments. This threatened the 'liberty of the subject', expressed in Parliament's debates, and in its protection of property rights. The Commons lawyers had fought back in defence of 'liberty', by asserting that Parliament, and not the king, had the right to take control of customs duties. These attacks had, in turn, prompted fears that if the Crown was too weakened, the monarch could end up in the financial pocket of a dominant faction of MPs. A strong king was seen as a protector against populist tyranny, ruling above faction and political interest.

Now, this new parliament, with a young and inexperienced king in grave need of money, meant fresh opportunities for champions of the 'liberty of the subject'. Charles had seen the difficulties his father had faced in the 1621 Parliament, but he was confident that MPs would now support him in a dangerous war that threatened the very safety of the kingdom. After all, he observed, they had voted in 1624 to engage in the war, 'and so were bound to sustain it'.[22]

On 18 June, Charles sat enthroned in the Lords Chamber, dressed in velvet and ermine, and prepared to give his opening speech. The benches beneath him were roped off with crimson tape, 'the Lords in their Robes, and the Commons present below the Bar'.[23] Buckingham was watching him, along with Henry Rich, Earl of Holland, who would join the Privy Council the following month. Holland's elder brother, Warwick, was also here.

Smiling out of a portrait by Daniel Mytens, Warwick sports a goatee, along with brilliant red breeches and a doublet sewn with a field of flowers. Even his enemies judged him a 'man of a pleasant and companiable wit, of a universal jollity'.[24] Yet behind the relaxed manner was a godly Calvinist who cultivated an inner life of reflection and prayer, and was a ruthless political strategist.[25]

Warwick was seen as a virtual king in Essex where he owned 20,000 acres, and had in his gift twenty-two livings – that is, placements for clerics – which he used to influence and organise prominent Puritan clergy.[26] In London his colonising activities in the New World had also linked him to a new merchant class, sprung from the ranks of shopkeepers and mariners. These men did not have the wealth to be granted access to the great merchant companies like the Levant and East India that traded across Europe, the Mediterranean, the Near and Far East.[27] They had instead been obliged to develop commerce in the New World where Warwick had helped Puritans found godly communities.[28]

In Parliament Warwick was known as one of the 'popular lords' who 'aimed at the public liberty' and the limiting of royal power. Another was his cousin, the thirty-four-year-old 'Robin' Devereux, 3rd Earl of Essex, son of Elizabeth I's last favourite. Pockmarked by smallpox and embittered after a disastrous marriage had ended in divorce, Essex had found purpose in spending his summers fighting for the Protestant cause in Europe.[29] In the winters he came home to recruit men, or attend Parliament. He was now returning from the siege of Breda, which had just fallen to the Spanish. Of the English force of 7,000 Charles had sent to save the garrison two months earlier, a mere 600 had survived.[30]

'I am unfit for much speaking,' Charles admitted from the throne, and he kept to the point.[31] The necessary supply of money for the war had to be voted quickly. Plague had broken out in north and east London – and was spreading rapidly towards Westminster.

Plague was a regular occurrence in summer. But this epidemic had fallen on a weakened population. Cheap imports of wool cloth had led to high unemployment and rain had ruined the summer harvest. The London poor were starving and easy prey to disease. One peer in Parliament knew the dangers better than most: he had had his shoemaker pull on his boots that morning, only to see the man drop dead in front of him.[32]

Charles reminded his listeners that the rapid granting of sufficient subsidies for the war was also vital for national and royal honour. 'This being my first action,' he said, 'all the eyes of Christendom will be on me.'[33]

Unfortunately, this matter of national and royal honour proved to be of less concern to his MPs than Charles had hoped. The news of the fiasco of Breda and distrust of Buckingham had killed confidence. 'We have given three subsidies and three fifteenths to the [Winter] Queen of Bohemia, for which she is nothing the better,' as one MP observed.[34] The funds that Parliament now voted were woefully inadequate for the needs of the war effort.[35] To make matters worse, the French alliance was threatened as the debates turned to the suspension of the anti-Catholic penal laws. The Puritan MP John Pym saw it as a Jesuitical plot to destroy not only 'us and our religion ... but also the possession of themselves of the whole power of the state'. If Catholics 'get but a connivance, they will press for a toleration, then strive for an equality, and lastly aspire to such a superiority as may work the extermination of both us and our religion.'[36]

Henrietta Maria became frightened that her promised religious freedom might even be taken from her. On her first morning in London there had been sour comments on the Mass being 'mumbled over to Her Majesty' at Whitehall, and her wearing 'a veil upon her head'.[37]

To ease Protestant anxiety Charles forbad his subjects from attending his wife's Catholic chapels, but the grumbling continued. It did not help that, after a brief experiment in his Protestant chapels when the congregation were invited to pray for their 'Queen Henry', Henrietta Maria's name was anglicised instead to 'Queen Mary', with its unfortunate associations with the last Queen Mary of England: the Protestant-burning Mary Tudor.[38]

Ever watched by hostile Protestant eyes, Henrietta Maria felt suffocated in her chambers that summer. There were always hordes of visitors at court. People came on matters of business, to see its entertainments or simply to escape 'the barbarous and insipid dullness of the countryside'.[39] To gain admission you needed only to dress the part and you could eat in hall at the king's expense – a part of his ancient duty of 'good lordship' – or watch the queen dine. One MP was entranced by her, 'a most absolute delicate lady … all the features of her face much enlivened by her radiant and sparkling black eyes' and her behaviour 'sweet and humble'.[40] Another visitor, however, witnessed a different side of the queen. In the roaring fires and the press of people, the fifteen-year-old's composure snapped, and 'with one frown … she drove us all out'. It seemed that 'howsoever little of stature', she had 'spirit and vigour' as well as 'a more than ordinary resolution'; 'I suppose none but a queen could have cast such a scowl.'[41]

In Parliament Buckingham attempted to reopen the subsidy debate, but merely irritated MPs, who judged he was taking advantage of a thinly attended Chamber. Most of their colleagues had fled London. The weekly toll of plague victims had risen into the thousands. One arrival in the City 'found nothing but death and horror, the very air putrefied with the contagion of the dead'.[42] But England was still at war, and Charles still needed the money to fight it. He adjourned Parliament to have it reopen on 1 August in Oxford, far from the plague. A courtier travelling on Henrietta Maria's barge en route for Oxford spotted the people of a Berkshire town stoning a man who was having a fit at the side of the road.[43] They feared the plague was following the court. And, indeed, by 27 July the first deaths from plague were already being reported in Oxford: a knight who had arrived from London had succumbed along with a doctor, staying in the same house.

In the febrile atmosphere of a town of sudden death, Charles now addressed his MPs' concerns about the prosecution of the war. He explained that money was needed to support his Danish uncle, the Lutheran Christian IV, who planned to attack Catholic forces in north Germany.[44] The remnants of Mansfield's army still needed paying. Meanwhile England's major contribution to the latest war effort was to be a joint military and naval attack on Cadiz. The financial estimates and plans were laid out in detail. The aim was to drive Spain to the negotiating table by destroying her ships and undermining her sea trade. Essex, who had at last arrived from Breda, was asked to take the role of vice admiral serving under the experienced soldier Sir Edward Cecil.

Buckingham's probity and competence as Lord High Admiral were, however, questioned. He was also attacked for his monopoly of power, for mismanaging the marriage negotiations, and for popish influences. Henrietta Maria was well aware of the pressure Charles was under to reimpose the anti-Catholic penal laws, and that Buckingham was encouraging him to do so in order to blunt the attacks on himself. As relations between France and England deteriorated so did they in royal marriage, and she treated Charles to 'disrespects' and 'little neglects'.* Bewildered, Charles confided his distress in Buckingham,

---

* One example Charles gave was that when he sent instructions that her household use the same rules as had governed that of his late mother, she had sent back an open rebuke, observing that she hoped he would allow her to look after her own household as she thought fit. He assumed she hadn't meant to be so rude and so raised the matter with her, 'calmly' explaining that she shouldn't have affronted him publicly and why she was wrong not to follow his mother's household orders. She told him exactly what she thought of this, and then insisted that when he wished to see her he make an appointment. *Letters of King Charles I*, ed. Sir Charles Petrie (1935), p. 43.

blaming her behaviour on 'the ill crafty counsels of her servants'. Henrietta Maria was equally convinced it was Buckingham who was stoking their quarrels.[45] According to one contemporary Buckingham had even reminded her 'that there had been queens in England who had lost their heads'.[46]

When Charles did reinstate the penal laws it failed to stem the attacks on Buckingham. It seemed to Charles that having betrayed their duty to support their king in a challenging war, some MPs were now attempting to appropriate his right to appoint his own ministers. In despair of getting his money, on 12 August Charles dissolved Parliament. The war against Spain would have to be fought with what cash he had – and without the French, who were busy crushing the Huguenot rebellion. In October the Cadiz expedition set sail with 5,000 sailors and 10,000 soldiers funded at a cost of £250,000.[47] This was more than double the money Charles had gained from the French for his wife's dowry, but the navy was still undersupplied and many of the ships in poor condition.

Rubens, toiling on his painting of Buckingham, was disgusted by the duke's role in the coming conflict. 'When I consider the caprice and arrogance of Buckingham I pity that young king who, through false counsel, is needlessly throwing himself and his kingdom, into such an extremity.'[48]

When the navy reached Cadiz the joint forces managed to capture a small fort, but this was followed only by the further capture of a large cache of wine. This was promptly drunk, turning the soldiers into a mob. Men who passed out on drink were left to have their throats cut by the Spanish as their ships then sailed away. 'Throw but a butt of sack* in the way of the English', the Spanish sneered, and 'it will do more harm in an English army than a thousand Spaniards can do in arms.'[49] Buckingham's choice of commander, Edward Cecil,

---

* A fortified white wine such as sherry.

had proved incompetent, and his pressed men undisciplined and poorly led.

On 24 November, a few days after his twenty-fifth birthday, Charles opened his first Chapter of the Garter at Windsor. The king walked down the quire under a golden canopy, leading his knights two by two.[50] Hierarchy, kinship, patronage and friendship mattered in England as much as impersonal institutions. So did the chivalric qualities of honour, duty and loyalty, of faith and courage.[51] The Garter represented all these things and defined Charles's ideals of kingship: *Honi soit qui mal y pense* (May he be ashamed who thinks badly of it) ran the motto. As spectators to the Garter procession gossiped nosily, Charles knew, however, that 'under the eyes of Christendom' a tragic scene was unfolding with the return of the Cadiz expedition.

Far from the music and ritual of the Garter chapel, contrary winds were destroying his navy. They crashed against the English coast, some ships wrecking as far as Scotland. There would surely be further loss of life in the fighting yet to come: 'For anyone can start a war when he wishes,' Rubens observed; 'he cannot so easily end it.'[52]

ENTER LUCY CARLISLE

THURSDAY 2 FEBRUARY 1626 WAS CORONATION DAY AND A YOUNG
lawyer was hoping to find a seat in Westminster Abbey. Although he
arrived early he couldn't get into the abbey and decided to watch the
procession instead. It was 'a fair day', winter bright, and Henrietta
Maria was also waiting near the palace gate where the procession was
due to begin. She had a good view from a room at a private house.
Charles had intended for the coronation to be a joint ceremony with
his wife. But since the penal laws against Catholics had been reinstated
Henrietta Maria felt she had to offer her co-religionists assurance that
she would not be cajoled into converting. She had therefore refused
to be crowned at the hands of a Protestant bishop.[1] Charles was disappointed: he had hoped to follow his parents' coronation ceremony in
every detail.

When the procession began it was strikingly orderly. Charles walked
under a canopy supported on silver staves and carried by peers, while
a choir sang a prayer for his long life – just as they had for James. It
would later be claimed that Charles was dressed in white, and would
be the first king ever to be crowned as such. For some the image of
the white robes would later recall the prophecies of the 'Dreadful
Dead Man': a prince in white who becomes 'lost in the eye of the
world ... and in the love and affections of his people'.[2] For others the
robes were the mark of a prince 'without one noted vice': a royal saint,

whose soul was pure as snow. The legend of the white coronation robes would earn Charles the sobriquet 'the White King'. In fact, although Charles wore white satin underneath his purple mantle, this was because his father had done so.

As the procession entered the abbey's west door the watching lawyer spotted another door 'guarded by one and thronged at by a few'. He seized his opportunity, sneaked inside and 'instantly settled myself at the stage on which stood the royal seat'. The officiating archbishop began by presenting Charles to the congregation as king, and asking them for a 'general acclamation'. The careful choreography of the occasion then broke down. People were uncertain what to do. After an excruciating period of silence, the Earl of Arundel stepped forward and 'told them they should cry out "God save King Charles!"' 'A little shouting followed.' Arundel tried again. Finally the abbey rang with the words 'God save the king.'[3]

The lawyer was now to witness the last coronation in England to use the medieval regalia and relics of Edward the Confessor.

Charles swore the same oath his father had sworn, and was presented with the regalia whose meanings James had recorded for him. The crown was a symbol of his people's love; the sceptre – handed to Charles by the Earl of Essex – represented royal authority. The robes resembled the clothing of a bishop because kings 'sit on thrones … as mixtae personae … bound to make a reckoning to God for their subjects' souls as well as their bodies'.[4] Finally, the anointing, carried out in cruciform, imprinted the king with God's mark. Charles had ordered the consecration of new oil scented with orange and jasmine for this symbolic moment. It was a statement of his just title, but also of sacral kingship and his status as Christ's image in England.

Two days later Charles opened his second parliament. Another fleet was in preparation and his need for money more urgent than ever. Charles had nominated (or 'pricked') the leading malcontents of the Oxford parliament as sheriffs, which made them incapable of sitting as MPs. But the failure of Cadiz was a new and serious addition to the charge sheet against Buckingham. Military defeat at Breda, and now Cadiz, heightened fears of the Counter-Reformation threat. Just as Parliament got under way, the favourite then made still more enemies by aligning himself with a revolutionary new movement within the Church of England, labelled 'Arminianism'.

The term 'Arminian', like 'Puritan', was intended to be an insult. It was drawn from the name of a Dutch theologian, Jacobus Arminius, who had attacked the Calvinist theology of predestination (that an elect was predestined by God for heaven, while everyone else was predestined to hell, whatever good they did in life).[5] In fact not all so-called Arminians had strong feelings about predestination. The leading anti-Puritan cleric, William Laud, observed that such mysteries were unknowable in this life. The Arminians did, however, wish to 'worship the Lord in the beauty of holiness', favouring ceremonial and ritual over Calvinist extempore prayers and sermons.[6]

It was a movement that had been encouraged by the example set in Elizabeth I's royal chapels. But it was becoming evident that Charles intended to reform the entire Church of England in line with these preferences, and not just enjoy them personally in his palaces as she had done. He believed that well-ordered Protestant church services, conducted within beautified interiors, offered something more than just pleasure to the senses. They offered a religious lesson in the value he wanted inculcated in his dominions: a reverence for divinely instituted authority and the framework it offered for duty and service.

A particular flashpoint with the Puritans was the writings of an Arminian royal chaplain called Richard Montague, who had down-played the differences between the Church of England and Catholicism and defended the use of religious images. At the Earl of Warwick's request there was a conference on Montague's writings at Buckingham's residence, on 11 and 17 February. The hope was that the conference would conclude in a robust confirmation of the Church of England's Calvinist traditions that would set Charles on a more conservative path. When, instead, it ended without any public repudiation of

Montague's doctrines by Buckingham, it became a turning point for Warwick and other hot Protestants. It would be almost impossible to change Charles's religious policy without Buckingham's backing. Since he would not give it, Buckingham's destruction became a priority.

The plan was to impeach Buckingham for corruption. The difficulty lay in finding anyone prepared to give evidence against the powerful favourite. But then, in April 1626, a new and shocking allegation was made.

A pamphlet had appeared accusing Buckingham of having murdered James with the plaster and syrup that he had supplied for the king in his last days. Written by a Catholic Scottish physician, it was a piece of Habsburg black propaganda, aiming to sow confusion amongst their English enemies. It worked brilliantly by confirming a long-held suspicion that behind the beautiful face painted by Rubens lay corruption and wickedness.[7] The pamphlet sold quickly and its contents were soon repeated in news-sheets. Ben Jonson's current play *The Staple of News* was satirising this fast-moving new media, with a character list of disreputable owners and disorderly writers. But news-sheets helped satisfy the contemporary thirst for comment and gossip and the media was far more powerful than Charles yet realised.

A parliamentary select committee immediately began cross-examining James's doctors. The evidence they uncovered was riveting. Buckingham had twice violated rules that only the royal physicians could prescribe and administer drugs, and one doctor insisted that what Buckingham had given James was 'no better than poison'.[8] Although there was no proof of murder, this implied more sinister secrets might yet be uncovered.

The House of Commons laid formal charges against Buckingham before the Lords on 8 and 10 May 1626. Behind the scenes, meanwhile, the MP John Pym had been working diligently to make the accusations as hard-hitting as possible. A heavy-set Puritan of forty-two, Pym preferred simple dark cloth and a collar of white linen to Warwick's lace and silk. He had begun his working life as a clerk in the office of the Exchequer, where, it was later said, he had improved himself by hard work rather than natural talent. Nevertheless, he had gained notice as an MP 'for being concerned and passionate in the jealousies of religion'.[9] He was politically and personally close to Warwick and he was involved in many of the same colonial ventures.[10]

Thirteen offences were listed. All the forms of corruption in royal government had converged in Buckingham, it was said, 'drawn like one line in one circumference'.[11] The last of these offences accused him of an 'injury' to King James in 'an act of transcendent presumption and of dangerous consequence'.[12] This threatened not only the ruin of Buckingham's career and reputation; potentially it also threatened his life. Yet the man who made the poultice and cordial Buckingham had given James was a respected doctor who was also employed by Warwick.

Charles dissolved Parliament on 15 June, before the impeachment case against Buckingham reached the Lords. Not only was Charles left without the subsidies he had sought, MPs had also refused him the traditional life grant of the customs duties known as Tonnage and Poundage, and described another customs duty, known as Impositions, as a 'grievance'. This had deprived him of income he needed for his very financial survival. But Charles believed the case against Buckingham nothing more than a surrogate attack on monarchical authority. Ensuring he got his subsidies, vital though that was, had, in the end, not been the most important thing to him. The war abroad had opened up a new front at home in which, he believed, he faced enemies who were less anxious to do their duty at a time of war, than to dictate royal policy and appointments. These men wanted to manipulate public opinion for their own ends, and their narrow interpretation of Protestantism only encouraged their sedition and demagogy. They were the forces of disorder that it was the duty of the monarchy to stand against.

Charles would have to find new means to raise money, since he had to push ahead with the war urgently. Louis XIII had signed the long-threatened Franco-Spanish peace, and the Habsburgs would now only be growing stronger.

Henrietta Maria's priests were, meanwhile, punishing the young king for his persecution of Catholics by persuading his wife to refuse him sex on the church's many Holy Days. They also ruined his mealtimes by saying grace as loudly as possible, in competition with his Protestant chaplains.[13] More seriously, with war approaching, Charles feared her household was riddled with spies.

In June 1626, a year after Henrietta Maria's arrival in England, Charles decided it was time to exchange her French servants for English ones. This was usual practice and many English families, anxious to see their relatives in the queen's household, had been busy ensuring their daughters had been practising their French. Buckingham, however, had persuaded Charles that his friends and relations should predominate. Their names included that of the woman Buckingham was said to have lined up to be Charles's mistress: the twenty-six-year-old Lucy Hay, Countess of Carlisle.[14] If so, this posed a formidable threat to the sixteen-year-old queen.

Like Henry VIII's Anne Boleyn, from whose sister she was descended, Lucy Carlisle's 'bright ... conquering eyes' held many men in their power.[15] The poet John Suckling confessed to voyeuristic fantasies, describing how watching her walking in Hampton Court's gardens 'I was undoing all she wore / And had she walked but one turn more / Eve in her first state had not been / More naked or more plainly seen.' Yet Lucy was more than merely the 'killing beauty' of the age. Powerful men stood 'in awe of her wit' and some were even a little afraid of her cruel put-downs. One victim described her as 'the most charming of all things that are not good, and the most delightful poison ever nature produced'.[16]

Lucy Carlisle's mother had been a Devereux, making her a first cousin to the Rich brothers, the earls of Holland and Warwick, as well as to the Earl of Essex, while her own brother headed the great Percy family of the Earls of Northumberland. As for her relationship to Buckingham – she was said to be his lover.

Henrietta Maria warned Charles 'she would never have confidence' in any of Buckingham's choices and had 'a great aversion' for Lucy Carlisle in particular.[17] Over the following weeks her French servants helped block the new English members of her household from attending on her.[18] In August Charles lost patience. Buckingham was told to 'send all the French' back across the Channel, 'like so many wild beasts'.[19] Henrietta Maria was allowed to keep several favoured priests, which meant her religious rights would be upheld. But the ill-tempered manner in which she had lost servants, whom she considered 'family', had left her distraught. Charles's 'wild beasts' had included a Mme St George, who had been like a surrogate mother to her since she was in the nursery.

In the closed private archives of Belvoir Castle lies one of the greatest collections of civil-war manuscripts in the world. Many of these documents are unknown to historians and among them are many royal letters. One was now written by Henrietta Maria to the banished head of her ecclesiastical retinue, the Bishop of Mende. She had been forbidden from communicating with anyone unless in the presence of her English servants.[20] She complained to Mende she had to hide away to write to him, 'like a prisoner who cannot talk to anyone, neither to describe my misfortunes, nor to call upon God to pity a poor, tyrannised princess and to do something to alleviate her suffering'. Miserably, she announced, 'I am the most afflicted person on earth. Talk to your queen [Marie de' Medici] my mother about me and reveal to her my woes. I say Adieu to you, and to all my poor servants, and to my friend St George, to the Countess of Tillières, and all the women and girls who (I know) have not forgotten me. I have not forgotten them either.' With all the drama that a teenager can summon she concluded, 'Is there any remedy for my suffering, which is killing me? Goodbye bitterness. Goodbye to those from whose actions I will die if God does not have pity on me. To the wise Father who prays for me and the Friends I hold to me always.'[21]

Henrietta Maria continued for a time to assure Charles she would 'find it very difficult to accommodate herself to the humours of the Countess of Carlisle'. Yet, within a few months, Lucy had become the queen's great favourite.

Henrietta Maria was bored by the formality of Buckingham's female relations. Unlike Charles, she was uninterested in the strict observation of hierarchy and had been used to a relaxed atmosphere with her French friends. Now they had gone, she found she enjoyed the intimate supper parties Lucy threw for her. In a court filled with cautious 'frenemies' Lucy was outrageously frank in her opinions. She joked and gossiped, her eyebrows plucked high, as if caught in mock surprise at her own words. Henrietta Maria also had a teasing wit and she ended up relishing Lucy's company.[22]* But Henrietta Maria had something more important in common with Lucy – both women were political animals and they were using each other for political ends.

For Lucy Carlisle, male admirers were a means to power and influence. In James Hay, Earl of Carlisle, she had married a Scotsman who was much older than herself and far from handsome: Charles's sister, Elizabeth, the Winter Queen, called him 'camel face'.[23] He was, however, a highly successful diplomat. Lucy's only child had died as an infant and the international political world of which Carlisle was part had become the central focus of her life. She had made sure she stayed close to Buckingham because he was the greatest man in England – after the king. Since Charles was too dutiful a monarch to take her as an official mistress, Lucy considered the advantages of a friendship with the queen. As Mme de Chevreuse's activities in Paris

---

* Years later the queen would recall how, once, trapped on a ship in a storm with her ladies-in-waiting, she had heard several of them shouting out confessions of their sins above the noise of the wind – afterwards when they were safely back on shore she had teased them mercilessly about their guilty secrets.

demonstrated, a queen's affections were a useful power base and one Lucy hoped to make good use of. Yet Henrietta Maria was no mere stooge. Although only sixteen, she had hard-headed motives of her own for making Lucy her favourite.

Charles's cause was going from bad to worse in Europe. His uncle, Christian IV of Denmark, had suffered a crushing military defeat in August. Buckingham, however, was now encouraging Charles into a war with France that would see the British kingdoms fighting both of the great powers – France and Spain – at once. His reasoning, as Lord Admiral, was that Richelieu's build-up of French naval forces posed a threat to England. Charles fretted that 'the chief design both of our enemies and our ill-affected friends is to dispossess us of that sovereignty in those seas to which ... all our ancestors have enjoyed time out of mind'.[24] Yet even Buckingham's own mother suspected that his anxiety over the navy also owed much to a personal sense of rivalry with the cardinal.

In the spring of 1627 the tensions exploded in a trade war, with English and French ships clashing on the high seas.[25] Buckingham wanted Charles to respond aggressively. Henrietta Maria believed Charles would do better to improve his relations with Louis so that France might aid him in his war against the Habsburgs. She sought reconciliation and showered favours on courtiers who advocated her policy. Principal amongst them were Lucy and her husband, who had a long history of being anti-Spanish and pro-French, in the same manner as Lucy's cousin, Henry Rich, Earl of Holland.

Lucy's political differences with Buckingham later inspired a series of scandalous accounts of her plotting with Richelieu against her former lover. This malicious (and untrue) gossip was later repeated in Dumas' *Three Musketeers* with Lucy's part reinvented in the character of the fictional Milady de Winter.[26] In fact, far from being deadly enemies, Buckingham remained on reasonable terms with Lucy 'Milady' Carlisle. As war with France became inevitable he needed her as a point of contact with Henrietta Maria.

*   *   *

It was not just Buckingham who pressed Charles to go to war with France. Charles's godfather, the Duke de Soubise, begged him to aid the Huguenots against Louis. The French king had used English ships, which had been lent to him for the war with Spain, against these Calvinist rebels, and then had broken a treaty agreement made in February 1627 to lift the siege of the Huguenot stronghold of La Rochelle. In April Charles travelled to Portsmouth to oversee in person the preparations for an attack which he hoped would relieve the French port.

To pay for his double wars Charles had resorted to some desperate, and in legal terms, highly dubious, forms of fundraising. He had deployed the royal prerogative to raise compulsory loans from his subjects. The reaction was widespread disobedience. Several 'patriot' peers refused to pay out, or gave as little as they could get away with. They included Essex and Warwick, along with Warwick's fellow colonising aristocrats, the 'proud, morose and sullen' William Fiennes, Viscount Saye and Sele, and his son-in-law, Theophilus Clinton, Earl of Lincoln.[27] The 'patriots' argued that the forced loan was part of a project to 'suppress Parliament' and they organised resistance in their home counties, warning that to pay it was to 'make ourselves the instrument of our own slavery'.[28]

Charles's Arminian clergy backed his actions from the pulpit, while Puritan divines helped promote the political initiatives of the 'patriot' peers. Amongst them was a radical preacher called Hugh Peter, whom Warwick had brought from Essex to London. Above average height, with a large nose and dark eyes set wide apart, Peter was the son of a merchant from Cornwall, and had a liking for good food, bad women and plenty of wine. Not, perhaps, a typical Puritan, but his sermons were fluent, witty and persuasive, with Peter issuing aggressive pleas for God to reveal to the king 'those things which were necessary for … government', and the queen to 'forsake idolatry'.

Charles threatened peers who refused to pay the loans with prison, and four were sacked from their local offices. Seventy-six gentlemen were punished more harshly. They were jailed for refusing to pay and

Charles made an example of five knights by denying them bail. Lower down the social scale, townsfolk across the country were threatened with having their houses torn down if they did not agree to the loans, while in London many of the City's handicraftsmen, shopkeepers and new merchants nevertheless also stood up to the Crown, egged on by preachers like Hugh Peter.[29]

Other unpopular measures taken in the war effort included soldiers being billeted on private households and martial law declared for reasons of national security. For Charles, however, the heavy political cost would all pay off in the event of a victory in France. Henrietta Maria, meanwhile, assured Buckingham that, although she had sought peace, now it had come to war, 'she must prefer her husband's honour before all the world'.[30]

On 27 June Charles launched the greatest naval offensive England had ever made against France. Over a hundred ships crossed the Channel under Buckingham's command. They disembarked at the Île de Ré near La Rochelle, on 12 July. Cardinal Richelieu took personal charge of the French response. A painting by the nineteenth-century artist Henri Motte imagines Richelieu in armour and scarlet silk, standing at the edge of a churning sea. The real scenes, as they unfolded, were scarcely less dramatic. Buckingham's cannon proved too few and too small to break the island's garrison fortress. The duke and his army were left trapped in heavy rains for weeks, with the men falling prey to illness and disease. Louis XIII entrusted the government north of the Loire to Marie de' Medici once more, as he joined his army on the mainland in person, to oversee operations along with Richelieu.

By October Buckingham was desperate for reinforcements, but a shortage of money and contrary winds saw a fatal delay in the promised arrival of a force under Henry Holland. Eventually, on 27 October, Buckingham withdrew his men through the island's salt marshes under attack by the French. It was said 'no man was more fearless, or more ready to expose themselves to the brightest dangers'.[31] But the casualties were heavy. Of Buckingham's 7,000 men only 3,000 reached

Portsmouth in November. Amongst those killed was Sir Charles Rich, younger brother of the earls Holland and Warwick.

It was an historic defeat, worse than the disasters of Breda and Cadiz combined. 'Every man knows that since England was England, it never received such a dishonourable blow', one Cornishman wrote. Reports of Buckingham's courage did nothing to dent public fury. He was accused in ballads and news-sheets of 'treachery, neglect and cowardice'. The angriest were those who had served under him and were now left unpaid. Buckingham had spent over £10,000 equipping himself and his servants for the campaign. His essentials had included £367 8s 6d for a silver perfuming pan. It was true that a duke was expected to keep up appearances, and perhaps also to be pleasantly scented, even while on campaign. Yet many of his men and their families were starving, and in February 1628 a group of sailors attacked his London house.

Charles's money was all spent and his debts were growing exponentially. Parliament was the quickest and most effective way to raise the taxes to pay them off. A number of Charles's councillors were anxious to call one and to use the opportunity to heal the wounds created by the forced loans. Charles blamed himself – and Parliament – for the failure to send reinforcements to the Île de Ré, and was appalled by the mobs at Buckingham's gate. Henry VIII or Elizabeth I would have thrown Buckingham to the wolves.[32] Charles did not yet understand it was more important for a monarch to inspire loyalty than to be loyal. He thought it honourable to take personal responsibility and feared for his friend. But he also feared for French Protestants. 'Louis is determined to destroy La Rochelle and I am no less resolved to support it,' Charles assured the Venetian ambassador, 'otherwise my word and my promises would be void, and that I will never allow.'[33]

On 20 February 1628, with deep reluctance, Charles duly called the third parliament of his reign.

EXIT BUCKINGHAM

'THIS IS THE CRISIS OF PARLIAMENTS,' ONE MP OBSERVED. 'WE SHALL know by this if parliaments live or die.'[1] On 17 March 1628 when Parliament opened, Charles had warned his MPs that if they failed to grant funds for the war he would revert 'to other courses'.[2] Dressed in chocolate-coloured silk trimmed in gold, Charles's expression in his portrait by the Dutch artist Daniel Mytens is resolute. MPs understood that if Charles was forced to rely on his own emergency tax-raising powers the institution could suffer the recent fate of the French parliament. Known as the Estates General, the French parliament had suggested tax cuts in 1614, rather than the increases the Crown had needed. It was dissolved – and had not been recalled since. Nor would it be for generations to come.[3] Charles still accepted that there were great benefits of working with Parliament, but he had come to wonder if this was still possible.

With both king and MPs anxious to reach an accommodation, Parliament voted for a bill that would grant Charles £300,000. In exchange Charles duly examined MPs 'grievances' – the traditional give and take between king and Parliament. Charles accepted that forced loans, the compulsory billeting of soldiers and the use of martial law against civilians were all 'unlegal'. He insisted, however, on the right to refuse bail without showing cause – as he had with the five knights who had refused the forced loan. Such uses of the royal prerogative were, he said, sometimes necessary for national security. The judges in the Lords agreed. MPs in the Commons did not. They protested instead that Charles was making his subjects 'slaves' by claiming 'a sovereign power above the laws and statutes of the kingdom'.[4]

A Petition of Right was drawn up to set out what MPs considered the rightful liberties of the king's subjects to be. Its careful wording avoided any repudiation of the king's prerogative, encouraging Charles to make a strategic retreat. But the entire argument between Crown and Parliament was made very public when MPs had the petition published.

In the past it was the Crown alone that had been largely responsible for the publication of political material. Now debates in Parliament were being printed and disseminated into the provinces. Six books had been brought to Bristol alone, describing the Commons arguments on the liberties of the subject. The publication of the Petition of Right took things further. MPs were, in effect, going to the country with a constitutional programme and raising the threat of public violence if Charles did not accept it. Charles angrily accused 'some of the members of the house, blinded with a popular applause' from trying to 'destroy our just power of sovereignty'. Nevertheless, on 7 June, he consented to the petition.

On another matter, however, Charles would not bend.

MPs issued a protest document known as a 'remonstrance', demanding that Buckingham be removed from office. Where Charles saw military failure as the consequence of disobedience and Parliament's refusal to honour the costs of war at a time of national danger, the remonstrance indicated that government incompetence and 'popery' were to blame. Concern was expressed at recent innovations in religion and in government that endangered the church, Parliament and the law, suggesting these were the cause of disasters at home and aboard, and 'at a time when our religion is almost extirpate in Christendom'.[5] It was met by Charles's orders to the Commons not to interfere in matters that did not concern it – namely a king's right to choose his own councillors.

What followed on this announcement was 'such a spectacle of passions as has seldom been seen in such an assembly'. There was weeping, shouting and further wild allegations. One MP claimed Buckingham was plotting to 'drive out the king' from his throne and take it for himself. Another that Buckingham 'has got all our shops, forts into his hands' and had 'soldiers in every place to cut our throats'.[6] As these speeches were disseminated throughout England, public anger against Buckingham rose to dangerous levels. Satires and songs even accused Buckingham of being in league with the Devil. A poem had Buckingham boast that he had got away 'in the poisoning of the monarch of this land' – King James – by using black magic.[7] His astrologer John Lambe was also said to be his 'familiar' – a species of witch's helper first identified during the reign of Queen Elizabeth.

An act of actual murder followed.

On 13 June Lambe was attacked in Cheapside by a mob calling him 'the duke's devil'. He lost an eye from the beating and died the following day. Soon a new ballad was sung in warning:

> Let Charles and George do what they can,
> The Duke shall die like Doctor Lambe.

Buckingham demanded justice. The City authorities did not oblige, even though two of the marshal's servants had witnessed the murder and knew full well who the perpetrators were.[8] Charles could have taken matters further. Others later argued that he should have made an example by executing the lynch mob's ringleaders. But his focus now lay elsewhere. On 26 June 1628 Parliament was prorogued for the summer and Charles left London for Portsmouth to prepare a new fleet for the relief of the Calvinist Huguenots of La Rochelle. The conditions in the besieged city were appalling. Dog meat had become a luxury with people reduced to eating leather boiled in tallow.

The Huguenots feared that if they surrendered they would face the same fate as Bohemia had suffered since the Battle of White Mountain. The kingdom's former privileges within the Holy Roman Empire had vanished, nobles had been executed, fortunes had been confiscated, and Bohemia was now being ruthlessly re-Catholicised. Desperately the Huguenots awaited Charles's fleet and salvation.

Henrietta Maria, meanwhile, had been writing secretly to her mother, asking her to work for peace. She feared another disaster would soon befall England and her husband.[9]

Now eighteen, Henrietta Maria's marriage to Charles had become much happier. It was commented on how loving they were towards each other. She still disliked Buckingham, however, and her feelings had not altered even after his wife had delighted her with an unusual gift: an eight-year-old child who, although perfectly proportioned, was only eighteen inches high. He was called Jeffrey Hudson. Henrietta Maria had commissioned Mytens to paint several portraits of herself and the tiny boy to be sent abroad as gifts to friends and relations.[10] We do not know if any of these were destined for Marie de' Medici, but the queen dowager had asked her daughter for a picture, and a letter in the Belvoir archive reveals Henrietta Maria had found an opportunity to send her one.

Henrietta Maria warned her mother the painting was rushed and the clothes done badly. Queens were expected to look their part. Many of her favourite summer dresses at this time were in a wavy silk called 'Genoese tabby', in white, black or a grassy green, each decorated with silver or gold.[11] She begged her mother to have the picture altered and the clothes in her portrait 'made more beautiful' – a fascinating insight into the attitude sometimes held towards artists whose works today hang in great museums.[12]

Shortly after this letter was sent Henrietta Maria received shocking news from Portsmouth.

Buckingham had been staying at the Greyhound Inn when, on 23 August, he was brought intelligence that an advance English force had relieved La Rochelle. He literally danced with joy. He then ate a hearty breakfast and ordered a carriage to drive him to the king, who was staying outside the town. Buckingham did not wait even to kiss his wife, who lay in their room upstairs, tired and pregnant. Whatever the nature of his past relationships with King James and Lucy Carlisle, his was a contented marriage.

The inn was already crowded as he walked towards the hall, pausing to speak with one of his colonels. They bowed to each other from the knee, one foot forward. As Buckingham straightened, he saw a man leaning over the colonel's lowered shoulder and felt a punch. 'Villain!' Buckingham shouted and, staggering back, he pulled out a dagger from his chest. He tried to draw his sword and move towards his attacker, but fell against other men in the press of the hall. Horrified and astonished, they lifted him onto a table.

Upstairs, Buckingham's wife heard the commotion and sent a friend onto the open gallery above to see what had caused it. From there her friend saw Buckingham lying on the table surrounded by moving heads and hands, his face turned up towards her and blood gushing from his mouth.[13] He was not yet thirty-six.

Henrietta Maria dashed off another letter to Marie de' Medici telling her she had just learned 'the duke is dead'. She guessed that by the time her letter arrived her mother would also know Buckingham had been assassinated, 'but not how'. She told Marie de' Medici that he was 'killed with a knife'. She was under the impression that he had been alone with his murderer and it had been quick. His only words were 'I am dead' while his unrepentant killer was now insisting that the murder was a job 'well done'.[14]

Marie de' Medici forwarded the letter to Richelieu, hoping it would be shown to Louis. 'You see what a state she is in,' she wrote of her daughter, 'and how worthy of compassion.'[15] With Buckingham gone

---

* They did not bow from the waist as breeches and doublets were worn fastened together.

Marie de' Medici wanted peace between her children and their warring kingdoms.

It soon emerged that Buckingham's murderer was an embittered soldier who had been wounded at the Île de Ré, and who was owed £80 in back pay. He was caught in the kitchens of the Greyhound, and in his hat, which he lost as he fled, were pages of Parliament's remonstrance demanding Buckingham be sacked.

Charles was hearing divine service when a messenger whispered to him what had occurred. As the horror sank in he 'continued unmoved without the least change in his countenance, till prayers were ended, when he suddenly departed to his chamber, and threw himself upon his bed, lamenting with much passion and with abundance of tears'.[16] His friend was dead, and, he later observed, he was 'so near me' the murderer might as well have aimed the dagger at his own breast. To add to his misery Charles was forced to hold Buckingham's funeral at night so that he could be buried at Westminster Abbey without disturbances.

Charles mourned Buckingham deeply. Buckingham had been a friend with a 'nature just and candid, liberal, generous and bountiful' and 'of such other endowments as made him very capable of being a great favourite to a great king'. Charles had him buried in the Henry VII chapel, previously reserved for those of royal blood, and near his father, King James, who had loved Buckingham so well.[17] Aged twenty-seven Charles had no more need for a mentor, however, and he would never again make the mistake of maintaining any other such great – and hated – favourite.

The news that Buckingham had been bringing to Charles proved false. La Rochelle was not relieved and in October 1628 the Huguenots surrendered to Louis XIII. Of a population of 27,000 only 8,000 had survived the siege and it was said they were so thin and frail they looked like ghosts. On All Saints' Day, 1 November, Louis made his entry into the port. The starving inhabitants lined his route on their knees crying out 'Long live the king'. The main church had undergone a ceremony of purification the previous day to convert it from Protestant to Catholic worship and there the 'Te Deum' – a Catholic prayer of thanks – was sung. The Counter-Reformation had won again.

Henrietta Maria now lavished her love on her grieving husband. She also put all her quarrels with Buckingham's relations behind her and went in person to see Buckingham's widow and his mother to offer her condolences. Her own favourite, Lucy Carlisle, left no comment for posterity on the murder of the man who was said to have once been her lover. She had nearly died herself that summer, having caught smallpox. Miraculously she had been left unscarred and Henrietta Maria had been one of the first to visit her. Indeed she seemed prepared to put her life at risk and there was 'much ado' to keep the queen away until Lucy had fully recovered.[18]

Lucy's place in the queen's affections was now more valuable to the Carlisles than ever. Come December, Lucy's husband was predicting that the queen's 'influence [which] was rather eclipsed by Buckingham's favour ... would now shine as her eminent qualities deserved'.[19] This made Lucy the favourite of a more powerful queen.

The end of Buckingham's dominance at court meant opportunities for others too. Henry Rich, Earl of Holland, had scarcely waited for Buckingham to be dead twenty-four hours before he had written to Charles asking for one of the duke's former offices.[20] He was soon given Buckingham's former position as Master of the Horse, a role that guaranteed constant attendance on the monarch. Others were hopeful that Buckingham's death also offered the possibility that the king's fractured relationship with his MPs would heal.

It was God – or rather the business of God – that ensured people's hopes were to be disappointed. Although one hated servant was dead, another highly controversial figure had been promoted. Charles had raised the notorious anti-Calvinist cleric Richard Montague to the post of Bishop of Chichester during Parliament's summer recess.

Charles intended for parish churches to become a vehicle for the propagation of a culture of deference to lawful authority and the promotion of sacral kingship. He was certain the military failures since 1625, and their damaging consequences to the monarchy, had been occasioned by the corruption of disobedience, for from that had followed the refusal to help pay for the war's necessities. There were MPs who wanted 'to reduce his power to nothing', Charles complained, 'Puritans', 'enemies of monarchs' and 'republicans'.[21] His efforts to change their rebellious culture had to be redoubled.

Accusations of Arminianism had followed a ban on sermons and public discussion concerning the theology of predestination. The ban existed, however, only because Charles feared such discussion was dangerous to public order. If good works played no role in saving your soul then, some believed, you might as well live as you pleased. It was religious practice, not theory, that mattered to Charles. 'Godliness is good manners', as one of his chaplains observed.[22]

In place of Calvinist preaching, emphasis was placed on set prayers, kneeling and standing. Churches were also gradually being reordered. Wooden Communion tables, kept in the centre of the church for parishioners to gather round for the Lord's Supper, were coming to be positioned like altars, east-wise under windows, and protected by rails to encourage a sense of reverence.[23] Plain glass windows were being replaced by stained glass offering valuable religious lessons. In Oxford, the new enamelled east window of the chapel of Lincoln College bore an image of Christ with Charles's face: a reminder that he was God's image on earth. Where James had promoted divine-right kingship in words, Charles was doing so visually.

Some parishioners welcomed the changes. They described their relief at Communion tables being protected by rails that prevented them being used to dump hats on. They also liked the beautification of their churches, and the new ritualised forms of worship. Others, however, feared that the placing of Protestant tables like Catholic altars was only a step away from tables being used as altars, and that all images in churches were idolatrous. Puritans raged against the new 'popish baits and allurements of glorious pictures, Babalonish vestures, the excessive number of wax candles at one time, and especially the horrible profanation of both sacraments with all manner of music'.[24]

The more active Puritan opponents to Charles's changes were punished in the church courts, as Charles sought to impose uniformity. In response, their protectors amongst the godly 'patriot' peerage plotted to use the American colonies as a base for opposition campaigns.[25] For the time being, however, the Puritans and their allies had Parliament as their platform – and religion was to be the focus of the first debates when MPs reassembled in January 1629.

There were many complaints on the floor of the Commons about the increase in popery since the reign of Queen Elizabeth. It transpired, however, that there was little agreement amongst MPs about what the Church of England should look like. Most wished to preserve the church's Calvinist character. Others, however, actively approved of the reverent style of Protestant worship that Charles encouraged, while a radical minority wanted further Calvinist reform that would abolish the episcopate. Eventually, exhausted by their own squabbling, MPs returned to the vital question of customs duties.

Tonnage and Poundage were duties that had been granted to English monarchs for their lifetime, for the past 200 years. Only Charles had been denied them. The 'patriots' wished to continue with this policy, and so make Charles more financially dependent on Parliament. The king's supporters feared this would tip power too far from the Crown and they too now had a name – the Royalists. This distinction between MPs, into opposing parties, was seen as a troubling development – and it was one that was about to see an explosion in violence on the very floor of the House of Commons.

* * *

On 1 March 1629, nine 'patriot' MPs met in a pokey room at the Three Cranes Inn just west of London Bridge.* They were convinced Charles was poised to dissolve Parliament, perhaps forever. A sharp-featured twenty-nine-year-old called Denzil Holles told his colleagues that as MPs they had a duty to their electorate to ensure 'that we go not out like sheep scattered: but to testify to the world we have a care of their safety'. The others agreed and, the following morning, as Parliament reassembled, the nine had their plans in place.

The Commons Chamber had been a royal chapel until the Reformation. MPs sat in the old choir stalls and a gallery that had been added since, creating a horseshoe shape, resembling a theatre.[26] Centre stage that day, beneath the Gothic windows of the old chapel, was the Speaker, Sir John Finch. In his mid forties he was a judged a 'good Speaker' and a 'good man'.[27] Charles had ordered Finch to adjourn Parliament for eight days, so he could negotiate a back-room deal on his prerogative taxes before MPs returned to their debates. Charles did not intend to dissolve Parliament as the nine MPs feared. But as Finch began to announce the adjournment, he was drowned out by shouts. He tried to stand, only to have Holles and a second MP grab him and force him down into his chair. The doors of the Commons were slammed shut and locked.

With Royalists and patriots throwing punches at each other, Holles shouted out a Commons resolution that anyone who supported 'innovations in religion', who advised the collection of Tonnage and Poundage, or who paid it, should be condemned as 'a capital enemy to the kingdom and commonwealth'.[28]

---

* The Three Cranes got its name from the timbers used to winch barrels of wine from boats on the river outside it. Drink here was cheap, and the playwright Ben Jonson described its regulars as 'Pretenders to wit' who had not 'a corn of true salt, not a grain of right mustard amongst them'. *Bartholomew Fair*, Act I, Scene I. Samuel Pepys later complained that even the best room in house was no better than 'a narrow dog-hole'.

With the session ending in chaos, Charles decided he now had to dissolve Parliament. In a speech in the House of Lords, he described the events of the past year as he understood them. He had seen an aggressive minority of MPs hijacking Parliament's proceedings hoping 'to bring our government into obloquy so that in the end all things may be overwhelmed with anarchy and confusion'. First they had attacked Buckingham as an 'evil counsellor'. Then, as soon as Buckingham was murdered, they had suggested 'new and causeless fears … to cast a blindness on the good affections of our people'. Now it was 'manifest the duke was not alone the mark these men shot at'. Buckingham had been merely a surrogate for an attack on the rights of the Crown. 'But be assured,' Charles said, 'we shall find honourable and just means to support our estate, vindicate our sovereignty, and preserve the authority which God has put into our hands.'[29]

The Tudors managed their parliaments by intimidation, messy compromises and words of love. For Charles, appeals to the emotions smacked of populism. His enemies used such tactics to raise 'new and causeless fears' to turn his people against him. He also found it difficult to gauge people's feelings and motives and so lacked confidence in his ability to manage his MPs as the Tudors had done. Hierarchy structured relationships in a way he understood and he felt intensely threatened by those who questioned his authority. Unfortunately that left his questioners also feeling threatened and encouraged disobedience.

Ruling without a parliament would now become a matter of royal policy. Without one, however, Charles could not afford to take any further role in the Thirty Years War. It was time to exit Europe, make peace with France, and Spain too, if that was possible.

Part Two

HIS WIFE'S FRIEND

'HAPPY IN THE LAP OF PEACE'

HENRIETTA MARIA WAS SIX MONTHS PREGNANT AND ALREADY SHE
was in labour. When the town midwife at Greenwich examined her,
she found the baby was breech and promptly fainted. With the midwife
carried from the room, and Henrietta Maria in great pain, the king's
surgeon was left to manage alone. The doctor asked Charles whether
he should save mother or child. Charles said the mother. Their son
died two hours later. Afterwards, Charles stayed at Henrietta Maria's
bedside, and wrote to her mother to give her the sad news.[1] It was
just over two months since the dissolution of Charles's last parliament.
He could no longer afford to be at war with Louis and this was his
first contact with Marie de' Medici since he had signed a peace with
France almost three weeks earlier. The baby was buried at Westminster
Abbey that night, 12 May 1629. Six pall-bearers, each the son of an
earl, bore the black velvet cloth over the tiny coffin.

Henrietta Maria had been only fifteen when she married and small
for her age. Four years had passed before she bore this short-lived
son. It may be that she had lacked the physical maturity to conceive
earlier. In the first of a further series of lost royal letters Henrietta
Maria refers sadly to the 'affliction' of her baby's death in correspondence
with Richelieu.[2] Her friend Lucy Carlisle knew the pain of losing an
infant, as did her sister Christine, the Princess of Piedmont, who also
commiserated. Christine's letter, however, announced the successful

delivery of her latest child. Charles answered it for his wife and found it in himself to be generous. He reassured Christine that her good news lessened their sadness, and announced himself optimistic that 'the unhappy accident that has befallen my wife' was the forerunner of better news.[3]

The following year Henrietta Maria was pregnant again, and this time she insisted she had her mother's midwife, Mme Peronne, present for the delivery of her baby. Peronne had travelled all over Europe for the birth of Marie de' Medici's grandchildren, but when she sailed to England accompanied by Henrietta Maria's dwarf, Hudson (who had been sent to the Continent to collect her), the ship was seized by Dutch privateers. For a time this had 'caused more upset at court than if they had lost a fleet'.[4] Peronne and Hudson were, however, soon released and the midwife proved her worth. At midday on 29 May 1630 Henrietta Maria delivered a healthy boy at St James's Palace. She had thus succeeded in the principal function of a royal consort – the production of a male heir. Charles was delighted and, while his wife rested on a bed of green satin embroidered with silver and gold, he sat with her, and wrote once again to Marie de' Medici.

'Madame, My joy, together with the speed of sending you the promptest news of the happy confinement of my wife, only allow me to tell you that, thank God, Mother and Son are doing very well.' He signed himself, 'Your most loving son and servant, Charles R'. Henrietta Maria interjected a comment that prompted him to add a postscript. 'My wife wanted me to write this in her name to show you that she is doing well, so her hand bears witness of this truth to you.' What follows is the very shaky handwriting of the exhausted new mother, signing herself in French, 'Your most humble and most obedient daughter and servant, Henriette-Marie'.[5]

Ordinary Londoners celebrated the birth of their prince with enthusiasm, enjoying an opportunity to 'so ply themselves with penny shots ... that at length they have not an eye to see withal or a good leg to stand on'.[6] The infant was named Charles after his father, though he in no way physically resembled him. Henrietta Maria wrote to a friend in France four months later describing her son as 'so fat and so tall he is taken for a year old'. But he had his mother's black eyes. Indeed, she wrote, the prince was 'so dark I am ashamed of him'.[7] It would earn him the later sobriquet 'the black boy'.

The birth of the future Charles II would ease the new negotiations for a peace with Spain. The recovery of the Palatinate was less urgent now that Charles's sister Elizabeth, the Winter Queen, and her sons were no longer his heirs – and Charles badly needed peace. Continuing the war would require him to call another parliament to raise the subsidies to pay for it. This in turn would provide the forum for a renewed attack on Arminian influence within the English church. The court was, however, bitterly divided between those who wanted to see the British kingdoms disengage entirely from Europe's wars and those who hoped the French peace was the prelude to a recall of Parliament and an Anglo-French campaign to check Habsburg power in the Old and New World.[8]

Henrietta Maria was for the French alliance. Philip IV's empire in Europe was like an aging elephant. The population of Spain was in decline, and internal poverty had become the price of external success. France, with its huge and growing population, was preparing to take down a lumbering and wounded beast – and remained a powerful potential ally for the Stuart kingdoms.

Surprisingly, however, the Carlisles, who had always been anti-Spanish (and, correspondingly, pro-French), held the contrary view, and wanted peace with Philip IV. Politics had been the basis of Lucy's friendship with the queen since 1626. It would now lead to the first serious breach in their relationship.

Rumours had surfaced as early as December 1628 that 'camel face' Carlisle had turned 'hugely Spanish'. Lucy had asked her husband for assurances that this wasn't so and had worked hard to protect him from the queen's anger. However unfaithful she was to her husband in the bedroom, Lucy was loyal to him in politics. After all, Carlisle's success or failure at court affected her own position.[9]

The rumours were true.

Although he remained deeply committed to the Palatine cause, Carlisle was indeed 'hugely Spanish'. France and Spain were falling out over their rival interests in Italy, and Carlisle judged that if they went to war, Spain would be desperate not to fight the British kingdoms as well as France. The return of the Palatinate could be the price of British neutrality. His differences with the 'pro-French party' thus concerned means rather than ends. But the division was nevertheless a bitter one, and viciously contested.

Tensions were high at court in June 1629 when the artist, and occasional diplomat, Peter Paul Rubens appeared in London in the role of Philip IV's envoy. Fifty-two years old, with a curled beard and moustache, Rubens' success as an artist had made him a rich man who 'appeared everywhere not like a painter, but a great cavalier, with a very stately train of servants, horses, coaches, liveries and so forth'.[10] Philip IV, who took 'an extreme delight in painting', had become his most devoted patron after Marie de' Medici, and for eight months, between August 1628 and April 1629, Philip had visited his rooms almost every day.

The Spanish king had matured into a hard-working and conscientious monarch, but also restless, depressive and indecisive. He took comfort in sex and his mistresses, while allowing himself to be overshadowed by his powerful minister, the Count-Duke of Olivarez, whose policies had yet to restore the Spanish monarchy to the glory Philip envisaged for it. 'The king alone has my sympathy,' Rubens observed. 'He is endowed by nature with all the gifts of body and spirit, for in my daily intercourse with him I have come to know him thoroughly. And he would surely be capable of governing under any conditions, were it not that he distrusts himself and defers too much to others.'[11] Rubens now had the opportunity to get to know Charles as well.

The King of England's eye as a collector had long impressed Rubens: even so, he was stunned to see Charles's 'incredible quantity of excellent pictures, statues and ancient inscriptions'.[12] Above all, however, Rubens fell in love with England, 'the beauty of the countryside', and 'the charm ... of a people rich and happy in the lap of peace'. Rubens' task was to arrange an exchange of ambassadors between Charles and Philip to begin peace negotiations. But that same month Richelieu had dispatched the French ambassador, Charles de l'Aubespine, Marquis de Châteauneuf, with instructions to persuade Charles into an alliance against Philip, and war.

An arch intriguer, Châteauneuf took up residence in the Holborn house of Lord Brooke, a London neighbour and friend of the Earl of Warwick, whose house was the hub of anti-Spanish lobbying. Warwick's brother, Holland, was Châteauneuf's principal co-plotter at court, where Holland served in key roles as the queen's High Steward, as well as Charles's Master of the Horse.[13] Châteauneuf assumed the pretty young Henrietta Maria had little interest in worldly affairs. Yet he also thought her potentially dangerous. It was clear that Charles loved her, and both Châteauneuf and Rubens feared she had a sexual hold over him. Women were believed to have higher sex drives than men and their ability to seduce men and make trouble was also well known.[14] They had brought evil into the world when Eve persuaded Adam to eat the forbidden apple in the Garden of Eden.

It was vital to Châteauneuf that Henrietta Maria be surrounded by pro-French and anti-Spanish influences. That meant Holland's promotion in the queen's household and the demotion of Carlisle's 'bright and sharp-witted' wife, Lucy. To this end Henrietta Maria was told that Lucy had 'abused her favour ... going so far as to make sport of her actions'. This the queen could well believe. In 'wild' moments, or 'very jolly' moods, Lucy would often show off her friends' letters and laugh at them behind their backs.[15] Lucy asked to see Henrietta Maria to defend herself. But the queen was persuaded that having such a conversation with a servant would be undignified. In January 1630

Charles advised Lucy to leave the court 'until the queen was appeased'.[16] She duly left for a month. On her return, she found that Henrietta Maria had a new best friend: Holland, who was seen out in the mornings riding 'with the king and queen in their chariot in St James's Park', and on such good terms with them that he kept his hat on.[17]

Rubens had been struck by Holland's extravagance – only 'camel face' Carlisle matched him in his appreciation of fine things and beautiful clothes. The earl was, in consequence, chronically in debt, but the war with Catholic Spain was not only a religious and patriotic duty to him, it was also good business. He had that year become governor of one of his brother's many privateering endeavours.* The Providence Island Company had been founded to plant a Puritan colony off what is now the Nicaraguan coast. Many of Warwick's colonising friends were involved: John Pym, Viscount Saye and Sele and Lord Brooke amongst them. The plan was for it to be a base from which to launch piratical attacks on Spanish shipping. The Dutch had captured much of the Spanish plate fleet in 1628, and gained 4 million ducats in gold. The Dutch fleet and its captive prize had put in at Portsmouth and Falmouth in December 1628, providing a revalidation in England of the claim that a naval war with Spain in the Caribbean could pay for itself.[18] It was also the kind of money that could buy Henry Holland a lot of suits.

Once Rubens had succeeded in arranging the exchange of ambassadors between Philip and Charles he prepared to leave England. But the future of his peace efforts remained uncertain. At his formal leave-taking of the court, on 22 February 1630, Henrietta Maria had offered a snub, deeming him 'not of that quality to require ... [a] solemn reception with the attendance of her great ladies about her'.[19] Rubens fretted she might yet undo all his good work, and persuade Charles into the French alliance. But Rubens need not have been so

---

* Warwick had sponsored about half the aristocracy's privateering ventures against Spain since 1626.

downhearted. Like Châteauneuf he had overestimated her political influence over the king. Charles wanted peace, which would free him from any immediate need to recall Parliament, and in producing an heir in May 1630, Henrietta Maria had given him a renewed incentive to pursue a treaty.

The peace with Spain was eventually signed in November 1630. Rubens' efforts in bringing about the peace were rewarded with a knighthood, £500 worth of diamonds and, in a personal gesture from Charles, the right to incorporate part of the royal arms of England as an augmentation of his own armorial bearings.[20] Carlisle, who like Rubens had worked for the peace with Spain, was made Groom of the Stool, which made him the first Gentleman of the Bedchamber and the man who controlled access to the king.[21] Since Henrietta Maria accepted Charles's decision, Lucy's former happy relationship with the queen began to be restored.

'What news?' asked a diary entry. 'Every man asks what news?'[22] War stories poured in daily from Bohemia, Austria, the Palatinate, the Netherlands and elsewhere. People sought to discover from the news-sheets the fate of the Calvinist churches abroad, 'seeing them as counterscarps and outworks of the Church of England'. As soon as any of them were threatened so the English and the Scots felt threatened, 'Apprehensions raising passions, passions leading to extremes both in action and judgement.'[23]

English, Scottish and Irish volunteers went to fight in large numbers alongside their co-religionists in Europe, despite the peace Charles had made. Atrocity stories brought many recruits and also ensured that the pressure for Charles to rejoin the conflict was often intense. Here no event was more significant than the fall of the German city of Magdeburg to Habsburg forces on 20 May 1631. At least 20,000 people were killed by soldiers 'in all sorts of merciless and wretched ways', or suffocated in cellars when the city burned. The mayor bemoaned that 'words alone cannot adequately describe these acts.'[24]

Words were, however, printed in plenty. At least 205 pamphlets appeared in one year in England describing the scenes.

But then at last Protestant revenge came. Four months later, the Lutheran King of Sweden, Gustavus Adolphus, inflicted the first major defeat on Catholic forces at Breitenfeld near Leipzig. He was promptly hailed as 'the Midnight Lion', the Protestant hero who, it had been foretold, would come from the north to defeat the Habsburgs.[25] Charles's courtiers began sporting moustaches and beards in the same style as the Swedish king. Charles dutifully sent an expeditionary force to Europe to act as auxiliaries, but would do no more – and his caution proved justified: Gustavus Adolphus was killed at the Battle of Lutzen the following year. In the same month, November 1632, Charles's brother-in-law, Frederick the 'Winter King', died of a 'pestilential fever' in Swedish-occupied Mainz.

Over nineteen years had passed since Elizabeth had married Frederick, and Charles had last seen his sister. The future Winter Queen had smiled so broadly on her wedding day that 'it was almost elated to laughter'.[26] Now, she told Charles, she was 'the most wretched creature that ever lived in this world'.[27] Frederick had called Elizabeth his 'heart's soul' and she had loved him in return.[28] Charles asked his 'dearest and only sister' to return to London and with 'as much haste as you conveniently can to come to me'. The apartments at Whitehall 'where she lay when she was a maid' were already prepared for her. Elizabeth, however, declined the offer. Frederick's letters to her, some with the sand used to blot the ink still clinging to them, are full of descriptions of the fashions he saw in Germany as he encouraged Elizabeth in their dream of returning to the Palatinate. It was a dream that she could not allow to die with her husband.

Elizabeth's eldest son, Charles Louis, was not yet of age. Until he was, she would seek covert ways to raise money for his cause in Europe, as well as initiating diplomacy and military action on his behalf. 'I … have become a stateswoman,' she admitted.[29] Charles, in turn, continued to send his sister what money he could to support her and her children, but he would not send an army. As one of his ministers observed, 'putting aside the bonds of consanguinity ... the Palatinate itself is as remote from his interests as it is from his dominions'.[30]

In Whitehall Charles hung a powerful anti-war painting, which Rubens had left him as a gift. Mars, the God of War, is held back, while Peace, in the form of a sensual nude, brings bounty. In the foreground children play: this bounty would be their future if peace prevailed.

Charles's own brood of children was growing. A daughter, Mary Henrietta, had been born in 1631. Lucy Carlisle was chosen as the princess's godmother. Lucy's differences with her cousin Holland were also resolved. They were even said to be having an affair. Come the new year of 1633, Henrietta Maria was pregnant again. The baby was to be a second son, named James.

Charles placed the Rubens picture in the gallery overlooking the old tilt yard. The money that used to be lavished on jousting and tilting was now spent instead on masques at the Banqueting House.[31] These were an exquisitely beautiful form of theatre, with words by Ben Jonson and gilded sets built by Inigo Jones shimmering in candle-light. Charles would often appear in these theatrical events cast as the sovereign of a chivalric elite, whose wise rule created order and harmony. They were, in effect, beautifully crafted political manifestos, and designed to provoke some of the wonder found in high art. Charles still wished to be seen as an heroic monarch, but in the absence of Parliament's subsidies to fight actual wars, these aspirations were transferred to the imaginary world of St George: an Arcadian fantasy of erotic delight, where the knight defeats the dragon and wins his lady.

Back in Antwerp Rubens completed a new painting celebrating the ultimate success of his visit to England. It was a vast canvas of St George and the dragon, set in an English landscape, and in which the faces of St George and his princess were those of Charles and Henrietta Maria. The dragon, lying dead, represented the conquering of strife and disorder, with the couple ushering in an era of peace and tranquillity. He knew his client well. Charles soon acquired the painting for his art collection.

The poet Thomas Carew described these years of peace as marking England's 'halcyon days'. While the Germans beat their drums, bellowing 'for freedom and revenge', it was for Charles's kingdoms to prosper. They could be 'rich and happy in the lap of peace', even as Protestant agony in Europe continued.

8

THE RETURN OF MADAME DE CHEVREUSE

LUCY CARLISLE'S HUSBAND DIED IN STYLE IN MARCH 1636. HE HAD suffered a stroke, but had several new sets of clothes made in his last days, 'to outface naked and despicable death'.[1] Lucy was saddened by this loss, but her grief was neither deep nor long-lived. Indeed, she was soon 'very jolly' and busy honing her political abilities.[2] Based in the Strand, she had, as a widow, gained that holy grail for the seventeenth-century woman – independence. 'Who shall control me?' asks a character in James Shirley's contemporary play *The Lady of Pleasure*. 'I live in the Strand, whither few ladies come / To live and purchase more than fame.' And what Lucy had was indeed more valuable than fame: she had influence.

'The gay, the wise, the gallant and the grave' flocked to Lucy's house.[3] Poets claimed her beauty outshone jewels, and her limbs left 'tracks of light'. Holland composed several such verses which were judged, even against this stiff competition, to be 'the worst that were ever seen'.[4] He did better with a gift of a diamond bracelet valued at the vast sum of £1,500.[5] And Lucy was worth it. As the powerful Lord Deputy of Ireland, Thomas Wentworth, observed, she was 'extremely well skilled how to speak with advantage and spirit for those friends she professes', promoting careers and speaking the truth to power.[6]

Lucy's success did little to improve the darker side of her character. Her sister Dorothy, Countess of Leicester, complained that she still

85

took pleasure in abusing 'most of her friends when they are absent'. Indeed she had grown 'greater in her own conceit than ever she was'.[7] Her gallants were her slaves and Lucy did not like playing second fiddle, even to the queen. Henrietta Maria scarcely dared ask her to perform in her masques for fear of being turned down.[8] Like it or not, however, Lucy owed much of her influence to her position in the queen's bedchamber, and Henrietta Maria too had grown in confidence, as had her husband, the king.

The outgoing Venetian ambassador described the thirty-six-year-old Charles in October 1637 as 'in the flower of his age'. Slender and muscular, he handled his 'arms like a knight and his horse like a riding master'. His hair was now short on the right side, and grown longer on the left in a fashionable lovelock. The Puritan pamphleteer William Prynne warned that lovelocks were used by the Devil to drag wearers down to hell for their 'shameful and uncomely vanity'.[9] But Charles's clothes showed just as little regard for pious restraint. Jacobean ruffs had given way to falling collars of intricate lace, and he wore silk suits with clashing coloured stockings: he bought enough to put on a brand-new pair four times a week. Sartorially, the most striking addition to his wardrobe was the new escutcheon of the Garter, which he had embroidered on his cloaks. A Cross of St George surrounded by glittering silver rays, it sparkled when he moved. Garter knights were expected to wear it in public 'at all times ... and in all places', along with their 'George': the badge of St George killing the dragon.[10]

There were no great favourites at court. The Venetian ambassador noted approvingly that in political affairs Charles selected 'his ministers not from affection, but from his opinion of their capacity'. In intellectual matters he showed 'literary erudition without ostentation, possessing what befits a king'. He was careful to set an example in sacred observance and his 'exercises in religion were most exemplary', while he showed 'no lusts or vices'.[11] The deeply charged physical and emotional relationship he had with his wife lay at the heart of the court, and continued to raise fears of her influence on him. 'The only dispute which now exists between us is that of our conquering each other by affection,' Charles admitted to Marie de' Medici.[12]

Turning twenty-eight in November 1637, Henrietta Maria was 'the happiest of women'. She loved 'beautiful clothes, physical elegance and witty conversation', as well as taking pleasure in her growing brood of children.[13] Prince Charles, aged seven, was full of energy and curiosity. The king would make him a Knight of the Garter the following year, to 'encourage you to pursue the glory of heroic actions', he told his son.[14] Lucy's god-daughter Mary, aged six, had her father's melancholic eyes and a wilful temperament. James, Duke of York, aged four, was as blonde as his brother was dark, and 'cared not to plod upon his games' but 'was delighted with quick and nimble recreations'.[15] As soon as he was five and allowed to wear breeches, he would be made honorary Lord Admiral. Sandy-haired Elizabeth was now almost two, while a baby, Anne – named after Charles's mother – was just eight months old.

In Stuart tradition the children were placed with governors, but the Stuarts were a close family by royal standards. The children of the Winter Queen later complained that she had preferred the company of her dogs to her offspring. By contrast, her brother Charles enjoyed measuring the growth of his children on a silver staff and accompanied his wife to play with them in St James's Park. They, in turn, adored their father, greeting him after he had been away 'with the prettiest innocent mirth that can be imagined'.[16] He placed their portraits where he could see them every day. He had commissioned several likenesses from Rubens' former assistant – another Catholic artist from Antwerp – the thirty-eight-year-old Anthony Van Dyck. Charles involved himself in many of the details, once asking why the youngest ones weren't painted in the aprons they usually wore to protect their expensive clothing.[17] Mary wouldn't stand still for her sittings, but Charles was delighted with the results. He kept one of the group portraits over his breakfast table. Another, of himself with Henrietta

Maria and the two eldest children, was hung at the entrance to his personal quarters at Whitehall. They advertised his success in maintaining the continuity of the dynasty.

Van Dyck was also painting many of the king's leading subjects. Installed in a house in the Blackfriars on a royal pension of £200 a year, and with the help of his studio, he churned out a picture a week. Not all Van Dyck's patrons were happy with his work. One countess demanded he make her figure 'leaner for truly it was too fat'. Even after his alterations she claimed 'the face is so big' it looked like a representation of 'the winds puffing'.[18] Most, however, felt differently. Native Protestant artists, uncomfortable painting nudity, lost commissions, for the ladies of the court loved his 'sweet disorder of the dress', with sky-blue silk falling off their bosoms and bare arms.[19] Men, meanwhile, were being painted for the first time with friends or brothers, their poses effortlessly aristocratic, lace tumbling down loosened shirts and foaming over tall leather boots: images that have come to define the Caroline court.

But Van Dyck was not the only artist to benefit from Charles's patronage. Diplomatic agents from Rome were wooing the king by helping to expand an art collection destined to become the greatest in English royal history.* Charles was like a boy at Christmas when these new paintings arrived. A papal agent once described him dashing to open the latest packages, taking Inigo Jones and Holland with him. 'The very moment Jones saw the paintings he greatly approved of them,' the papal agent reported, 'and in order to be able to study them better threw off his cloak, put on his eyeglasses and, together with the king, began to examine them very closely, admiring them very much.'[20]

Inigo Jones had started his professional life as a London joiner, before spending much of his twenties learning about art and

_____

* Henrietta Maria was particularly grateful for the introduction to Bernini, the greatest sculptor of his day. Van Dyck had painted the king's head from three angles, so he could do a bust of him.

architecture in Italy. He had arrived at court as a set and costume designer for masques. Ben Jonson complained he remained a control freak even at sixty-five years of age, insisting on being 'the main Dominus *do all* in the work'. Charles, however, was grateful 'that he educated workers constantly day and night in our service'.[21]

Charles had commissioned nine ceiling canvases from Rubens for Inigo Jones's Banqueting House. The neoclassical building begun in 1619 had been inspired by the town palaces of Palladio and Scamozzi that Jones had seen in Italy, and the exterior was coloured in contrasting bands of pale gold Oxfordshire stone and the redder burnt gold of Northamptonshire.[22] The ceiling, still a work in progress, would depict King James being transported to heaven as God's former representative on earth, and celebrate the rich benefits of peace now being realised under Charles. Beneath it would hang tapestries celebrating the history of the Order of the Garter.[23]

The king had transformed his finances since he had dissolved his last parliament in 1629. With the British kingdoms at peace and Europe at war, merchants were shipping their goods through English ports despite the high customs duties Charles charged. There was also unprecedented growth in trade with southern Europe, the Mediterranean and the Near East. Out of Charles's estimated total income of £900,000, almost £400,000 now came from customs duties.[24] The most productive tax Charles raised was, however, the reinvention of a prerogative tax dating back to the Middle Ages known as Ship Money, so called because it paid for the navy.

Eleven new ships of the line had been built with the Ship Money tax, including the *Sovereign of the Seas*, which, with 102 bronze cannon, was the most heavily armed battleship in the world. As Charles foresaw, the Royal Navy was key to Britain's future wealth and power. Nevertheless, the tax was traditionally raised only on coastal areas in time of war. Charles was raising it in peacetime and had extended it to inland areas without any parliamentary scrutiny. Indeed, this money was helping Charles rule without Parliament being called at all. As such the tax was seen as a threat to property rights as well as to 'the liberty of the subject'. And some opponents refused to pay.

Charles had sought to make an example of one repeat offender in non-payment: a member of Warwick's American colonising circle called John Hampden.[25] The former so-called 'patriot' party had high hopes when the case came to court that Ship Money would be declared illegal. But in November 1637 the judges declared for the king. It was now said that Charles was 'more absolute than either the King of France or the great Duke of Tuscany'.[26]

Yet John Hampden was widely treated as a hero, and Charles's future was looking far from secure. The departing Venetian ambassador thought Charles would 'be very fortunate if he does not fall into some great upheaval'.[27] He cited not only the 'diminution of the liberty of the people', but also Charles's religious reforms, spearheaded in England by the man he had made Archbishop of Canterbury in 1633: William Laud.[28]

Described by his social superiors as a 'little, low, red-faced man', 'of mean birth, bred up in a college', William Laud was a prelate with a mission and not much tact. The son of a clothier from Reading, Laud was, in private, a gentle intellectual who loved his cats and kept a dream diary in which he wrote of erotic encounters with the late Duke of Buckingham. In public, however, he was 'arrogant' with 'an uncourtly quickness, if not sharpness', a man who could 'not debate anything without some commotion'.[29] He was uncomfortable with women and his efforts to cultivate Lucy Carlisle had fallen on stony ground. He did, however, have Charles's ear.

Charles had given Laud a secular role as a privy councillor. This gave the archbishop more political power than any churchman had in England since the days of Henry VIII. Laud had no interest in living in the grand manner of a Cardinal Wolsey. He dressed modestly and teased clerics with a taste for the good life as 'the church triumphant' – that is, those who had already achieved heaven. He did, however, hope to return to the Church of England something of the standing of the pre-Reformation English church. To do this he sought to restore the wealth of the church as an institution. That meant regaining some of the lost church lands. Land meant power, and Laud believed the Church of England could be a power for good – and not just in terms of the political support the church could give the king.

Laud wanted to root out corruption in society. This had to begin with rooting out clerical corruption, and Laud was willing to use the ecclesiastic Court of High Commission against bishops as well as more junior clergy. More controversially Laud also took on rich and powerful gentry. The protection of the weak is a Christian duty and Laud used the Star Chamber in this spirit, prosecuting the mighty for such malefactions as hoarding grain for profit while the hungry starved, or enclosing the common land the poor used to feed their animals. In the parishes too, the clergy were encouraged to stand up to large landowners in the public interest. At the same time, however, the traditional roles of the gentry in their local communities were protected. 'Lawful recreations' such as archery and dancing, usually carried out on Sundays under the patronage of the local landowner, helped foster the community ties that Charles wished to cultivate, and so were permitted to continue – in the face of Puritan disapproval.

Puritans also wanted to reform the morals of their fellow countrymen in order to help transform England into a new Jerusalem. For Puritans that meant encouraging a strict observance of the Sabbath, as well as opposing the new ceremonial style of worship that was central to Charles's policy of building a more deferential society. Laud was ruthless in crushing such dissent, censoring the press and using the Court of High Commission and the Star Chamber to bring Puritans to heel. The punishments Laud meted out to troublemakers could not be compared to those suffered by opponents of Henry VIII's Reformation. There were no executions without trial, no one was starved to death in their cells, or burned alive. There were, however, fines, prison and, most horribly, mutilation, such as cropping men's ears.

Puritans continued to flee abroad to join the colonies in New England where they hoped their communities would become beacons of godliness, acting as 'a city upon a hill', inspiring their homeland by their example.[30] At home, meanwhile, large crowds came out to witness the suffering of the Puritan martyrs. Some came principally because they sympathised with Puritan religious beliefs. Others were more anxious about Charles's rule without Parliament, which was backed from the pulpit by the Laudian clergy, and many were alarmed by what they had heard of the growing influence of their Catholic queen, Henrietta Maria.

In 1625 Charles had forbidden his subjects from attending Henrietta Maria's chapels. Yet Henrietta Maria now had a splendid new chapel at Denmark House designed by Inigo Jones, and when the chapel had opened in December 1635, there had been three days of festivities that had attracted numerous non-Catholics. Charles had even donated a Rubens painting of the Crucifixion. There had since been many conversions amongst ordinary members of the public who had attended the Catholic Mass out of curiosity. Meanwhile, the rough-clad Capuchin priests in Henrietta Maria's household had achieved a number of further conversions, especially amongst her ladies-in-waiting.

It seemed to Puritans that Charles's queen was behind his religious changes, and that they were part of a popish plot to turn England over to Roman tyranny. 'Ordinary women can, in the night time, persuade their husbands to give them new gowns' so could not Henrietta Maria, 'by her night discourses, incline the king to popery?'[31] In fact, Charles was appalled by the Catholic conversions and used both stick and carrot to encourage conversions the other way – from the Catholic Church to the Church of England. He vigorously collected the fines that fell on Catholics for their refusal to attend Church of England services, and pushed on with his reforms, convinced that when Protestant worship was as impressive as Catholic ritual, he would be able to 'deal with ... the Pope as wrestlers do with one another, take him up to fling him down'.[32]

There was no attempt by Charles to modify the Elizabethan Thirty-nine Articles, which remain the defining statements of the doctrines of the Church of England. But anxiety was such that the more Charles and Laud beautified English liturgy 'the more the Puritans cling to the bareness of their worship', the Venetian ambassador noted, 'and what is worse, many other Protestants, scandalised by the new institutions, become Puritans from fear of falling into Catholicism.'[33]

Time, however, was on his side. Charles was young and had sons to succeed him. Rather than be intimidated by opposition to his reforms he was extending them, determined to succeed where his father had failed – in achieving religious uniformity across the three kingdoms. In July 1637 he had introduced a new prayer book into Scotland to bring the kirk and the Church of England into closer alignment. Instead it would unleash the very forces he most feared.

It is often said – and not inaccurately – that the first blow struck against Charles in the civil wars was a woman throwing a stool. On 23 July 1637, as the Dean of St Giles, Edinburgh, read from the new Scottish prayer book, a row of women sitting at the front of the congregation on fold-up stools began to clap and shout. They called him Satan's spawn and the stout Bishop of Edinburgh, sitting near the dean, was abused as 'a beastly glutton'. It was when the dean continued to read that the stool was thrown. He ducked, but the man who tried to stop a second such projectile was set upon, 'his gown rent, his prayer book taken from him and his body pitifully beaten and bruised'. The plump bishop then fled down the street, with women in pursuit screaming abuse, throwing clods of mud and threatening to cut his throat.

The stool-throwing was a pre-planned protest organised by the most firmly Presbyterian ministers of the kirk, along with leading aristocrats who resented the growing secular power of the bishops, and feared the restoration of church land at their expense. The passion of the matrons of Edinburgh expressed in the riot was real nevertheless, and not manufactured. Charles had underestimated the extent to which the stripped-down Calvinism of the kirk was bound up with the national, and even personal, identity of the Scots. His sole visit to Edinburgh as king was in 1633, for his coronation, which had been carried out in a manner many Scots had found offensive, with candles and crucifixes, a railed-in Communion table and bishops in surplices.

When Charles had subsequently purged awkward nobles from high office, replacing them with pliable lawyers and grateful bishops, ordinary Scots had begun to wonder what this outsider from England might introduce next.

Then came the Scottish prayer book.

It had been drafted by a committee of Scottish bishops and vetted by the Scottish Privy Council. But it was introduced on the royal prerogative alone, without consultation with the Scottish Parliament or any recent General Assembly of the kirk. It was now widely judged to be even more 'popish' than the English prayer book, which the Scots had always despised. Most notably it left out several words that denied any belief in the physical presence of Christ in the Eucharist – the core difference between Lutheran and Calvinist belief.

Further riots followed, along with a petitioning campaign against the prayer book and the bishops. But this was as much an aristocratic and nationalist rebellion as a religious one. By early 1638 Scottish dissidents had set up what amounted to a provisional government. Its aim was to limit the exercise of the royal prerogative, and to replace low-born bishops and lawyers as well as other 'evil' councillors with members of the traditional ruling elite.[34]

This sedition had to be confronted. In February 1638, Charles announced that opponents of the new Scottish prayer book would be treated as traitors. This sent shock waves south of the border. The Tudors had dealt with opponents of their religious reforms with the utmost savagery. Warwick and other colonising aristocrats wondered if the time had come for them to join the emigration to Puritan New England.

While they dithered, the Scottish dissidents responded aggressively by issuing a public contract known as the 'National Covenant'. Inspired by the Old Testament covenants made between God and his people, its signatories swore to protect their Calvinist kirk against popish influences. Loyalty was sworn only to a covenanted king – in effect a Presbyterian – who ruled according to the laws of the realm. It swept the central and southern Lowlands, raising political consciousness there in a way that had never been achieved in Scotland before. Its subscribers, irrespective of rank, were now political actors in God's design for their nation in the overthrow of popery. Charles believed, however, that this was the work of only a few dangerous malcontents who were in league with Louis XIII and Cardinal Richelieu.

Seditious alliances of fiery ministers and lairds dated back to the earliest days of the Scottish Reformation. James had described the consequences in his 'how to rule' handbook, the *Basilikon Doron*, and the last example had resulted in the execution of the Ruthven brothers on the day that Charles was born. The involvement of the French in Scottish affairs was even longer-standing. For centuries France had used Scotland as a 'bridle' on England, fomenting anti-English feeling in Scotland to ensure kings of England had to divert resources to their northern border, while confronting France to the south. It appeared to Charles that Louis was playing this old game.

France and Spain had been at war since 1635. The result was that Louis, the 'first son of the [Catholic] Church', and his cardinal chief minister were doing far more for European Protestants in their battles against the Habsburgs than the Stuart kingdoms ever had.[35] But renewed hopes in Paris of an Anglo-French alliance against Spain had risen and fallen over the course of 1637.[36] Louis feared that Charles might even make an alliance with Spain instead. An angry Charles now encouraged those concerns by welcoming to court a long-standing enemy of Richelieu. This was no less than Holland's reputed former mistress, the glamorous intriguer with the serpentine ringlets, Mme de Chevreuse.

* * *

On 7 September 1637 Mme de Chevreuse had left the Loire and ridden for the frontier with Spain. Successive quarrels with Richelieu had forced her to flee France, and she was disguised as a boy. Accompanied only by two grooms she successfully reached the Pyrenees and safety, changing back into her fine clothes at a remote monastic hospice. From there she had made her way to Madrid. As a favourite of Anne of Austria, she received a friendly welcome at the court of Anne's brother, Philip IV, and had spent December and January being banqueted and feted. Then, in February 1638, she had left Madrid for refuge in England.

Charles could not easily have forgotten the woman who had prepared Henrietta Maria for his wedding night. On her departure from England in August 1625 she had left behind her portrait dressed as an erotic shepherdess with one breast exposed.[37] She had later entangled not only English courtiers, but also Henrietta Maria in her plots against Richelieu. It was only in recent years that Richelieu had begun to build a better relationship with Henrietta Maria. Louis feared Chevreuse would again now 'perform unfriendly offices' against his government in England.[38] And, indeed, when she disembarked at Portsmouth in April 1638, Mme de Chevreuse had every intention of doing exactly that.

Chevreuse believed that France would benefit from making peace with Spain, just as Charles's kingdoms had benefited. Richelieu was an impediment to these hopes, but if Britain went into alliance with Spain this would force Richelieu's downfall. Her allies could then bring France to the negotiating table.

Charles sent her former lover, Henry Holland, at the head of a welcoming party of twenty-five coaches to bring her to Whitehall. Holland remained high in royal favour at court and had succeeded Lucy's late husband as Charles's Groom of the Stool. He also had a key position in helping raise money for the king by enforcing the medieval Forest Laws. At the palace Mme de Chevreuse was granted the privilege of being permitted to sit in the royal presence while the wife of the French ambassador was publicly denied a similar honour – an ominous snub to Louis XIII, whose representative her husband was. Charles also loaned Chevreuse a house in Whitehall's gardens. In it he hung a portrait by the high-baroque Italian artist Guido Reni depicting the biblical figure of Judith holding the decapitated head of her enemy, just as Chevreuse would have liked to do with Richelieu: Charles's joke.

Mme de Chevreuse was soon enjoying herself immensely. Charles paid her expenses while Henrietta Maria supplied her with fashionable clothes. 'She has renewed her old acquaintances and is making new ones,' a diplomat noted, 'all the lords pay her court and she passes the time merrily.'[39] Although she was personally pious, Henrietta Maria's friends were often rakish: there were drinkers, gamblers and fornicators amongst them. Chevreuse too liked to shock, and one day went swimming in the Thames, inspiring poets who compared her body to a galaxy of stars, shooting through the water like the Milky Way.[40] But she also spent more respectable hours attending the queen's masques. Often they depicted representations of the love Henrietta Maria shared with Charles, which in turn reflected the peace and order Charles had brought his kingdoms.

Yet worthy as these masques sound, to hot Protestants they demonstrated a moral threat every bit as much as Mme de Chevreuse swimming in public view. Henrietta Maria had revolutionised the English stage by introducing women who both spoke and sang. The Puritan William Prynne railed against this, arguing that women, standing on stage, 'perchance in man's apparel and [with] cut hair', subverted woman's divinely ordained submission to man. They were 'notorious whores', he wrote, both 'sinful and abominable'. His ears had been struck off for his words, and the masques with their transient kingdoms of gilded board continued. 'O shows! Shows! Mighty shows! / The eloquence of masques!' the underemployed Ben Jonson scoffed. 'What need of prose / or verse ... / You are the spectacles of state!'[41]

The court conversions also continued. In May 1638 one onlooker complained that it seemed 'Our great women fall away [from the Protestant faith] every day.'[42] Mme de Chevreuse made great play with the queen of trying to also convert Holland. Chevreuse knew very well that Holland would never become a Catholic. His support for Puritans was linked both to family solidarity and a genuine horror of popery, even if he was not a Puritan himself. But at court the distinction between those Calvinists, like Holland, who were Church of England conservatives, and as such disapproved of Charles's innovations, and those who were full-blooded Puritans and active dissidents, was being blurred. Lucy's brother, the Earl of Northumberland, complained that 'To think well of the Reformed religion is enough to make the archbishop one's enemy.'[43] Chevreuse's 'failed' efforts to convert Holland were designed to tar him with the Puritan-dissident brush, while reminding the queen that Chevreuse was a fellow Catholic and a much older friend. Holland remained viscerally anti-Spanish, and that was not an influence Chevreuse wanted anywhere near the queen.

While cutting Holland out from Henrietta Maria's circle, Chevreuse also busied herself making friendships with court Catholics to whom the queen was close, and began the promotion of the alliance when she 'artfully threw out some project of a marriage between the Princess Mary ... and the prince of Spain'.[44] Added pressure could be brought on the queen through her mother.

Marie de' Medici had been living in the Spanish Netherlands since a failed coup against Richelieu in 1630. Henrietta Maria was concerned about her, and Mme de Chevreuse persuaded the queen to press Charles to invite her mother to England. Laud was aghast at this development. Marie de' Medici was well known for her Counter-Reformation commitment, and Laud was already at his wits' end over the court conversions. Chevreuse, he observed, was 'a cunning and practising woman', and Marie de' Medici's imminent arrival with her 'seditious, practising train' would be a most 'miserable accident'.[45]

Charles, meanwhile, also dreaded the expense. He would have to pay to support Marie and her household at a time when financing his sister and her son, the Prince Palatine Charles Louis, was stretching his resources. The plan, however, had the advantage of further annoying the French. As the situation in Scotland continued to deteriorate, he agreed at last to his wife's request, and offered to welcome Marie de' Medici to England.

'A THING MOST HORRIBLE'

THE MOTHER-IN-LAW HAD LANDED, HER ARRIVAL ON THE ENGLISH coast heralded by storms. In London the 'great winds' of October 1638 were dubbed 'the queen mother's weather'. Having disembarked, Marie de' Medici took 'to her bed to recover from the discomforts of the sea and had recourse to medicine'.[1] Meanwhile, Henrietta Maria awaited her arrival at court anxiously. Marie had regularly admonished her little daughters to be compliant, demanding in her Tuscan-accented French that they were 'well behaved and obedient'.[2] Discipline had been strict and Henrietta Maria still felt a childlike need to please her.

A state entry to London was organised of a grandeur appropriate to Marie's rank as 'a mother of three kings' (her son being Louis XIII of France, and her sons-in-law Philip IV of Spain and Charles I of Britain). She was processed down Cheapside by Charles's entire court, along with six of her own coaches, seventy horses and 160 followers. There were monks and dwarves, dogs and nobles, while the crowd enjoyed at least the hope of also glimpsing the queen mother. In her youth she had been the embodiment of Rubens' ideal of beauty, all full curves and chestnut-gold hair. Even now her curvaceous body was reminiscent of those imposing saints and angels depicted in baroque churches, stampeding towards heaven in rolling waves of marble: indeed she was almost the Counter-Reformation in physical form.

Henrietta Maria greeted her mother, accompanied by her five children, and despite being heavily pregnant, threw herself at Marie's feet.

Although state apartments had been made ready for Marie at St James's Palace, Henrietta Maria was supervising the upgraded redecoration of the passage between her mother's bedroom and a Catholic chapel. Marie, meanwhile, pronounced her 'extraordinary satisfaction' at 'the great progress of their holy religion in the kingdom where it had formerly been so persecuted'.[3] Henrietta Maria had done well in fulfilling the written instructions she had been given at their parting in France.

Charles visited Marie daily and also proved generous.[4] By 5 November a warrant had been issued giving Marie an allowance of £100 a day.[5] Pensions of leading courtiers were, however, being stopped. Charles needed the money to face down the Scots.

That same month a General Assembly of the kirk had formally backed the Covenanters, condemning the new Scottish prayer book as popish and declaring episcopacy unlawful. This marked a challenge to Charles's authority across his kingdoms, for if bishops were 'unlawful' in Scotland, then it could be argued they were unlawful in England and Ireland too. The royal supremacy in religion that gave the king the right to direct religious policy in England was under threat, and so were his secular powers. Leading Covenanters, such as the Highland chief Archibald Campbell, Earl of Argyll, were pushing reforms through the Scottish Parliament that stripped Charles of his 'prerogative' rights, instituted the calling of regular sessions of Parliament, and denied Charles the power to veto legislation – thus allowing themselves to make law without royal consent. This included the abolition of the episcopal system, which Charles, like his father, believed had been ordained from the earliest Christian times and was a pillar of the monarchy itself.

'The aim of these men is not religion as they falsely pretend and publish,' Charles observed, 'it is to shake all monarchical government and to vilify our regal power, justly descended to us and over them.'[6]

As for their 'damnable Covenant': so long as it 'is in force I have no more power in Scotland than as a Duke of Venice, which I will rather die than suffer'.[7]

Already Van Dyck had begun to produce portraits of Charles in the guise of a military leader. In several Charles stands in armour, his hand resting on a helmet. Surviving studio copies of a lost original show the same image, but in these the king's hand rests instead on a transparent sphere. The inspiration came from a Titian in Charles's collection. Entitled *An Allegory of Marriage*, it shows a woman holding a transparent sphere as a symbol of the fragility of human happiness.[8] It was usual for a globe to be used as a symbol of terrestrial power. The weighty orb in the coronation regalia was one example. Yet, here, under Charles's hand, this symbol of power is as delicate as glass, as transient as a soap bubble.[9]

On 3 January 1639 Sir Henry Slingsby, the thirty-six-year-old deputy lieutenant of the West Riding of Yorkshire, went to Bramham Moor to see the light horse practising for battle. He had contributed two horses to support the king in the coming confrontation with Scotland, but he felt no pride as he watched his horses being trained. 'These are strange, strange spectacles to this nation in this age that have lived thus long peaceably without noise of shot or drum,' he wrote in his diary. That Englishmen should be poised to fight fellow subjects of the king was 'a thing most horrible'. He compared it to the freakish horror of looking up and seeing in the sky 'a flock of birds … fight and tear one another'.[10]

The effect on Charles of the coming conflict also should not be underestimated. Kings existed to ensure peace, prosperity and justice, ruling above the narrow interests of faction for all a nation's people. He had promised harmony in his court masques. This rebellion was a failure of kingship. A hundred years earlier, in the wake of another religiously motivated rebellion in 1536, Henry VIII had changed his burial wishes, moving his planned tomb from Westminster Abbey to

St George's Chapel, Windsor. He did so in order that he could be buried with the protagonists of the Wars of the Roses, with himself depicted as the embodiment of national reconciliation between the rival royal houses from which he claimed descent: a mark of his trauma in the face of the new divisions he had opened. This Scottish rebellion was equally a body blow to Charles's self-esteem. Even if he defeated the Scottish rebels, he mourned that 'It is my own people who will by this means for a time be ruined.'[11] Nevertheless, a war that neither side wanted was now almost upon them.

To pay for their army the Covenanters were raising taxes on a scale that far outstripped what Charles had ever asked of his Scottish subjects. Battle-hardened Scottish veterans were recalled from Europe, where the Dutch and the Swedes allowed Scottish merchants to buy munitions and ship them home. The Covenanters also sought the support of fellow Calvinists in England. At the forefront of those ready and most able to help were Robert Rich, Earl of Warwick, along with his fellow colonising aristocrats and their allies. If their treasonous dealing with the Scottish rebels were discovered, they intended that Puritan New England would be their safe refuge. A fort at the mouth of the Connecticut River was being reinforced, just in case they needed to defend themselves there from royal attack.[12]

Meanwhile, in London, Mme de Chevreuse and Marie de' Medici had persuaded Henrietta Maria of the benefits of a Spanish alliance against Louis. Lucy Carlisle was the first to report that she had 'heard the queen use strong violent persuasions to the king such as must presently make us ill with France'. The French ambassador was so concerned he encouraged Louis to 'foment the war in Scotland', just as Charles believed he was doing already.[13] With the French, the Swedes and the Dutch now lining up alongside the Covenanters, and the queen – and possibly the king – with Spain, the rebellion in Scotland risked bringing the Thirty Years War to England. Yet this was to be a fight not of Catholic against Protestant, but for the kind of

Protestantism that would be practised in Scotland – and ultimately in England too.

It was in this tense environment that, on 20 January 1639, Henrietta Maria delivered a daughter at Whitehall. The baby, named Catherine, lived only a few hours, but was no less loved for that. Just as today parents keep mementos of babies that have died, so the king and queen commissioned elegies and verse to memorialise her.[14] Over the next days Charles moved, distracted, from his traumatised wife's bedroom to his councils of war. The campaigning season would begin when the roads were dry enough to move large numbers of horses and heavy equipment. He planned to lead his own army, and as Henrietta Maria struggled to recover from the death of her baby, she did her best to contribute to the war effort. She began a fund-raising campaign amongst English Catholics and organised a weekly fast in her household, asking all Catholics to follow suit. It was supposed to offer a demonstration of the English Catholic community's moral and practical support for their king against rebels. But away from the court, English Catholics were terrified to now find themselves in the spotlight.

However powerful the Habsburg cause in Europe, at home English Catholics belonged to a small and threatened minority. They had survived, rubbing along with their Protestant neighbours by keeping a low profile. The fundraising and fasts raised that profile and encouraged suspicions that Catholics had a vested interest in the defeat of the Calvinist Scottish rebels.

Not only Catholics were viewed in England with suspicion, however. So were the Church of England's bishops, many of whom were also raising funds for the king's campaign. Archbishop Laud was said to have personally given the king £3,000. These actions were seen less as a mark of patriotic loyalty than as offering support for authoritarianism, since the money raised for the royal army helped – if only in a modest way – to ensure Charles did not have to call Parliament to pay for it. England had not gone to war without a parliament being called since 1323.

As the Rubens ceiling glorifying the divine right of monarchy and the riches of peace was being installed at the Banqueting House, in March 1639, the rebels struck. A Covenanter army of over 15,000 seized the royal castles of Edinburgh and Dumbarton. Despite the historic contempt the English had for the Scots, many English Puritans celebrated their victories. The Venetian ambassador judged that London was 'entirely favourable to the constancy and interests of the Scots'. This was, however, an exaggeration. There were plenty of non-Puritans who agreed with the Yorkshireman Henry Slingsby that the Scots were making 'religion a pretence and cloak for wickedness': that their true goals were to take power from the king for themselves.[15]

Slingsby marched north for Scotland with the king's army in a troop under Henry Holland's command. Holland had advised Charles against the war, but had nevertheless lobbied for his commission as second in command of the royal forces. Other peers had responded well to Charles's personal call to arms, bringing followers with them, 'some ten, some twenty, some more'.[16] The county militias, which constituted England's only peacetime army, had also been raised, ensuring the royal army was a match for the Scots in terms of numbers. Yet their equipment was poor and many of the troops were pressed men. 'I dare say there was never so raw, so unskilful and so unwilling an army brought to fight,' one officer commented: 'they are as like to kill their fellows as the enemy'.[17]

Charles still hoped that battle might be avoided. If he appeared in Edinburgh as King of Scots, and 'show myself, like myself', it would surely be enough to end the rebels' 'follies', 'impertinencies' and 'mad acts', he asserted.[18] Indeed the Scots were fearful of war. They had seen defeat at English hands many times in past centuries.

On 4 June Charles, camped with his army near Berwick, received intelligence that a Covenanter force was by the border town of

Kelso. He gave Holland orders to reconnoitre the Scots' position and to drive them out. Holland duly came upon an army 10,000 strong. The enemy was strung out in a shallow formation that made their numbers look still more impressive. He beat a swift retreat and passed on an exaggerated estimate of the Covenanter strength. It may be that Holland had seen what he wanted to see – a reason to give Charles pause. By the following evening, when the same Covenanter army appeared within sight of the king's pavilion, there were rumours they had 45,000 in their ranks. The royal army stood to arms for three hours, the responsibility of decision weighing on the king.

If Charles defeated the Scots decisively, it would shut down sedition in Scotland and weaken his critics in England. On the other hand the consequences of engaging in battle and then losing were unthinkable. Charles sent a page to start negotiations. A treaty was signed the same month. It was tragic for Charles to then discover that the Covenanters had had logistical and financial problems. His campaign might well have succeeded had he accepted battle. Instead all he had gained was time.[19]

In the New Year of 1640 Charles took part in the first court masque to be performed at the Banqueting House under the Rubens ceiling. The drama began with the arrival of the Fury named Discord, stating her intention to put the whole world into chaos. In response Charles appeared as King Philogenes, the lover of the people. Discord was put to flight and the king was rewarded by the appearance of his queen and her ladies. The last scene in the masque depicted London beneath a cloud-filled heaven from where a chorus sang, 'All that are harsh, all that are rude / Are by your harmony subdued.'[20]

This was the dream.

The reality was that both Covenanters and king were already preparing for a second 'Bishops' War'. Holland was to be demoted and Charles brought in his principal hard man to take charge of the coming campaign: the tall, forty-six-year-old Lord Deputy of Ireland,

Thomas Wentworth, who Charles raised that January 1640 to the rank of Earl of Strafford as a mark of royal confidence.[21]

Strafford was judged a man with a 'cold brain', 'of great observation and a piercing judgement into both things and persons'. He was, however, 'stooped at the neck', a sign of mental stress, and even in repose his 'countenance was cloudy'.[22]

Strafford had been the king's servant in Ireland for the past seven years, ruling the colony with a rod of iron. Three-quarters of the population were native Catholic Irish, persecuted for their religion and despised for their ethnicity. The next largest group was the Anglo-Normans, who had settled in Ireland during the Middle Ages. Most of them were also Catholic. As such they had lost the high office they had held until the mid-Tudor period in favour of more recent Protestant settlers from England and Scotland. Both James and Charles had encouraged these colonists by permitting them to expropriate Catholic land, especially in Ulster and Munster. Strafford supported the policy vigorously, seeing it as a means of further controlling the Catholic Irish, 'with their habitual hatred of the English government'.[23]

Strafford also argued that the king should seek to have a large standing army in the kingdom, supported from Irish revenues. In the longer term, and with Ireland tamed, Strafford intended that Charles could use this army 'in any part of Christendom', or, indeed, against rebels at home.[24] Meanwhile, Strafford had imposed royal control not only on Catholics in Ireland, but also on dissident Protestants, in terms of both the economy (ensuring Ireland paid for itself) and religious orthodoxy (he was a close friend of Laud). It was a policy he described as 'thorough' and it had earned him the thorough dislike of almost everyone in Ireland. In England, meanwhile, Strafford was regarded no better. He had thwarted courtiers used to enriching themselves at the king's expense and his 'sour and haughty temper' alienated many others.[25] Holland, in particular, detested him.

Strafford was rumoured to have once suggested to the king that he execute Holland after the flamboyant earl had got involved in a near duel. Holland now told the queen that Strafford was insane. When Strafford complained, Holland explained that he was referring to Strafford's constant illnesses. He had 'hypochondriac humour', Holland observed, and sniffed, 'If I mistake not the English', that meant 'civilly and silently maddish'.[26] Strafford, however, had at least one friend at court, and one whom Holland also admired: Lucy Carlisle. The hard man and the court beauty had even exchanged full-length portraits.

Strafford backed Lucy's financial interests in Ireland and helped promote her relatives into ever-higher office.[27] Lucy, in turn, provided him with information and contacts. Her sister, the Countess of Leicester, reported that Lucy was currently 'more in favour [with the queen] than she has been in a long time'.[28] This was, perhaps, because Lucy and Henrietta Maria's friend Mme de Chevreuse were now constantly together. Although they were certainly not natural allies, given Lucy's Calvinist Protestantism, Lucy was pivotal in brokering meetings between Strafford and Mme de Chevreuse.

Charles not only needed money to pay for an army to take on the Scots. Sooner or later England would have to fight the Dutch. The previous October they had attacked a Spanish fleet in full view of the castles of Dover, Deal and Walmer, thereby destroying Charles's claim to sovereignty over the English Channel. Mme de Chevreuse assured Strafford that Philip IV would supply Charles with a loan of £100,000 and 'on very favourable terms'.[29] Strafford believed that in the meantime, however, Charles would also need the money he could gain from parliamentary subsidies. To this end he encouraged Charles to call a new parliament, pointing to his own recent success in Ireland. In March 1640 MPs in Dublin had granted subsidies totalling £90,000 for an army. Strafford was certain he could pull off a similar coup in London. With Strafford's impressive record for getting things done

Charles was convinced. In April 1640 he called his first parliament in eleven years.

There were many new faces in the Commons when it assembled on 15 April 1640. But, unfortunately for Charles, the MPs also included some of his most long-standing opponents: Warwick in the Lords, and Pym in the Commons, amongst them. The grievances were similarly old and had only been sharpened by time. There was anger at the loss of liberty represented by eleven years of personal rule and taxes raised without parliamentary consent. Charles had also given them fresh reasons to fear a 'popish' Counter-Reformation conspiracy. Charles had entered into diplomatic relations with the papacy to support his picture-buying. He had allowed Catholic aristocrats to practise their religion in the queen's chapels. Now he was prepared to use Spanish gold and an Irish army (containing Catholic as well as Protestant troops) against fellow Calvinists in Scotland.

Warwick and Pym intended to use Parliament to force Charles to turn his policies upside down. Abroad, they wanted friendship with his Scottish Covenanter enemies and an aggressive anti-Spanish war, focused on taking Spain's colonies in the West Indies. At home, they wanted Charles's religious reforms reversed in favour of a more thoroughgoing Calvinism and the king to be stripped of many of his prerogative powers. Pym's long experience as an MP ensured he 'understood the affections and temper of the kingdom ... had observed the errors and mistakes in government, and knew well how to make them appear greater than they were'.[30] A majority of MPs were therefore prepared to withhold subsidies until Charles had reformed the kingdom's 'abuses'. Pym stretched these to produce a list of thirty-six and demanded they be examined at length. This was intended to undermine the war effort, ensuring a long delay before any possible monies would be voted for an army to fight the Scots.

On 4 May 1640 Charles promised to give up Ship Money – the most hated of all the arbitrary taxes – in exchange for twelve subsidies worth £650,000. The offer was refused, even though the subsidies proposed were less valuable than the tax. Strafford, who had met with Philip IV's envoys only five days earlier, was now confident, however, that Charles would have enough aid from Spain to dispense with any need for the MPs' subsidies. Holland counselled Charles against dissolving Parliament, as did Lucy Carlisle's powerful brother, Northumberland.[31] Strafford advised otherwise. 'Go vigorously on,' he urged the king. Parliament had not met its responsibilities, so the king was 'absolved from all rules of government being reduced to extreme necessity'. 'You have an army in Ireland you may employ here to reduce this kingdom. [I am] as confident of anything under heaven the Scots shall not hold out five months.'[32]

Charles dissolved what became known as the 'Short Parliament' on 5 May. Against all precedent, he insisted that the deliberative body of the Church of England, known as Convocation, nevertheless continue sitting. He wanted his actions backed by the bishops and they duly gave him their support. Requirements were issued for clergy to make regular pronouncements from the pulpit on the divine right of kings and for them to swear loyalty to the Church of England's 'archbishops, bishops, deans, and archdeacons etc'. Puritan trouble-makers suggested the 'etc' might even include an oath to the Pope.[33]

In May it emerged that there was to be no aid from Spain. A major rebellion in Catalonia had broken out, and Philip IV needed every penny he had. This meant Charles could no longer afford to offend France. Mme de Chevreuse was encouraged to leave court. She departed for Flanders in June 'accompanied by the royal coaches and the Spanish ambassadors' as well as a parting gift from Henrietta Maria of a 'rich jewel worth 12,000 crowns'.[34] This was particularly generous, given that Charles was now forced to rely on voluntary contributions, loans, sales and the further exploitation of his prerogative rights to pay for his army. Pro-royal forces in the City, including the elite merchant companies, lent Charles £250,000 and also engineered a loan which provided a further £50,000 in ready cash.

James VI of Scotland and I of England, father of Charles I, in his English coronation robes

Henry Stuart, Prince of Wales, elder brother of Charles I

Elizabeth Stuart, Electress Palatine and 'Winter Queen' of Bohemia, elder sister of Charles I

Philip IV of Spain in 1623, the year Charles visited Madrid

Cardinal Richelieu,
Chief Minister of
Louis XIII of France

George Villiers, Duke of
Buckingham, the man King
James called his 'wife'

Title page of a plague
pamphlet from 1625.
On the right is a group
of people fleeing from
the plague. In response
to their words, 'We fly,'
Death answers, 'I follow,'
as it did when court and
MPs moved to Oxford

The mother-in-law has landed: Marie de' Medici, 'mother of three kings' and one-time regent of France, as depicted in one of a series of twenty-four paintings by Rubens celebrating her life and achievements

Charles I, *c.* 1628

Charles's queen, Henrietta Maria,
in masque dress

Robert Rich, Earl of Warwick:
privateer, colonialist and rebel

Henry Rich, Earl of Holland:
courtier, knight and turncoat

Henrietta Maria

Lucy Hay (née Percy),
Countess of Carlisle,
descendant of Mary
Boleyn, was 'the most
delightful poison ever
nature produced'

(Left) John Pym, the Puritan
leader later known as 'King Pym'

(Right) The victorious
Louis XIII and Cardinal
Richelieu at La Rochelle

Anthony Van Dyck's triple portrait of Charles I was commissioned
to enable the sculptor Gian Lorenzo Bernini to create a bust of
the king as a papal gift for Henrietta Maria

Marie de Rohan, Duchesse de Chevreuse, as Diana. The goddess was
seen as gender-fluid and used as an icon of women with aspirations to
power. The French kings Francois I and Henri II both chose to be
depicted as Diana as, at times, would Henrietta Maria

(Left) Charles I and Henrietta Maria dining at court

(Right) The glass sphere in Titian's *Allegory of Marriage*, which formed part of Charles's great art collection, represented the fragility of human happiness

In 1637 Charles paid Van Dyck £100 for this picture of his five eldest children, Mary, James, Charles, Elizabeth and Anne. In 1625 one of the suits Buckingham wore in Paris was said to be worth 'fourscore thousand pounds'

Many of Charles's subjects were, nevertheless, deeply troubled that Parliament had not supported the war effort against the Scots. The institution was an integral part of English political culture in a way that the Scottish-born Stuarts had never understood. In Dorset, when troops learned Parliament had been dissolved, they went home.[35] Rumours, meanwhile, were spreading that dark forces were behind the king's actions – a conspiracy linked to Spain that would see the overthrow of Protestantism. Mob attacks began on altar rails and images in churches and soon turned more violent. Two officers suspected of popery were murdered at the hands of their own men, and London, in particular, became a dangerous place for anyone perceived as Catholic, or even a supporter of Charles's religious reforms.

Warwick and other dissident aristocrats with links to the American colonies were galvanising radical support amongst London's small traders, the 'new merchant' class and the Puritan clergy, with whom they had worked for years. The English nobility might no longer have had the great feudal following they had enjoyed in the Middle Ages, but they were now set to ride the tiger of a popular mass movement.

On 10 May notices were pinned up at prominent places across London calling people to defend their liberties, and to assassinate Laud and Strafford. The lynch mob, last seen in the death of Dr Lambe in 1628, was back.[36]

The next day several hundred youths stormed Lambeth Palace looking for the archbishop, 'with the purpose of slaying him'. Most were apprentices who had come out 'with the connivance of their masters, Puritans for the most part'.[37] There was an element of spontaneity in these riots, but they were also planned events, like the stool-throwing Edinburgh riot against the Scottish prayer book in 1637. Where the Scots had led, the English opposition was following, but to deadlier effect.

As Laud fled the mob across the river to Whitehall, several signs were put up outside the royal palaces. They warned that the king himself could not save Laud or Strafford from being killed. Charles was forced to react.

On 12 May it was reported that the Earl of Warwick, Viscount Saye and Sele, Lord Brooke, John Pym and the Ship Money martyr John Hampden had all been arrested and their papers searched. Charles was looking for evidence of treasonous collusion with the Scottish rebels so they might be put in prison. Nothing was found beyond a discourse by a New England minister against the Church of England's liturgy, and the men were released.[38] Charles's suspicions remained, however – and with good reason. The dissident peers had invited the noble Scottish Covenanter leadership to invade their homeland.

Henry VIII, Mary I and Elizabeth I had each introduced dramatic religious change. But they had used Parliament to give their actions legal force with MPs both seduced and terrorised into giving their support. History was to label the period that Charles ruled without Parliament as the 'Eleven Years' Tyranny'. But it had seen no political or religious executions. To some contemporaries it seemed rather that Charles's Eleven Years' Tyranny had not been nearly tyrannical enough. In England 'a prince's awful reputation' had always been 'of much more defence to him, than his regal, nay legal, edicts'.[39] Charles had been merciful. Now he faced emboldened traitors not only in Scotland, but also in England.

In the middle of August 1640 word reached Charles's council in London that the Scots were poised to cross the border. Charles immediately announced that he would place himself at the head of his threatened people. On 20 August he left for York. The Scots crossed the river Tweed on the same day. The English commander, the Earl of Northumberland, claimed he was too ill to fight and the army, betrayed by Warwick and his allies, proved able to muster only limited resistance. On 28 August, following a brief skirmish, the Scots took Newcastle, ending the second Bishops' War in the king's defeat. Strafford summed up the full gravity of the situation: 'The country from Berwick to York [is] in the power of the Scots to the universal affright of us all.'[40]

With Charles in York, his council in London ordered out the royal bodyguard to protect his wife and children from the traitors in their midst. Henrietta Maria had a new baby – Henry – not yet two months old. Days later a petition was being widely circulated in manuscript in London bearing the names of twelve peers.[41] The signatories included Warwick, Saye and Sele, Brooke, Essex, and Essex's brother-in-law, William Seymour, Earl of Hertford.[42] It listed a 'heap of complaints' concerning religion and the personal rule. There was also a sinister demand for 'evil' councillors to be given up to a new parliament for 'condign' punishment. That meant probable death for Strafford, and perhaps Laud as well.

Only Parliament could now raise the money necessary to pay for another army to fight the Scots or to pay them off, so they would go home. Charles was the victim of a coup in the north and in London – and he knew it.

'A BROKEN GLASS'

IT WAS DUSK WHEN CHARLES APPROACHED LONDON FROM YORK ON 31 October 1640. A humiliating armistice had been signed with the Scots. Under its terms the Covenanters had been promised £850 a day to maintain their armies on English soil. Newcastle, and the northern counties of Northumberland and County Durham, remained in enemy hands, along with the Tyneside collieries. This meant the Scots controlled the coal Londoners needed to heat their homes, and winter was now upon them.

Charles's Privy Council had fortified Whitehall Palace and artillery pieces covered the landward approaches. Behind the palace gates, meanwhile, in the Great Court, *caballeros* or 'Cavaliers', as they were coming to be known, awaited the king, dressed in wide-brimmed hats and tall leather boots.* Some of his bodyguard were on horse, others on foot, ready to protect the king from his own subjects.[1]

The opposition's latest political weapon was the mass petition. Charles had been brought a document in York which expanded on the 'heap of complaints' offered by the twelve-peers petition and bore the signatures of 10,000 London citizens. Not all the signatures represented the genuinely aggrieved. Bully-boy tactics also got names

---

* Shakespeare used the term 'cavaleros' in *Henry IV Pt 2*. It is from the same Latin root as the French word '*chevalier*'.

on paper. It would become commonplace to be called to the houses of powerful neighbours late at night, and those who would not sign the latest petition told that they were 'neither good Christians nor honest men', and could be ostracised – or worse.[2]

Charles, too, knew what it was like to have his hand forced.

Although the king had announced in York, 'I have of myself resolved to call a parliament,' the truth was he had had little choice. What would become known as the Long Parliament was due to open on Tuesday 3 November 1640. Warwick gave friends the news, crowing that 'the Game was well begun!'[3] The opposition's next move in their power play was to provoke fears of an internal Catholic threat. This would encourage MPs to help them take power from the king. Spreading fear and slander was not difficult – the opposition could speak to thousands through print and pulpit – but sometimes actions spoke even louder than words.

On the night of 2 November Catholic homes in London were searched for arms. The message this sent was that Catholics were about to rise up and turn hidden weapons on sleeping Protestants. A story spread like wildfire that Marie de' Medici had 'secretly given the king advice against the liberty and religion of the realm': that the king himself could not be trusted.[4] Charles did not therefore dare risk the usual grand procession through the streets to Parliament for its opening. Instead, he arrived at Westminster on 3 November by barge, unseen by his people: a small victory for his enemies.

But Charles had friends here, as well as foes. One nobleman had written in advance to a fellow peer instructing him to come to Parliament armed 'with zeal and with the sword of eloquence' so they might 'cut in two the Puritans and chop off the heads of the anti-Monarchists'.[5] Another called the petitioner peers 'traitors and Covenanters' who 'deserved to be hanged'.[6] Such men awaited Charles's lead.

The Lords Chamber was filled with MPs and peers, while Lucy Carlisle stood with other courtiers who had come to watch the proceedings. The king sat on the throne dressed in ermine robes with his ten-year-old heir at his right hand. He had a sensitive face. In several portraits, a favourite baroque pearl earring hangs by his cheek like a falling tear. But his melancholic eyes could also reveal determination: 'if fair means will not [achieve my aims], power must redress it,' he had once said.[7]

Addressing the gathered MPs Charles asked that they consider their fellow countrymen living under the heel of the Scottish enemy. A third campaign against the Scots was necessary to free the north. Charles did not go on to allude to those who had betrayed the English army to the Scots, but he planned to act against them. Strafford had been summoned from York to discuss how to use the royal armies in the north and in Ireland also, to crush both the Scots and their English allies.

Strafford reached London on 10 November. The next morning he proposed to Charles that those who had invited the Scots into England now be accused publicly of high treason. Just a short walk from Whitehall, in Parliament, Strafford's impeachment had, however, been launched and John Pym was already summarising the accusations in the Commons Chamber. Strafford and the king had taken their decision too late.

Pym had a 'grave and very comely way of expressing himself, with great volubility of words, natural and proper'.[8] MPs listened intently as he exposed Strafford as a secret papal agent provocateur. Strafford's plan was 'to provoke the king to make a war between us and the Scots that thereby we might consume one another'. With England at war with Scotland, Strafford would then bring over the Irish army and, with the help of English Catholics and foreign powers, he would subdue England entirely and 'bring in the papist party'.[9]

To counter this threat a parliamentary committee had already begun to draw up plans to constrain Catholics more tightly. Pym would go so far as to suggest Catholics be forced to wear distinctive clothes, an idea inspired by the badge of shame worn by Jews in medieval Europe.[10]

The truth was that Strafford was an orthodox Protestant whose wife came from a Puritan family. The accusation that he sought a Catholic takeover was absurd, but in the fevered atmosphere Pym's alternative truth was believed.

That evening, still innocent of the proceedings against him, Strafford arrived in the Lords. Holland was amongst those present.[11] It was said that if Warwick was the visible head of the Puritans, Holland was now the 'invisible' head 'not because he means to do either hurt or good' but because he thought it 'gallantry' to act as the opposition's future go-between with the king.[12] The debates on the impeachment charges were still in progress and Strafford was greeted as he entered by shouts of 'Withdraw! Withdraw!' He duly left, shocked, only returning when the debates had concluded. He was then informed he was to be placed in custody while the charges were further investigated.

Henrietta Maria later recalled that Strafford had the most beautiful hands she had ever seen. Did they tremble as he gave up his sword? He was escorted from the Chamber under guard, 'all gazing', their hats on in a mark of contempt, 'to him whom before that morning the greatest in England would have stood'.[13]

Strafford had recovered his composure by the time Lucy Carlisle visited him in the Tower. She told everyone he was 'very confident of his overcoming all these accusations' and 'I never saw him for one minute discomposed.'[14] But those who had conspired with the Scots knew they had to destroy Strafford if their lives were ever to be safe. They could not trust Charles to grant them amnesty for their treason unless they had control over him. That meant not only stripping Charles of power, but also taking the roles of his senior councillors for themselves, and making sure any royal servant capable of fighting back on the king's behalf was incapacitated by ruin, imprisonment or death.

Charles's Secretary of State, Sir Francis Windebank, fled to France, rather than risk his own arrest. The Lord Chancellor, John Finch, would also do so. Laud stayed. His radical vision of an empowered Church of England would have changed the face of

English society. He understood better than Charles that for the landowning classes, who had benefited from the land released by the dissolution of the monasteries under Henry VIII, it looked like a potential reversal of their fortunes, as well as a threat to the Reformation itself. He had long expected their revenge.

On 18 December Laud was impeached in the Commons for high treason. The charges laid against him were of endeavouring to bring in arbitrary government, alienating the king from his English subjects, hindering justice, bringing about the war with Scotland, altering the true religion, persecuting godly preachers and working secretly to reconcile with Rome.

Laud was not yet locked in the Tower. He was instead placed in the custody of the Gentleman Usher to be sent for trial in due course. The diminutive and grey-haired archbishop was not a man to raise or lead armies. He did not pose the same sort of threat to the opposition as did Strafford – the leading advocate of force.

The queen was, however, now also at risk. The opposition's narrative of popish threat had a part for her too. A verbal assault against that 'popish brat of France' was unleashed in Puritan pulpits and violence then followed. A Puritan mob came to 'my own house', she wrote to a friend, attacking people emerging from Mass in her chapel, 'furiously with stones and weapons'.[15] There was no respite for Henrietta Maria even when the death of the three-year-old Princess Anne was announced on 16 December 1640. The heartbroken king and queen had known the deaths of infants, but never of a child whose growth they had measured, and with whom they had played. It had been but 'a brief sickness' and the Venetian ambassador described their 'intense grief'.[16]

Just at the time they had lost one child, however, they had to plan to send another away: nine-year-old Mary, the little girl who had refused to stand still for Van Dyck's portraits. Charles needed money and allies. Marie de' Medici had suggested a marriage for Mary that would gain both, while also pleasing his kingdoms: a Protestant marriage to the fourteen-year-old William of Orange, heir to the ruling house of Holland. He was Calvinist – so there could be no accusations of popery – and he was rich. Indeed, Marie argued, he could help provide Charles with an army of 20,000 men.[17]

Already power in England was slipping from Charles's grasp. The majority of Parliament's electorate had been troubled by his authoritarianism. They wanted Parliament to reassert its place in the 'ancient constitution' and MPs to ensure that the 'liberties of the subject' were secured. Similarly many wished to see the Calvinist character of the Elizabethan church renewed, and its growing political power stripped back. These aims were conservative, but to achieve them, the majority of MPs were prepared to back those who were leading the way in imposing new ways of constraining the king.

A new law was passed that Parliament must be called every three years. There could be no further eleven years of personal rule. Charles was also denied his right to raise customs revenues under the royal prerogative. There would be no further taxation without representation, and Charles was left fiscally dependent on Parliament. No longer would Puritan gentlemen have their ears cropped, or Puritan ministers be punished for opposing the anti-Calvinist changes in the Church of England. Parliamentary committees were appointed to abolish any court that did not adhere to common law. These included the Star Chamber (used in trials for sedition) and the ecclesiastic Court of High Commission (used against dissident clergy), as well as the regional judiciaries of the Council of the North and the Council of the Marches of Wales.

Yet there remained a dark undercurrent to this return to a functioning 'mixed monarchy' and Puritan liberation. Despite tougher penal laws being introduced against Catholics and Charles ordering the expulsion from England of Catholic priests, attacks on innocent Catholics in general, and on Henrietta Maria in particular, continued. In one of the lost royal letters preserved in the archives of Belvoir

Castle's secret rooms, Henrietta Maria feared she faced her 'utter ruin'. Written to the French Secretary of State for Foreign Affairs, the Comte de Chavigny, this letter prepared the ground for her possible flight to Paris.[18]

Charles's leading opponents and their allies were now so powerful they were being called the 'Junto'. And this too was troubling for many. The Junto had the appearance of an emerging oligarchy with its own radical agenda. Warwick's London house was serving as the kingdom's new exchequer, and channelling money to the Scottish occupiers. His Scottish friends now intended to use their victory to impose their religious views throughout Britain and Ireland. Like their allies in England, the Covenanters needed to secure themselves against any future trial for treason. If episcopacy was not acknowledged to be intrinsically wrong then they too would never be secure from Charles's future revenge. They therefore had demanded that episcopacy be abolished across the three kingdoms. But in doing so they had asked something of Charles that he would never give them.

In his coronation oath, Charles had sworn to defend the rights granted to the clergy by Edward the Confessor, 'according to the laws of God, the true profession of the Gospel established in this kingdom'.[19] He was not a man to break such an oath, nor to deny his sacral kingship, as God's lieutenant on earth. When he learned the latest price of peace with the Scots, his anger was such it was said 'the king he runs stark mad'. But the demands of the Scots were also the shock that brought the moribund Royalist party in England back to life.

Like the king, the majority of MPs saw episcopacy and Henry VIII's royal supremacy in religion as an integral part of England's constitutional arrangements. Upending them could undermine the rule of law and the entire social order.[20] The legislation Parliament had put through limited the king's freedom to act without the direct co-operation of the landed classes. This was what they had wanted to achieve. What they did not want was to introduce to England a Scottish-style Presbyterian system of church government. There was also widespread dislike for another Scottish demand: the Scots wanted a new confederal constitutional arrangement between the two kingdoms that would support a military agenda aimed against the native Catholic population of Ireland. Few English MPs wished to see any kind of political union with Scotland.

Within the Junto itself there was also a division between hard-line and more moderate elements.[21] But they were all at least partially dependent on the support of London radicals who wanted revolutionary change.[22] Most striking was a radical petition to Parliament, bearing 20,000 signatures, that demanded episcopacy be abolished 'root and branch'. As with other such petitions it was backed by the threat of mass violence. Moderate MPs fought against having the petition even considered, 'because tumultuously brought'.[23]

When Charles's sister, Elizabeth, in The Hague, received a letter from a friend with the 'news of Parliament', it was a tale of cold civil war: 'We are full of distempers, all is like a broken glass,' her correspondent wrote, 'our world of happiness is near an end.'[24]

STRAFFORD ON TRIAL

ON 22 MARCH 1641 THE VAST SPACE OF WESTMINSTER HALL WAS packed with spectators for Strafford's impeachment trial. There had never been a trial like it, with tickets sold to the public. Demand for the tickets outstripped supply and onlookers who could not get inside crowded at the doorways. The Junto's intention was to see Strafford 'sacrificed on the altar of public satisfaction', the Venetian ambassador reported.[1] What was said and seen in that room would be reported by word of mouth, in letters, and in print to a national audience.

The southern end of the hall had been set out in the same rect-angular shape as the Chamber of the House of Lords, England's court of last resort. The peers sat in long rows on benches opposite each other, dressed in crimson and ermine, the judges, bareheaded, sitting amongst them. Holland was absent, although he was due to be called as a prosecution witness. This may have been because of his hopes of being a bridge between the king and the more moderate members of the Junto. For the first time the entire Commons was also present with MPs seated on a grandstand of sharply rising tiers, juxtaposed on either side of the peers' benches.[2]

Strafford stood in a panelled dock between the grandstands, his hair uncombed as a symbol of grief, his black suit adorned only with his George, the insignia of the Garter with the figure of St George killing the dragon of rebellion.[3] He faced the raised dais on which sat the king's empty throne and, beside it, a seat for the Prince of Wales. Viscount Saye and Sele had argued a few days earlier that the king's sovereign authority was vested in the two Houses of Parliament while it was in session, and that his physical presence in the court would violate this premise. On this basis a committee of peers had decided that Charles would not sit on his throne, but in a box, of the kind seen in theatres, placed near the throne, but where he would be hidden behind a lattice screen. Court officials would not bow to the king, but to 'the state' represented so strikingly by the empty chair.[4]

Charles entered the hall at 9 a.m. with his wife and his tall, dark eldest son. Charles's cloak glittered with the areole of the Garter Star. The prince, graceful in his movements, went and stood next to his seat, at the right hand of the throne. Charles walked on past the dais with the queen. When he reached the box allocated for him he sat down with his wife, then tore down the lattice screen. He would be seen, his visible expressions showing the support for his servant that he was determined to give.

The Scots and Strafford's enemies in Ireland had been lobbying hard against Strafford, but this theatre of justice was no mere show trial. They did not have the judges and peers in their pockets. Strafford, meanwhile, was prepared to fight hard for his life. He had a wife, a son and three daughters waiting at home. He was also confident he had a strong defence, 'which certainly he has much reason for', Lucy Carlisle remarked, 'both from his own innocence and the weakness of his charge.'[5]

Twenty-eight articles of impeachment were read out that first morning. The following day the prosecution began, led by Pym. It was easy to see why Pym had been chosen. He 'was at that time … the most popular man and the most able to do hurt that has lived.'[6] He could be a powerful performer in the Commons where his right-eous conviction gave his speeches emotional force. But he was never-theless humourless, bad at reading an audience, and slow to respond to a change in mood. Strafford, meanwhile, had no intention of allowing himself to be simply ploughed down by Pym's rhetoric.

The most serious accusation Strafford faced was of seeking to introduce illegal and arbitrary government. Here the prosecution case suffered one outstanding difficulty. Pym argued Strafford had committed treason against the state. In English law treason was to act against the king. Charles's evident support was a reminder that Strafford had acted *for* the king. 'Sure,' Strafford observed, 'it is a very hard thing, I should here be questioned for my life and honour, upon a law that is not extant, that cannot be shown.'[7]

For over two and a half weeks Strafford picked apart the articles laid against him, calmly, politely, and with occasional flashes of scornful humour. Even a hostile spectator admitted, 'when he speaks he does so with so much bravery ... as begets admiration in all the beholders.'[8] By contrast Pym's 'language and carriage was such' it seemed he was expressing 'personal animosity' rather than seeking justice.[9] Pym's inner conviction was, this time, playing against his performance.

The Scots and their allies feared that Strafford might even be found innocent. If so, he could return to office and strike back against them on Charles's behalf. The Irish army was still standing, as was the humiliated English army, its soldiers left unpaid while money poured into Scottish coffers. English officers were now petitioning their desire to get back at the invaders, 'if the perverse endeavours of some [traitors] do not cross us'.[10] The Junto knew that drastic action had to be taken to bring the trial to its conclusion and the guilty verdict they needed.

The key witness against Strafford was a former Secretary of State, Sir Henry Vane, whose enmity was personal. Vane claimed Strafford had intended to use the Irish army to subdue the English and not merely the Scottish rebels. His testimony was uncorroborated and flatly contradicted by other councillors. Vane's son and namesake, a youthful former governor of Massachusetts, had, however, found his father's council meeting notes and had passed them on to Pym. With the prosecution case slipping away, Pym decided to deploy Vane's stolen documents.

On 10 April the prosecution lawyers asked to introduce their new evidence. Strafford countered that, if so, then he should be allowed to introduce new evidence of his own. This would inevitably drag out proceedings and, given Strafford's winning performance thus far, would likely cost the prosecution their case. When the Lords accepted Strafford's request, the Commons men in the grandstands erupted in anger. Pym's party shouted at the prosecution counsel, 'Withdraw! Withdraw!' In the heat of the moment many MPs heard this as 'Draw! Draw!' and reached for their swords. To calm the situation the Earl of Southampton called for the Lords to adjourn, but as the peers filed out of the hall, the Commons followed still in 'great confusion', crowding at the doors in a 'tumultarie'.

Strafford looked on, smiling in the knowledge that he might now be saved. Charles, in his box, laughed aloud.[11] Their celebration was to be short-lived.

Strafford's enemies had already found a way around the difficulties of a trial. In the crush at the doors, heading for the Commons Chamber, was Lord Brooke's brother-in-law Sir Arthur Hesilrige.[12] He had in his pocket a white scroll in which the charges against Strafford had been redrafted as a bill of attainder. The plan was to deny Strafford any further hearing. The trial had failed but he could simply now be pronounced guilty, and condemned by Act of Parliament. A fellow MP, Sir Philip Stapilton, introduced the bill in the House of Commons that afternoon.[13]

Attainder was not a tool, however, likely to appeal to anyone who revered common law, and some MPs saw it as threatening 'judicial murder'.[14] Time also remained on Strafford's side. Anti-Scots and anti-Junto feeling was building, not least over Scottish demands for the abolition of episcopacy. Plenty of Englishmen wanted 'leave to make laws in England ourselves without their directions', and prayed 'God for the church's safety' from Presbyterians.[15]

Charles sent Strafford a letter reassuring him 'upon the word of a king, you shall not suffer in life, honour or fortune'. This was 'but justice and therefore a very mean reward from a master to so faithful and able a servant'. The king signed himself 'Your constant, faithful friend, Charles R'.[16]

Charles hoped to bring round the more moderate elements within the Junto to find a compromise that would preserve Strafford's life. Henrietta Maria, encouraged by Holland, was also anxious to help. Not only was her own safety threatened by the Junto radicals, so was that of the king's Catholic subjects, whom it was her duty to protect. In an unpublished letter to Richelieu, recommending the merits of a Catholic who had fled into exile, she described a 'storm that is falling upon the poor Catholics of this land'.[17] The role of conciliator was a traditional one for a queen. Henrietta Maria seized this opportunity to take it up. Years later, in France, she would give dramatised accounts of the night-time conferences she now had with 'the worst' members of the opposition – by which she meant Pym. Their meetings took place at the foot of the back stairs to the rooms of one of her ladies-in-waiting, their faces lit only by the torches they carried.[18]

Pym not only had clandestine meetings with the queen. He also saw the king. Charles offered high offices for Junto members in exchange for assurances that Parliament would grant the Crown adequate revenue to replace his tax-raising powers, that episcopacy in England would be preserved – and that Strafford's life would be spared. Junto moderates were willing to accept this. Unfortunately there were also several figures who shared the Scots' view that the only way to guarantee that Strafford would never again be restored to office was to cut off his head. 'Stone-dead hath no fellow', as the Earl of Essex put it.[19]

The arrival in London of the fourteen-year-old Prince William of Orange should have been a cause for national celebration. He represented the valiant Dutch rebels against the might of Habsburg Spain, as well as being the groom for Mary, to whom her father had given the title 'Princess Royal'. Prince William had, reportedly, brought gifts worth upwards of £23,000 as well as a substantial sum in gold. This generosity had, however, raised concerns amongst Junto hardliners that Charles would use it to pay the army's arrears. There were already rumours of a Royalist plot by discontented army officers. If Parliament was now adjourned for the wedding celebrations, the army might ensure Parliament would never be recalled.[20]

On 21 April a crowd of 10,000 'ready at command' of the hardliners and 'upon a watch word given', descended on Westminster.[21] Three officers of the City militia handed in a petition carrying 20,000 signatures calling for Strafford's death. With the mob at the gates, MPs passed the attainder bill against Strafford and sent it up to the Lords. Strafford asked for mercy, that he might 'go home to my own private fortune, there to attend my own domestic affairs, and education of my children'. But, he observed, if things went differently and 'I should die upon this evidence, I had much rather be the sufferer than the judge'.[22]

On 26 April, the peers passed the first reading of the attainder bill. Army officers, meanwhile, issued a new petition complaining of 'ill-affected persons' using mob violence to overawe Parliament and threaten the king. A diplomat reported nervously that 'Every one fears that if the fire of these differences is not extinguished by the more prudent, it will finally break out in a terrible civil war.'[23]

On 1 May, following another, failed attempt to reach out to hardliners, Charles went to Parliament to intervene himself in the debates on Strafford's fate.

Again he sought compromise. He accepted that Strafford had committed misdemeanours which required punishment, but not that he had committed treason. Kings were answerable directly to God for their actions. To sign the death warrant of someone he believed to be innocent would be a grave sin. 'I hope you know what a tender thing conscience is,' Charles told the Lords, 'and no fear or respect will make me go against it.'[24] He then issued a warning. He would not disband the Irish army until the Scots had left England. This statement left open the possibility that he might yet deploy the Irish army in England. The king's speech 'astonished us', an MP recorded. This was, perhaps, what Charles intended. He had given notice that he was taking a stand.

The following day was Princess Mary's wedding. The mood in London was fearful and behind the scenes Charles had made one of his 'extreme resolutions'.[25] The ceremonies were to provide cover for a plot to spring Strafford from the Tower.

12

GIVEN UP

ON SUNDAY MORNING, PRINCE WILLIAM'S CARRIAGE MADE ITS WAY down the Strand in a cavalcade of coaches heading for Whitehall Palace. He was a good-looking boy with long brown hair, dressed in red and gold. Not to be outdone, his companion Henry Rich, Earl of Holland, wore silver and gold. Holland had taken what should have been Warwick's place in the carriage. Warwick had claimed he was too busy with 'affairs of state' to attend the wedding.[1] It was a troubling absence and an extraordinary snub for Charles, who had made Warwick a privy councillor only days earlier.

Did Warwick know what was happening at the White Horse Tavern near St Paul's, where Sir John Suckling was now assembling a planned force of a hundred armed men?[2] Suckling was the poet who had once written verses on the fantasy of stripping Lucy Carlisle naked while she walked in Holland Park. Slim, of middle height, with a small head and long fair curls, the thirty-two-year-old cavalier had 'a brisk and graceful look'.[3] He was a cousin of the queen's current favourite, Henry Jermyn. Yet he was no blind supporter of Charles's policies. Suckling had argued that Charles needed to pay court to the people, in the traditional manner of an English monarch and as Elizabeth I had done so successfully.[4] But he also believed that men like Warwick and Pym were self-seeking and dangerous – and had to be stopped.

While public attention was focused on the marriage ceremonies, Suckling planned that his hundred men would march to the Tower, where the lieutenant had verbal instructions to grant them entry. Once in, they hoped to overpower the wardens and release Strafford.

Prince William, meanwhile, had reached Whitehall where he was escorted into the royal chapel. There he awaited his bride on a railed platform near the Communion table. The nine-year-old Princess Royal entered the chapel dressed in silver and escorted by two of her brothers: the ten-year-old Prince of Wales, and seven-year-old James, Duke of York. William had not been permitted to kiss Mary when they had first met, but thought her 'beautiful'. She was wearing a necklace of huge pearls lent by his mother. 'I love her very much and I believe she loves me too,' he had told his parents. Behind Mary and her brothers followed sixteen small bridesmaids of her own age, ushered by Mary's governess, the old Countess of Roxburghe.[5] The king entered next, with a number of senior peers. Then came Henrietta Maria and the stately Marie de' Medici, attending the ceremony as spectators rather than co-worshippers.

Since Charles had been left financially dependent on Parliament, Marie de' Medici's allowance had been stopped, obliging the 'mother of three kings' to dismiss her household, with its dwarves and noblemen, and to live 'the frugal life of a private lady'.[6] She was also now showing signs of poor health. Her life in England was under constant threat and the strain was taking a toll. Holland had asked his fellow peers to provide money for a guard, reminding them that if anything were to happen to their royal guest, 'it would be a great dishonour to the Nation'.[7] The money was denied and so she still faced the danger of being killed by a rogue fanatic just as her husband, Henri IV, had been.

The children's wedding was presided over by the Bishop of Ely, Matthew Wren, who was personally closer to Charles even than Laud, and promoted a devotional style far closer to baroque Catholicism than that of the archbishop. Light filtered through 241 feet of modern stained glass, while music was played on a magnificent organ. Charles gave the bride to the groom and William put a ring on her finger.[8]

This was not a marriage of the stature Charles had wanted for his daughter. The Prince of Orange was the stadholder, or 'place holder', of the province of Holland, and as such merely the hereditary head of state of a Dutch republic. Charles would have preferred a King of France or Spain for Mary and would never have agreed to the marriage had he not desperately needed Dutch money. But Henrietta Maria told her sister Christine that 'although [William] will not be a king I have no doubt she can be just as happy. I know well that it is not kingdoms that bring happiness.'[9]

As the wedding ceremony ended, Suckling counted only around sixty men at the White Horse Tavern: two-thirds of the number he had expected. He decided to delay the enterprise until the following night. But word of this threatening group of soldiers was spreading through London, even as Charles enjoyed the wedding breakfast with his family in the withdrawing chamber.[10] Here there was a notable absence. Charles's eldest nephew, the twenty-three-year-old Prince Palatine, Charles Louis, had arrived in England in February hoping to prevent the Dutch alliance in order to marry Mary himself.[11] Charles had tried for years to find rich brides for his nephews.[12] He had always been generous to the family of his sister Elizabeth. Now that Charles was himself in financial straits, it was ungrateful of Charles Louis to have tried to claim Mary as his bride, and his coming to England was unhelpful on another front. For years there had been Puritans who believed the thoroughly Calvinist Charles Louis would be a more worthy King of England than Charles, or Charles's sons by the Catholic Henrietta Maria.

At around 10 p.m. the ambassadors returned to Whitehall to witness the ritual consummation that would ensure the marriage was irrevocable. They were escorted from the withdrawing chamber to the bedchamber where William now lay with Mary, as Charles and Henrietta Maria looked on. Since Mary was only nine it was

considered sufficient that what was witnessed was the children 'asso-
ciating', as the Venetian ambassador put it.[13] The ceremony was given
drama by the queen's dwarf, Jeffrey Hudson, who produced an enormous pair of shears to cut the stitching on the nightgown into which
the princess had been sewn. William then could touch her leg – flesh
against flesh made the ritual complete. Afterwards William was taken
back to his own quarters. He would return home at the end of the
month. It was not expected that Mary would leave her parents for
The Hague before her twelfth birthday. They did not want the sexual
act to take place before she was physically mature. Charles wanted
her to be fourteen, at least.

At eleven o'clock that night, with the wedding over, Charles learned
that the plan to spring Strafford had failed. Notices had gone up that
an attempt to free Strafford was planned and a crowd of around 1,000
people was now gathered in the darkness outside the Tower. By
morning the crowd had shifted to Westminster and their numbers had
grown. MPs were informed of the Tower plot and of a further
conspiracy to bring the English army in the north to London to institute a coup. Warwick had indeed been busy. MPs promptly drew up
a protestation in defence of the Protestant religion. Over the following
days several of those wanted for interrogation about the Tower plot
fled aboard. The queen's favourite Henry Jermyn was amongst them,
as was Suckling. The Countess of Leicester – sister of Lucy Carlisle –
saw Suckling in Paris soon after and pronounced him still 'good
company, but much abated in his mirth'.[14] A year later he vanished
and was rumoured to have taken poison rather than live in poverty.

Lucy Carlisle was interrogated in front of a Commons committee
about what she knew of the Tower plot.[15] She learned more from them
than they did from her – and the lesson she took away was that it was
time to distance herself from her former affiliation to Strafford. Pym
and her cousins Warwick and Essex were the new force in the land.
Charles's power, meanwhile, continued to diminish with a law passed

that Parliament could not be dissolved without its own consent.[16] Henrietta Maria would henceforth refer to it shrewdly as the 'perpetual parliament', for why would MPs ever vote themselves out? The law opened the door to the absolute power of whoever controlled Parliament. Currently that meant the Junto – and their mobs.

MPs who had abstained from the attainder bill against Strafford were publicly named and shamed, with news-sheets and pamphlets driving the verbal assaults on them as 'enemies of their country'.[17] They were also abused by the crowds that filled New Palace Yard, and peers, who had yet to take their final vote, had to push their way through men chanting at them 'Justice! Justice!', and 'with great rudeness and insolence pressing upon those lords whom they suspected not to favour the bill'.[18] Attendance in the Lords dropped from seventy peers to around forty-five. Catholic peers in particular kept away, unwilling to sign the protestation and fearful of 'having their brains beaten out' if they voted against the attainder.[19]

On Saturday 8 May the attainder passed its third reading, leaving Charles confronted with the decision of whether or not to give his assent to Strafford's death. He could hear the baying of a crowd of around 12,000 men and women pressing at Whitehall Palace's gate, threatening his life and that of 'all the royal house'.[20] It was too late to send his family away. The French ambassador had warned Henrietta Maria that the roads were now too dangerous.

The Bishop of Lincoln, John Williams, assured Charles that in signing Strafford's attainder his 'public conscience as a king might … oblige him to do that which was against his private conscience as a man', in order to 'preserve his kingdom … his wife … his children'.[21] In Christian religious teaching governments have the right to do what individuals do not, such as executing a guilty criminal, when the public good demands it. But the key word here is 'guilty'. Charles did not believe Strafford was guilty. Strafford himself, however, wrote urging Charles to sign his death warrant as the price of the public good, and the preservation of the kingdom.

The next day, Sunday – a week after Mary's wedding – Charles Louis saw his uncle the king break down in tears at the council table as he struggled with his decision. Come the evening, outside the Tower, another violent crowd had to be subdued by rifle fire, leaving three dead. Charles's fears for his people and his family sapped at his resolution to hold firm; at nine that night it broke, and he signed the attainder. Charles said if it was only his life at risk he would 'gladly venture it' to save Strafford, but 'seeing his wife, children and all his kingdom was concerned in it, he was forced to give way'.[22] 'In this he showed himself a good Master, a good Christian and at last a good king,' Charles Louis wrote to his mother Elizabeth, with smug satisfaction.[23]

The only hope left to Charles was that the Lords could yet be persuaded to show Strafford mercy. On 11 May, the day before the execution was due to take place, Charles sent his eldest son to plead that Strafford's beheading be commuted to life imprisonment. The prince entered the Lords Chamber and duly delivered the message on which a man's life depended. These were his father's 'natural counsellors' and Charles informed them he had sent his son as the person 'that of all your House is most dear to me' to ask them to accept his plea for mercy. To one Royalist, looking back, this 'strange submission of himself to the power and courtesy of his people' amounted merely to a diminishment of majesty.[24] Charles had humbled himself – and to no avail. The reply, delivered to Charles later that day, denied mercy on the grounds that sparing Strafford's life could not be achieved 'without evident danger to [the king] himself, his dearest consort the queen, and all the young princes, their children'.[25] Strafford's fate was sealed.

'I was persuaded by those that I think wished me well, to choose rather what was safe than what was just,' Charles later recalled.[26] Strafford's blood was now on his hands. He would never forgive himself.

* * *

Strafford sent a message to his fourteen-year-old son, William. They were 'the last lines you are ever to receive from a father that tenderly loves you', he wrote. He sent blessings for his daughters and asked his son to care for them, along with the boy's stepmother.

On Tower Hill, where the scaffold was built, the crowds began gathering before dawn. When the sun came up on 12 May it was estimated 100,000 or more had flocked to witness Strafford's death. The Lieutenant of the Tower feared his prisoner would be lynched on the walk from the Tower gates to the Hill and so Strafford was given a military escort. Spectators were perched on the tiered benches of the grandstands like birds on the branches of a great tree. From up on high they watched Strafford, a figure in black, moving on the scaffold, speaking, praying. When he lay prostrate on the block he vanished from the view of those on the lower stands. Then the axe was swung, his fallen head was raised up for all to see, and in the shadow of the Tower the spring morning rang with the ugly song of their cheers.

'THAT SEA OF BLOOD'

EDINBURGH WAS A BEAUTIFUL, IF SMALL, CITY, 'HIGH-SEATED, IN A
fruitful soil and wholesome air'.[1] With building restricted by defensive
walls built to keep English invaders out, and the population growing,
many of its houses were very tall – some eleven to fourteen storeys
high. This gave a sense of an enclosed space along the high street
where on 17 August 1641 Charles was processed in scarlet and ermine
to the Parliament House. Newly built, it was a fine building with a
hammer-beam roof, by the Kirk of St Giles. Charles's crown was carried
before him in a display of majesty. Yet he was a defeated king at the
mercy of his Scottish subjects. The treaty he signed eight days later
gave the Covenanters almost everything they wanted in exchange for
the withdrawal of Scottish forces from England.[2] Charles planned,
nevertheless, to win back what he had lost. He would deal with the
Scots once he had regained the upper hand in England. There the
Junto's position was, at last, weakening.

People were becoming increasingly alive to the dangers the Junto
now posed both to national stability and to the traditions of the Church
of England. Warwick, Saye and Sele, Brooke, Essex, Pym and the rest
claimed to be the protectors of the law against the king's arbitrary
rule. Yet they had encouraged violent demonstrations not only in
London, but also in the provinces, where Puritan mobs were vandal-
ising local churches. The Church of England also faced a new threat

from the radical and formerly clandestine congregations, run by extreme Puritans known as the 'sectaries'. To many who had sought a conservative reaction to Charles's political and religious innovations, the Junto were proving even worse: a 'pack of half-witted lords' using the sects to 'stir up sedition' and get rid of 'all reverend ministers'.[3]

In September the Junto attempted to regain control of the iconoclastic attacks on churches by issuing orders through Parliament for an orderly destruction of images and altar rails. This, however, provoked fury in those parishes that did not share their distaste for religious art. At Kidderminster in the west Midlands, 'the poor journeymen and servants' ran 'together with weapons to defend the crucifix and the church images': a reminder that Charles's reforms also had their supporters in the Church of England's congregations.

The Junto's most potent means of uniting people behind them remained their insistence that there was a popish conspiracy from which only the Junto would protect them. To demonstrate their point they had driven Marie de' Medici out of England. She had arrived in Dunkirk in June, diminished and seriously ill. The flamboyant former regent would not survive much more than a year, dying in Cologne in a house that had once belonged to Rubens and with her servants burning her furniture to keep her warm. Ordinary Catholics were now in the firing line, facing a persecution even many Protestants later judged to be of 'preposterous rigour and unreasonable severity'.[4] Orders had been issued for all priests to leave England. But at the centre of Catholic religious practice is the Mass, which cannot be performed without a priest: so several had stayed to serve their communities.

The first execution was of an elderly scholar and priest called William Ward. Ward had failed to meet the deadline and was condemned under an Elizabethan law that made it treason simply to be a priest in England. He was hanged at Tyburn and, when almost dead, was cut down from the rope, dragged by his heels to the fire, his belly ripped open, his heart cut out and thrown into the flames.

His head was then cut off, his body dismembered, and the parts placed on the gates of the city. He was eighty-one years old.

The death warrants for a further seven priests had been drawn up and were awaiting Charles's signature, for when he returned to London.

Meanwhile, Charles's family also remained under attack, with Henrietta Maria facing 'disgraceful pasquinades' posted up in London's streets.[5] Until the conclusion of Strafford's trial she had been a vital intermediary between the king and the Junto, a role facilitated by her long-standing friendship with Holland, who was her high steward. But saving Strafford had been key to hopes of compromise and those hopes were now as dead as he was. The gloves were off in the Junto-led attacks on the queen. It was the traditional resort of the enemies of queens to question their chastity, and Henrietta Maria was accused of adultery with her favourite, Henry Jermyn. She felt, she confessed, 'almost crazy with the sudden change in my fortunes'.[6] She lost weight, and suffered headaches and cold sores, while her doctor dosed her with opium to help her sleep. And in that drug-induced slumber what dreams did come? Of the mobs at the palace gate that May, of the old priests screaming as their guts were torn out, or of a time long ago, when she was carried as a baby at the funeral of her murdered father?

The ailing queen had asked Parliament for permission to escort the Princess Royal to Holland, so she might visit spas for her health. Secretly she also hoped to raise money in Europe for Charles. She had, however, been denied a passport and was instead assured that everything possible would be done to ease her stress. 'I give many thanks to both Houses of Parliament for their care of my health,' she replied sarcastically. 'I hope I shall see the effect of it.'[7] Since she could not now help Charles from Europe, she agreed with him to do what she could from home. In the 1630s Henrietta Maria could afford to think 'little of the future, trusting entirely in the king'.[8] Now with his

Privy Council packed with members of the Junto, Charles needed someone close to him he could trust and could play a political role.

Charles had told his acting Secretary of State in England, Edward Nicholas, to consult Henrietta Maria while he was in Scotland, explaining that she had been thoroughly briefed and 'knows my mind fully'.[9] He was writing to her from Edinburgh at least three times a week when, on 23 October, just two months after he had signed the peace treaty with the Scots, shattering news arrived of a rising in his third kingdom: Ireland.

From across the sea, Irish Catholics had looked on, appalled, at what was happening to their English co-religionists. It seemed only a matter of time before they faced something still worse – genocide. These fears were justified. The confederal arrangement the Scots sought with the English was designed to support a military agenda against Irish Catholics, and there had already been leading English advocates of genocide as a legitimate tool of colonial conquest there.[*]

The Irish declared theirs a Royalist rebellion: 'to vindicate the honour of our sovereign, assure the liberty of our consciences, and preserve the freedom of this kingdom under his sacred Majesty'.[10] But their 'liberty of conscience' and 'freedom' represented, on the contrary, a challenge to royal authority. The aim of the rebels was to force Charles to grant them the same degree of religious autonomy, and the same political rights, that he had given the Scots. But Charles would never permit Catholics the free practice of their religion on equal terms with the Church of England. On this one matter Charles and the Junto were agreed: England needed to raise an army to bring Ireland under control.

---

[*] The Elizabethan colonist Edmund Spenser (author of *The Faerie Queen*) in 'A Brief Note on Ireland' had declared that the sword would never effectively wipe out Irish Catholics so 'famine must be the means'. Twenty per cent of the population of Ireland would die under the Commonwealth to famine and the diseases that followed in famine's wake.

In Ulster, Protestant settlers were now being stabbed, hanged and burned in their homes by native neighbours they had known for years. Often the Catholic Irish humiliated their victims by stripping off their clothes, and then leaving them exposed to the elements in the unusually bitter weather of that winter. An English sailor described how his own little daughter, naked and freezing, had tried to comfort her shivering parents, insisting 'she was not cold nor would cry'. She died of hypothermia that night. The parents only saved their four other children by finding shelter in 'a poor shack' and lying naked on top of them 'to keep them in heat and save them alive'.[11]

The colonial administration's reaction to the rebellion was equally savage. In Munster 200 Catholics prisoners were hanged without trial 'for terror', while in Leinster, Catholics were simply murdered in their beds. Soldiers were actively encouraged to target women, 'being manifestly very deep in the guilt of this rebellion'.[12] 'Our men burned the house, killed a woman or two, marched on,' noted the diary of one English officer with indifferent brutality.[13]

Charles called the Irish rebellion 'that sea of blood'. For the Junto, however, it represented a powerful propaganda tool: it made the dangers of Catholic conspiracy real. Although the truth was terrible enough, the Junto and their allies exaggerated the stories of atrocities against settlers to help push through Parliament ever more radical means of reducing Charles's powers. There had been a brief flash of royal teeth on 12 October when a plot was uncovered to arrest (and possibly kill) leading Covenanters in Edinburgh after luring them to Holyrood Palace. Charles denied any foreknowledge of this 'incident', as it became known, but he was not believed. It had involved his childhood friend William Murray and was all too reminiscent of the army plots in England earlier that summer. This 'incident' and its potentially murderous consequences were a terrifying reminder to the Junto of their likely fate if they failed to coerce the king successfully.

The Junto's principal concern now was that they control the army that would have to be raised to crush the Irish rebellion. Traditionally armies were raised in the name of the king. That had to be prevented if they were to ensure that Charles could not then turn the army against them.

As the Junto plotted their next moves, they met at Henry Holland's house in Kensington. Built by Inigo Jones, it was hung with no less than five fabulously expensive Mortlake tapestries, as well as other works of art: an exquisite place for what was often almost a family gathering. Along with Holland's privateering brother Warwick and their dour soldiering cousin Essex was their mutual cousin, the lovely Lucy Carlisle. It was said that since Strafford's demise she had taken a new gallant in Pym and become a Puritan 'she saint'. She was even seen taking notes during sermons.[14] Yet she also remained close to the queen.

Lucy was a spy, although for which side was yet to emerge.

Holland, on the other hand, was certainly not the royal favourite he had once been. He had been moving closer to his brother's position since the dissolution of the Short Parliament, and the offices and grants on which Holland relied for the bulk of his income, and which were in the gift of the king, were now under threat – at least until the Junto deprived Charles of his powers of appointment, as they intended to do. Others were also calculating that Charles could no longer afford to reward great servants: Lucy's brother, Northumberland, amongst them.[15] It would be unfair, though, to suggest that Holland's decision to move against the king was wholly about money. He was an anti-papist 'very much by my breeding', as he himself noted. The Irish rebellion had given him a final push to align with the most ruthless opponents of the rebels – the Junto.

The planned means of attack on the king in Parliament was that form of protest document known as a Remonstrance. This, however, was to be a Grand Remonstrance, listing over 200 individual acts of 'misgovernment'. It was designed to show that religion, liberties and law were intertwined and, as such, they had to be defended together against a popish plan to destroy Protestantism. The 'actors and promoters' of this supposed Jesuitical threat included the Church of England's own bishops, 'along with the corrupt part of the clergy who cherish formality and superstition'.[16] Once passed by MPs the Grand Remonstrance would be published, so allowing the Junto to go straight to a thoroughly alarmed people with the programme they intended: the removal from the Lords of all bishops and Catholics, a vigorously Calvinist reform of the Church of England, and the employment only of royal councillors approved by Parliament.

Henrietta Maria was under no illusion what the Irish rebellion would mean for her. Already, in November, she was named as a suspect in encouraging the revolt in Ireland and blamed for the deaths of Protestant settlers. She knew too that this would be used against her husband. With the family facing such dangers the best she could do in the short term was to try to smuggle his senior heirs – the Prince of Wales, and James, Duke of York – out of the country. To this end she had the boys brought the eight miles from their residence at Richmond Palace to where she was at Oatlands Palace in Surrey. The Junto promptly dispatched Holland to tell her to return them to their governors.

Holland framed the Junto's demands politely, in terms of their anxiety that the princes' education would suffer if they missed their lessons. She did as she was asked, but her punishment for her attempt was swift.[17] As the princes left Oatlands her priestly confessor – the man who acted as her spiritual guide and mentor – was taken away for interrogation concerning his 'involvement' in the Irish rising and also accused of attempts to convert the Prince of Wales. When the priest later refused to swear his answers on a Protestant Bible, he was placed in the Tower. His loss was a very personal blow to the queen, while the fate of the ordinary Catholics whose protection she saw as her responsibility was becoming ever more concerning. A proclamation had been issued demanding that all Catholics bring their names to Parliament: the assumption was that they would then be expelled from the country as the Jews had been in 1290, or at the very least lose their property.[18]

Charles, however, had written to assure the queen that he was on his return journey from Scotland to London. He had left Edinburgh on 4 November and was already riding through the towns of northern England, where the streets were lined with cheering crowds and strewn with flowers: a reminder that the Junto only represented part of the nation. Together Charles and Henrietta Maria now plotted a strategy that was tried and tested in England: the king would make a spectacular entrance to London and woo the affections of his people, as the Tudors had done successfully in countering threats that they had faced from disaffected subjects.[19] The royal fightback was about to begin.

On 22 November, with Charles still a few days from London, the debate on the Grand Remonstrance opened in the Commons. It was met with ferocious opposition.[20] MPs complained that Charles had already answered so many grievances that it was 'unseasonable' to now welcome him home from Edinburgh with a 'volume of reproaches for what others had done and he himself had reformed'.[21] The Remonstrance was passed by a mere eleven votes, and at 2 a.m. when most MPs were in bed. Later that morning another row erupted over whether it should be published. This would be a blatant act of troublemaking. 'I did not dream that we would demonstrate downwards, tell stories to the people and talk of the king as of a third person,' one MP observed with disgust.[22] An interim decision was made for the Remonstrance to be released in manuscript, rather than printed.

On 24 November, Charles reached Theobalds just outside London. Henrietta Maria had gathered a large greeting party that included an impressive array of loyal peers as well as their elder sons. The next day they all accompanied the king towards London. Four miles from the City Charles was met by the lord mayor and his aldermen, along with 600 other leading citizens, all on horse and dressed magnificently.

The mayor presented Charles with the keys of the City and Charles delivered a speech. He blamed the riots earlier in the year on the 'meaner' sort, and vowed to protect the Protestant religion. He and the princes then mounted horses and rode into the City.

The church bells pealed and fountains ran with wine while Charles 'was received everywhere with universal acclamations'. He responded with 'gestures and speech', causing the crowds to erupt in 'a renewal of the shouts of welcome'.[23] At the Guildhall, the aldermen had laid on a feast and, afterwards, the king and queen were escorted to Whitehall by torchlight, the crowds roaring their approval. In the old tilt yard by the palace hundreds of mounted cavaliers awaited Charles, illuminated by tapers, and when the king entered the gates they cried out, 'The Lord preserve King Charles'.[24]

That same day Essex's command as Lord General of the southern army lapsed, as did Holland's command of the army north of the Trent. Charles had promoted them to these roles in the hopes of gaining their goodwill. But he was no longer willing to try and buy the Junto's favours. The king's next move would be to take control of the army needed for Ireland.

With the peace treaty signed in Edinburgh the English army had been disbanded. It would have been a relatively simple matter to recruit it again to fight the Irish. But the soldiers viewed the Junto as traitors and so the Junto wanted instead to raise an army of pressed men – that is, draftees – to be led by their own hand-picked officers. To achieve this they first needed to pass an impressment bill. Charles was determined to mobilise Royalists in Parliament to stop them.

The king's party had a majority in the Lords, thanks to the presence of the bishops, while in the Commons the Junto's majority was reliant on intimidation: moderates had been kept away by the mobs. Charles had to persuade these moderates back. To do so, on 12 December Charles issued a proclamation summoning 'all members of both

Houses of Parliament' to return to Westminster by royal command on or before 12 January 1642. With moderates obliged to attend under this order, Pym's claims to represent the people would be exposed as a sham. Already his pretentions to power had earned him the mocking sobriquet 'King Pym'. It was time to bring his reign to an end.

But 12 January was a month away.

The City radicals were still churning out pamphlets filled with tales from Ireland of babies on pikes and of Protestant families burned in their homes.[25] Those who could not read heard similar stories broadcast from Puritan pulpits. The exaggerated numbers of victims quoted by Puritan ministers at times surpassed the entire Protestant population of Ireland.[26] When Pym's Remonstrance, with its depiction of an England in the grip of a Counter-Reformation takeover bid, was now printed and circulated, the scaremongering was spread far beyond London. In York, the future Parliamentarian general Sir Thomas Fairfax wrote to his father at Westminster, describing how he was living in terror of Catholics hiding in homes all over York, poised to take advantage of the Christmas season, when 'joviality and security chase away fear', to attack ordinary folk when they least expected it.[27]

Meanwhile, back in Westminster, pressure was being maintained on MPs by mobs of 'factious citizens' who descended on Parliament 'with their swords by their sides, hundreds in companies'. The atmosphere in London grew still more violent as the capital filled up in turn with cavaliers. One day there were blows at Whitehall between 'citizens carrying clubs and swords', shouting abuse outside the gates, and 'gentlemen of the Court, who went over the rails striking at them with drawn swords'.[28] On 27 December the Archbishop of York, John Williams, a moderate Calvinist and former friend to the Junto, got out of his coach at Westminster only to have to fight off thugs with his fists. It had become unsafe for bishops to attend the Lords. This removed the Royalist majority in the Upper House and, as moderate MPs had not yet answered Charles's summons to attend Parliament, the Junto retained its majority in the Commons. They were free to push through any bills they wanted.

Archbishop Williams urgently petitioned the king for a suspension of parliamentary business, arguing that without the bishops the Lords were not fully constituted. The Junto-packed Commons promptly had ten of the twelve bishop petitioners arrested for treason and incarcerated in the Tower.[29] Charles's last powers could now be dismantled long before 12 January when moderate MPs would return to Parliament. Charles made a last-ditch effort to reach out to his enemies, offering Pym the coveted post of Chancellor of the Exchequer. Pym turned him down.

Something drastic now had to be done if Charles was not to risk becoming a puppet king. He decided to use the familiar process of impeachment to charge six of the Junto with treason, such 'as stirring up the apprentices to tumultuous petitioning'. Five were members of the Commons: John Pym, Sir Arthur Hesilrige, Denzil Holles, John Hampden and a fanatic called William Strode. The one peer, Viscount Mandeville, was Warwick's son-in-law. Warwick himself and the other great peers were to be left until Charles was in a stronger position. Meanwhile, Charles hoped the impeachment proceedings would clog up parliamentary business until the vital 12 January date.

On Monday 3 January the Attorney General duly presented the House of Lords with the impeachment articles. The Lords would then usually have moved to examine witnesses, as they had with Strafford. Instead, they appointed a committee to decide if the charges were lawful. When the serjeant-at-arms arrived at the Commons to arrest the five members, he was turned away. The Junto then went on the attack, striking as close to the king as they dared.[30]

That night news reached Charles that Parliament was to deprive the queen of most of her household clergy. Henrietta Maria believed this was the prelude to her own arrest. A whispering campaign had been building, accusing her of seeking 'to overthrow the laws and religion of the kingdom'. It was said, furthermore, that a 'queen was only a subject': as such she could be tried and executed as other queen consorts had been before her.[31]

At 10 p.m. Charles ordered that the cannon at the Tower be armed and made ready to overawe the capital. London was eerily quiet the next morning. Then, at three o'clock in the afternoon, Charles suddenly emerged from his quarters at Whitehall. He called out to the multitude of armed Royalist gentry who were standing around: 'Follow me, my most loyal liege men and soldiers.' As they walked behind him he strode out of the palace and commandeered a carriage off a man in the street. He asked to be taken to Parliament. With him went his nephew, Charles Louis, and the seventy-year-old Earl of Roxburghe. The Scottish peer had been urging Charles to intervene directly. Charles Louis was a more reluctant companion. Charles had kept his nephew, and potential replacement, at his side so that the prince would be associated with his action.

MPs may have ignored the arrest warrant for the five members delivered by Charles's serjeant-at-arms, but Charles was certain they could not also ignore an order from his own mouth. And that was what he now intended to deliver.

As Charles's carriage rumbled towards Westminster, Henrietta Maria assured Lucy Carlisle that the king was poised to reclaim his realm, 'for Pym and his confederates are arrested before now'.[32] Henrietta Maria had feared that unless the five members were imprisoned, she would be forced to flee England for her own safety. She had warned Charles the previous night, 'pull those rogues out by the ears – or never see my face more!'[33] What she did not know was that Lucy had then betrayed her, sending a message to an MP friend – possibly Pym – that a plan was being laid against the five members, although she had not known what it was.[34]

Now, as the king's carriage continued down the street followed by 400–500 armed men, a soldier who had served in Buckingham's disastrous French campaign asked what was happening. When he was told, he squeezed past the cavaliers and ran ahead to warn the Commons.

With the soldier's warning delivered, the five members were asked to leave the Chamber to avoid 'combustion in the House'. Strode tried to stay, but a friend dragged him out. At that same moment the king entered New Palace Yard, just outside Westminster Hall. Charles's cavaliers entered the hall first and lined up on either side of the long room in order for the king to pass between them. The MPs sitting in the Commons Chamber then heard the clatter as the king came up the stairs followed by his men. Charles entered the Commons alone, to stunned silence. The five members were by now hiding in the neighbouring Court of the King's Bench. The MPs who remained seated could see old Roxburghe behind the king, holding open the door to the stairs and a crush of soldiers beyond. One held a pistol in his hand, already cocked. A twitch of a finger and MPs' blood would spill on the Commons floor.

Charles walked centre stage to the Speaker's Chair and addressed his MPs. He requested the five members be given up, looking around hoping to spot where they were. 'I do not see any of them,' he said, 'I think I should know them.'[35] The birds had flown and there was nothing left to do but leave. The humiliation of his position was evident. As Charles walked out the silence gave way to shouts of 'Privilege! Privilege!', the thunderous voices pursuing him down the stairs.[36]

A petition was delivered to the king from the City Council on 7 January, informing Charles that the fears prompted by the rebellion in Ireland 'were exceedingly increased by His Majesty's late going into the House of Commons, attended by a great multitude of armed men'. They saw the potential 'ruin of the Protestant religion, and the lives and liberties of all his subjects'. The action Charles had taken had proved disastrous. As one Royalist recalled sadly, 'All that [the Junto] had ever said of plots and conspiracies against Parliament, which had before been laughed at, [was] now thought true and real.'[37] Henrietta Maria was blamed for the attempted arrests, and her life was left at even greater risk than before.

Charles, fearing for the safety of his wife and children, informed the Junto that the royal family would leave London. Holland and Essex tried to persuade Charles to stay, while Lucy Carlisle spoke to Henrietta Maria. Lucy was now open in her support for the Junto, to whom she had for some time been communicating 'all she knew and more of the dispositions of the king and queen'.[38] Lucy had always liked winners, and in common with Holland she was dismayed by Charles's new poverty. England's purse strings now seemed to be in the hands of the Junto. She may also have felt Strafford had betrayed her. She had learned he had profited personally to the tune of thousands of pounds after persuading her to sell vast tracts of her Irish lands to the king.

In any event, Henrietta Maria was not inclined to listen to the advice of her treacherous lady-in-waiting. Later when the queen helped pick code names for the king's party, using their enemies' names to confuse those who intercepted their post, Henrietta Maria chose for herself the code name 'Carlisle': a mark of her contempt for her former favourite, now turned foe. Charles too was angered by the 'ingratitude of those' who 'having eaten of our bread and being enriched with our bounty have scornfully lift themselves up against us'.[39] Holland's desertion was particularly painful for the king: he was a fellow Knight of the Garter, a former Captain of the Guard and Groom of the Stool, as well as a long-standing friend of the queen. Yet Holland's advice was worth listening to. Abandoning London, the 'seat and centre' of Charles's empire, was to prove a major error.

The royal family left Whitehall on Monday 10 January, travelling by barge to Hampton Court, with few courtiers but a large number of officers from the disbanded English army.[40] A Royalist saw the King of England arrive in a 'most disconsolate, perplexed condition, in more need of comfort and counsel than they had ever known him.'[41] It was icy cold at Hampton Court and there were few beds made up. Charles, Henrietta Maria and the children slept together. There was surely some comfort in the warmth of their bodies against each other on that January night. Soon they would be separated forever.

Part Three

HIS TURNCOAT SERVANT

14

'GIVE CAESAR HIS DUE'

AS CHARLES SAID FAREWELL TO HENRIETTA MARIA AT DOVER ON
23 February 1642 it seemed he 'did not know how to tear himself
away from her'.[1] He had banished bishops from the Lords and signed
the impressment bill so that she would be permitted to accompany
their daughter Mary to The Hague. Nevertheless it was hard to see
her go. He stood 'conversing with her in sweet discourse and
affectionate embraces', neither of them able to 'restrain their tears'.[2]
'Pray God for me,' Henrietta Maria asked a friend, 'there is not a more
wretched creature in this world than me separated from the lord my
king, my children and my country.'[3] It was nearly seventeen years since
she had arrived as a child bride from France, and England was now
her home. As her ship sailed away, Charles rode along the shore,
waving his hat until the mast disappeared from view and he was 'left
to his loneliness'.[4]

The youngest of the royal children – Henry, aged nineteen
months, and Elizabeth, aged seven – were installed under the care
of Parliament at St James's Palace. They had lost not only their
mother and Mary, but also their governess, the Countess of
Roxburghe, who was to care for Mary in Holland. It was evident
that the elder princes also 'grieved at the going away of their mother
and sister'.[5] On 9 March, the Prince of Wales wrote to tell Mary his
news in a few 'sad lines'.

The prince was now in Newmarket where their father was 'much disconsolate and troubled'.[6] Henry Holland had arrived and had handed the king a declaration which referred to 'advertisements' in foreign parts that Charles had 'great designs in hand for the altering of religion and the breaking of the neck of your Parliament'. Briefly the king's iron self-control had snapped: 'That's false!' he had shouted. ''Tis a lie!' He feared more 'for the true Protestant profession, my people and laws than for my own rights or safety'.[7] The prince assured his sister that despite everything, their father's small band of followers were 'as we may, merry; and more than we would sad, in respect we cannot alter the present distempers of these troublesome times'. They were now set for York, the second city of the kingdom, 'to see the event or sequel of these bad unpropitious beginnings'.[8]

The Prince Palatine, Charles Louis, complained to his mother, the Winter Queen, that he would have to sell a diamond garter to pay his own travel expenses.[9] He was most unused to putting his hand in his pocket, but there was no avoiding it. The king was so poor, one courtier wrote to his wife, that some nights he had no wine, some nights no candles, and 'he cannot feed them that follow him'. The courtier pitied a monarch 'so friendless yet without one noted vice'. The trouble was, he believed, Charles was too 'good-natured'. Charles's last-ditch efforts to offer Pym the post of Chancellor of the Exchequer had looked like weakness. 'If he had been of a rougher and more imperious nature, he would have found more respect and duty,' another Royalist ventured.[10] Charles himself concurred: 'Had I yielded less, I had been opposed less, had I denied more, I had been more obeyed.'[11]

Before leaving Newmarket, Charles met Holland again. The earl headed a delegation from Parliament and had been picked for his diplomatic skills, as well as his knowledge of the king. His brief was to persuade Charles to reverse his refusal to cede control of the militia to the Junto. This was England's only peacetime force, raised on behalf of the king by the Lord Lieutenants of the counties in times of military need. Holland's wheedling got him nowhere. Parliament was asking things of him, Charles said, 'that were never asked of a king, and with which I will not trust my wife and children'. As king, it was for him alone to lead the fight against the rebels in Ireland. Parliament may have beggared him, but, he declared emphatically, 'I can find money for that!'[12]

Charles had always prided himself on his ability to control his emotions under pressure. Now, 'lost in the eye of the world ... and in the love and affections of his people', his reign had reached a nadir and his anger was visceral.[13] As Charles and his small train of followers set off for York, they stopped at Cambridge. Women threw stones and shouted at him to return to his Parliament. 'Poor king,' another of his subjects wrote, 'he grows still more in slight and contempt here every day.'[14]

Henrietta Maria's arrival in The Hague was, meanwhile, greeted with lavish entertainments laid on by her daughter's father-in-law, Frederick Henry, Prince of Orange. Charles's sister Elizabeth offered a cooler reception. Her son Charles Louis had been writing home describing Henrietta Maria as a harridan who dominated Charles and was determined on war. Elizabeth was convinced that all her 'dear brother's' problems must stem from his wife. Meanwhile Charles Louis' siblings reacted unsympathetically to the visible effects on Henrietta Maria of months of illness and weight loss, not to mention the wreck of one of the ships accompanying her to Holland.[15] Charles's niece, Sophie of the Rhine, wrote cruelly of her skinny arms and of loose teeth 'protruding from her mouth like ravelins from a fortress'. The description is still quoted to imply Henrietta Maria was plain. In fact as soon as she won Sophie round, the girl began to notice that the queen 'had very beautiful eyes, a well-formed nose and a lovely complexion'.[16] Charles had been confident Henrietta Maria's charm would also ensure that 'my wife and my sister will be very good friends'.[17] And indeed, the Winter Queen admitted that her sister-in-law 'uses me and my children extremely well', showing 'civility and kindness'.[18]

Henrietta Maria was in Europe, however, not only for her own safety. She had a job to do. Having smoothed over family relations, Henrietta Maria took up her new role as Charles's diplomat and party leader in Europe, as well as his arms buyer. The situation in Ireland was, for both sides, now only the pretext for the gathering of arms and men to fight on English home soil. Henrietta Maria had been set a formidable task, and in the Dutch Republic she faced anti-Royalist prejudice. When she tried to sell the royal jewels she had brought with her, obstacles were put in her way. In one of her lost letters to Charles she warned, 'Dear Heart ... can you send me a warrant under your hand, which gives me full power to deal with my jewellery, since the merchants say a woman cannot sell jewellery during the lifetime of her husband.' The gems included Crown possessions such as the famous Burgundian jewel, the 'Three Brethren', a pin of rubies and diamonds that Charles had flaunted in Madrid to dazzle the Spanish in 1623.[19] Once they were sold she was confident she could 'buy gunpowder, arms and cannon here'.[20]

Charles responded quickly and a further letter from his wife followed. She had his pearl buttons 'taken out of their gold setting and made into a chain'. It proved a great success: 'You cannot imagine how pretty your pearls were.' Nevertheless the dealers in Breda struck a hard bargain. The buttons went for half what they were worth.[21] As she began using the money to buy arms, she also deployed her political skills to undermine Parliament's efforts to gain European support for their cause. In a further lost letter Henrietta Maria informs the French foreign minister Chavigny that 'The English rebels, under the name of Parliament', had sent an agent to Holland, claiming that 'the king and I' wanted to re-establish Catholicism in England: 'I hear they have also sent an agent to France on the same pretext of religion. Whoever he is I hope he will not be heard nor received, since he comes from rebels against God and against their king.'[22] In a later letter she thanks

Chavigny for 'the services you give me'.[23] What kind of services is indicated a few months later when she thanks him for stopping a shipment of 'arms prepared for the rebels'.[24]

Charles arrived in York on 19 March with the Prince of Wales and a mere thirty or forty gentlemen. He accepted that he had to agree to many of the new restrictions that Parliament had placed on him if he was to gather recruits. In the meantime, there was a truly grim decision to be made. After the scaremongering about Catholics hiding in houses in York at Christmas, he needed to reassure the frightened townsfolk that he was committed to protecting them from a popish conspiracy. This necessitated his lifting a stay of execution on a local Catholic priest. The unfortunate man was hanged, drawn and quartered on 13 April, along with another priest, a native-born Yorkshireman aged eighty-seven.[25] At least the man was guilty of the crime of which he was convicted – albeit only of being a priest and being in England.

In the shadow of these deaths Charles planned the annual Garter feast. A glittering march-past of Charles's knights was intended to be an affirmation of the loyalty and companionship of his leading nobles, a theatrical reminder of the ethos of order and a projection of the mystery of royal power.[26] Only four knights came. It did achieve one thing, however: the arrival of James, Duke of York, for his election to the Order, escorted by the Marquess of Hertford, and upwards of 900 horse.[27] This marked a decisive break between Hertford and his brother-in-law, Essex, with whom he had always been close. Many friendships and families were beginning to see similar divisions. But Charles needed to do much more to recruit Royalists. His next move was to advertise his role as the true guardian of the law against radicals who were bringing disorder and terror to England.

The Junto-controlled Parliament had issued an order, without the necessary royal consent, for the munitions kept in Hull since the second Bishops' War now to be moved to London.[28] Henrietta Maria urged Charles to act quickly and seize the magazine for his future army. His hopes of compromise made him vacillate, and she warned him, 'You should never take half-measures. This is what you have always done, started well and continued badly.'[29] She had a point. Charles was attracted to adventurous exploits, but the considered, scholarly side of his nature, and dislike of violence, also made him draw back. The result was that while he was open to suggestions of bold action, he had often proved not to have the ruthlessness to take personal charge or to follow through the consequences. On this occasion, however, Charles's restraint had solid reasoning behind it.

Charles hoped to create a theatrical scene that would make it clear the Junto had committed an act of rebellion. He ignored his wife's call to take soldiers to fight for the magazine and instead, on 22 April 1642, two days after the Garter ceremonies were finished, he sent James to Hull. There the eight-year-old, boasting his new George, politely informed the governor, Sir John Hotham, that the king was approaching and expected to be granted entry. Hotham greeted the little Duke of York in Parliament's name with 'every demonstration of respect', but when the king appeared he refused him entry. This was out-and-out treason.

On 30 April Charles asked the Yorkshire gentry for their aid in defending his person and that 'he may be vindicated in his honour'.[30] On 12 May he issued a further call to arms. 'You see that my magazine is going to be taken from me (being my own goods) directly against my will ... I have thought it fit to have a guard that I may be able to protect you, the laws, and the true Protestant profession.' In this he required their 'concurrence and assistance'.[31]

As recruits began to flock to the Royalist cause in York, Charles issued resolutions announcing the disarming of all Catholics, reiterated his commitment to 'true religion', and his openness to discussing all disputed matters. Personal letters were also sent out to every peer, commanding each on his allegiance to offer his counsel. A steady stream of noblemen duly began to head north. Then the Junto helped the king further by taking a false step. Charles was presented by

Parliament with nineteen Propositions to which he had to agree if civil war was to be avoided. If accepted, these Propositions would have reduced him to the status of a puppet king, without the right even to supervise his own children. What Charles called their 'horrible novelty' antagonised moderate opinion and his official 'Answer' in June became a major propaganda victory.[32] It warned that Parliament had become an 'upstart authority' and that it was moving to destroy the constitutional balance by usurping royal powers. If the king were left undefended, the entire social order would collapse 'into a dark equal chaos of confusion'.

Multiple editions of Charles's 'Answer' were printed and given wide circulation. It tapped into a deep vein of anxiety that power had tipped into the hands of an oligarchy that was working hand in glove with extremists. This anxiety had, furthermore, a basis in fact. The leading oppositionists were dependent for their lives and political programme on the Presbyterian Scots and the radicals of the London mass movement. The majority of the political nation did not hold radical or Presbyterian views and were horrified at the explosion of extremist religious literature seen over the last year since the abolition in the summer of 1641 of the Court of Star Chamber, which had addressed cases of sedition. In terms of church structure the maximum most envisaged was a 'lowered', or less powerful, episcopacy, not its removal. They were now ready to defend the king and the Church of England against attack by Presbyterians, Independent Congregationalists and the wilder fringes of Protestantism represented by the sectarians.

Petitions in support of episcopacy began to be issued in the counties and a new sense of optimism took hold around the king. Charles and his sons were described as 'well and cheerful, the court full of lords, many of the House of Commons and multitude of other brave gentlemen'.[33]

By July only about a third of MPs and a quarter of peers were attending Parliament.[34] As Charles had highlighted, it scarcely looked like a legal body. Nevertheless, Holland, Warwick and Essex were successfully raising large sums of money for Parliament's army.[35] Emigrants were also returning home from the Puritan colonies to help in the regime change. Amongst them was Warwick's bibulous protégé Hugh Peter, who had spent six years in New England serving as a minister in Salem and overseer of Harvard College. Such 'Americans' found it was 'a notion of mighty great and high respect to have been a New English man'. They were welcomed to serve as MPs, clergymen and soldiers.[36] A constitutional revolution in the City of London government had, meanwhile, seen the lower house gain power over the upper, and the Royalist lord mayor sent for trial.[37] For opponents of the regime, London had become a place of fear. Half the judges were jailed, along with many Royalist laymen, ministers and bishops.

As they prepared for war, the Junto justified acting against the king – which was how treason was defined – by using the theory of the 'king's two bodies'. This made a distinction between the physical body of the king (which might be incapacitated) and the Crown as a body of authority. According to their argument Parliament, as the highest court, had the right to act on Charles's behalf, as it might if he were insane. This did not have the rallying quality of the Royalist appeals to loyalty to their king. But the Junto could, and did, continue to mine the atrocity stories from Ireland.* It was ironic that the 10,000 men raised to defend the Protestant settlers in Ireland were to be used instead against the king. But then the popish threat was, supposedly, threatening England itself.

For English Catholics the Junto's jabbing at religious and ethnic prejudice had terrifying consequences. Their houses and goods were being plundered by mobs and there were further hangings, drawings

---

* In June Ireland's Catholic leaders had formed a Confederation with its own General Assembly and Supreme Council. It would govern Catholic Ireland for the next seven years and raise its own army and navy against the feared threat of an English invasion. The Protestant Lords Justices had, meanwhile, issued orders that their men could execute people without trial under martial law.

and quarterings of priests. Near Dorchester, one tortured cleric was left alive for half an hour during his disembowelment. 'His forehead was bathed in sweat and blood and water flowed from his eyes and nose,' a witness reported. A woman watching as pieces of his liver were being extracted begged for him to be put out of his misery. When at last he was, his decapitated head was used as a football in the crowd.[38]

Essex was now named as Parliament's Lord General. Although the fifty-one-year-old's military career in Europe had ended seventeen years earlier, with him holding the rank of a mere colonel, his father's name still held its magnetic force. The legend of the 'valiant knight of chivalry', who had fallen victim to royal injustice under Elizabeth I, lived on in his son who had a stoical authority and attracted a large popular following. Indeed, one Parliamentarian later asserted that if he 'had refused that command our cause in all likelihood [would have] sunk'.[39]

Warwick was also a key figure in gaining Parliament military power. After Essex, he was England's premier fighting lord, and had almost single-handedly carried the fight to the Spanish in the Americas for over two decades. Many sailors were attracted to his reputation, and when he appeared at the Downs naval base at Chatham in north Kent on the river Medway, all but five of the royal ships came over to him immediately. That night he persuaded a sixth captain to join them. The following day Warwick besieged the remaining four ships. He described to Pym how he fired cannon shot over the last two holdouts and then sent a message saying, 'I had turned up the glass upon them.' When the sand ran out their time was up. He attacked, the ships were boarded and their captains arrested.[40] Warwick had thus successfully seized control of the navy for Parliament.

Both sides were now recruiting for their armies across England and Wales. Towns and villages everywhere saw 'fierce contests and disputes'.[41] The term 'Cavalier' was used as an insult to conjure images of popish caballeros while 'Roundhead' associated Parliament with Puritans who kept their hair 'close round their heads with so many little peaks as was something ridiculous to behold'.[42] The corporation of Coventry was amongst those that strove to remain neutral, and the ordinary people of north Devon refused even the most diligent recruitment efforts. People were certain that the war would begin and end with one great battle, as had so often been the case during the Wars of the Roses. There was no desire to commit when it would soon emerge who the victor was to be.

There was, furthermore, no profound ethnic or religious hatred amongst the people of England and Wales, despite the narrative of a popish threat. The numbers of Catholics were too few. This was to be a war of Protestant against Protestant over the nature of the Church of England, and where the balance of power between king and Parliament should lie in a 'mixed' monarchy. Neither Royalists nor Parliamentarians held a homogeneous view on the outcome they desired. As, gradually, the kingdom began to splinter, so each side held within it the certainty of further splits that would see Royalist turn on Royalist, and Parliamentarian on Parliamentarian.[43] The question was, would moderates win, or something extreme?

Charles's cause was slowed by his desire to demonstrate his reluctance to make war. The 'king is content to look on quietly, and to tread the path of peace', one royal servant had observed in June.[44] It was a risky strategy. Parliament was already strongest in the richest and most populous regions of London and the south-east, of East Anglia, and much of the south and east Midlands.[45] But in August Charles at last ordered his supporters to rally to his standard at Nottingham Castle.* Charles Louis promptly deserted his uncle to sail for Holland. He would later issue a public call for Charles to reconcile

---

* In a previously unrecorded letter by Charles of 4 August he orders the herald William Dugdale to disarm the castles of Warwick and Banbury held by Lord Brooke, and if they resist to declare them traitors. I have passed on details to Sarah Poynting, who is editing a comprehensive volume of Charles's writings. The letter is held by a Dugdale descendant.

with Parliament and condemn his younger brothers Rupert and Maurice of the Rhine, who landed in England to join the king's cause just as he left.[46]

It was raining when, at six in the evening on 22 August, Charles's sons the Prince of Wales and James, Duke of York, rode with their father up the hill at Nottingham Castle, to raise his standard. The cloth was pennant-shaped and cloven at the outer edge. It was sewn with an image of the king's heraldic arms, along with a bloody hand pointing to a crown and the words 'Give Caesar his due'.[47] This allusion to Christ's instruction to 'render unto Caesar what is Caesar's' was a reminder of a subject's duty of obedience to a king's divinely sanctioned authority. It must, nevertheless, rank as one of history's least inspiring rallying cries. Raised against a dark sky, the cloth hung limp from a blood-red pole, the rain lashing down as the drums rolled. The standard was planted in the ground, trumpets blasted, and 1,000 Cavaliers cried out, 'God save the king.'

In The Hague, Henrietta Maria pronounced herself happier with events than she had been in two years. She had sent Charles powder, muskets, pistols and carbines, field pieces and cash for the battle ahead. Victory would be theirs, and 'Hay then! Down go they!'[48] She and her 'Dear Heart' would be together in 'a month', she assured him.[49]

But in Nottingham, Charles's face looked stricken.

The Royalist commander Sir Henry Slingsby had, like the king, glimpsed the horrors ahead. 'Neither one nor the other can expect to see advantage by this war,' he predicted; 'the remedy will prove worse than the disease.'[50]

15

'EDGEHILL

THE TOWN OF WORCESTER AND THE COUNTRY AROUND IT IS 'so papistical, atheistical, and abominable, that it resembles Sodom and is the very emblem of Gomorrah'.[1] That, at least, was the judgement of one Roundhead. His brothers in arms should, therefore, have been on the lookout for trouble when they reached Wick Field by Powick Bridge on 23 September 1642. Instead they blundered into a troop of Royalist cavalry under Prince Rupert of the Rhine. Aged twenty-two and over six feet tall, Rupert had, it was said, the face of an angel and the temper of a demon. But it was his younger brother, the strapping twenty-one-year-old Prince Maurice, who promptly shot a Roundhead dead. In the ensuing melee the princes both received cuts to the head before the Roundheads were overcome. Around 150 were killed, and some of the wounded were finished off with daggers and their bodies mutilated.[2]

Rupert was a child of the Thirty Years War and already an aggressive soldier. He had fought against the Habsburgs under the Calvinist Prince of Orange from the age of thirteen, and at nineteen was a prisoner of war. He had been released the previous year 'in perfect health, but lean and weary'.[3] He had with him a rare large white hunting poodle called Boy: a gift of the Royalist Earl of Arundel from the litter of a bitch known as Puddle.[4] Rupert had sworn not to fight the Habsburgs again as a condition of his release, and since soldiering was his only business, he had come England with Boy and Maurice to fight for his uncle. Rupert's years on the battlefield had left him with little courtly polish, but Charles had given him command of the horse and the most energetic and talented Cavaliers had flocked to take service with him. Within weeks of his appointment Rupert's cavalry was 2,500 strong, in an army of 12,500. At Powick Bridge his reputation amongst Cavaliers was sealed.

That night, as his men tasted their success, 'swearing most hellishly', Rupert wrote to Parliament's general, the Earl of Essex, and challenged him to duel or battle. Parliament's official orders were for Essex to seize Charles from his evil councillors. Rupert accused the earl of an ambition instead to usurp the throne. 'I need not fear, for what I do is agreeable both to the law of God and man, in defence of true religion [Rupert was a Calvinist], a king's prerogative, an uncle's right, a kingdom's safety.' Justice would be 'delivered in a larger field than this small piece of paper, and that by my sword, not by my pen'.[5]

Brave words. But without good maps both armies were moving blind. Slipping and sliding over the wet rutted roads of the Midlands, 'neither army knew where the other was' and they 'gave not the least disquiet ... to each another'.[6]

Meanwhile both Roundheads and Cavaliers were hungry and tired, each soldier carrying up to sixty pounds of armour, helmets, swords and knapsacks. The musketeers had their guns, slung off one shoulder, and bandoliers of gunpowder chargers. The pikemen stood out for the size and strength they needed to carry weapons sixteen feet long that juddered as they marched.[7] Royalists were here to fight the tyranny of the Junto and for the king as the protector of the law; Roundheads to fight the tyranny of the king and for Parliament to preserve their just liberties. Essex had brought his coffin with him, to show his men he was ready to die amongst them. There were, however, many on both sides who were ready to fight for the pay, the plunder and the adventure. 'I will learn to swear and drink and roar / and (gallant like) I will keep a whore', hoped the ploughman of one contemporary ballad.

Such a man could earn more in a day robbing a dead gentleman than he could earn in a year on the farm. Very few had any experience of soldiering and some had friends or family on the other side.

On the evening of 22 October Rupert and his men ran into a party of Essex's quartermasters looking for billets for their troops at the Warwickshire village of Wormleighton. It was the kind of luck that would make the Roundheads begin to wonder if Rupert had magical powers. Having taken the Roundheads prisoner, Rupert sent out a patrol to find the main body of their army. It was spotted seven miles to the west, camped at Kineton. Rupert dispatched a message to Charles advising that Essex be intercepted at a 300-foot escarpment called Edgehill. Stretching north from the high ground there was a meadow known locally as the Vale of the Red Horse. It was perfect ground for Rupert's cavalry, but the request triggered a row with Charles's Lord General, the fifty-nine-year-old Robert Bertie, Earl of Lindsey. When the king backed Rupert, Lindsey resigned. Since he was not considered fit to lead the army, he would, he declared, 'die a colonel at the head of his regiment'.*

It was four in the morning when Rupert at last received Charles's reply: 'Nephew, I have given order as you have desired.'[8]

Charles's army immediately began moving onto the ridge. Come the morning, their conspicuous position offered a direct challenge to Essex and his forces. By noon Essex had deployed his men in response. He chose his ground on a small rise in the ground facing Edgehill just to the south of Kineton. His was the better-equipped army. He had all the supplies from Hull, and had made good use of the wealth and munitions industry of London and the south-east. Warwick's navy had, furthermore, captured several ships filled with munitions that Henrietta Maria had sent for Charles from Holland. Some of Charles's

---

* Lindsey had already lost one argument with Charles's Scottish field marshal, Patrick Ruthven, Earl of Forth, over whether or not to use a Swedish or Dutch deployment, with Charles ruling in favour of the former.

foot soldiers were armed only with cudgels and the cavalrymen were lucky if they had 'pistols or carbines for their two or three front ranks, and swords for the rest'.[9] The major advantage the Royalists had was psychological: the presence of the king himself amongst his troops.

Essex had to try to keep his men from seeing that they were taking up arms directly against their king – and that wasn't easy. It was 'as fair a day as that season of the year could yield'.[10] Charles could be seen clearly in the brilliant sunshine riding his charger 'up to the forefront of the head of his army'. There he addressed his men. 'Friends and soldiers, I look upon you with joy to behold so great an army as ever King of England had.' He thanked them for standing by him, 'with high and full resolution to defend your king, the parliament, and all my loyal subjects'.

Although the opposing army became known as the 'Parliamentarians', nearly half of those originally selected as members of the Commons for the Long Parliament had taken the king's side, as did most of the House of Lords.[11] Charles would always claim that he was the true defender of Parliament. 'Heaven make you victorious,' the king prayed. The last preparations for battle then began.[12]

On the cusp of 3 p.m. Essex ordered the opening salvos of artillery. 'Go in the name of God,' he reassured his men, 'and I'll lay my bones with yours.'[13] His men, most of whom were unused to any loud noise beyond the peal of church bells, now heard 'the cannon's thundering voice'. The shot exploded in the Royalist ranks.[14] It was 'dreadful', one recalled, as 'brains and bowels blew in our faces'.[15] When the king's artillery returned fire the first shots fell short in ploughed fields.[16] Rupert, however, was now preparing the first great cavalry charge England had seen since the Middle Ages. Riding from one wing of the army to the other he gave orders to the horsemen to ride 'as close as was possible, keeping their ranks with sword in hand, to receive the enemy's shot without firing either carbine or pistol'. Only when he gave the word could they return fire. The cavalry advanced slowly before breaking into a canter. Facing the remorseless drum of horses' hooves and the war cries of their riders as they began a headlong gallop, the untested Parliamentarian troops broke in terror. A few fired off their pistols before fleeing, while one brigade of foot 'wholly disbanded and ran away, without ever striking stroke, or so much as being charged by the enemy'.[17]

It was now the turn of the Royalist infantry to move forward. One commander knelt and prayed, 'Oh Lord, thou knowest how busy I must be this day. If I forget thee do not thou forget me.' Then he got up and shouted, 'March on, boys.'[18] James, Duke of York, just a few days past his ninth birthday, watched fascinated as the men walked towards the enemy with 'a slow steady space and a daring resolution'. Only the centre of Essex's army was still holding. Essex himself dismounted his horse. He later described to Lucy Carlisle how he 'put himself at the head of his regiment of foot, with a pike in his hand' like an ordinary soldier.[19] He expected to fight to his death. But the Royalist cavalry, which should have helped their infantry finish the job they had started, continued to rush blindly forward. They were joined by the king's reserve horse 'with spurs and loose reins', out of the control of their commanders.[20] This was Charles's first battle, and he could not stop even his own mounted bodyguard, the scarlet-clad Life Guard of Horse, getting caught up in the thrill of victory and galloping in pursuit of the fleeing enemy. Amongst them were his Stuart cousins, the thirty-year-old Duke of Richmond and his young brothers, Lord Bernard Stuart, Lord John Stuart and Lord Aubigny.

As the infantry from both sides collided, Essex deployed his own cavalry to join the melee. Orange scarves distinguished many Roundheads, red the Cavaliers. Pressed between the heaving masses of friends behind them, and the slashing ranks of enemy opposing them, men fired off pistols, sending up blinding clouds of smoke, while others hacked with swords or struck out with clubs.* Strange sights

---

* Two centuries later, in another civil war on the other side of the Atlantic, at the Battle of Gettysburg, it was noticed that the stress on the heart caused men to fall asleep in the middle of the fighting.

confused and dismayed, with the smoke playing tricks, making the enemy seem bigger than they were, like ghouls rising from the fog of a nightmare. In the Royalist ranks, those without proper weapons stepped on the bodies of the fallen and 'took up the arms which their slaughtered neighbours left them'.[21]

On the Parliamentarian side chaplains 'rode up and down the army, through the thickest dangers ... exhorting the soldiers to fight valiantly and not to fly'.[22] The Life Guard of Foot, protecting the royal standard, faltered under their intense assault. The standard-bearer Sir Edmund Verney killed the Parliamentarian soldier who cut down his body-guard, but Verney was in turn killed. He 'would not put on armour or buff coat' that morning: he had prepared to meet the enemy dressed as if he were greeting family – which in a way he was. His eldest boy was in the opposing army. Verney's body was left so badly mutilated that it would never be found. The standard was taken, fought over ferociously for six minutes and retrieved by a Captain Smith.

Elsewhere in the battle another old soldier, the former commander the Earl of Lindsey, was shot in the thigh. He was carried from the field a prisoner, bleeding heavily. His son, Lord Willoughby, dashed to help his father and was taken prisoner with him.

Charles, despite the bullets flying over his head, and with his men falling around him, refused to leave the fray, showing 'as much dexterity, presence of mind and personal courage as any'. His visibility shored up morale and another witness believed that 'had he not been in the field we might have suffered'.[23]

He needed, however, to ensure that his young sons Charles, Prince of Wales, and James, Duke of York, would not be harmed or taken prisoner. They were already under fire when he ordered his personal escort and a few other trusted soldiers to take his children and 'with-draw to the top of the hill'.

Dusk was falling when the boys saw a body of horse moving towards them. It was unclear if they were friend or foe. An equerry rode ahead to check. The Prince of Wales saw the equerry beaten off his horse, left for dead and stripped. Their small party promptly changed course.[24] 'We drew behind a little barn not distant from them, which was encompassed by a hedge,' James later recalled, and 'several of the king's wounded were there'. It was a grim spectacle for a child, with the cries of the dying. He also realised that if they were attacked they would be overrun. Charles understood that too and had ordered for his sons to be moved to nearby Edgecote. Before these orders could be carried out, however, James witnessed the battle's conclusion.

It seemed incredible to James that the exhausted and frightened men on either side still stood their ground, blacksmiths and dyers, gentlemen and lords, all 'continuing to fire at one another even unto night'.[25] At last, however, darkness ended the fighting. The icy weather finished off many of the wounded that night. Yet the cold saved at least two severely injured officers. They had been robbed and stripped, and their surgeons believed the chill had 'stopped their blood better than all their skill and medications could have done'. The Royalist physician William Harvey, who was at the battle, confirmed their hypothesis after he discovered the circulation of the blood.[26]

The old general, Lindsey, protected from the cold in the 'poor house' where he was prisoner, was less fortunate. He died of shock and blood loss from his wounded leg. His fellow Royalists had suffered the heavier casualties, especially amongst the higher ranks. Lord Bernard Stuart estimated 'what is killed and run away I think is about 2,500'. Perhaps the most tragic death to him was that of his twenty-four-year-old elder brother, Aubigny. A young man 'of gentle and winning disposition', he was shot in the back by a Dutch mercenary he had punished earlier for poor discipline.[27]

Charles stayed out on the hill that night, by a fire. He could hear the groans of those still dying and 'bemoaned the loss of so much blood'.[28] 'There was a great deal of fear and misery about the field that night,' a trooper wrote to his mother. Another soldier, suffering post-combat shock, found that although he was hungry, his jaws were clenched so tight he could barely eat. An MP on the Parliamentarian side found the same. As a result, 'We almost starved,' he remembered.[29] When the sun came up on the Monday the traumatised men of two armies remained in a state of stupefaction.

> Edgehill, with graves looked white,
> With blood looked red
> Maz'd at the numbers of the dead.

So wrote the Cavalier poet Edward Benlowes.

Hours passed as the soldiers stared at each other across the field, unmoving. In the Roundhead camp, it was said there was 'much trouble and disorder in the faces of the Earl of Essex and the principal officers about him, and so much dejection in the common soldiers, that they looked like men who had no further ambition than to keep what they had left'.[30] Both sides had believed this one battle would end the war, but now it was obvious there was no clear victor.

Essex was on the point of breakdown. Instead of writing the official report of the battle that evening, as was customary, he did nothing. Six junior officers took it upon themselves to fulfil the task. Only the young Prince Rupert recognised the danger of post-battlefield lethargy, arguing that Charles should press on to London immediately. Others thought it inadvisable to take London 'by conquest', fearing Rupert might even 'fire the town', as the Habsburgs were reputed to have done at Magdeburg in 1631.

Charles decided to push for peace, but prepare for war.

On 24 October 1642, Henry Holland and his cousin Northumberland headed a delegation from Parliament to the City government in London, and gave 'pithy and pathetical speeches'. Londoners had been pressing Parliament to make peace. Holland and Northumberland assured the City government that Parliament had 'no evil intention to the king', but, they warned, his councils would result in the destruction of true religion, and 'he intended to expose the wealth of his good people, especially of London, to the rape and spoil of his cavaliers and soldiers'.[31]

On 12 November Rupert crossed the Thames, sacked the Parliament garrison at Brentford and plundered the town. Frightened Londoners, fearing what Rupert might do next, readied themselves to defend their city. The king's youngest children – Elizabeth aged six, and the two-year-old Henry, Duke of Gloucester – trapped in Parliament's control since their mother had left for Holland, were moved from St James's Palace to Lord Cottingham's house on Broad Street, to be used as hostages or human shields.[32] If Rupert fired London, his little cousins would die in the flames.

The following day the opposing armies met on the west road from London, at the village of Turnham Green. Parliament's forces now had the 'trained bands', London's militia, formed in regiments and many thousands strong. It was an army double the size of that of the Royalists.

Rupert's advice to Charles was to avoid battle, march south, turn and attack London from Kent. Charles, anxious to avoid large numbers of civilian casualties, instead retreated up the Thames Valley to Oxford. London was spared violence, but a vital opportunity for Charles was lost.

In the New Year, Charles's sister Elizabeth in The Hague received the latest reports of the war from an old friend: 'I wish I had nothing to write,' he told her, 'for no news is good news.' The king was 'at Oxford strongly quartered; the Earl of Essex at Windsor and both have flying armies like fiery dragons everywhere destroying'. In the west of England and south Wales a Royalist army was consolidating control of Cornwall, Wales and the border counties. In the north the forces of the Royalist Earl of Newcastle (soon to be made a marquess) were overrunning much of Yorkshire and establishing a bridgehead in the Midlands at Newark. Yet there seemed to be no part of England that did not also see Parliament's troops. All hope that the war would be over soon was dashed.

'TIGER'S HEART'

SIXTEEN WARSHIPS HUNTED HENRIETTA MARIA THROUGH THE HIGH waves of the North Sea. It was February 1643 and Robert Rich, Earl of Warwick, acting as Parliament's High Admiral, wanted her captured or killed.[1] The stormy weather helped her lose her pursuers and poor visibility cloaked her disembarkation at Bridlington Bay on the Yorkshire coast. She spent that night in a cottage on the pier. It was 5 a.m., and dark, when Warwick's captains located her. Four of Parliament's ships entered the bay and opened fire. Henrietta Maria was still in bed; 'the balls were whistling upon me', she told Charles, and 'you may easily believe I loved not such music'.[2] She grabbed her clothes, and dashed with her ladies to the shelter of a ditch. In her arms she clutched her dog, an ugly little mutt called Mitte. The shot, 'singing around us in fine style', killed a sergeant only twenty paces from her. His body lay 'torn and mangled with their great shot' as the women lay in the ditch, 'the balls passing over our heads and sometimes covering us with dust'. It was two hours before the tide turned and Warwick's ships were forced back out to sea.

Charles publicly condemned what he saw as Warwick's attempt to kill his wife, complaining the cannon fire at Bridlington Bay was 'not casually but purposely committed'.[3] No other spoilt princess of Europe had to face such dangers. But Henrietta Maria was every inch the daughter of the great warrior king Henri IV, and she had risked her life to good purpose. As soon as the firing had stopped she ordered a guard for the munitions she had brought. 'I must act the captain,' she joked, even 'though a little low in stature'.[4] Her men, money and arms would now join her in Yorkshire where they would help the Royalists soon gain superiority in the county.

Meanwhile peace efforts were in process. If they failed, the finger of blame was already being pointed at Henrietta Maria, with fears expressed that 'her ardent French temper may inspire the king ... to vigorous resolution'.[5] She was even compared to another French-born Queen of England, Margaret of Anjou, that 'tiger's heart wrapped in a woman's hide', blamed for much of the bloodshed of the Wars of the Roses. The truth was rather different.

Many had expected Essex to win a decisive battlefield victory over the king at their first engagement. Charles had arrived in York in 1642 with only thirty or forty followers. His achievements since then had been extraordinary. He had not only survived the Battle of Edgehill, his forces were now on the attack. The future the Parliamentarians faced was either total defeat by the king, or a long civil war that would threaten the established order, bankrupt the country, and hand power to military men. This prospect had split the Junto. There was now a war faction and a peace faction, with the Rich brothers, Holland and Warwick leading figures in the opposing camps.

Both king and Parliament controlled a portion of Holland's income, making any further extension of the war financially ruinous for him. In common with Northumberland, and several other peers, he was also concerned about the risks to the country of continued instability. They were, therefore, working with a moderate faction in the Commons for a peace treaty that left the king with most of his preroga-tive powers, and the Church of England with its bishops. It was a peace treaty that Charles was likely to accept. Warwick and the other leaders of the war party included those who had been complicit in the 1640 Scottish invasion, and whose lives remained at risk until Charles was stripped of all meaningful power. They did not want – and could not afford – a 'moderate' peace. They included Pym in the Commons and Warwick's old allies in the Lords, Viscount Saye and Sele and Lord Brooke.

The vast majority of the ordinary English people were with the peace party, sharing Holland's desire for an end to the war. But they no longer had any real representation in Parliament. With no immediate prospect of having to face re-election, MPs lacked accountability to the ordinary voters. They were subject instead to manipulation by the leaders of the war and peace parties – the 'grandees', as they were now known. Policy was being made, and patronage distributed, in back rooms, through the operations of the grandee-dominated 'executive standing committees'. It was the peace-party grandees who had a treaty delegation sent to Charles in Oxford.[6] But the war-party grandees had ensured the proposed terms were far tougher than the king was likely to accept. They included demands that the armies be disbanded before peace negotiations began, and that Charles's leading friends be delivered up for justice – in other words, death. This was knowingly 'to propose an impossibility against the making of peace'.[7]

The war-party grandees realised, however, that they also had to convince the moderate majority of MPs to follow their lead. Here, raising fears of popery still remained their most effective method of persuasion. They therefore now launched a fresh assault on the papist-in-chief – Henrietta Maria.

In March 1643 one of Warwick's former clients, an Irishman called Sir John Clotworthy, led a party to destroy the images and books in the queen's Denmark House chapel. He personally slashed the faces in the Rubens masterpiece of the Crucifixion that had been Charles's gift to her, and then 'thrusting the hook of his halberd under the feet of the crucified Christ ripped the painting to pieces'.[8] It was the greatest single loss to art of the war. Destroying papist paintings remained mere surrogacy, however, for the more important business of destroying actual papists. Henrietta Maria was therefore indeed anxious to stiffen her husband's resolve not to accept the war party's terms. 'If you make a peace and disband your army before there is an end to this perpetual parliament, I am absolutely resolved to go into France,' she told him, 'being well assured that if the power remain with them that it will not be well for me in England.'[9]

In Oxford those Royalists who were as anxious for peace as Holland nevertheless urged Charles to remain flexible in his dealings with Parliament. On 24 March 1643, in a letter written in cipher and neatly in his brown ink, Charles told Henrietta Maria that he was being 'terribly laboured to grant Parliament base articles of cessation', with some of his councillors particularly 'fierce in it'. But he assured her, 'What I have done concerning the Treaty I am confident will not displease thee.'[10] The war-party grandees had succeeded. The terms had been rendered unacceptable to Charles. His final rejection of them was made public in April 1643, to the relief of the queen.

Less than two months later, the Commons began investigating Henrietta Maria for treason and drew up articles of impeachment accusing her of 'having levied war against Parliament and kingdom'.[11] A Royalist newsletter now wondered that 'good women live the while in a wretched age, who cannot be assisting their husbands in their great necessities ... without being traitors to master Pym and some of the good members of both houses'.[12] Charles concurred: Henrietta Maria's only true crime was 'that she is my wife'.[13]

Based in York, Henrietta Maria shared both the celebrations of victories and the pain of losses with the Royalist troops, often eating in the sight of the soldiers. She attracted many fresh recruits with her drive, courage and charm. But at the end of June 1643, while Parliament was pursuing her impeachment 'with great energy', she told Charles she was obeying his orders to join him at Oxford, and was on her way.[14] 'I carry with me 3,000 foot, thirty company of horse and dragoons, six pieces of cannon, and two mortars,' she wrote. Listing the commanders, she added self-deprecatingly that this left 'her she Majesty, generalissima' only with the 'baggage to govern' – not that this was a small task. It included 150 wagonloads of essential supplies.

Essex sent cavalry to intercept the queen, but she escaped him on the roads, just as she had escaped Warwick on the high seas in February. Still en route to meet Charles, she even found time to capture Burton upon Trent in a 'bloody' and 'desperate' battle. Over 400 Parliamentarian soldiers and officers were taken prisoner. She confessed to Charles that her soldiers had 'plundered so much that they cannot march with the bundles'. A day had to be put aside for them to sell their goods before they could continue.[15] She was bone-tired, having not slept more than three hours in a night for days, and travelling on little food. Loyally she told Charles exhaustion and hunger were 'pleasure to me in regard it is for you; and to let you see by all my actions that I have no delight but to serve you'.[16]

It had been seventeen months since Charles had parted from his wife at Dover in February 1642 and he was 'infinitely desiring' to see her.[17] On 13 July, the victorious Henrietta Maria met her husband and her two elder sons at Edgehill. The joy at being reunited was tempered by memories of the battle losses there, witnessed by her sons, and by the fact it was only a partial family reunion. The youngest two children, Elizabeth and Henry, remained in Parliament's hands. Yet there was much to celebrate. Charles's armies had enjoyed a slew of recent victories. There was another that very day, at Roundway Down in Wiltshire. A medal struck in its commemoration was to feature Charles and Henrietta Maria with a speared dragon at their feet: St George and his lady, conquering the sin of rebellion.[18] It seemed that a final victory over Parliament was now within Charles's grasp.

As the king entered Oxford with his queen, the Prince of Wales and James, Duke of York, the church bells rang in celebration and crowds cheered them along the streets.

The people of Oxford were living in a strange new normality in Charles's wartime capital. The university town had a mint producing the king's new currency, printing presses churning out witty newspapers that did 'as much prejudice' to Parliament as 'any of the cavalier armies', and there was a gibbet by St Mary's Church, where Parliament's spies were hanged.[19] All Souls served as the royal arsenal; New College housed a powder magazine.[20] Henrietta Maria and her household resided at Merton College and Charles was based at Christ Church, where the main quadrangle also served as a cattle pen. Undergraduates helped build fortifications in their spare hours, or joined the soldiers training in the once sleepy meadows. Ann, Lady Fanshawe – who was both young and pretty – nearly lost her life when a volley of shots fired in her honour sent 'a brace of bullets not two inches above my head'.[21]

The more battle-hardened Cavaliers were 'neat enough and gay in their appearance' but also 'vain, empty and careless'.[22] Duels, drunken brawls, killings and assaults were regular occurrences. This extended even to the high-ranking servants in Charles's bedchamber. John Ashburnham, the treasurer and paymaster of his army, fought a duel with Charles's cousin, the twenty-one-year-old Lord John Stuart.[23] This also reflected another problem: the bitter rivalries within Royalist ranks. The high stakes put everyone under strain. As Charles found, it was much easier to control a court in time of peace than an armed party amid the general lawlessness and chaos of a civil war. Anyone would have struggled to discipline Cavaliers whose tempers were up, and Charles had little stick or carrot available to empower him. His means of offering patronage and reward were limited, especially by the loss of London, and he could not easily afford to punish the misdemeanours of loyal and useful followers. Instead of removing Ashburnham from the bedchamber Charles ignored the duel. With such leniency 'nothing but disorder can be expected', Charles's Secretary of State, Sir Edward Nicholas, moaned, and reported to his correspondent a further recent shooting and a wounding as a result of private quarrels.[24]

Nevertheless, Royalists still continued to come to Oxford to support the king, and to stay there. The streets were thick with aristocrats who had moved from fine houses to little more than garrets. They were, Ann Fanshawe recalled, 'like fishes out of water ... as poor as Job, [with] no more clothes than a man or two brought in their cloak bags'. Their talk was all of 'losing and of gaining towns and men', while from their windows they saw 'the sad spectacle of war, sometimes plague, sometimes sickness of other kinds by reason of so many people being packed together'. Even the smallest dwelling in St Aldate's, which was one room up and one room down, housed several soldiers sleeping together like sardines. For the most part, however, Ann Fanshawe found people bore their suffering with 'cheerfulness'.[25]

On 26 July 1643 there was a further major success for Charles when Prince Rupert took Bristol with men that Henrietta Maria had brought from the north. Charles promptly issued a declaration advertising his commitment to a new peace process. He attached all blame for the war to a 'committee of a few men' – essentially the war-party grandees and their radical allies.[26] Mercy was promised to everyone else, if they now returned to their former loyalty to their king.

On 2 August, Holland and his Parliamentarian allies responded, instigating the setting up of a parliamentary committee to prepare new preliminary peace propositions.[27] Holland hoped to win his cousin Essex over to the peace party. If he succeeded Essex's army could ensure the war party complied with the peace terms. It was a dangerous situation for the war-party grandees and London once again now simmered with barely suppressed violence. The war party had satires and invective printed across the capital with 'fiery-spirited citizens' calling for Holland and his allies to be arrested and punished. Nevertheless, on 5 August the Commons voted to consider the peace propositions that had been outlined in the Lords. The response on 7 August, also instigated by the war party's City friends, came in the form of a 5,000-strong mob descending on Westminster Palace. The intimidated Commons MPs then rejected the peace proposals by a majority of seven. When Holland left the House of Lords, along with two other peers, they too were abused by the mob with shouting and waved fists.

The next day it was the turn of the peace party to bring their own supporters down on Parliament. A crowd of women arrived and battered the door of the House of Commons for an hour, demanding that Pym, Strode and other Roundheads be thrown into the Thames. The hope may have been that using women would prevent bloodshed. If so, that hope was disappointed. When the women returned on 9 August and stoned the guards with pebbles and brickbats, the soldiers fired live rounds at the rioters, killing two men orchestrating the attack. Undeterred, the women continued to shout 'Give us that dog Pym!' A company of horse then 'hunted the said women up and down the back Palace Yard and wounded them with their swords and pistols with no less inhumanity than if they had been brute beasts'.[28] Amongst the victims was the daughter of a man who sold spectacles outside Westminster Hall, and who was shot dead while passing by on an innocent errand.[29]

Many peace-party MPs left the Commons for good, too frightened to return. Six of the peace-party peers went further and defected to the Royalists. Holland was amongst them, gambling that his former closeness to the king and queen would see him quickly restored to favour. Northumberland went home, preferring to watch and wait. He was glad he did. Holland soon discovered that there was to be no fatted calf to welcome the prodigal peers when they reached Oxford. Charles endeavoured to be polite, but his long-standing supporters viewed Holland, in particular, as a Judas. This was a mistake. A welcome would have encouraged Northumberland and other potential defectors to come over.

But Holland also did himself few favours by offering no apology to the king for his past actions. Holland believed that he had acted from the beginning on noble principles. He wanted Charles to accept an Elizabethan-style Calvinist religious settlement and for constitutional liberties to be enforced. Any disloyalty on his part had, in his view, been 'cancelled by the merit of coming to the king now, and bringing such considerable persons [as the other five peers] with him disposing others [such as Northumberland] to follow'.[30] Nevertheless he was prepared to prove his renewed commitment to the king, even in battle. To this end, Holland headed west with Charles and the elder princes for the siege of the city of Gloucester.

Henrietta Maria had argued Charles should instead make for London and take advantage of the divisions between the war and peace parties. The capital had been rocked by anti-conscription riots since the failure of the peace and five people had been killed. Essex's army had also dwindled through desertions from lack of pay, and deaths from disease. It seemed to the queen that London had been ripe for the taking. Whether that was true or not, with the king besieging Gloucester, Parliament was given a breathing space to bolster Essex's army. This enabled Essex to take 15,000 men to relieve Gloucester on 5 September. He then headed back to London with his army. If Essex's army was cut off before he reached his destination, the Royalists knew they could yet attack a weakly defended London – and very possibly win the war. First, however, Charles had to find him. He described it as hunting a fox.

On 14 September Charles wrote he 'cannot yet get him out of his woods and holes into a fair field, the Earl of Essex keeping altogether in the byways'.[31] On 20 September the fox was found – and the opposing armies met for battle at Newbury. Holland rode with Charles's regiment of horse, who 'showed a kind of contempt for the enemy' and 'charged with wonderful boldness'.[32] Newbury was, however, a battle of artillery with pieces given names like 'Sweet Lips', in memory of a notorious whore from Hull. One Royalist captain described their deadly kiss: 'A whole file of men, six deep, with their heads struck off with one cannon shot of ours.'[33] The battle ended only when the Royalists ran out of ammunition.

The next day, several Royalist nobles were seen riding up and down the fields 'to view the dead men and to seek for some lords or earls

which they lost'.[34] Amongst those cut down was young Robert
Dormer, Earl of Carnarvon, a favourite of the queen, who had been
shot late in the battle and died in the king's arms. Charles ordered
the mayor of Newbury to care for the remaining injured, including
Roundheads, even 'though they be rebels and deserve the punishment
of traitors'.[35]

Charles had been unable to prevent Essex continuing to London.
But there was worse news coming. The Parliamentarian war party was
working hard on persuading the Scottish Covenanters into a military
alliance, one that would see the Scots join the English civil war on
Parliament's side.

With Charles now on the back foot militarily, Holland once more
pressed for him to begin peace negotiations. Holland was often seen
in his elegant clothes at Merton, where Henrietta Maria was based,
talking with Charles alone by a window. Charles was astonished that
Holland 'behaved himself with the same confidence and assurance
as he had done when he was most in his favour'. It seemed that
Holland expected immediately to 'have his key [to the bedchamber]
restored to him'.[36] Charles now disabused him of that notion, giving
Holland's former post as Groom of the Stool to the Marquess of
Hertford, who had been a Royalist since 1642. He also made it clear
that he would not seek peace from a position of weakness, and that
is exactly what he would be in if the Scots joined the war and he was
left heavily outnumbered.

The more aggressive Royalists – who gathered around the queen –
wanted Charles to match the Scottish army with his own troops from
Ireland. His army there was not doing much good in its war against
the Catholic rebels. He could not afford to properly resource it, and
it was losing badly. If, on the other hand, Charles were to arrange a
ceasefire with the rebel government, the Confederate Catholics of
Ireland, this would both ease the burden on loyalist Irish Protestants,
who were being killed in large numbers, and also free his army to

come home to England in the Royalist cause. Coming to terms with Irish Catholics was, however, too much for others to stomach.

When Charles indeed signed a cessation of arms with the Confederates, Northumberland was so appalled that he joined the most aggressive Parliamentarians, accepting Scottish intervention as a necessary evil to secure the king's utter defeat. Equally, for Holland, any compromise with Irish Catholics was anathema and he returned to London and to the Parliamentarian side once more. Four of his fellow defectors would soon join him.[37]

The war party in Parliament was now in the ascendant. Pym was dying of cancer and he looked 'a sad spectacle'. Even so, he had worked hard to complete the negotiations with the Scottish Covenanters. In return for their military intervention Parliament agreed that every Englishman over the age of eighteen would sign a new Solemn League and Covenant. Under this, Scotland's established religion – Presbyterianism – was to be imposed on both England and Ireland.

The Scots entered the English civil war in January 1644, when troops under the Earl of Leven crossed the river Tweed. In an effort to reach out to Parliament, and prevent a civil war across the three kingdoms, Charles summoned all his MPs and peers to assemble for a parliament at Oxford, where they could debate a way forward. Most of the House of Lords and about a third of the Commons came. But those who remained in London, knowing the Scottish army gave them military superiority, spurned the Oxford parliament's efforts at renewed peace negotiations. Holland had little influence. His reputation with Parliament would never recover from his period in Oxford. Instead of peace the spring brought a new campaigning season, more battles and further bloodshed.

Henrietta Maria was pregnant and 'weary not only of fighting', she told a friend, 'but of hearing of it'.[38] On 29 March 1644, Charles's duelling young cousin, Lord John Stuart, was killed at the Battle of Cheriton near Winchester. This Royalist defeat ended all hope of a successful assault on London and it meant that Parliamentarian forces would soon focus an attack on Oxford. Henrietta Maria wanted to leave for somewhere safer to have her child.

Charles said goodbye to his distressed wife on 17 April at Abingdon, eight miles from Oxford. Holding her in his arms, he comforted her, saying, 'madam, extreme remedies are requisite for extreme evils'. It all seemed so unreal to Henrietta Maria that she recalled, 'I found myself ten leagues distant from him before I became conscious that I had left him.'[39] She stayed in hiding for over two months, travelling from town to town. It was a difficult pregnancy and sometimes she was in such pain she believed she was dying. Eventually, Charles asked their trusted doctor, 'for the love of me … go find my wife'. The old man was with her when her baby girl was born at Exeter on 16 June. 'I thank God my wife is well delivered,' Charles confided in Prince Rupert.[40] As 'for the christening of my younger and, as they say, prettiest daughter', he instructed Henrietta Maria that 'it should be in the Cathedral [of Exeter] if the health of my little baby will permit it, and in the same way of the Church of England as all the rest of my children have been'.[41] His wishes would be carried out on 21 June, when their daughter was christened Henrietta, in the presence of her servants.

Henrietta Maria had fled the city. With Essex's army approaching she had been forced to abandon her newborn infant. France now seemed her best option. Richelieu had died in 1642 and Louis XIII in May 1643.[42] Anne of Austria was regent for the five-year-old Louis XIV. She was sympathetic to her fellow queen and had already lent Henrietta Maria £20,000.[43]

On 13 July Henrietta Maria wrote to Charles from the coast at Falmouth. 'Adieu, my dear heart. If I die believe that you lose a person who has never been other than entirely yours.'[44] She was described by one witness as presenting 'the most woeful spectacle my eyes yet ever beheld'.[45] Once again the Earl of Warwick sent ships to pursue her. This time they fired a hundred cannon shot on the queen's little fleet.[46] She would not permit Charles to make compromises to save her life if she was captured so she ordered the captain of her ship to blow the gunpowder in the hold if they were overrun. Happily for all on board, her ship escaped. Henrietta Maria was rowed ashore at a wild, rocky cove in Brittany, half blind, suffering symptoms of what may have been tuberculosis, and in agony from a breast abscess. With her bedraggled court of England ladies, her favourite Henry Jermyn, and her dwarf Jeffrey Hudson, she must have looked, she later recalled, more like a distressed wandering princess from a romance than an actual queen.

Yet as Henrietta Maria made her slow progress towards Paris she was greeted in town after town with the same grand ceremony with which she had left France in 1625. Cannons were fired, and she was processed beneath golden canopies, along streets lined by crowds anxious to cheer this brave daughter of Henri IV.

She stopped to take the spa waters of Bourbon-l'Archambault to try and gather strength.[47] Anne of Austria's former favourite Mme de Chevreuse was also in the town, but now Anne was ruling France, she saw Chevreuse in the same light as Richelieu had: as a troublemaker. Henrietta Maria was asked privately not to 'receive the visits of a person at variance with Her Majesty' and so she politely declined Chevreuse an audience.[48]*

Henrietta Maria reached Paris in November and commissioned a silver ship as a gift for the Cathedral of Notre Dame to thank God for

---

* When Henrietta Maria reached Nevers in October 1644, her dwarf Jeffrey Hudson challenged the brother of the captain of her guard to a duel. The weapons chosen were pistols on horseback. The cavalier didn't take it seriously, and arrived armed only with a giant squirt with which to 'extinguish' Hudson and his powder. Hudson shot him in the head. Henrietta Maria had raised Hudson since he was seven years old, when he had sprung out of a pie, eighteen inches high and perfectly proportioned. At Henrietta Maria's request he was spared execution for murder, though he was obliged to leave her household. She would never see him again. He was captured at sea by Barbary pirates and he was to spend the next twenty-five years as a slave. His freedom from his Muslim captors was then purchased along with those of other English slaves. In England, however, he was imprisoned for his Catholic faith in 1676, and though eventually released in 1680 he died only two years later.

her survival crossing the Channel.[49] But she remained 'very weak and ill, like one in a deep consumption'.[50]

It was twenty years since Henrietta Maria had last lived in the Louvre. Then, she had been wholly French. Now, she hung her rooms with English Mortlake tapestries and her servants were British. She had changed – and so had France. The government had become increasingly centralised and autocratic under Louis XIII and the taxes needed to support the war with Spain were heavy. These taxes would become all the more resented now France was under the rule of two foreigners – the Habsburg Anne and her chief minister and rumoured lover, the Italian-born aristocrat Cardinal Mazarin.

It was, however, events in Britain on which Henrietta Maria remained focused. Despite her ill health she would continue to raise arms for her husband, while looking for rich brides for their sons. She sent Charles most of the income Anne of Austria gave her and assured him, 'although I am well treated here that will not prevent me from desiring to return to England. I have there what I have not here, that is YOU.'[51]

Henrietta Maria would, in fact, never see Charles again. 'I ought never to have left the king my lord and husband,' she later reflected to their eldest son.[52] What Charles faced, he would have to face without her.

'ENTER OLIVER CROMWELL

THE GREATEST BATTLE OF THE WAR SO FAR WAS ABOUT TO TAKE place at Marston Moor in Yorkshire. On 2 July 1644 an Anglo-Scottish army of 30,000, under the Scottish Earl of Leven and Parliament's Earl of Manchester, faced 20,000 Royalists under Charles's nephew, Prince Rupert, and a former governor of the Prince of Wales, William Cavendish, Marquess of Newcastle. It was said that Newcastle was of 'no religion, feared neither God nor the Devil, believed neither in heaven nor hell'.[1] He had a reputation for fighting with utter fearlessness. When a battle was over, however, he would retire to his music and 'his softer pleasures', refusing to be disturbed 'upon what occasion 'soever'.[2] This could be awkward for junior commanders, whom he had a record of ignoring for two days at a time. Nevertheless, he inspired the devotion of his men.

The low open countryside of the moor's battleground was 'the fairest ground for such a use as I have ever seen in England', a soldier recalled.[3] The armies were laid out ready for the fight almost like the toy model armies Charles had played with as a boy: infantry in the middle, and cavalry in the wings. The weather, however, was unseasonably cold. It had been a day such as this for the Battle of Towton during the Wars of the Roses: winter ice clinging to heather in summer bloom. The shattered bones of the Towton dead still lay under Yorkshire soil, waiting to yield up their terrible evidence of slaughter and desperate violence: pulverised skulls and forearms cut where they had been raised in self-defence from merciless blows in a *guerre mortelle* – a battle to the death.

The usual preliminary for a battle began at Marston Moor late that afternoon with a Parliamentarian bombardment. It stopped at 6 p.m. to be succeeded by the rich sound of men singing psalms. When a hailstorm broke, Rupert and Newcastle retired for supper in their carriages. The singing also ended. It seemed the day was to end peacefully and battle would come in the morning. Then at 7.30 p.m., beneath the staccato of raining ice, a deep rumble began. The Roundhead cavalry of the Eastern Association was moving down a low hill 'in the greatest order and with the greatest resolution that ever was seen', under the command of their forty-five-year-old general, Oliver Cromwell.[4]

Oliver Cromwell was a descendant of a sister of Henry VIII's ruthless vicar general, Thomas Cromwell. The family had changed their name from Williams and Oliver sometimes referred to himself as 'Cromwell aka Williams'. A gentleman born, Cromwell was nevertheless not a rich man, and before the war he had lived more like a yeoman. There had been periods of depression and he had thought himself to be 'a chief, the chief amongst sinners'. Everything had changed on the day he became convinced he was 'among the congregation of the first born', one of God's elect predestined for heaven, despite his sins.[5] This certainty had inspired him to powerful religious preaching, and this in turn had earned him a place in Parliament as MP for Cambridge. There, in the Commons, his passion and self-assurance had ensured he stood out from the crowd.

One fellow MP remembered first noticing Cromwell at the beginning of the Long Parliament in November 1640. 'I vainly thought myself a courtly young gentleman,' the MP recalled, and 'came into the House well clad'. Cromwell was speaking on behalf of a servant of William Prynne – the Puritan whose ears had been cropped for sedition after he had suggested the queen was a whore.[6] Stocky and balding, with a thick nose, Cromwell was dressed in a 'cloth suit, which seemed to have been made by an ill country tailor. His linen was plain and not very clean; and I remember a speck or two of blood [from shaving] on his little [neck] band, which was not much larger than his collar'. Cromwell was nevertheless a striking figure, above average height, a 'sword stuck close to his side: his countenance swollen and reddish: his voice sharp and untunable and his eloquence full of fervour'. By the time he had finished speaking 'one would have believed the very government itself was in danger', were Prynne's servant not to be forgiven his indiscretions.[7]

Cromwell had 'no ornament of discourse, none of those talents which use to reconcile the affections of the bystanders'.[8] But his sense of mission ensured that, when it mattered, and the hour came, 'he was to act the part of a great man'.[9] Before Charles had raised his standard at Nottingham, and while others dithered, Cromwell had moved decisively, recruiting men and seizing the arms stored at Cambridge Castle. As the war got under way he 'had a special care to get religious men into his troop'. He did not care whether or not they were orthodox Protestants and he was equally unconcerned with the social rank of his officers. 'I had rather have a plain russet-coated captain that knows what he fights for and loves what he knows, than that which you call a gentleman and is nothing else,' he once wrote. It sounds romantic, liberal even, but many of his men were judged fanatics.

Moderate Puritans balked at the fervour they found in Cromwell's cavalry. 'Proud, self-conceited, hot-headed sectaries had gotten into the highest places and were Cromwell's chief favourites,' one Parliamentarian officer complained.[10] Cromwell's own commander, the forty-two-year-old Manchester – who had purged the clergy in the eastern counties of Laudian clerics, and personally ordered the destruction of crosses and other 'superstitious images' – viewed them with equal distaste, expressing dismay at this 'swarm' of those 'that call themselves the godly: some of whom profess they have seen visions and had revelations'.[11] At Marston Moor, however, Cromwell's sectaries had their opportunity to show their fighting worth.

As the rumble of Cromwell's advancing cavalry grew to a roar there was panic in the dozing Royalist camp. Then the tall, slender figure of Rupert was seen with his white hunting poodle Boy, dashing for his horse. He shouted at his confused cavalry, 'Do you run? Follow me!' They did as they were asked, mounted their horses, and attacked the Roundheads with gusto. 'Cromwell's own division had a hard pull of it: for they were charged by Rupert's bravest men', one Parliamentarian recalled, and the two sides 'stood at swords point a pretty while hacking at one another'.[12] Cromwell was injured in the neck and forced to leave the field bleeding heavily, but the Scottish regiments halted the ferocious Royalist advance and Cromwell's men then killed Rupert's horse from under him.

With Rupert and Cromwell out of action on the east wing, the Royalist cavalry on the right wing was cutting through the Roundhead lines. They were supported by Newcastle's 'Whitecoats', foot soldiers in undyed uniforms – men Henrietta Maria had known during her months in the north. For one Royalist the noise of battle was such that 'In the fire, smoke and confusion of that day I knew not for my soul whither to incline.'[13] Sir Thomas Fairfax's cavalry regiments were put to flight, and the whole of the allied Roundhead–Covenanter third line and two regiments of the fourth also broke, some without firing a shot. Almost half the allied army was now on the run, including the men under Sir Thomas's father, Lord Fairfax, over half the Scots and Manchester's regiment of foot. The Royalist northern horse chased the enemy for miles and the news spread that the Royalists had won the day.[14] But the remaining Scottish regiments withstood the Royalist charges, and after Cromwell's cavalry had gone to the aid of the allied right wing the battle began to turn. Rupert remained trapped behind enemy lines, unable to act as the general he was and give direction.

Newcastle, who had arrived late on the field, was reduced to fighting almost as an ordinary officer. By nine o'clock Cromwell's men could boast, 'we had cleared the field of all our enemies'.

Newcastle escaped, but the Whitecoats were trapped against hedgerows. They died where they stood in ranks and files, the last of the wounded lying on their backs thrusting their weapons at the horses that rode over them. Only thirty survived. Fleeing Royalists were chased to within a mile of York, a full moon allowing the killing to continue for hours, and their bodies were left scattered along three miles of road.[15] 'God made them as stubble to our swords,' Cromwell remarked with satisfaction. Manchester felt differently. He asked his men to thank God for their victory. But the slaughter – worse than any battle since 1642 – had convinced him there was little that was holy in this terrible civil war.

The next day, the sun rose on a grim spectacle: 'thousands lay upon the ground, dead and not altogether dead'.[16] Bone-white corpses twisted in unnatural shapes lay stripped of clothes and valuables, their stillness contrasting with the frantic activity of the living. Lord Fairfax had lost his younger son, Charles, while his elder son, Sir Thomas, had his face cut open with a sword slash. Lord Fairfax's own role had been less courageous than that of his children. Having fled the field he had remained away from the battle. Now he had his men hunting down the Royalist 'colours' (the flags representing the honour of the individual Royalist units). He sent to London 'so many as upon a sudden we could as yet receive from the soldiers, who consider it a credit to keep them'.[17]

Prince Rupert had, like Newcastle, escaped capture, but his white dog, Boy, had not been so fortunate.

The great hunting poodle whelped by Puddle had become legendary after appearing in a Royalist spoof on a Puritan pamphlet entitled 'Observations Upon Prince Rupert's white dog called Boy'. Printed in 1643, it had followed an earlier poem about Boy, also designed to poke fun at the Puritan determination to root out popish 'superstitious' practices, expressed in what the Royalist pamphleteers judged the Puritans' own superstitious fears of witchcraft. According to the spoof pamphlet Boy was Rupert's familiar and had magical powers that made the Prince bulletproof. These Royalist jokes had, however, backfired. On the eve of the Battle of Newbury in September 1643, Roundhead soldiers had killed a local woman as a witch, believing she was working for Rupert. There were Roundheads who had taken the stories about Boy as evidence that Rupert – and even the king – really were in league with the Devil.[*]

When Rupert's horse was shot from under him, Boy was seen bounding after his master, but he never made it to the bean field where Rupert had hidden. The Roundheads crowed that it was a magic bullet, fired by a Puritan soldier 'who had skill in necromancy', that had brought Boy down. Numerous woodcuts were printed depicting the poodle's lifeless body, often by the bean field. In some a witch stands over the dead dog, weeping as if he were her own child.[18] Boy was gone, but, it seemed, witches remained.

In Oxford bonfires were lit to celebrate the Royalist victory that had come so close at Marston Moor.[19] It was days before the truth of their defeat filtered through: the king had lost the north. The Parliamentarian press reported Rupert had renamed Cromwell 'Ironside', reputedly after a flanking attack on Cromwell's cavalry that had failed. It was from this that Cromwell's troops gained their famous sobriquet the 'Ironsides'.

---

[*] Their new Scottish allies were enthusiastic witch burners. King James, who had burned many witches in Scotland, had even written one of his famous tracts on witches. Charles viewed the obsession with English disdain. Witchcraft in England had been made a capital offence in common law under Queen Elizabeth and there had been several efforts to tar leading Catholics – even members of the royal family – by accusing them of witchcraft, but it had not been very successful. A few English witches were burned during James's reign but he lost enthusiasm for the stake as his rule in England went on. Catholic Ireland had still fewer cases.

The Parliamentarian Earl of Essex did not rejoice at this Parliamentarian victory, however: the achievements of rival generals, in contrast to his own weak performance, were reducing his influence and his popularity had waned dramatically. In London graffiti depicted him as a lazy glutton, with a glass of wine in his hand. He needed desperately a victory of his own. He was now on his way west, heading into Cornwall, the most Royalist county in England. Charles, who had been in the Midlands, followed him. A victory in June, at the Battle of Cropredy Bridge in Oxfordshire, had already restored Charles's fortunes in the south. Now, in the far west, the two armies fought for eight days in Cornwall's thick hedgerow country. Essex's army was squeezed and squeezed until it had little room or life left.

On 2 September 1644 Essex's surviving 6,000 troops surrendered to the king, while Essex fled ignominiously in a fishing boat. The so-called Battle of Lostwithiel was, Essex admitted, 'the greatest blow we ever suffered'. Charles had gained over 5,000 muskets and pistols, hundreds of swords, forty-two guns, and several wagons laden with powder and match.[20] The men taken prisoner were 'so dirty and dejected as was rare to see'.[21] They were now to face further humiliation. The losses of the long battle of attrition had embittered the victors and the prisoners were 'abused, reviled, scorned, torn, kicked, pillaged, and many stripped of all they had'. Royalist officers beat their men off their traumatised Roundhead prisoners with the flats of their swords. But the local Cornish joined in. One group grabbed a female camp-follower, who had given birth just three days earlier, 'took her by the hair of her head and threw her into the river'. Charles hanged the culprits for murder. He could not, however, prevent the impoverished Cornish from stripping other Roundhead women of clothes and valuables.[22]

There were now further victories for the king's cause in Scotland, led by a former Covenanter, the thirty-two-year-old James Graham, Marquess of Montrose.[23] Parliament's invitation to the Scots to join the war had been intended to defeat Charles quickly and end the fighting. It had helped them to win Marston Moor, but it had also brought the war to Scotland. Montrose's followers, from Ulster and the Western Highlands, were far fewer in number than the Covenanters, but were excellent warriors. Their fighting abilities ensured the Covenanters could not now help Parliament make the decisive thrust into Royalist territory in the south that was needed to finish Charles. The Scottish army in England had to stay close to the border for any time it might be needed to join their forces at home to fight Montrose.

The fear also remained for Parliament that Charles could yet bring outside forces into England, as they themselves had done. Warwick had issued orders to the navy for the summary execution of any soldiers coming from Ireland captured at sea.[24] On 24 October this was followed by a decision in Parliament of historic shamefulness: that no quarter be granted to any Catholic Irish found in England or Wales. While both Royalist and Parliamentarian forces had committed acts of murder and even massacres, this was new: the legal sanctioning of killing on ethnic and religious grounds.* The majority of soldiers coming from Ireland (seven to one) were, in fact, English-born, and had been sent to Ireland from England only after 1641, to suppress the Irish revolt.[25] The victims of Parliament's ordinance would therefore largely be either English Catholics or Welsh Gaelic-speakers: if they also happened to be women it would prove to be all the worse for them.

* * *

---

* A notable Royalist massacre had taken place in Bolton – known as the Geneva of the north – on 28 May. Parliamentarians claimed 1,600 defenders were slaughtered after Rupert stormed the town. Seventy-eight were listed in the parish register, but this would not have included soldiers from outside the town. They did include the names of two women. Royalists said their anger had been triggered by the murder of a soldier who had served against the Irish rebels for the king, but was hanged by the Roundheads as a papist. Many Royalist soldiers had been raised in Lancashire, a county which still had many Catholics. Later on 11 July after a skirmish in Dorchester, Parliamentarians had captured eight 'Irish' prisoners. Seven were hanged – the eighth spared 'for doing execution on his fellows'. This in turn provoked further Royalist reprisals in the killing of prisoners; http://www.british-history.ac.uk/rushworth-papers/vol5/pp677-748.

Charles's generals and councillors quarrelled constantly. He tried to weigh up the best advice. 'If thou knew what a life I lead,' he sighed in a letter to Henrietta Maria, 'I dare say thou would pity me, for some are too wise, others too foolish, some too busy, others too reserved, many fantastic.'[26] He tried to find the balance between being too cautious and too reckless, but this was no easy task and Charles was no great military strategist himself. He was, however, resilient. He was also a brave soldier who inspired great loyalty. As such he continued to prove an extraordinarily tough enemy to defeat, despite all Parliament's advantages in terms of holding London, in terms of wealth, and in terms of the superior military numbers handed to them by the Scottish alliance.

Three days after Parliament had passed the 'no quarter' ordinance Charles escaped vastly superior Parliamentarian forces at a second Battle of Newbury. Manchester's men were exhausted, but on 9 November 1644, with an opportunity to meet the king again in battle in Berkshire about to be passed by, Cromwell stood up at a Council of War to demand action. The campaigning season was about to end and if they did not fight the king now, Cromwell warned, then come the spring they could be facing a French army sent by the queen to make war alongside the Royalists. Manchester demurred: the French were too busy fighting against the Habsburgs in Europe to invade England. Seeking a battle now would also be a mistake. Their men were tired after the fighting at Newbury and a defeat would be disastrous for them. 'If we beat the king's army never so many times, [even] if a hundred times, yet he is king still and so will his posterity be after', Manchester reminded Cromwell, and 'if he beat us once, then we are every one of us undone'. In other words, their war aims were no more than a successfully negotiated peace with Charles. If they lost, they would all be hanged as traitors.

Cromwell snapped back that Manchester 'had as good have said that we are resolved to have peace upon any terms in the world.'[27] Unlike the earl he could imagine a future in which there was no certainty of survival for Charles as king, or for his posterity to succeed him. Hugh Peter, the radical from Massachusetts who was now the leading chaplain in the Parliamentarian army, concurred. Why make a fetish of the need to come to terms with the king, 'as if we could not live without one'?[28]

Manchester's arguments prevailed at the Council of War, but with the campaigning season now ended, the disagreements between the generals shifted to Westminster and the benches of the House of Commons and the House of Lords. The split in the Junto that had emerged after Edgehill between war and peace factions now disappeared, and these factions were replaced by what were in effect England's first two political parties.[29]

The party associated with Cromwell was called the Independents. They were set on the absolute defeat of the king and included (but were not limited to) many members of the old war-party faction.[30] These men had previously agreed to Scottish demands that Presbyterianism be imposed on England because it was the price of the military support that would achieve Charles's defeat. Since the Scots had failed in this task, the Independents had moved their religious and foreign policy away from being pro-Scots and Presbyterian. Instead they looked to the most ruthless English generals, men like Cromwell, who favoured Independent Puritan congregations that the Scots saw as incubi for heresy and civil disorder.

Manchester was associated with the second party, the 'Presbyterians', who favoured a negotiated peace with Charles. They included Essex, who feared religious anarchy and social upheaval under the Independents. Holland was also a leading figure. His brother Warwick, meanwhile, was, if not a fully fledged 'Presbyterian', then certainly no enthusiast for the Independents. There was an international dimension to this. The Scottish Covenanters were close to the French – the traditional allies of the Scots. The French were the great enemies of Spain – whose ruin Warwick had sought all his life, and he was therefore inclined to the Scots.[31] Where once he had led events, however, now Warwick trailed uncertainly in the wake of Essex, Manchester, and the rising power of their rival Oliver Cromwell.

Despite the religious labels for the two parties, their goals were each primarily secular.[32] Both Independents and Presbyterians wanted to gain for themselves the political and military power necessary to impose their choice of peace settlement upon the king and his kingdoms. Their leaders – or grandees – each hoped for a restored monarchy in which they would be the ones holding senior office. The difference was that while the Presbyterian party was prepared to rely on the king granting them senior office freely, following a negotiated peace, the Independents wanted to crush Charles militarily and reduce him to the status of a puppet king.

The struggle for power between the new parties began on 19 November 1644, when Parliament's Anglo-Scottish executive body, the Committee of Both Kingdoms, began to consider how best to reform – or remodel – Parliament's failing army. The intention was to streamline its command to make it more effective. A new proposal was then made in the Commons for a 'Self-Denying Ordinance' under which members of the House of Lords and House of Commons would resign their commissions. This would clear the decks. Warwick duly lost the navy, while Essex and Manchester resigned their commissions on 2 April 1645.[33] Cromwell was also obliged to resign. In their place the army was given a consolidated command under the thirty-three-year-old Sir Thomas Fairfax. He was a commander of proven ability – but also a family friend of the Independent grandee the Earl of Northumberland. Although a former peace-faction supporter, Northumberland had lost all confidence in Charles since his cessation of arms with the Irish Catholic Confederates, and had allied with Cromwell.

The Independents had won this round of the power struggle. Cromwell would soon be made the one exception from the Self-Denying Ordinance and would act as lieutenant general of Fairfax's cavalry. The civil war was now also to enter a more ruthless period.

Essex had noticed a key change between Fairfax's new commission in 1645 and his own in 1642. The phrase that had called for 'the preservation of the king's person' had been omitted. Essex tried, and failed, to have it reinstated. It had once been treason even to imagine the death of a king. No longer. And Charles warned Henrietta Maria that 'this summer will be the hottest for war of any that hath been yet'.[34]

'EVIL WOMEN'

ON THE DAY OF HIS DEATH, 10 JANUARY 1645, THE DIMINUTIVE Archbishop of Canterbury, William Laud, dressed in his habitual black. Laud had been a chief supporter of Charles's rule without Parliament. Facing trial for his life had been no less than he had expected. Nevertheless, this death had been a long time coming. He had spent four years in the Tower, writing memoirs, as well as penning defences of episcopacy and the liturgy. He might have been left there and forgotten if it had not been necessary for him to appoint bishops at Parliament's request. When he had refused to appoint an individual who had once been rejected by the king, his enemies in Parliament were reminded that they had unfinished business in his regard.

For Laud, the Church of England was a pillar of a Christian society, which, along with the Crown and a well-established social hierarchy, would protect the weak from the strong. Others saw him as an apologist for tyranny and an enemy of the godly. Popery had been the leading accusation made against Laud at his trial, and he had defended himself from it vigorously. He had 'laboured nothing more, than that the external worship of God might be preserved', he told his judges. Puritan neglect of places of worship was a kind of sacrilege while ritual and ceremony were together 'the hedge that fence the substance of religion from all the indignities which profaneness ... too commonly put upon it'. Since the essence of religious ceremonies was that the whole congregation took part, so uniformity of religion in the community had been at the heart of his reforms. Enforcing it had in turn been allied to royal authority.[1]

It was defiance of royal authority that had cost Laud's prosecution lawyer, the Puritan polemicist William Prynne, his ears and had branded his face. Defiance of Parliament's authority was to cost William Laud his life.

As with Strafford, the prosecution had failed to achieve a conviction at trial. Laud had been condemned by Parliament. The Act of Attainder was passed on 4 January 1645: the same day that Parliament abolished the Book of Common Prayer, and with it the old Jacobean and Elizabethan liturgy of the Church of England. Now, six days later, the seventy-one-year-old was being escorted to Tower Hill. The white-haired old man was harangued and harassed by a mob all the way to the scaffold. Even here his tormentors were so numerous that they barred his way to the block.* 'I did think', Laud commented drily, 'that I might have room to die.' Despite the clamour he met his end 'supported by remarkable constancy'.[2]

Charles was certain God would now punish Parliament for their actions. He ascribed his own misfortunes to divine retribution for having agreed to send the innocent Strafford to his death in May 1641. Charles bore no such responsibility for Laud's beheading. This Act of Attainder had not borne his signature. It was Parliament's turn to feel divine retribution, Charles assured Henrietta Maria, 'this last crying blood being totally theirs'.[3]

Charles now had to win the war outright or be crushed. He confided in Henrietta Maria that there was no longer any realistic prospect of a negotiated peace. The Independents would expect him to sacrifice his religious beliefs, deny his sacramental kingship, and his monopoly

---

* The hostile crowd included Sir John Clotworthy, the man who had destroyed the Rubens in Henrietta Maria's chapel.

of legitimate force. He was equally resolved that he would 'neither quit episcopacy, nor that sword which God hath given into my hands'.[4] To defeat his enemies, however, he had to have Irish troops. He was now prepared to drop the penal laws against Irish Catholics in return for their help, although he drew the line at giving them the right to practise their religion with equal status to Protestants. While negotiations with the Irish continued, those of his councillors who remained strongly opposed to his bringing in foreign troops were sidelined. Several were appointed to a council to advise the fourteen-year-old Prince of Wales. Charles had appointed the prince as leader of the Royalist forces in the west, explaining that 'himself and the prince were too much to venture in one bottom', for if they were captured together it would 'ruin them both'.[5] The Independents could make the prince a usurper, just as the infant King James and been made a usurper of his own mother's throne.

The Prince of Wales and his council duly left Oxford for the west in March. Charles, meanwhile, prepared to go on the attack in the Midlands.

Dawn on 20 May 1645 was heralded in Leicester by the blast of cannon. The besieged townsfolk were firing at the royal army as they built a battery for the king's heavy guns. Over the last month they had addressed weaknesses in the town's defences, and fortified Leicester's crumbling walls. Scottish soldiers as well as local recruits had joined the 900 or so men of military age already in the town. Nevertheless, Leicester remained short of arms and some of the recent recruits were described as 'being very malignant, with many coming in who did not intend to fight'.[6]

At one o'clock the king's cannon fired two great shots at Leicester: a warning of what would come if the Town Committee did not agree surrender terms. The townspeople worked to further strengthen the fortifications while the committee continued to drag out the negotiations for as long as they could. At three o'clock Prince Rupert lost patience and the Royalist battery began to 'play' on the town walls. The defenders fought back ferociously with cannon and musket. At six o'clock Royalist cannon breached the wall on the south side of Leicester.[7] The townsfolk dug earth frantically and grabbed woolsacks to fill the gap, with the 'women and children giving the most active and fearless help'. It took six hours to seal the breach and a Royalist assault then began at two other points.

The defenders fought back 'with great courage and resolution'. 'We were thrice repulsed,' Charles admitted to his wife. Nevertheless, at midnight the Royalists broke through the fortifications and poured into the town.[8] In the darkness attackers and defenders fought hand to hand and street by street, without quarter given.[9] A Royalist commander recalled 'the very women ... did take their parts ... they fired upon our men out of their windows, from the tops of houses, and threw tiles upon their heads'. There were bodies lying everywhere when resistance ended at around two in the morning, and Rupert's black colours were raised above the battery.[10] Yet still the killing continued. Captured town councillors were shot or hanged in cold blood. Finally, the plundering began.

Many of the Royalist troops were from the poor, mountainous regions of mid Wales and they robbed Leicester without mercy. Churches, hospitals and homes were all 'made prey to the enraged and greedy soldier'.[11] A resident claimed years later that he saw Charles riding through the town in armour, indifferent to attacks on innocent civilians, declaring, 'I do not care if they cut them three times more, for they are mine enemies.' At the time, however, a Parliamentarian newspaper allowed that the civilians had only been killed in the angry confusion of battle, 'rather than on purpose'.[12] What the accusations against Charles truly reflect is the bitter legacy of this siege.

One townsman, William Summers, had lost his house and all his possessions, his son was killed and he saw his wife go mad with grief.[13] Just how many others must have been left ruined or grief-stricken is indicated by the 140 cartloads of spoils listed as taken from the town, and the parish registers that reveal 709 burials immediately after the siege. But, however terrible the events in Leicester, at last the end of the war seemed to be in sight. 'If it shall please God to bless me,' Charles wrote to Henrietta Maria, 'it may make us see London this next winter.'[14] A few days later, his spirits rose further when he learned good news from Scotland, where Montrose had enjoyed further victories. 'Since this rebellion my affairs were never in so fair and hopeful a way.'[15] It seemed that God had indeed taken up the king's cause.

Fairfax was ordered by Parliament to avenge Leicester. His army of 14,000 outnumbered Charles's forces by at least 5,000 men, and Cromwell had again been given command of Fairfax's cavalry. But the king viewed what Royalists referred to as the 'New Noddle Army' with contempt. It was made up from units of the former Parliamentarian armies of the Earl of Essex, the Eastern Association (which had been under the command of the Earl of Manchester) and the Southern Association (formerly under Sir William Waller). In addition there were pressed men from Parliamentarian-held areas. The reforms had cleared out the old leadership, but there were rumours the New Model Army's morale was poor. The soldier Sir Samuel Luke, writing on 9 June, thought it 'the bravest for bodies of men, horse and arms, so far as the common soldiers, as ever I saw in my life': but many of the officers were inexperienced, and he worried that you could barely tell them apart from their men.[16]

On 14 June 1645, Charles received news that Fairfax's army had been spotted close to his headquarters in Market Harborough, Leicestershire. With their smaller force, the best chance for the Royalists was to attack early so catching the enemy off guard before sweeping them from the field with maximum ferocity.[17] With this in mind Rupert deployed the main body of the Royalist army on Dust Hill, facing the Northamptonshire village of Naseby. The Royalist cavalry was in the wings, infantry in the middle, with a reserve line of two infantry regiments.

The battle began at about 10 a.m., 'the first charge being given by Prince Rupert, with his own and Prince Maurice's troop' – the right wing of the cavalry. They rode 'with incredible valour and fury' and routed at least two of the cavalry regiments they confronted.[18] They then wheeled round to hit the enemy right wing in the rear – only to find around 3,000 New Model pikemen and musketeers blocking their path. Rupert was trapped and so unable to order up the reserves. Meanwhile, the Royalist cavalry in the left wing was in a struggle against overwhelming odds. They stood their ground although 'outfronted and outpoured by their assailants' until 'still more [Roundheads] came up to their ranks and put them to the rout'.[19]

Charles, seeing Cromwell's cavalry riding in pursuit of the broken Royalist left wing, moved to lead a countercharge. It put him in a direct line of fire from Fairfax's regiment of foot. The Earl of Carnwath*. grabbed the bridle of the king's horse and, swearing several full-blooded Scottish oaths, warned, 'Will you go upon your death in an instant?'[20] With Charles's horse abruptly pulled up, the entire charge juddered to a halt. Orders were shouted out for the men to turn right. They turned, only to face a vast force of Roundheads. They turned again in panic and fled, galloping hard 'upon the spur, as if they were every man to shift for himself'.[21]

With confusion and flight on the right, the Royalist infantry in the middle was inflicting heavy casualties on the New Model Army. Unfortunately, with neither Rupert nor Charles present to give orders, the reserve lines never moved forward. The infantry were worn down by sheer weight of numbers and Cromwell used his cavalry reserves to complete the Royalist defeat.[22] The ensign of the last regiment to resist was killed by Fairfax with his own hand.[23]

---

* According to a legend that appears in a Victorian history of Montrose by Mowbray Morris, Carnwath's bastard daughter led a troop of cavalry alongside Montrose the previous year. Mrs Pierson, aka Captain Frances Dalzell, rode under a standard that bore the image of a naked man hanging from a gibbet and the motto 'I dare'. Disappointingly the story may be too good to be true.

Charles and Rupert tried to rally their broken troops, but it was too late. There was not a Royalist left on the battlefield who was not a prisoner or dead by one o'clock that afternoon. Charles had been in the heart of the action and the bodies lay 'most thick on the hill the king's men stood on'.[24] The remnant of his army was now in flight, the king among them, riding hard towards Leicester. When Charles found his escape blocked by soldiers on the county boundary, he charged his horse across a small brook, dashed through ranks of surprised Roundheads – and got away by the skin of his teeth.

Elsewhere, in a field between Naseby and the village of East Farndon, the 500 or so women who rode with the baggage trains of the Royalist army were less fortunate. Unarmed and on foot, they were being slaughtered.

Between 100 and 400 women were killed at Naseby. The rest were mutilated, their faces cut into 'the whore's mask', noses slit and mouths slashed. This was not part of a general massacre.[25] Only these non-combatants – the laundry women, the wives and lovers of the Royalist soldiers – were treated without mercy.

Since the beginning of the civil war Parliament's pamphleteers had claimed that popish Irish and Welsh whores were following the king's army in large numbers, that they carried knives and that some were witches.[26] The stories about Boy had heightened interest in the occult. Now racism and religious hatred had come together to find full expression. The parliamentary press, reporting on the massacre, observed that the women had had their just deserts. They had 'cruel countenances', and were paying for the humiliation of the parliamentary camp followers in Cornwall, who had been robbed of their clothes.

The camp followers at Naseby were not, however, the only women to be murdered in large numbers that summer. Three days later the events of another mass killing would be set in train. Thirty-six people – the vast majority of them women – were tried for witchcraft at the assizes in Essex. They were the weak, the frail, the unconventional, those who had made enemies and had no powerful defenders.

Nearly half were in their sixties. Although there was no concerted policy against witches either by Parliament or its leading supporters, the Earl of Warwick, whose interests dominated this area, appears to have done nothing to stop this breakdown in public order. The mob was given its head. Only one of those accused of witchcraft would be found innocent, and eighteen were hanged on one afternoon. In total about a hundred 'witches' would die in 1645: more than had died on such charges thus far in the whole of English history.

Meanwhile, on 21 June 1645, a week after Naseby, the captured Royalist soldiers were being paraded through London escorted by the Green and Yellow regiments of the London trained bands. Fairfax had destroyed Charles's principal field army outside the west. While the king licked his wounds at Raglan Castle in Wales, the New Model Army now marched into the west. On 10 July they defeated the king's main field army there at the Battle of Langport, south of Bristol. A different kind of blow then followed.

A parliamentary newspaper reported that the capture of the king's correspondence at Naseby had proved more valuable to Parliament than 'all the wealth and soldiers that we took'.[27] Around 200 letters had been gathered, including many between Charles and Henrietta Maria. Often Charles's letters to her concerned matters of state, but all were infused with the language of love. She was his 'Dear Heart' and he was 'eternally' hers. Thirty-seven letters had been carefully chosen for translation and transcription. These were now published, with commentary, under the prurient title *The King's Cabinet Opened*. This exposed what was, supposedly, the king's darkest secret: proof that he, and not his 'evil councillors', was responsible for policy, and that he, in turn, was the vassal of a foreign, Catholic wife.

Henrietta Maria was depicted in *The King's Cabinet Opened* as a transgender perversion of nature, with the official commentary pointing to shocking examples of her mannishness during the civil war, such as when 'you see she marcheth at the head of an army and calls herself the Generalissima!' Those letters from Henrietta Maria in which she wrote of wishing only to serve her husband were excluded from *The King's Cabinet Opened*. Those that referred to Charles's concern about her poor health were carefully edited of such material. The information Charles had been sent regularly from France about his wife's desperate illness had made him protective.[28] His criticisms of her ideas were thus always made obliquely; where he agreed with her he did so ringingly – and such endorsements were underscored in Parliament's commentary: 'It is plain', the commentary ran, 'that the king's councils are wholly managed by the queen.' Particularly damaging for Charles was the material that suggested he might agree to his wife's wish that he allow his Catholic subjects the free practice of their religion.[29] 'This', one parliamentary journalist wrote, 'is the Dear Heart which hath cost him almost three Kingdoms.' Here was 'the true controller of the breeches'.

Charles's public reaction to *The King's Cabinet Opened* was less one of embarrassment, however, than of disgust. It was 'barbarous' to publish his private letters for public view. They had lost 'that reputation for civility and humanity which ought to be paid to all men'. He, on the other hand, had lost only his papers. These offered nothing for him to be ashamed of, as good people would judge, for 'bees gather honey where the spider sucks poison'.[30] Royalists concurred, noting that Henrietta Maria had done nothing that did not 'befit a wife'. It was natural for women to advise their husbands, and as the wife to an English king, and mother to the heir to the English throne, she was, effectively, English. But this was Royalist bravado. There were many more spiders sucking poison from the letters than bees finding honey.[31]

The success of Parliament's propaganda, built as it was on deep-rooted gender and religious prejudices, would be long-lasting. Henrietta Maria still remains in much popular memory the hysterical and domineering wife depicted in *The King's Cabinet Opened*, and even responsible for the loss of Charles's kingdoms.

* * *

Charles's leading general, Prince Rupert, accepted that the recent battlefield defeats meant the king could no longer hope to win the war. He advised Charles to begin negotiations for peace. Charles refused, angrily. He was well aware, he told Rupert, that 'there is no probability but of my ruin'. He would not, however, agree to any terms against 'the defence of my religion, crown and friends'. He reminded Rupert that 'as a Christian I must tell you that God will not suffer rebels to prosper, or this cause to be overthrown'.[32] He still firmly believed God would grant ultimate victory to his cause, although he accepted this might come after his own death, either in battle or by assassination. 'It is very fit for me now to prepare for the worst,' he wrote to his heir. The Prince of Wales now needed to save himself. If it looked as if he was at risk of falling into rebel hands he should flee England for France, Charles advised.[33] Later Charles changed his mind, and suggested the prince go to Protestant Denmark instead.

Further military defeats followed like hammer blows. On 10 September 1645 Rupert surrendered Bristol. On 13 September Montrose's army was defeated in Scotland at the Battle of Philiphaugh. Then, on 14 October, Oliver Cromwell arrived in north Hampshire at the long-besieged Basing House, stronghold of the Catholic Marquess of Winchester, and a leading Royalist fortress.

Cromwell had an army of 7,000 battle-hardened troops. Basing House had 300 defenders, including clergymen and priests, actors and artists, women and children. The seventy-two-year-old Inigo Jones had used his talents as an architect to help plan the defences, and the women had been taking lead from the roof to cast bullets. They called Basing 'Loyalty House' and they had carved these words in the windowpanes. Cromwell saw it merely as 'a nest of Romanists'.[34]

Cromwell's first cannon shot killed two of Lady Winchester's ladies and his troops soon overwhelmed the house. A hundred survivors of the attack were killed on the spot, 'many whereof in cold blood'.[35] 'You must remember what they were', a parliamentary newspaper noted: 'they were most of them papists; therefore our muskets and our swords did show but little compassion'.[36] Six of the Catholic priests were murdered with four others kept alive only so they might be drawn and quartered in public executions. But there were not only Catholics here. One Protestant clergyman, who had been severely wounded, saw his daughter's head split open with a sword after she had abused Cromwell's men as Roundheads and traitors. Past insults were equally costly. A comedian from Drury Lane, who had mocked Puritans in his routines, was killed by a Roundhead major doing 'the Lord's work'.[37] Charles had once observed that while dull comedians are condemned, the witty are more hated.[38] The comic from Drury Lane had been far too witty for his own good.

When the killing was finished, the house was plundered of its famous riches, and the remaining civilians stripped of anything of value, including their clothes. Warwick's former protégé, Hugh Peter, now the New Model Army's chief chaplain and propagandist, saw '8 or 9 gentlewomen of rank running forth together' as they were grabbed at and stripped by the Roundhead soldiers. A fire then began and soon the great palace and its works of art were in flames. Inigo Jones was carried out wrapped in a blanket through billowing smoke as the palace burned. In the cellars, meanwhile, the remnants of the garrison were dying in the flames. Hugh Peter reported hearing their last futile cries for quarter before the nest of Romanists was at last snuffed out.[39]

The victors of that summer did not represent the whole of the Long Parliament as elected in 1641, or even that part of Parliament that had opposed Charles after 1642. They represented one party, the Independents. They had in their control the New Model Army, which had matured into a disciplined fighting force, and that was, crucially, regularly paid and so less prone to desertions than Essex's army had been.[40] There still remained, however, a very substantial Presbyterian party, not only in Parliament, but also in the City of London, where many people were fearful of 'the increase of heresies, sects and schisms' encouraged by the Independents.[41] Together with the Scots, the

English Presbyterian party, still including Holland, now offered secret peace terms to Charles. They agreed that Charles could keep many of his powers. In return, however, he would have to accept the Covenant. Henrietta Maria urged her husband to accept this offer. Charles ignored her. He would never equivocate on his belief in the divine origins of a Protestant episcopate.

Charles returned to his capital at Oxford, and prepared to play the Presbyterians and the Independents off against each other. It would buy him time and let God do his work.

'THE GOLDEN BALL'

IT HAD BEEN YEARS SINCE CHARLES HAD WORN COSTUME FOR A masque. Now, once more, he was dressing for a part. At midnight, on the eve of 27 April 1646, his cousin Richmond and his Gentleman of the Bedchamber, John Ashburnham, began to trim the king's beard and cut off his lovelock. Charles had dressed as a groom, and he put on a peaked hunter's cap to hide his face. Oxford was under siege and he needed to escape the city undetected. The clock struck 3 a.m. as he rode across Magdalen Bridge. A friend bade him 'Farewell, Harry' – the name he had chosen for the road – then he was away, riding from Oxford into the witching hour along with Ashburnham and a royal chaplain called Michael Hudson.[1]

Charles had left behind the twelve-year-old James, Duke of York, who was living on half rations in solidarity with ordinary Royalist residents of the city. The road was thick with Independents from the army and Charles had been warned that, if he were caught, they 'would treat him very barbarously'. He did not want that for his son.

Charles's options now remained limited. His last significant body of infantry had been defeated at Stow-on-the-Wold in March. Nevertheless, he intended to make the best use of those cards that he had left to play. 'I am endeavouring to get to London,' he explained to a friend, 'being not without hope that I shall be able to draw either the Presbyterians or Independents to side with me, for extirpating the one or the other.' If he failed, 'I desire you to tell all my friends that, if I cannot live as a king, I shall die as a gentleman.'[2]

The Independents anticipated Charles's possible return to the capital with considerable anxiety. They knew it could well trigger a London uprising in his favour. Charles's reinstatement as king was seen as essential to restoring the normality people yearned for, and at the very least, his appearance would 'attract hearts'.

Charles lingered west of London waiting for intelligence. The French allies of the queen's party had assured Charles that he would be well received by the Scots and, when a messenger arrived warning him not to expect favourable terms in London, he made the decision to ride instead to the Scottish garrison at Southwell, near Newark in the Midlands.[3]

To avoid detection Charles and his companions took a circuitous route, skirting the Fens and riding north-west from Huntingdon. They stopped for the night at the wayside cottages of Coppingford, using aliases. Charles tried to sleep on the floor at the inn, but the snores of the innkeeper kept him awake. The next day the tired king rode on, evading capture until he pulled up his horse at the garrison courtyard of the Scottish army on 5 May 1646. Their commander reported to London that Charles's sudden appearance 'filled us with amazement and made us like men that dream'.[4] They could hardly believe their luck as the king announced his surrender.

The Independents, by contrast, were 'drooping sorrowful' when they heard the news. Possession of the king was vital to the political calculations of all parties. No settlement was deemed possible without the king's consent, and now the Presbyterians would be the ones negotiating with him.[5]

The Scots promptly took Charles north to Newcastle. Charles knew it as a beautiful city of over 10,000 souls, described in England as 'inferior for wealth and buildings to no city save London and Bristol'.[6] But, to Charles's horror, his servants were removed as soon as he arrived and he was shut in the governor's house with guards beneath his windows. He was not to be an honoured guest of the Scots, as he had been led to believe, but their prisoner.

It was vital for the Scots that Charles now agree to sign the Covenant. The English Parliament had already established Presbyterianism in England that March. In place of the king and his bishops, the parishes of the Church of England were to be governed by a minister and ruling elders. They were, in turn, placed under the government of Parliament. The Scots called this secular control 'a lame ... Presbytery'. Yet it was better than no presbytery at all – and that was the threat posed by an un-Covenanted king. Only if Charles accepted that episcopacy was an illegitimate form of church government would the future of Presbyterianism in Scotland be truly secure from any future royal threat.

On 19 May 1646 Charles ordered his remaining armies to lay down their arms. He was ready to admit he was defeated militarily. The civil war was over, leaving a kingdom bled white by deaths from war and disease greater as a percentage of population even than the losses in the trenches of World War One. Foreigners noted the very character of the English people had changed: they were hardened and embittered. Nearly everyone assumed that Charles would now agree to the Covenant. But while he might give up his armies, Charles would not surrender his conscience. The Scottish commissioners were reduced to tears and to chasing him from room to room in their efforts to persuade him to give way on this vital matter. Some believed the king needed only to be properly educated in the right religion. Charles, however, was unimpressed by the sermons their ministers delivered to him. One homily, given at his dining table, was brought to a close by the king impatiently stabbing at his meat with his fork. On another occasion, he ended a church sermon by rousing the congregation to sing Psalm 56 – a prayer for relief from your tormenters. It was said that people sang who hadn't raised their voices in years.

Henrietta Maria joined the Scots in pleading with Charles to sign the Covenant. To the queen, London was well worth the mitres of a bench of Protestant bishops. This only provoked Charles to turn on his wife, railing against the 'false' dealings of her Scottish friends and their 'barbarous usage' of him. To their faces, however, he kept his temper as far as he could, playing golf with his jailors, and asking only for James to be sent to him.

Charles regretted that his energetic second son had missed out on his studies during the war. He remained a father as well as a king and he hoped earnestly only that one day James would 'ply his book more and his gun less'. He also had to consider, however, that if the Prince of Wales succeeded in fleeing to France (as he would do in June) then James could be made king in their place. Charles needed James to be either out of the country like his elder brother, or under his own care. For the time being, however, James remained in Oxford, where negotiations for the surrender of the town continued.

The besieged inhabitants of Oxford and Fairfax's army were still exchanging cannon fire on 30 May. The Royalists let off 200 shot, killing a Roundhead colonel, and a man victualling the army. The Roundhead 'cannon in recompense played fiercely upon the town, and much annoyed them in their works and colleges'.[7] Later that day, however, a cessation of 'great shot' was agreed. To encourage Oxford to continue the surrender negotiations, Fairfax sent James a 'brace of bucks, two muttons, two veals, two lamb and six capon', to remind him of the food that he – and other residents – were missing.[8] There was no response from James, but in one of Charles's lost letters, written to Oxford in cipher, he asked his supporters to take 'care particularly' of the university when agreeing the final surrender terms, and 'to try to get the Duke of York sent hither to me'.[9] That proved impossible.

On 17 June there was a general cessation of arms and drunken fraternising between the two forces, as Royalists and Roundheads celebrated the end of the fighting. Three days later Oxford made its official surrender and James was handed over to Fairfax. Four carriages and six horses were ordered to take him to St James's Palace. There he was to be placed under the supervision of the Earl of Northumberland, who already had the care of James's younger siblings Henry and Elizabeth, whom James hadn't seen for four years. Charles's wartime capital could now return to its former role as a university town. Up to 3,000 Royalist troops left Oxford on 24 June, 900 marching over Magdalen Bridge with all the honours of war, and between lines of rebel forces. They were replaced by three regiments of Roundhead foot, Puritan soldiers taking the rooms in the town formerly inhabited by Cavaliers.

The king's spirit rose briefly when he learned in July that the baby of the royal family, the two-year-old Henrietta, had, at least, escaped Parliament's control. Her godmother, Lady Dalkeith, had snatched her from Oatlands Palace in Surrey, with the connivance of the palace servants. His pretty baby girl had been disguised as a boy, dressed in patched clothing, and was called 'Peter', a fact the little princess had resented deeply. Before she boarded the boat to France, she told people firmly that she was not a 'Peter', and her clothes were not her own.[10] In Paris, Henrietta Maria had been thinking of her abandoned daughter 'a hundred times a day', and when she saw Henrietta 'she embraced, she hugged again and again that royal infant'.[11] Henrietta would grow up to be one of the brightest stars of Louis XIV's court. But Charles, who had only ever seen his daughter once and briefly, after her christening at Exeter in July 1644, must have wondered if he would ever do so again.

The latest terms for Charles's restoration as king in England and Scotland, hammered out between the English Independent and Presbyterian parties, and presented to him in Newcastle by Parliament on 28 July, were, he declared, repugnant to his 'conscience, crown and honour'.[12] Charles had to agree to the abolition of episcopacy, the twenty-year suspension of his powers over the militia, and the handing over of fifty-six supporters to almost certain death. Charles was ready to accept a temporary compromise on the matter of the bishops, as with the militia. But he would not agree episcopacy was intrinsically wrong.* Nor would he agree to the execution of fifty-six of his friends – not even one. Strafford's death still haunted him.

The Scots, who had backed the Newcastle Propositions, were losing patience with Charles. Yet they dared not risk keeping their army in England. Their presence was bitterly unpopular and this damaged the English Presbyterian party led by the Earl of Essex. Reluctantly, therefore, they prepared to hand Charles over to the divided English Parliament and to withdraw their army. They relied on Essex to continue to look after their interests in Parliament.

But, just as a £400,000 payment to the Scots for their part in helping Parliament win the war was agreed, Essex suffered a massive stroke. He died four days later on 14 September 1646, with his cousin and political ally, Henry Holland, at his side.[13]

Essex was given a regal funeral in Westminster Abbey based on the funeral rites given to Charles's elder brother in 1612. Vast crowds came out in the rain to see the cortège as it passed through London's streets. Essex's funeral effigy, lying on his coffin, was dressed in his buff-coloured military coat, scarlet breeches and parliamentary robes. Essex had dedicated his life to what he had seen as a movement of aristocratic virtue, one in which the nobles worked for the public good, protecting their liberties and 'true' religion. He had never been in sympathy with the sectarians allied to Cromwell, and doubted their attachment to any liberty other than the freedom to do whatever they wished.

With Essex dead the Scots were more anxious than ever about handing Charles over to an unstable Parliament. By early 1647 the

---

* He was prepared to agree that the Presbyterian religious status quo in England be maintained for three years (or even five), while twenty Presbyterians, twenty Independents, plus twenty of his own divines thrashed out recommendations for the future of the church. These would then be put to king and Parliament. The militia he was prepared to give up for ten years, or even his whole lifetime, so long as the traditional royal powers would revert to his son on his death.

Presbyterians had gained a majority in both the Lords and the Commons. This was not, however, because Presbyterianism was popular with MPs. It was merely judged to be the most effective means of repressing something worse: the growing tide of religio-political radicalism. The Independents could still overtop the Presbyterian party and the king would then be in their hands. The Scots, therefore, asked for assurances of the king's honourable treatment, and that no settlement would be made against Scottish interests. The message came back that Parliament would dispose of matters as it saw fit, with Independents pointing to the fate of Mary, Queen of Scots, as an example of the power they could wield. This was a threat to Charles's life – and it was one that Charles himself took very seriously.

If Charles were killed his son, the Prince of Wales, would succeed him. Charles knew his heir was intelligent and able, but to observers 'he seemed to have no sense of religion'.[14] Theology had not been a priority of his former governor, the Marquess of Newcastle, under whom he had learned instead to dance and ride very well, and to enjoy literature. The education the prince might have had to rectify this later had not been possible during the war. Instead the traumas the future Charles II had been through were shaping a charming young man, who was also deeply cynical. The prince was now in France where he would be subject to the influence of the queen's party, who believed the king had to accept Presbyterianism in order to be restored to his thrones. If the Church of England was to keep its bishops Charles needed to stay alive.

The king's best hope was escape. He now wrote in secret to his fifteen-year-old daughter Mary, asking her to send a warship that would take him to Holland. Mary's marriage to William of Orange, arranged during the crisis winter of 1640–1, was not a particularly happy one. When she had left England in 1642 Charles had instructed her governess that the marriage should not be consummated until she was at least fourteen. But in February 1644, when Mary was still only twelve, the prince had bullied his way to her rooms and had sex with his child bride. Mary had never warmed to this selfish man, but she was deeply loyal to her father. In November 1646 a thirty-four-gun Dutch warship duly arrived at the Tyne. Its gilded stern was carved with figures of Mary and William of Orange, and between them an orange tree laden with fruit representing their future children. A Yorkshirewoman took advantage of the spectacle to pretend she was Mary. The con artist installed herself in fine accommodation and the locals came to kiss her hand – until the truth was discovered and she was whipped out of town. Meanwhile, the Dutch admiral met Charles, ostensibly to deliver a letter from his daughter, but in reality to plot Charles's escape.

Unfortunately, just before Christmas, a letter from Charles urging James also to escape was discovered at St James's Palace. James was interrogated, an incident reminiscent of the Victorian painting *And When Did You Last See Your Father?* by W. F. Yeames. It depicts a golden-haired boy, dressed in silk, facing a panel of dark-clad Parliament men, just as James surely faced. James was asked why he had kept his father's letter hidden. He had acted 'out of obedience to the king's command and in kindness to his father', he replied, reminding them 'he had so many obligations from a loving father as to command secrecy from him'.[15]

Guards were now placed in Charles's apartments, and on 30 January 1647, soon after the first £100,000 down payment on their £400,000 was paid, the Scottish army handed Charles to the English Parliament, and abandoned Newcastle for Scotland. The Covenanters, Charles observed, had 'sold him at too cheap a rate'.[16] Without him they had lost all leverage in England while earning contempt for 'betraying of my safety and honour for their own advantages'.[17] He was right on both counts. They had sold the life of their king for silver and even a fellow Covenanter-Scot warned that 'the dogs in the street would piss upon them' for what they had done.[18] The townsfolk of Newcastle threw stones at the backs of the Scots as they left for their homeland. When Charles left the town on 3 February, under the guardianship of commissioners of the English Parliament, more crowds came out, but this time to cheer.

Hatred of Parliament's Scottish allies had revived pro-Royalist feeling in the north. Along the route south people brought out victims of the skin disease scrofula for Charles to cure with his royal touch, just as Christ had cured the lepers. Their enthusiasm reflected, however, not only the belief that he was a king chosen by God, but also the national yearning for peace. People complained their condition was 'in every way worse than before this [perpetual] parliament began'.[19] Even those areas of England that had avoided battles and plundering were being impoverished by taxation. Parliament's monthly wartime levy alone amounted annually to ten times Charles's controversial Ship Money tax of the 1630s, while an excise duty on consumption of many common goods, copied from the Dutch, fell particularly hard on the poor.

England urgently wanted a return to the 'old, known ways' of a king ruling with his Parliament. But the question set at the outset of the war remained: where should the balance of power lie between king and Parliament in England's mixed monarchy?

Charles's new prison, the Elizabethan palace of Holdenby House in Northamptonshire, had 'a pleasant, spacious and fair garden' with walks, orchards, fishponds and bowling alleys.[20] The Presbyterian-dominated Parliament did not permit him use of the now banned Book of Common Prayer, but he was able to hunt, and be entertained by the local gentry. These pleasures came to an abrupt end on 3 June 1647, with the sudden arrival at Holdenby of over 500 New Model horsemen: more than enough to overawe Parliament's garrison of fifty or sixty men. Charles could only guess what was happening, but Royalist agents had been keeping him abreast of dramatic political developments in London that suggested a possible coup.

The Presbyterian majority of Parliament lacked the military power they needed to force the Independents to accept the peace they wanted to agree with Charles. To achieve this they had been moving to create an army answerable to them. The Presbyterians planned to do to the New Model Army what the Independents had done to the armies of Essex, Waller and Manchester in 1646. It was to be broken up and those commanders they wanted to be rid of – Independents such as Oliver Cromwell – retired. The disbandment of the New Model infantry had duly been announced on 25 May, with soldiers offered a mere two months' arrears in pay. Parliament was virtually bankrupt and the regular pay the army had enjoyed had come to an end. The arrears offered were far less than the soldiers were owed. Over the following days, however, Cromwell's house in Drury Lane had seen the arrival of a stream of religious radicals and New Model officers, united in their anger. While Mrs Cromwell fed her husband's visitors bread and butter washed down with small beer, the men talked and plotted. On 31 May they included a twenty-nine-year-old cornet – the lowest rank of commissioned officer – called George Joyce. It was he who commanded the horsemen that now appeared at Holdenby.

There was an agony of waiting for whatever would happen next. The following night, Charles was disturbed by the sound of arguing outside his door. It was possible that the moment of his assassination had arrived. This was the usual fate of a deposed King of England. His servants were now refusing Joyce entry. Anxious for their safety, Charles commanded that Joyce be admitted. He was confronted by a thickset Londoner and former tailor, with fashionable long brown hair. Joyce demanded the king accompany him from the house. The young radical believed that the garrison commander had gone to get help and he had made the decision that Charles must be removed to somewhere more securely in the army's control. Charles agreed to leave if Joyce offered him assurances that he would not be harmed, that his servants might accompany him, and that he would now be allowed to practise his religious beliefs. Joyce accepted his terms.*

At six the following morning Charles emerged from Holdenby and stood on the front lawn under the June sky. Joyce had his troopers drawn up smartly in ordered ranks. On his command his men shouted out their adherence to the promises of the night before. This strange democracy prompted Charles to reflect that he had not yet seen Joyce's orders, so he asked, 'What commission have you to secure my person?' Joyce blustered. Charles persisted, 'Have you nothing in writing from Sir Thomas Fairfax, your general, to do what you do?' Still receiving no straight answer, Charles pressed further: 'I pray you, Mr Joyce,' he demanded, 'what commission you have.' Joyce gesticulated, 'Here is my commission!' 'Where?' Charles asked, bewildered. Joyce then turned in his saddle and pointed at his soldiers, 'It is behind me.' 'It is as fair a commission, and as well written a commission as I have seen in my life,' Charles observed drily.[21] He began his journey with Joyce without further protest, 'rather', he noted, 'than be carried by neck and heels'.[22]

The king was, in Fairfax's phrase, 'the golden ball cast between two parties'. The faction that had possession of Charles had control of the peace process. The New Model Army now had him, and hoped to make good use of their prize.

---

* Fairfax and Cromwell would deny giving Joyce any orders to remove Charles from Holdenby. It seems likely they had ordered him only to take control of the house.

'A CLOUDED MAJESTY'

CHARLES MET FAIRFAX AND CROMWELL OUTSIDE NEWMARKET ON 7 June 1647. Fairfax kissed the king's hand. Commonly known as 'Black Tom' for his dark colouring, he had been shot twice in battle, once in the shoulder and once in the wrist, while his face remained badly scarred by the sword thrust he had received at Marston Moor. A Yorkshireman of few words, he was 'the only judge' in the army's Councils of War. Yet the decision to secure the king at Holdenby had been made by Cromwell without his authority.[1] Cromwell too now bowed his head to the king. It was the first time Charles had met the man who would be his nemesis.

The New Model Army's leading generals were allied to Parliament's Independents. They were also, however, racing to catch up with the radical mood of their men. The soldiers had been angered by their poor treatment at the hands of the Presbyterian party and the diversity that had once been a feature in their ranks had now ended, with Presbyterian officers, sympathisers and former Royalists driven out. Three days earlier, under Fairfax's auspices, a General Council of the Army had begun drawing up a political programme. This council was made up of senior officers and elected representatives known as Adjutators, or Agitators. They included two officers from each regiment, and two from the ranks. On 14 June, a week after the generals had met the king, the council was ready to issue their public 'Declaration'.

'We were not a mere mercenary army, hired to serve any arbitrary power of a state,' the army asserted. They were men 'called forth and conjured by the several declarations of Parliament to the defence of our own and the people's just rights and liberties'. Parliament had failed to secure those rights, and, *in extremis*, safety demanded that the army 'would now proceed in our own and the kingdom's behalf'. Parliament was to be purged of 'corrupt' members and set a date for its own dissolution. There would then be new and regular elections.[2]

Almost certainly written by the army's commissary general and chief penman Henry Ireton, who was Cromwell's son-in-law, it both threatened Parliament (with a purge and dissolution), and offered to save the institution from itself (with new and regular elections).

With this message delivered, the New Model Army moved their valuable prisoner nearer London.

On 25 June Charles arrived at the Earl of Salisbury's palace at Hatfield House, where he was to be allowed his own chaplains and use of the prayer book. On 3 July, he was moved again, to the house of the fabulously rich Lord Craven, at Caversham on the banks of the Thames. The following day, Charles had a further interview with Cromwell, this time without Fairfax.[3]

The Puritan general was used to letting others talk so he could 'know their inmost designs'. Charles was used to keeping his innermost designs to himself. He appeared to impress Cromwell, who assured one of the king's servants that he thought Charles 'the uprightest and most conscientious man of his three kingdoms'. But the army needed Charles's goodwill to enable them to achieve the peace settlement they wanted.[4] Cromwell therefore not only flattered Charles, he also promised him visits from his three children. At that Charles could not hide his delight.[5] He hadn't seen Elizabeth and Henry in five years.

Charles left no record of his first impressions of Cromwell, but he wrote to James that same day, 'I am in hope that you may be permitted, with your brother and sister, to come to some place betwixt this and London, where I may see you.' He suggested James ask permission to come to him 'for a night or two. But rather than not see you, I will be content that you come to some convenient place to dine, and go back again at night.' He signed himself 'your loving father', adding as a postscript, 'Send me word as soon as you can.'[6]

An overnight visit was not permitted, but twelve days later the royal children were brought by carriage to the Greyhound Tavern in Caversham. Their father arrived under escort an hour later, at 11 a.m. Cromwell described the family reunion as 'the tenderest sight that ever his eyes beheld'.[7] The seven-year-old Henry, Duke of Gloucester, was bewildered, and when Charles asked, 'Do you know me child?' he answered, 'No.' 'I am your father, child,' Charles explained, 'and it is not one of the least of my misfortunes that I have brought you and your brothers and sisters into this world to share my miseries.'[8] James and Elizabeth then began to cry.

Charles sat his younger children on his lap and comforted Elizabeth. She was now eleven and very changed from the energetic girl he remembered. She had broken her leg running across a room three years earlier. Having been confined inside for months she had begun to study. She could now read and write in French, knew some Italian, Latin, Greek and Hebrew. She had also become a girl 'of great observation ... both of things and persons'. Her captors called her 'Temperance', but she watched them and made her judgements.

As the battle-scarred Fairfax entered the room, Elizabeth asked who he was. Charles had labelled Fairfax the rebels' 'brutish general'.[9] But when Elizabeth was given Fairfax's name she thanked him profusely for allowing her 'the great happiness she enjoyed' to see her 'dear father', and said she would return the favour, if ever she could.[10]

Only Charles, however, was in a position to deliver what Fairfax wanted.

The General Council of the Army was already drawing up a draft peace settlement with their Independent allies in Parliament. The terms of what was known as the Heads of Proposals proved to be very generous. Charles would get control of the militia and appoint his own councillors after ten years. They even allowed for the return of an episcopal church, so long as other Protestants were permitted to worship in their own way. To sweeten the deal further, the Independent-dominated Committee for the Revenue was using public money to bombard the king with luxury accessories, horses and clothing, painting themselves and their military friends as part of a loyal and generous court-in-waiting for the restored king.[11]

Henrietta Maria, having lost confidence in the Scots, now wanted an accommodation made with the Independents as soon as possible. Many Royalists agreed.[12] Charles, however, wondered what legal force any settlement with the army could have. As Charles reminded Cromwell, 'the power of Parliament was the power by which [they] fought'.[13] It seemed to him that his best hope remained in extracting more from the Presbyterians.

In London the Presbyterian grandees, including Henry Holland, were meeting regularly in Lucy Carlisle's rooms at Whitehall Palace, where they plotted how to get the king back in their hands.[14] While the Royalist nobles had eked out the war years in cramped quarters in Oxford, Lucy Carlisle had continued a life of relative glamour and comfort in Parliamentarian London. Nevertheless, the echoing palace of Whitehall was not the same without the court. She also no more trusted the army with its radical rank and file than Holland did, and she had thrown herself instead into the Presbyterian cause, along with many other former adherents of their late cousin the Earl of Essex. They had powerful allies in the City, where Presbyterians continued to dominate municipal and church government.

On 26 July 1647 the Presbyterians raised a huge mob of apprentices and disbanded soldiers who invaded Parliament. They ordered the Speaker to put to a vote an invitation for Charles to come to London to conclude a personal treaty. The terrified MPs obeyed while, in a grim farce of popular representative government, several of the mob joined in the voting.

When the army formally presented their Heads of Proposals to Charles two days later, the king had heard that the City's defences were being raised against the army, and that the Scots were now ready to fight for his restoration rather than see the Independents triumph. The army was on the back foot and Charles played hard ball. He outlined to the officers two main concerns. The first was to protect leading Royalists. He recalled the fate of the Earl of Strafford in 'tart' and 'bitter' language and said he 'would have no man suffer for his sake'. His second concern was to have the Church of England re-established. The army needed him, Charles reminded them, 'you cannot be without me. You will fall into ruin if I do not sustain you.'[15]

Amongst the official army delegation to see Charles was a thirty-seven-year-old colonel called Thomas Rainborowe. He struck an unprepossessing figure, with his hat removed respectfully, and a few strands of fair hair hanging to his shoulders from his bald head. Born in Wapping, he had been a mariner in his youth and then a currant trader. He was now a firebrand leader of the army's rank and file. For three hours Rainborowe joined other New Model officers in trying to persuade Charles to accept the Heads of Proposals. But he left the meeting early having concluded that it was time to force a settlement on the king.

Charles's immediate hopes of the London Presbyterians proved misplaced. Political power by 1647 depended more than ever on military strength. On 6 August Fairfax marched his men into London. His battle-hardened 14,000-strong New Model Army had little trouble in intimidating 400,000 Londoners. Cromwell rode at the head of the cavalry while Fairfax sat in a carriage along with Mrs Cromwell. Presbyterian peers and many of their supporters now fled London, or were imprisoned. But Lucy Carlisle remained, still plotting against the army she despised.

Fairfax and Cromwell now moved Charles still nearer London, to Hampton Court. They remained desperate for Charles to accept the Heads of Proposals and quickly, before radicals like Rainborowe demanded a thoroughgoing reform of the constitution, as well as the imposition of a settlement on the king. Soldiers were becoming subject to the influence of a movement within the London radicals soon to be known as the 'Levellers'. The term had originated in peasant rebellions against the enclosure of common land earlier in the century and referred to the flattening of hedges. It was now being used to suggest a desire to flatten England's political hierarchy. The Levellers hoped to see Parliament, king, legal and clerical establishments made subject to a new constitution that would be agreed to by all freeborn Englishmen.[16] This excited considerable fear in the New Model Army's leading generals and in the wider population, who equated democracy with mob rule.

Plague had broken out in the stables at St James's Palace, and the royal children were now moved to the Earl of Northumberland's Syon House near Hampton Court.[17] They continued to be brought regularly to see their father, and often 'spent a long time in the garden, running and playing before the king'. At dinner James sat on Charles's right, 'His Majesty ... loving to all the children', and Elizabeth in particular was 'often in his arms'.[18]

We have a snapshot of Charles at this time in a double portrait commissioned by Northumberland from the artist Peter Lely. It depicts the teenage James, full-cheeked and dressed in silk, reaching out to his father, who looks prematurely old. An admirer of Lely's thought the artist had caught perfectly the king's 'clouded Majesty', Charles's face showing 'sorrow ... without a tear', and 'humble bravery'.[19] Charles still hoped to salvage from the peace what was most important to him – an episcopal Church of England, the lives of his friends, and the rights of his heirs to raise the militia, but it also seemed probable to him that he would be murdered first.

When alone with his children, Charles reminded them of their religious and dynastic responsibilities in the event of his death. He told them to hold true to the Church of England and to be loyal to their eldest brother, Charles, Prince of Wales. He warned Elizabeth not to marry without the consent of the prince or that of her mother, Henrietta Maria. He asked James to escape to Holland, and told little Harry that if anything happened to Prince Charles then his loyalty must be to James, as the next in line.

There was a prime example of family disloyalty in a less welcome visitor to Hampton Court. Charles's eldest nephew, Charles Louis, the Prince Palatine, had returned to England in August 1644 to appeal to Parliament for the money with which Charles could no longer supply him. He had moved into lodgings at Whitehall and had signed the Covenant. His brothers Rupert and Maurice, who had fought for so long for the king, had been permitted to return to Europe. Charles Louis chose to remain and urged his uncle to compromise his terms. Charles snapped in reply that it seemed to him that Charles Louis would do anything, however base, 'to have one chicken more' on his dish.

The strategy of holding out for better terms was going well. There were good reasons to believe that a new alliance between the three kingdoms in Charles's support was becoming a real possibility. The military might and political power of the New Model Army, alongside the nationalistic imperialism of the Independents, were perceived in Scotland and Ireland as offering a dangerous new dimension to English dominance within the three kingdoms.

The Scots also still feared that the influence of sectaries and other radicals in England threatened the stability of their Presbyterian kingdom. A new moderate group of Covenanters under the Duke of Hamilton, many of whom had opposed the intervention in England in 1644–6, had now taken control of the Edinburgh Parliament and they were prepared to reach terms with Charles without him having to sign the Covenant.

In Ireland the heavy-handedness of officials employed by England's Parliament was also producing a new coalition of Irish Presbyterians, Episcopalians and Catholics, that could yet send an army to aid

Charles. The king's former Lord Lieutenant, the Calvinist James, Marquess of Ormonde, visited him at Hampton Court and was soon on his way to France to lay further plans.

In England itself, meanwhile, the army and the taxation to sustain it were exciting growing anger amongst ordinary people, while the unity of the army itself was also crumbling.

On 18 October 1647 radical-minded and Leveller-influenced soldiers published a new manifesto, entitled *The Case of the Army Truly Stated*. This document, which had not been agreed by either the Army Council or the leading generals, argued that a settlement should begin not by establishing the powers of Parliament, but with the people's rights, which, it argued, each individual had from birth. The people therefore had the right to consent to those who represented them. The *Case* called for a widening of the electoral franchise, as well as biennial parliaments and the imposing on Charles of a peace settlement. Amongst the soldiers responsible was Colonel Rainborowe, whose experiences in trying to persuade Charles to accept the Heads of Proposals had convinced him that the king should have no further say in the terms for his restoration.

Fairfax, Cromwell and Ireton all viewed the proposals outlined in the *Case* with horror. They did not believe people had any rights by nature, apart from the right to life. All political rights and liberties were established through Parliament, which had generated laws and customs over time. These had enabled men to hold property, and to enjoy the rights and privileges that stemmed from this. Amongst them was the right to vote, because in purchasing a 'fixed interest' in the kingdom through property ownership you bought into the nation's customs and laws. Those without property were considered too easy to manipulate and too dangerously unpredictable to be enfranchised.[20]

On 28 October the generals of the New Model Army confronted the radical agenda at the church of St Mary the Virgin, Putney. *The Case of the Army Truly Stated* was to be debated by the Army Council.

This was, however, set aside when Agitators representing junior officers and the ranks read out a new document, *The Agreement of the People.*[21] This called for the abolition of the House of Lords, and a written constitution with a parliamentary electorate 'proportioned according to the number of inhabitants'. Rainborowe expressed its democratic views in ringing terms: 'Really I think that the poorest he that is in England has a life to live [just] as the greatest he. And therefore, truly, sir, I think it is clear that every man who is to live under a government ought first by his counsel to put himself under that government.'

Ireton replied with the warning that the *Agreement* would lead to anarchy and communism. If every man had a natural-born right to the vote then, Ireton observed, 'by that same right, he has an equal right to any goods he sees: meat, drink, clothes, to take and use for his sustenance; he has a freedom to the land, to take the ground, to exercise it, till it; he has the same freedom to any thing'.[22] A trooper, in turn, reminded the generals of the earlier Declaration of the Army Council on 14 June, and which had stated that they had fought 'to the defence of our own and the people's just rights and liberties'. He and his fellow soldiers 'have engaged in this kingdom and ventured our lives, and it was all for this: to recover our birth rights and privileges as Englishmen'; yet, he noted, 'It seems now, except a man has a fixed estate in this kingdom, he has no right in this kingdom. I wonder we were so much deceived.'[23]

With the debates likely to raise fears of army radicalism across England, the generals imposed a news blackout. Even the internal records of the debates soon ceased. From what has survived it seems a majority proved in favour of an extended suffrage, but that there was also agreement that a peace settlement must start with Parliament. The deepest divisions lay over whether to treat with the king, and on what basis. Some wanted to see the Lords and the monarchy abolished. The angriest called for 'an immediate and exemplary justice on the chief delinquent' of the civil war – the king.[24] As the Putney debates came to an end, Cromwell and Fairfax demanded that every soldier sign a declaration of loyalty. This would include accepting the Heads of Proposals, and the terms it offered to the king, as the army's manifesto.

The army's next general rendezvous, due to take place at Corkbush Field near Ware in Hertfordshire on 15 November, would be the key moment when Fairfax and Cromwell would discover whether or not they could rein in the Leveller-influenced minority in the army and so restore unity. Only if Fairfax and Cromwell prevailed would they be able to make good their promises to Charles. If 'they were over-topped' by the radical Levellers, then, Charles observed, 'they must apply to the king for their own security'.[25]

There had been demands at Putney that Charles be tried as a 'man of blood'. This was a biblical reference: 'the land cannot be cleansed of the blood that is shed therein, but by the blood of him that shed it'.[26] Those making the demand wanted Charles convicted in law and then executed. On 9 November Hugh Peter was reported as having assured the Agitators that the king was 'but as a dead dog'.[27]

Yet murder remained the simplest way to dispose of Charles. There was no precedent for placing a King of England on trial. The English judges of Mary, Queen of Scots, had argued that the English crown had long claimed suzerainty over Scotland, making her a subject of Elizabeth, against whom she had committed 'treason'. Murder, dressed up as accident or misfortune, did not raise any potential legal difficul-ties and there were plentiful examples of regicide in English history – it was how Henry VI, the last King of England to lose a civil war, had met his end.

On 11 November Cromwell sent a letter to Hampton Court warning the governor of rumours of a planned assassination attempt on Charles. 'Have care of your guards. It would be accounted a most horrid act,' he wrote.[28] In his rooms, Charles received a further letter warning his assassination was imminent. He was loath to flee Hampton Court. To do so would be to break his parole, and his word. Being in army hands also had the advantage of maintaining pressure on the Hamiltonian Scots to come to an agreement with him. A Royalist treaty with the Scots was already 'very near to a conclusion'.[29] This would not be much use to him, however, if he were murdered.

It was a Thursday, the day when Charles was in the habit of writing letters in his bedchamber for the foreign post. It would be some hours before his disappearance was noticed. It was too good an opportunity to miss. At about six that evening Charles and three of his companions made their way by the cellar stairs to the garden and from there they rode to the river. Eventually one of his guards, thinking the king had been 'remarkably retiring', decided to open the doors.[30] He found Charles gone.

ROYALIST RISING

IT WAS COLD AND RAINING AS CHARLES RODE INTO THE NIGHT with his companions. They had fresh horses waiting for them at an inn in Sutton, south of London, on the lower slopes of the North Downs. Lost for a time in the dark, they arrived only at daybreak, on 12 November 1647. By then the inn had a local parliamentary county committee meeting taking place. It was too dangerous to stop. Charles called for his fresh horses, and they rode on without rest. The next stop would be Place House in south Hampshire, the seat of the Royalist Earl of Southampton.[1]

Charles had left two letters behind in his bedchamber at Hampton Court. In one he thanked his jailors for their care and asked them to look after his beloved dogs, a greyhound called Gypsy and a spaniel called Rogue. Another letter informed Parliament that he had fled Hampton Court in order 'to be heard with Freedom, Honour and Safety' and to 'show myself ready to be Pater Patriae' – father of his people.[2] The question was, where could he go 'to be heard with Freedom, Honour and Safety'? Some of Charles's supporters advised that fleeing to the French or the Scots was unpatriotic and that he needed to stay in England, albeit somewhere his physical safety could be assured. Charles believed there was no longer anywhere truly safe in England.

Southampton's mother was expecting the king and welcomed him on his arrival at the tall turreted gatehouse. Place House had once been the Abbey of Titchfield, a long-established stopping point on the way to France. Charles was told, however, that there was no ship available for him. He could not stay undiscovered long at Place House.[3] His Gentleman of the Bedchamber, John Ashburnham, 'whom the king loved and trusted very much', suggested that the young governor of the Isle of Wight, the Parliamentarian Colonel Robert Hammond, might prove sympathetic. Hammond's uncle was a devoted royal chaplain and Hammond was surely no Independent.[4] Charles agreed an approach should be made. Ashburnham left immediately with another of Charles's devoted companions, the forty-year-old Sir John Berkeley.

On the Isle of Wight, Hammond went white as Berkeley and Ashburnham presented him with the royal request for asylum. It meant he either had to betray Parliament by helping the king, or betray the king to Parliament. Hammond began to shake so violently Berkeley thought he was going to fall off his horse. He agreed to help, but he persuaded Ashburnham that it was better Charles give himself up than risk being caught by more dangerous men. Ashburnham and Berkeley duly returned to Place House with Hammond and a small escort of Hammond's men. As Berkeley waited downstairs with Hammond, John Ashburnham went to tell Charles. 'Jack, thou hast undone me!' the king exclaimed.

At Syon House, James, Duke of York, swore as he was told of his father's capture. When one of Northumberland's servants rebuked the fourteen-year-old, James grabbed his longbow and had to be tackled to the ground. James understood what Ashburnham had not – that his father's situation was rendered more dangerous than ever.

On 19 November 1647, Charles celebrated his forty-seventh birthday at the formidable medieval fortress of Carisbrooke Castle. He had swapped Hampton Court, a stone's throw from London, for isolation on the remote Isle of Wight. 'He could not have come to a worse place for himself' was the view of one local gentleman, Sir John Oglander.

Charles would also now have to negotiate with a reunited army. Fairfax and Cromwell had confronted and punished mutineers at the Corkbush Field army rendezvous, riding into the ranks of men wearing copies of *The Agreement of the People* in their hat bands, and beating the soldiers with the flats of their swords until they threw their manifestos away. Three ringleaders were sentenced to death and, after lots were cast, one was shot on the spot. It marked the doom of the Leveller cause – and perhaps of Charles's cause too.

The generals and their allies were now to take a much tougher bargaining position. Charles had betrayed their trust in breaking his parole, and his stubbornness in not accepting the Heads of Proposals had risked a radical backlash that had placed the constitution, and the protection it offered the propertied classes, at risk. As Christmas approached Charles's favoured bedchamber servants were replaced by Parliament-appointed spies. He was also confined within Carisbrooke's outer line of defence.[5] Charles spent his days walking his dogs, Gypsy and Rogue (who had been brought to Carisbrooke), around the castle perimeter. It offered 'a delightful prospect of land and sea' – a taste of the freedom he was now denied. In due course, a bowling green would also help while away the hours, but he spent much of his time with his books: '*Dum spiro, spero*', he wrote in his copy of Shakespeare's plays; 'While I breathe, I hope'.[6] He kept up his spirits with reading the comedies.[7]

The latest proposals from Parliament were delivered on Christmas Eve. They included a demand that Charles lose control of the militia in perpetuity. Only if he agreed would Parliament treat with him on other contentious issues. Charles pretended to consider their proposals in order to keep pressure on the Scots, with whom he was still negotiating. On 26 December he enjoyed success. The Scots signed a secret treaty with Charles known as the Engagement. It promised a Scottish invasion of England, allied with an army from

Ireland under the Marquess of Ormonde. In return, Charles agreed to establish Presbyterianism for three years, crush the radical Protestant sects in England and work for a union of the kingdoms that would protect Scottish autonomy.[8] The stage was now set for a second civil war. All it would take to light the touchpaper was a Royalist rising in England.

One of the most hated aspects of Parliament's rule was the Puritan reform of manners. The *Book of Sports* with its implicit encouragement of fun and games on Sundays had long been overthrown. But that summer the old Catholic holy day of Christmas, with its drinking, plays and dancing, had also been abolished.[*] This interference in the traditions and fun of the average Englishman proved too much for many to stomach. There were a number of violent incidents across England in December with serious riots in Norwich, Ipswich and Oxford. The most spectacular reaction, however, took place at Canterbury in Kent.

On 25 December the Puritan mayor saw that several shopkeepers had closed their stores and decided to make an example of one. Orders were issued for the man to be taken to the stocks where he would be left overnight. The shopkeeper might well have died of exposure if it wasn't for the angry crowds that had gathered as he was taken. They jostled the mayor, who lashed out. This proved to be the trigger for a town revolt. The mayor was knocked down, grabbed by the heels and dragged through the gutter. Games of football then began at either end of Canterbury, with balls kicked through Puritan windows. Two days later the Christmas rebels were

---

* Christmas had been banned in Presbyterian Scotland in 1640. The English Parliament had done so in June 1647, when Easter and Whitsun were also abolished. The celebrations of Thanksgiving in the United States and Hogmanay in Scotland are reminders that Christmas was not celebrated amongst the Puritan settlers in America or amongst Presbyterian Scots until very modern times. In the United States Christmas only became a public holiday in 1870, in Scotland not until 1958.

in control of the city, decorating doorways with branches of holly and adopting the slogan 'For God, King Charles and Kent'.

Meanwhile, on 29 December, as the Canterbury riots spread through neighbouring villages, a former Royalist officer called Burley attempted to lead a storming of Carisbrooke Castle on the Isle of Wight. He failed and by the end of December the army had managed to contain England's Christmas riots. But when Burley was executed in February a rumour began that he was a holy martyr and 'that where he was quartered is a spring of blood'.[9] Kent was restive again and there were fresh riots, this time in London.

Charles, meanwhile, continued to encourage James to try to escape. When another of his letters to James fell into Parliament's hands, James was threatened with the Tower. The boy was sufficiently frightened to give up the cipher he used to communicate with the king, but he refused to betray his accomplices, who included a female attendant of his twelve-year-old sister, Elizabeth. He wrote a letter to Parliament instead, swearing: 'I will engage my honour and faith never more to engage in such business.'[10] He was rewarded with a pay rise: £500 a year just to spend on his recreations and field sports – a little taste of how sweet life would be for him, if he turned away from his loyalties to the king.[11]

On 20 March 1648, Charles himself tried to escape. With his guards drunk on a gift of wine, he squeezed through his barred window, ready to drop to the ground from a silk rope. Unfortunately the bars were too narrow even for his slim frame and, 'sticking fast between breast and shoulders, he was not able to go forwards or backwards'. There was a long and painful struggle before the king, with a groan, retreated back into his room.[12] Undaunted, Charles then acquired nitric acid and saws to remove the bars. But on 20 April, James vanished from St James's Palace, ensuring his father would be watched more carefully than ever.

James had used a game of hide and seek in the gardens of St James's Palace as cover for a secret rendezvous. Playing with his younger brother and Northumberland's own children he had hidden in the bushes, where he met with a Royalist spy called Joseph Bampfield. They arranged to meet again that night. When it was dark James pretended to go to bed, but instead went to say his goodbyes to his sister Elizabeth. Her little black dog followed him back to his room, so he shut it in, and took a back stairway to the garden. He tripped in the dark and the crash convinced him he must have been heard. He dashed back to his room and pretended to read. When no one came he set off again, down the stairs, out of a back door into the garden and from there he ran into St James's Park.

Bampfield, waiting with a wig and cloak, took James by carriage to a safe house, where Bampfield's mistress was waiting with another disguise for James. 'Quickly, quickly dress me,' the boy demanded. She did as she was asked, lacing James into a gentlewoman's waistcoat with a scarlet petticoat and over them a mohair overcoat that had been made especially for him. She 'thought him very pretty in it'.[13] From the house James was taken to the river. As the lights on his fishing boat were dimmed, and it slipped out past the Tilbury–Gravesend blockhouses that guarded the Thames, James knew he was free. Only the open sea lay ahead before he would reach Holland. There he was reunited with his sister Mary, 'the affectionateness of which meeting I cannot express', he later recalled.[14]

The opening shots of a rising had by now been fired. In south Wales, on 23 March 1648, a former Parliamentarian major general and his colonel had led a mutiny and declared for the king. Many other former Parliamentarians also now joined Royalists against the New Model Army and the Independents. In the north of England, on 28 and 29 April, Berwick and Carlisle fell to their forces.

Petitions were also being circulated across the country calling for a personal treaty with the king, an end to high taxes and the suppression of the sects. On 4 May the formerly staunchly Parliamentarian county of Essex delivered one such to Westminster bearing 20,000 signatures, and with 2,000 people marching in train. That same month the trial of the Christmas rioters in Kent ended with the jury throwing out the charges and a Royalist rising in the county. The rebels seized control of Rochester, Sittingbourne, Faversham and Sandwich. On 27 May this, in turn, triggered a Royalist mutiny at the Downs naval base. Warwick, who had been obliged to resign as Lord Admiral in 1645 under the Self-Denying Ordinance, was reappointed to his former naval post.[15] Even he, however, could not win back the mutineers. Nine of Parliament's ships joined the small Royalist navy. Warwick's sailors would be facing largely their own former comrades.

Fairfax and a force of 4,000 New Model Army veterans quickly crushed the Kent rebellion, but 1,500 Royalists escaped across the Thames into Essex. In June parliamentary forces were still putting out brush fires across England and it was a bloody business. The former royal chaplain, Michael Hudson, who had led a rising in Lincolnshire, was cornered on the roof at Woodcraft Hall. He and his last companions were thrown off the building and, when Hudson managed to grip on to a drainage spout, his fingers were slashed with a sword. He fell into the moat below, where he was found still alive. He was then finished off and his body mutilated.

A week later Fairfax drove the Royalist forces in Essex behind the walls of Colchester, and the town was placed under siege. Fairfax's men had suffered 500 fatal casualties so far in this rising. More were expected, for the New Model Army would soon have to fight the Scots – and perhaps the Irish too. At a prayer meeting at Windsor a momentous resolution was passed. If they won this new war of the Engagement they would call 'Charles Stuart, that man of blood, to account for the blood he has shed'.

It was not, however, Charles, isolated on the Isle of Wight, on whom the Royalist war command was now centred. It was instead the frail figure of his thirty-eight-year-old queen in France. Henrietta Maria had grown so thin with her illness that she was almost disfigured, her large mouth out of all scale to her face. The French courtier Mme de Motteville recalled that 'there was something so agreeable in her expression that it made her beloved by everyone', but also admitted there was 'no trace remaining of her past beauty'. The loveliness of her youth 'had lasted a morning and left her before midday'.[16] It was, nevertheless, necessary for the ailing Henrietta Maria to project strength. To raise money for the Royalist forces her creditors had to believe that one day she would be able to pay them back.

Henrietta Maria played to the hilt the part of a great daughter of France, who would be backed by her Bourbon relations until Charles's ultimate victory. She dressed with magnificence at royal ceremonial occasions in Paris and at court entertainments she amused and charmed. Her childhood education had been limited, but it seemed to Mme de Motteville that 'her misfortunes had repaired that defect, for grievous experience had given her capacity'. Henrietta Maria had developed 'infinite wit, and a brilliant mind'.[17] She used her considerable skills to raise large sums of money for Charles's cause. This included a recent bill of exchange for 80,000 Dutch florins from a Parisian banker called Canatrini, and a further 10,600 French livres from a Jacques Mauchias, which she used to buy arms for Ormonde's Irish army.[18]

In July 1648, Mme de Motteville saw the queen at a Carmelite convent, where Henrietta Maria had been busy writing dispatches 'of great importance'.* All of Wales, save for Pembroke Castle, was already back under parliamentary control and the imminent prospect of a Scottish invasion in support of Charles had diminished enthusiasm

---

* A previously unrecorded letter by Henrietta Maria kept in a private archive in Warwickshire offers an example. Written 3 August, it requires free passage out of France for Sir William Dugdale (who is carrying dispatches to England), his men and baggage.

for the Royalist cause in the north. But her son, the Prince of Wales, had sailed to his father's aid at the head of the newly expanded Royalist navy. He was now a grown man of eighteen and Henrietta Maria hoped that, if a planned rising in the south-east of England could coincide with the Royalist navy anchoring off London and with the planned Scottish invasion, the Royalists could yet divide and destroy the New Model Army.

Henrietta Maria sipped out of a little gold cup as she talked with Mme de Motteville. It was, she told her friend, the only gold she had left, and her servants were bombarding her with demands for money.[19] She was, however, in regular contact with her former favourites, those Janus-faced cousins Henry Holland and Lucy Carlisle, who had been gathering forces for the crucial new rising.

Lucy had sold a pearl necklace valued at £1,500 to raise money 'for officers and other provisions'.[20] Holland, meanwhile, was commissioning men. Amongst them were the two young sons of the murdered Duke of Buckingham. George Villiers, 2nd Duke of Buckingham, was now twenty and Francis Villiers, who had been born after their father's murder, was eighteen, and like his father 'of admirable beauty'.[21] When they were young children they had been raised with the Prince of Wales and the Duke of York, but they had taken no part in the war and had just returned from a two-year educational tour of Europe. Looking for sophisticated companionship they 'fell easily into the friendship of the Earl of Holland' and he soon persuaded them 'to embark themselves in his adventure'.[22] It was, Holland believed, a 'good and pious thing, to rescue our country from the misery and slavery they were now under'.[23]

By 2 July Holland's efforts to smuggle large numbers of horses into the country had been discovered. Unable to wait any longer for the expected Scottish invasion, Holland decided to press on with the southern rising, gambling that it would trigger a major rebellion in London. Taking the Villiers brothers with him, he travelled south-west and, on 5 July, they arrived at Kingston upon

Thames in Surrey along with 500–600 men. They immediately began to recruit more.[24] Two days later they were caught up in a deadly skirmish on Surbiton Common. The teenage Francis Villiers had his horse killed under him, but fought on, trapped with his back to a hedge. There he was struck down and the nose cut off his beautiful face.[25] Holland and young Buckingham escaped and arrived at St Neots in Cambridgeshire, eighty-seven miles away, on 9 July, with around 300 survivors.

The fifty-seven-year-old Holland 'was so weary and shaken in his joints that he had a better will to his bed than his horse'. He retired for the night in a local inn. Just before dawn their pursuers caught up with them. A cry went up amongst the Cavaliers: 'To horse! To horse!' Buckingham fought his way out with 200 of his horsemen. Around twelve Cavaliers were killed and the rest were captured. Holland was taken at the inn. His captors claimed that he had taken so long over his elaborate toilette that they had caught him still in his under-clothes.[26] Amongst the personal effects they confiscated was his George – the insignia of the Garter – with its blue ribbon and badge of St George killing the dragon.

The punishment for turncoats was harsh in this second civil war.* Holland's life, however, was spared, so 'that he may turn round once again', an enemy report observed sarcastically.[27] The fact his brother Warwick was the Lord Admiral of the Parliamentarian navy had helped to save his life, for the time being. Yet Holland remained unrepentant. From prison he consoled his wife and daughters, 'where there can be no shame let there be no sorrow'.[28] The Independents and the army were governing by 'power, not love', and with 'a rod of iron'.[29]

---

* In Wales former Parliamentarian officers were court-martialled and shot. Later reports indicate that this was also the fate of a former quartermaster general to the Earl of Essex, a Dutchman called Dolbier, captured at St Neots.

'It is Scotland, and Scotland only can save the king and England,' a friend now wrote to Lucy Carlisle.[30] The long-awaited invasion had at last arrived, with a Scottish army of 4,000 horse and 10,000 foot crossing the border into England.

THE RED-HAIRED MISTRESS

IT RAINED CONSTANTLY, BREAKING THE WHEAT IN THE FIELDS, clinging to clothing, dripping down Carisbrooke's stone walls. Charles was a physically energetic man, and he suffered, he admitted, from this 'base imprisonment, cooped up'. The only person with whom he had private contact was the illiterate woman who emptied his stool pan. It was she who smuggled his private letters. He wrote one to Lucy Carlisle after the disaster of St Neots on 9 July 1648. She had been accused of being responsible for the discovery of his escape attempts, and he was reminded that in the past she had 'proved faulty'. Nevertheless, he said, 'I think she now wishes well to me.'[1] Indeed, she proved her worth. Despite the failure of the southern rising, she was working to persuade the Parliamentarian Vice Admiral William Batten to defect to the Royalists along with his ship, the *Constant Warwick*. It would not be long before she succeeded.

Meanwhile, Charles had received a letter from a red-haired spy who was angling to become his mistress. A striking, 'tall, well-fashioned and well-languaged gentlewoman with a round visage', Jane Whorwood was thirty-eight and had a full life behind her.[2] She had survived smallpox and a violent husband before taking on the dangerous role of a Royalist agent. She had helped plot the king's escape attempts in the spring and was now staying in the local town of Newport. Charles was intrigued by her suggestion of an assignation. He had been, by royal standards, an extraordinarily faithful husband and he still loved Henrietta Maria. He wore her portrait always, keeping it in a case behind his George. But he enjoyed sex and missed it now.* He had not seen Henrietta Maria for four years: he knew he might never do so again. So when Jane wrote that she wished to 'satisfy' her 'desires', Charles was anxious to oblige.

This was not to be a public love affair that would produce acknowledged bastards and threaten the legitimate succession of the Prince of Wales. It would be a brief sexual encounter, of a kind he had been willing to commit when he was young and chasing a she 'who must not be named'.[3] 'Sweet,' he told Jane, 'there is one possible way that you may get a swiving [fucking] from me.' While he was having dinner the stool-pan woman could smuggle Jane into the privy which was in his bedchamber. He estimated 'I shall have three hours to embrace and nip you' before the spies who acted as his servants returned. A few days later he suggested another plan. She should arrange to dine in the castle with one of the officers. He would then come in by surprise, 'and between jest and earnest get you alone into my chamber and smother Jane Whorwood with kisses'.[4] These planned encounters were, for the time being, just a desperate fantasy. The endgame was approaching.

Two days after St Neots the Royalist holdout at Pembroke Castle in west Wales fell, and Oliver Cromwell marched north to confront the Scots. He was certain God would grant him victory. His allies in Westminster were less sanguine. The royal fleet and the Prince of Wales were in the Thames Estuary and Royalist feeling in London was running high. On 12 July several of the ordinary Royalist prisoners brought from St Neots were freed by a London mob. The pressure from the City for an unconditional treaty with the king was

---

* He was furious when Henrietta Maria's priests limited his access to her bedchamber on religious days, and their numerous children are testament to the importance of the physical side of their marriage.

overwhelming, and on 28 July MPs agreed to hold negotiations without preconditions.

Charles was watched more closely than ever. Still, his messages to Jane continued. He sent two on 17 August, the same day as Cromwell's Ironsides met the Scottish and English Royalist forces at the Battle of Preston in Lancashire. The Scottish infantry was poorly armed and poorly trained. Nor was there much trust between the Scots and their former enemies in the English Royalist army. Nevertheless, they fought ferociously before their forces broke. At least 1,000 men died in the battle and its aftermath. Over 4,000 were taken prisoner.

As Cromwell marched on to Edinburgh and further victory, the besieged town of Colchester lost heart at the news from Preston and capitulated. Fairfax accepted the surrender on 28 August. The Royalist commanders, Sir Charles Lucas and Sir George Lisle, were then informed they were to be shot. They had given their word at the end of the first civil war that they would not take up arms again. In breaking their promise they had forgone any right to quarter. They were led into a yard where three lines of musketeers made up the firing squad. At the first volley of fire Sir Charles fell dead. Lisle 'ran to him, embraced and kissed him'. Lisle then turned to the musketeers and asked them to move closer, so they wouldn't miss him. One of them said, 'I'll warrant you, sir, we'll hit you.' Lisle smiled and said, 'Friends, I have been nearer when you have missed me.'[5] A second volley of gunfire followed, and his body fell.[*]

The short-lived blockade of the Thames Estuary also ended. The Royalist navy had proved to be so riven by dissent as to be virtually useless. The Presbyterian–Royalist faction (which included the queen) had wanted the ships to take the Prince of Wales to Scotland and to have placed him at the head of Hamilton's army. Others had preferred

---

[*] A third officer, who had already cast aside his doublet, ready to be shot, was told he was to be spared. His birth in Florence had saved him. The Parliamentarians didn't want their own relatives to suffer a revenge attack if ever they toured Italy.

the fleet to go to Ormonde in Ireland, where there were those loyal to an episcopalian Church of England. Having failed to engage an inferior Parliamentarian squadron, the Royalist navy returned to Holland.[6]

The war of the Engagement had ended with the New Model Army the victor in England and Scotland. But Ireland remained under arms and the vast majority of ordinary people in England and Wales still wanted a peace that would see a return to a king ruling with Parliament. Fear of the all-conquering and embittered soldiery of the New Model Army made Charles's agreement to peace terms all the more desirable. To gain his co-operation, MPs once again relaxed the conditions of his imprisonment.

The day after Colchester's surrender, Charles was permitted to spend time alone with Jane and take from her what comfort he could. Over the following fortnight he was allowed to see her several further times. Jane left the Isle of Wight shortly before the formal treaty negotiations opened at Newport on 15 September. Charles wanted her in London to monitor the mood in Westminster and the City while he and the parliamentary commissioners hammered out the terms of his restoration.

Charles sat for the negotiations on his throne under a canopy of state, flanked by several of his former councillors: his cousin, the Duke of Richmond, who had lost three younger brothers in the first civil war; the Marquess of Hertford, Royalist brother-in-law of the late Earl of Essex; the Earl of Southampton, at whose house Charles had been captured; and the Earl of Lindsey, whose father had been killed at Edgehill.

Those who had not seen the king since he had escaped Hampton Court were shocked by his appearance. His hair had turned completely grey and 'he had sorrow in his countenance'.[7] The terms Charles was now required to agree to were draconian. He would have to accept responsibility for the war, and also the abolition of epis-copacy; he would lose the militia; and Parliament would have control of court appointments.

Charles remained determined, however, to push back, even against seemingly impossible odds. He had been writing a justification of his actions for years. These papers had been professionally edited, rewritten, expanded and supplemented by a clergyman called John Gauden. Charles was now revising and approving the developing work. It was to be called 'The King's Sigh, or the Royal Plea'. At the end of September Charles alerted his publisher to prepare for publication.[8] Meanwhile, Ormonde was working successfully towards a treaty that offered generous terms to Ireland's Catholics in an effort to build a Royalist coalition. The possibility of facing a united Irish army of Catholics and Protestants, backed by the Prince of Wales's navy, was a horrifying prospect for the New Model Army. Charles hoped that this threat would strengthen his hand.

The New Model Army was, however, no longer interested in negotiation. Charles's flight from Hampton Court, so breaking his parole, and the subsequent war of the Engagement, had united generals, officers and men in a resolution that he should now face some kind of formal reckoning. On Monday 13 November Jane sent a courier from London with an urgent warning for Charles. The army had prepared a Remonstrance demanding that Charles be tried, along with his elder sons, on a charge of making war on the people.[9] On 20 November the army presented its Remonstrance to Parliament, just as Jane had predicted. The document came close to demanding that Charles be executed, calling for 'exemplary justice ... in Capital punishment upon the principal author ... of our late wars'.[10] This Remonstrance did not, however, have the backing of the English people. It was laid aside by Parliament, with MPs implicitly rejecting its demands for a trial.

Charles believed the army would now react as it had when Parliament had angered the soldiery the previous year. They would seize him from Carisbrooke, just as they had seized him in June 1647 from Holdenby. Only this time his fate would be less comfortable.

On 28 November the treaty negotiations were suspended and Charles took formal leave of the parliamentary commissioners in the town hall at Newport. He had accepted thirty-eight of Parliament's demands. But he maintained absolutely his promise to support episcopacy and his refusal to give up his supporters to the block. The negotiations on such matters were expected to continue, but Charles's farewell speech foresaw no such future. He told the commissioners that he did not believe he would see them again, and that he was ready to submit to what God 'shall be pleased to suffer men to do with me'. The end of the 'old known ways' of a king ruling with his Parliament was approaching. In this, he warned, they too faced danger: 'My Lords, you cannot but know that in my fall and ruin, you see your own.'[11] Many of those present wept.

He wrote to the Prince of Wales the next day. Charles advised his heir to seek peace and told him that when he became king he should never take more power than he needed for the good of his subjects: 'These considerations may make you a great prince, as your father is now a low one.'[12]

A new detachment of soldiers arrived at Carisbrooke in howling winds on the night of 30 November 1648. Word immediately reached Charles that the army planned to move him. Richmond and Lindsey did their best to persuade Charles to flee that instant, but he refused point-blank. There was something undignified in trying to escape yet again and he was doubtful that an attempt would succeed. The arresting officers came for him before breakfast the next morning. They did not say where he was being taken. He was simply told to bid farewell to Richmond. Both king and cousin were visibly distraught.

Charles was taken by carriage to the coast and then by boat to the sea-swept fortress of Hurst Castle. Marooned on a spit, it was 'a dismal receptacle or place for so great a monarch'.* The rooms prepared for

---

* Even today it remains a formidable sight as you approach it by sea from the Isle of Wight.

the king were so small and dark that he needed candles from midday. He managed, however, to write to his daughter Elizabeth, who had been pleading with him for news, a reminder that beyond politics there was a family. 'It is not want of affection that makes me write so seldom,' he explained to his daughter. 'I am loath to write to those I love when I am out of humour lest my letters should trouble those I desire to please.' He had nothing much to say, he added, 'but God bless you!' He asked her to send her little brother Henry another blessing from him 'with a kiss'.[13]

Although the peace terms Charles had agreed fell short of what had been hoped by MPs, Parliament confirmed on 5 December that they offered the basis for further negotiations. This was not what the army wanted to hear. One night, Charles heard a drawbridge fall, and wondered if his long-expected assassin had at last arrived.[14] The army, however, was otherwise occupied. At 7 a.m. on the blustery morning of 6 December 1648, army regiments were on the streets shouting for Londoners 'to go home and look to their shops ... and their wives'.[15] By 8 a.m. soldiers were stationed in New Palace Yard, Westminster Hall, the Court of Requests, and on the stairs and lobby outside the House of Commons. Others patrolled nearby streets.

Arriving MPs walked up the stairs to the Commons to find Colonel Thomas Pride flourishing a list of MP's names. He was an officer trusted by Fairfax, Cromwell and Ireton and was acting on their orders. Those on the list were taken away under guard. William Prynne, who had had his ears cropped for his long-ago attack on the queen, was indignant when Pride barred his way, reminding the colonel 'that he was a member of the House and was going into it to discharge his duty'. Prynne pushed up a couple of steps before Pride and others soldiers overwhelmed him. He was then dragged away, shouting that it was 'a high breach of the privileges of Parliament'.[16] Other arrested MPs demanded from the army chaplain, Hugh Peter, by what power they were held. The answer was blunt: 'By the power of the sword.'[17]

* * *

On 14 June 1647, the army's Declaration to Parliament had demanded an election to clear out 'corrupt' MPs. There had been no such election. Ireton, who had also composed the army's Remonstrance of November 1648, believed that these 'corrupt' MPs had threatened the safety of the English people by their willingness to negotiate with an untrustworthy king. It was this supposed threat to public safety that justified the army's purge of MPs. With that carried out, it was now necessary that Parliament's authority be reasserted and that Charles accept the institution's absolute primacy in a public trial. But to achieve that required more than just the seizure of Parliament – the army also needed to seize the City. What followed was the manipulation of qualifications for voting and office-holding in London. This transformed the balance of power in the municipality towards the Independents and radicals.

Charles was moved again, arriving at Windsor on 23 December. It must have been painful for the king to see the changes in the Garter chapel there. He had, over the years, commissioned an array of gorgeous religious plate, which had all since been broken up as idolatrous. The treasures had included a prayer book with a golden cover. On one side it had depicted the 'the king healing the Evil': a miraculous sign of his status as God's represented on earth. On the other side there had been an image of the Angel of Incense from Revelation, who turns the prayers of the saints ('thy kingdom come') into the fire that destroys the earth. This boasted the ancient heritage of the Church of England, the prayers of its adherents dating back to the first Christians and the Apostles from whom his bishops claimed descent.[18]

Charles did his best to honour the banned feast of Christmas. He dined on 25 December under a canopy of state and dressed in a new suit. There were no traditional mince pies or plum puddings, however, and he read the service himself from the banned Book of Common Prayer.

Elsewhere, Ireton and other army leaders were discussing their plans for the king's fate. There was agreement that Charles had to be

Charles I in armour on the eve of the first 'Bishops' War'. In the Van Dyck
original, commissioned by the king, Charles's hand rests on a helmet. In this
contemporary copy it rests on a sphere, usually a symbol of power, but
here made of glass like that in Titian's *Allegory of Marriage*

(Right) The atrocities of the Irish rebellion as reported in England

Companyes of the Rebells meeting with the English flyinge for their liues falling downe before them cryinge for mercy thrust theire into their Childrens bellyes & threw them into the water.

(Above) Marriage portrait of Mary, the Princess Royal, aged nine, and William of Orange, aged fourteen

(Below) Stands were built for the thousands who witnessed the execution of Thomas Wentworth, Earl of Strafford

THE TRUE MANER OF THE EXECUTION OF THOMAS EARLE OF STRAFFORD. LORD Lieutenant of Ireland. vpon Tower hill. the 12th of May 1641.

(Above) The organ case at St Nicholas Church, Stanford on Avon, Leicestershire, is part of an instrument made for Magdalen College Oxford in 1637, and is a rare survivor of the destruction of organs during the civil wars and under the Commonwealth

A witch mourns the shooting of the poodle, Boy, at Marston Moor

(Left) Boy's master, Prince Rupert of the Rhine

(Below) The fingernail of Thomas Holland, who was hanged and quartered in 1642 for the capital crime of being a Catholic priest in England. His body parts were displayed on London's gates

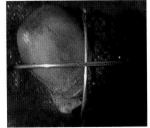

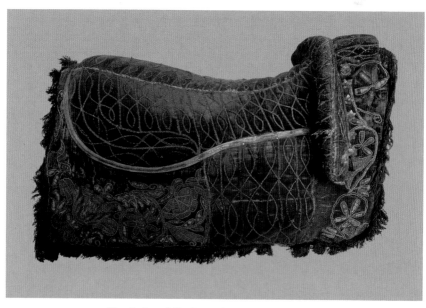

Charles's saddle from the Battle of Naseby

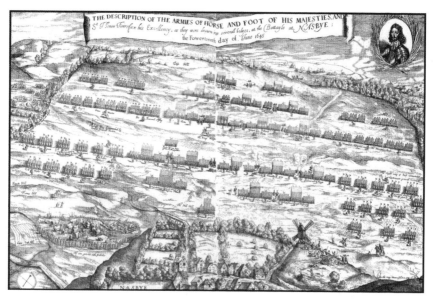

The battlefield at Naseby

(*Above*) The captive royal children, Elizabeth, James and Henry

Anne of Austria, queen consort of France, with her son, the future Louis XIV

Charles's daughter Mary, Princess of Orange

Oliver Cromwell

'Black' Tom Fairfax

Charles I at the time of his trial

A series of mica overlays chart the life and death
of Charles I on a portrait miniature

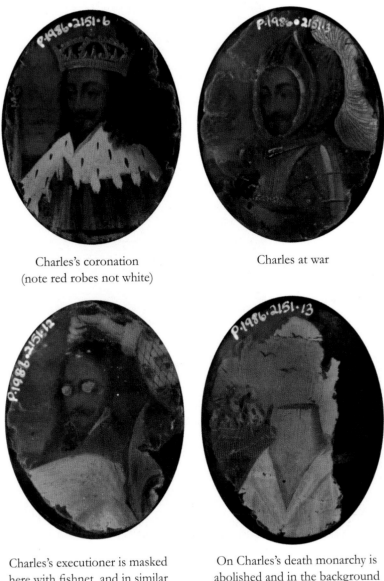

Charles's coronation
(note red robes not white)

Charles at war

Charles's executioner is masked
here with fishnet, and in similar
contemporary images

On Charles's death monarchy is
abolished and in the background
of this image the crown is broken

(Right) Henrietta Maria as a widow

(Above) A pearl earring said to have been worn by Charles I at his execution

(Above) St George's Chapel, Windsor, where Charles I is buried

(Above right) Frontispiece of the *Eikon* (pronounced 'icon') *Basilike* or 'Royal Portrait' depicts Charles giving up his earthly crown for that of a martyr

brought to trial 'and Hugh Peter did very gravely show the necessity for it'.[19] It was hoped that Charles would submit to the proceedings and in so doing effectively accept the superiority of Parliament. There were rumours in London that the Parliamentarian Earl of Denbigh had gone to Windsor to explain to Charles that his life would be spared if he agreed to be a powerless monarch.[20] If Denbigh was there, however, Charles never saw him.

The courtesies due to an English monarch were now stripped from Charles as a mark of his diminished status. It was ordered that he should no longer be served on bended knee and the number of his servants reduced.[21] The principal compiler of 'The King's Sigh', Dr Gauden, had meanwhile added an essay on Charles also being denied his chaplains. The collection of Charles's edited and expanded writings were being hastily renamed the *Eikon Basilike* – Greek for 'Royal Portrait'.[22] It was as if he were already dead. Charles was not, however, resigned to martyrdom and ordered a hold on publication.

The Thirty Years War had ended in Europe in October with the signing of the last in a series of treaties known as the Peace of Westphalia. Bohemia, where it had all begun, remained under Habsburg rule, but the Winter Queen saw her husband's heirs returned the diminished inheritance of the Lower Palatinate, with a devastated population one-tenth of what it had been before the war. Spain now recognised the United Provinces of the Dutch Republic as a sovereign state, while the French gained most of Alsace-Lorraine. The French or the Dutch, freed from European battlefields, might now seek to profit from England's weakness and disarray.

The aftershocks of the Thirty Years War were still being felt in Britain. Once the Stuart kingdoms had been uniquely at peace, but foreigners said that 'Winter here had too many tears' and that there had grown in England 'a monstrous kind of wild liberty ... for law, religion and allegiance are here arbitrary', and where it used to be the saying 'the king can do no wrong', it was now said 'the king can receive no wrong'.[23]

Only Charles, however, could prevent a war in Ireland that might easily spread to England if the kingdom's European rivals became involved there. He was certain this threat allowed him, even now, to hold out for the peace terms he wanted.

On 1 January 1649 the MPs left in the purged House of Commons passed an ordinance to establish a High Court of Justice. This declared it treason for an English king 'to levy war against the Parliament and kingdom of England'. The Lords rejected the ordinance. 'Not one in twenty of the people of England are yet satisfied whether the king did levy war against the Houses first, or the Houses against him; and besides, if the king did levy war first we have no law extant that would make it treason.'[24] So spoke the Independent grandee the Earl of Northumberland, but his words were an irrelevance. Parliamentarian peers had remained a powerful force right up to Pride's Purge. No longer. The only MPs who now mattered were those permitted to sit in the Commons by the army.

On 4 January the Commons declared 'That the People are, under God, the Original of all just Power.'[25] As the people's representatives the Commons MPs held this power in trust, and their acts alone had the force of law. At a stroke the declaration broke the traditional constitutional trinity of king, Lords and Commons. But what had replaced it? The absolute power of the Commons, looking strangely frail in a Westminster guarded by Pride's men, patrolling its corridors armed with muskets and swords.

THE KING'S TRIAL

THE PAINTED CHAMBER IN THE PALACE OF WESTMINSTER WAS A wonder of the thirteenth century. There were scenes from the Old Testament that had inspired crusades against the Muslim invaders of the Holy Land. Its brushwork, as fine as lace, had glowed in brilliant lapis blues, vermilion reds, glittering silvers and gold. But the shining armour of the chivalrous knights was now tarnished, and the faded images obscured by tapestries. The medieval world barely intruded into the new on 8 January 1649, when men in military buff coats or plain Puritan suits sat at trestle tables and debated the fate of their king.

Two days earlier a High Court had been established that would for the first and only time try a King of England. This was justified on the practical grounds of preventing Charles from raising further 'commotions, rebellions and invasions', and on a matter of principle: that the king should have no impunity from the law. The 135 trial commissioners – or judges – who had been appointed by the Commons were mostly army officers and radical MPs. Eighty-three of them attended this first meeting. They included the generals Fairfax and Cromwell.

A legal opinion had been given to Cromwell that deposing a king was treason.[1] He argued, however, that the king's trial was not the action of 'any man [who] has carried on the design of deposing the king', but an expression of God's will. 'I cannot but submit to Providence,' he observed.[2]

Charles was to be charged with having 'a wicked design totally to subvert the fundamental laws and liberties of this nation, and, in their place, to introduce an arbitrary and tyrannical government': crimes, it was declared, that deserved 'exemplary and condign punishment' – in others words, death.[3] But there was no certainty of outcome. Executing the king risked provoking foreign reprisals, another rising, or further mutiny in the navy. On the other hand, if Charles accepted the legality of the tribunal, he would effectively be accepting that he had no 'negative voice' – the contemporary term for a veto that could block Commons decisions. This would mean he could be returned to the throne without any danger to Parliament, 'a sword always over his head [and] grown grey in the documents of misfortune'.[4] Yet the judges were faced with a grim fact: as Cromwell reportedly warned them, if the king refused to plead, then in order to confirm the supreme power of the Commons, they would have to 'cut off his head with the crown on it'.

This was not what Fairfax had expected. His wife Anne, a Presbyterian, had virulently opposed the king being tried for his life, and one of the purged MPs had implored him to stop the trial, with the biblical warning 'who can stretch forth his hand against the Lord's Anointed, and be innocent?'[5] The army's December discussions about the trial had led Fairfax to believe that Cromwell backed him in seeking an outcome which would stop short of Charles's execution, even if he refused to plead. There were rumours of Charles's deposition being considered, and young Henry, Duke of Gloucester, being made king in Charles's place. Fairfax now felt betrayed. He would never attend a meeting of the judges again. Nevertheless, Fairfax would not prevent the trial as he was urged to do. That would risk tearing his beloved army apart. Having delivered Charles up for judgement, he washed his hands of what he feared would follow.

A letter written to Fairfax, as well as to the Speakers of the Houses of Parliament, in which Henrietta Maria begged permission to see her husband, was not even opened.

The remaining judges elected the veteran London radical and Chief Justice of Chester, John Bradshawe, as their Lord President and agreed the trial would take place at Westminster Hall. Fearful of how people would react to the upending of the constitution and the insults to their king, dissidents were taken into custody under martial law, the vaults under the Painted Chamber searched for gunpowder then sealed, and London's printing presses shut down. The first edition of the *Eikon Basilike* was destroyed at its printing house. Royalists promptly set up a new press outside the city.[6] A second edition was being prepared as Charles was brought with maximum discretion from Windsor to London on 19 January 1649. Few noticed the return of the king to the capital he had fled in 1642.

After a night at St James's Palace Charles was brought by barge to a private house next to Westminster Palace.[7] It was bitterly cold, with ice knocking against the sides of the boats on the river. Charles would have little privacy in his rooms during his trial. The house was watched over by thirty guards who would be changed regularly and had permission to open the doors to his rooms whenever they wished. Two were actually to be stationed in his bedchamber where they could drink and smoke.[8] In the grounds a further 200 soldiers were posted. At Westminster Hall, meanwhile, a raised dais had been built for the judges at the southern end. On it were benches covered in red baize, a raised chair and a desk. Facing these was another chair, covered in red velvet. It was here that Charles would sit.

It must have seemed appropriate to the king that he was to be tried in the same spot as Strafford had been. Westminster Hall had been packed for that trial – and so it was again, with a full audience awaiting the trial of the king.

Charles was escorted out of the back of his lodging at 2 p.m., twenty soldiers tramping ahead and more behind. They passed through the private garden, then between the buildings that huddled close against Westminster Hall and down a series of passages. At last he entered the hall through a doorway close to where the judges sat.

Inside, the sound of marching boots heralded a slight figure dressed in black silk. Charles wore a tall hat and around his neck was the blue ribbon of the Garter from which was suspended his George, the badge of St George and the dragon carved in onyx and studded with diamonds. At his elbow the silver rays of the Garter escutcheon sparkled. His beard was full. It was said he had refused to use the barber Parliament had provided for him, in case the barber was an assassin awaiting orders to cut his throat.[9]

The serjeant-at-arms conducted Charles to the railed-off area known as the bar. Charles stood there in his high hat. Everyone could see that it remained on his head: a highly visible reminder that no one there was his equal and so, legally, no one there was able to be his judge.

Charles's gaze was directed first at the court. Then he turned round to a wooden partition which ran from wall to wall. A few feet behind it was a strong railing and a line of guards armed with halberds. Behind them more soldiers lined the walkway between the spectators who filled the rest of the space. Charles ignored them and looked up at the far corners of the room where there were galleries accessed from private houses. These were filled with people of high status, and there were guards here too. According to legend the Lord President Bradshawe had had his hat lined with lead to protect him from possible snipers.[10] Charles moved to sit, but seemed to think better of it and turned again, his eyes sweeping the lowlier spectators, before he faced the court once more.

The Act of the Trial of Charles Stuart, King of England was read out and Charles accused as 'a tyrant, traitor, murderer, and a public and implacable enemy to the Commonwealth of England'. The roll call of the judges then began. Each of those present stood as his name was called. Many had chosen not to show up and their names were greeted only by silence – save for that of Fairfax. When his name was read a masked woman in the galleries shouted, 'He has more wit than to be here!' It was said to have been his wife, Anne. Cromwell, and many of the commissioners, would have recognised her voice.

It was a disconcerting beginning, but Bradshawe's nerve held. He rose from his chair and addressed the king: 'Charles Stuart, King of England, the Commons of England, being assembled in Parliament, being deeply sensible of the calamities that have fallen upon this nation (which is fixed upon you as the principal author of it), have resolved to make inquisition for blood.' It was for this that they had 'constituted this High Court of Justice, before which you are brought'.

The neat forty-year-old prosecuting counsel, John Cooke, who stood on Charles's right, now prepared to speak, but Charles tapped him on the shoulder with his cane. 'Hold,' he said. As Cooke moved to continue, Charles tapped again, 'Hold!' Bradshawe urged Cooke on and so Cooke asked for the charge to be read. As the clerk of the court began, Charles once again said, 'Hold!' This time his cane struck Cooke hard enough to send its silver head crashing to the ground. A hush fell across the room as it rolled on the floor. Charles waited for someone to pick it up. No one did. So he bent forward to retrieve it himself and put it in his pocket. Charles wondered if Hugh Peter had tampered with it deliberately.[11]

As the clerk continued Charles stood up and looked around him again before sitting and laughing contemptuously. Bradshawe now asked Charles to answer the charge. Charles could have argued that all he did was in self-defence, but he did not take that bait. 'I would know by what power I am called hither,' he demanded. He reminded the court he was at the point of concluding treaty negotiations with Parliament and, that being the case, what was their authority? 'I mean lawful – there are many unlawful authorities in the world – thieves and robbers by the highway – but I would know by what authority I was brought from thence.' There was none of the old stutter in his speech. 'Remember I am your king, your lawful king,' he continued, 'think well upon it.'[12]

Bradshawe retorted that Charles was being tried 'in the name of the people of England, of which you are elected king'. 'No,' Charles returned, 'England was never an elected kingdom but an hereditary kingdom for near these thousand years, therefore let me know by what authority I am called thither; I do stand more for the liberty of my people than any that come to be my pretended judges.'[13]* And if the people were represented by Parliament, which was a court, where was Parliament, Charles wanted to know. 'I see no House of Lords here that may constitute a Parliament.' Indeed, he noted, 'You have shown no lawful authority to satisfy any reasonable man.' 'That is your apprehension,' Bradshawe snapped; 'we are satisfied who are your judges.' ''Tis not my apprehension, nor yours either, that ought to decide it,' Charles retorted.

As the court was adjourned Bradshawe commanded the guards: 'Take down the prisoner.' 'The king, you mean,' Charles corrected. Shouts of 'God save the king!' broke out as he was escorted from the hall. The guards countered: 'Justice! Justice!'[14]

That night Charles refused to go to bed until his guards were removed from his room. It was a small victory. And there had been another. Ormonde had concluded a treaty with the Irish Confederates. Charles's bargaining chip of a Royalist Ireland had become more substantial.

On the Monday Charles was back in court. Bradshawe again asked him to plead. Charles again asked by what authority he was being tried, 'For', he said, 'if power without law may make laws [then] I do

---

* Was it true that England had been an hereditary kingdom for 1,000 years? Henry VII, the first Tudor king, had not ruled by hereditary right – he had none. Henry VII had claimed his right by divine providence. His 'right' (never described) was affirmed by parliamentary statute in 1485. Elizabeth I, a bastard in law, owed her right to the throne to statute. King James had succeeded the last Tudor by hereditary right, but the proclamation in 1603 had been signed and approved by representative peers, gentry and councillors. Without that backing it would not have happened – and it was considered necessary to confirm James's right in statute the following year. England was not quite an elective monarchy – but it was not merely hereditary.

not know what subject he is in England that may be sure of his life, or anything that he calls his own.' Bradshawe repeated that the judges sat by the authority of the Commons. 'I deny that. Show me one precedent,' Charles asked. 'The Commons of England was never a Court of Judicature. I would know how they came to be so.'[15]

Bradshawe ordered the guards to remove him. Charles said he required more time to explain his refusal to plead. 'Sir, 'tis not for prisoners to require,' Bradshawe sneered. 'Sir, I am no ordinary prisoner,' Charles retorted. 'Serjeant,' Bradshawe continued, 'take away the prisoner!' When Charles nevertheless continued to speak Bradshawe lost his temper, saying, 'How great a friend you have been to the laws and liberties of the people, let all England and the world judge!' Charles was stung. It was, he said, 'for the liberty, freedom and laws of the subjects that ever I took ...' He stopped himself, realising that if he said he had taken up arms, it could be construed as an admission that he was the aggressor in the civil war. He quickly corrected himself: ' ... *defended* myself with arms. I never took up arms against the people but for the laws.' Bradshawe ordered sharply, 'The command of the court must be obeyed!' Charles was hustled out, huffing, 'Well, sir!'

On the third day of the trial Charles was yet again asked to plead. He in turn again asked on what authority he was called. Bradshawe's irritation at Charles's claims to stand for the liberties and privileges of his subjects remained evident. 'Truly, sir,' he told Charles, 'men's intentions ought to be known by their actions; you have written your meaning in bloody characters throughout the whole kingdom.' As the soldiers moved to escort Charles out, Bradshawe reiterated, 'You are before a court of justice!' Eyeing the brute force of the armed soldiers, Charles commented coolly: 'I see before me a power.' Only then did he rise from his chair to leave.

By now pressure to halt the trial was growing. Ministers fulminated from pulpits against the sin of regicide while the Scots, French and Dutch ambassadors pleaded for Charles's life, and made veiled threats about what they might do if he were to be executed. Charles was, after all, a King of Scots, the uncle of the King of France and father-in-law of the now Prince of Orange. Charles himself believed that his judges had to see sense, and come to terms with him. Only he could end the risks of war in Ireland, and the intervention of one or more European powers.

The prosecuting counsel, John Cooke, was frustrated at Charles's refusal to plead. Cooke had hoped, amongst others matters, to cite in his case the 'murder' of King James by the royal favourite Buckingham. Over the course of the civil war Charles himself had come to be accused of involvement in poisoning James with potions and poultices. Referring to Charles's supposed patricide would help justify the king being tried for his life. After all, in English law, treason was committed against the king, not the 'commonwealth'. Charles might then have been convicted, leaving the purged Parliament to commute his sentence, subject to his good behaviour, in a supreme act of parliamentary sovereignty. But Charles had not pleaded.

That night a former pupil of Cooke's stopped him on his way home, tugging at his sleeve. The pupil wanted to know what to expect from the trial at this crucial juncture. Cooke replied bitterly: 'The king must die and monarchy must die with him.' In refusing to accept the jurisdiction of the court, Charles had denied that the Commons was the superior power in the kingdom. The cost of keeping Charles alive was now greater than that of his death. He had left them with no choice but to cut off his head.

Allies of the serving judges worked until dawn that night trying to persuade Fairfax to rejoin them on the court benches so they could better present a united front. He declined to do so. But nor would he stop the trial taking its course. There were few senior officers he could rely on for support if he insisted on a last-minute royal reprieve, and the probable result was mutiny in his army and a renewed civil war. Yet he had been 'much distracted in his mind, and changed purposes often every day'.[16]

* * *

In the Painted Chamber the judges now reviewed evidence and thirty-three witness statements were heard. The next day they were read out in a public session to help justify what was to come. The statements included that of the citizen of Leicester who claimed Charles had urged his troops to kill unarmed civilians in the town. Cromwell and his close allies insisted the judges hold their course, and by the following day, 26 January, the judges had finally agreed that Charles would suffer execution – if he refused a last offer to plead. A death warrant was drawn up and signatures began to be gathered.

On the morning of Saturday 27 January, as Charles was brought back into Westminster Hall, Hugh Peter raised the guards to a chorus, 'Execution! Justice! Execution!' Charles tried to speak. He was cut off. Bradshawe, dressed in red robes, reminded the court that Charles was brought before them on a charge 'of treason and other high crimes' and that this was carried out 'in the name of the people of England'. At that a woman's voice rang out from the gallery, 'Not half, not a quarter of the people of England. Oliver Cromwell is a traitor!' 'What whore is that?' muttered a musketeer officer. His men levelled their weapons at a masked woman being restrained by another woman, also masked, sitting beside her. The voice was again that of Anne Fairfax, and the woman beside her was a sister of another judge who had chosen to absent himself.[17] The guards in the gallery dragged the women out.

Bradshawe offered Charles a last opportunity to acknowledge the jurisdiction of the court and speak in his own defence. Charles, instead, asked 'that I may be heard in the Painted Chamber before the Lords and Commons'. The time had come, at last, to negotiate – or so Charles believed. But in asking to see the Lords as well as the Commons he was again denying the supremacy of the Commons.[18] The sentence was now to be handed down. The prisoner was not allowed his title as king, but addressed as one 'Charles Stuart', 'tyrant, traitor, murderer and public enemy', and, as such, he was to be 'put to death by severing his head from his body'.[19] The court stood.

Charles began to panic. He suddenly realised there was to be no negotiation. They really were going to cut off his head. He now had to make his defence for posterity. 'Will you hear me a word, sir?' he asked. 'No, sir,' replied Bradshawe, 'you are not to be heard after the sentence.' 'No, sir?' Charles asked. 'No, sir,' Bradshawe repeated, 'guard, withdraw your prisoner.' Charles was indignant: 'Sir, I may speak after the sentence ever?' The guard began to move. 'By your favour [hold] the sentence, sir,' Charles insisted, 'I say, sir, I do.'

He turned to those standing by. 'I am not suffered to speak,' he said. 'Expect what justice other people will have.'

In the passageways behind the hall the soldiers lining the route blew pipe smoke in his face, and jeered and mocked. Years before, when Charles was still a prince, his father had described such a scene in his last political work. Dedicated to Charles and titled 'A Pattern for a King's Inaugeration', James had reviewed for his son the significance and meaning of the coronation ceremony. He had recalled Christ's suffering during the last hours before His crucifixion, how in 'the public place for the administration of justice', the Common Hall, 'soldiers had mocked our Saviour, with putting the ornaments of a king upon him' and crowned him with thorns. James had warned Charles to prepare himself 'for the worst' so he might become worthy of the kingdom of heaven.

At the printers, the cover for the *Eikon Basilike* now bore an image of Charles carrying a crown of thorns. In the portrait he looks up at the heavenly crown to which he aspires, while at his feet lies the earthly crown he will leave behind.* The image was designed to send a powerful message: a debased Parliament was executing the envoy on earth of Christ the King.

---

* The crown in the upper right corner is '*beatam & aeternam*' (blessed & eternal), which is to be contrasted with the temporal crown at the king's foot, '*splendidam & gravem*' (splendid & heavy). He holds the martyr's crown of thorns, '*asperam & levem*' (bitter & light).

'EXECUTION'

CHARLES WAS BROUGHT FROM WESTMINSTER TO WHITEHALL IN A closed sedan chair. He was sealed from his people, 'as they carry such as have the plague'.[1] Witnesses would remember the silence of the foot soldiers lining King Street and the onlookers gathered at windows and shop stalls, many in tears.

It took only minutes for Charles to arrive at Whitehall, the Tudor palace he had hoped to replace. Even at Carisbrooke Castle he had continued to work on plans for a vast new classical building: England's Versailles before that palace was even a glint in the eye of Louis XIV. The architect Inigo Jones, having survived the conflagration that had ended the Basing House siege, had travelled, drawings in hand, to the Isle of Wight. This was the world in which Charles was happiest: a world of beauty and order in which he had time to choose his options, calmly and rationally. Yet it was also one of human warmth. In private Charles had always been very different from his chilly and regal public persona. Outside his family he was most relaxed in the company of the creative and knowledgeable commoner. 'With any artist or good mechanic, traveller or scholar, he would discourse freely,' others remembered. He was interested to learn from them, but also contributed from his experience, giving 'light to them in their own art of knowledge'.[2]

Now even the theatre Charles had built at Whitehall was closed. Parliament had banned all plays in England. The magnificent organ he had bought for the chapel was also sold off, while the bedchamber where he rested had been stripped of his collection of art.[3] The full-length portraits he had hung there of his wife, his brother and his sister were all up for sale. For the time being he still had the books in his personal library. These included his volumes on the Order of the Garter, bound in purple velvet or green leather, some with silver mounts and clasps. Many had been gifts from his mother when he was Prince of Wales.[4] He had little time to enjoy them now.

Two hours after Charles arrived at Whitehall he was moved again.[5] This spared him the sound of the scaffold being built outside the Banqueting House. He was taken instead to St James's Palace. Here much of his great art collection still remained, although these pictures too were awaiting sale. The family portraits included one of his sister and her children. A 'whole table of monkeys with my proper self', she had written jokingly when she had sent it to him as a gift in 1629.[6]

Charles's eldest nephew, Charles Louis, was still in London. Charles suspected he would ask for a last interview, as would many of his friends. He didn't want to see any of them. 'My time is short and precious,' he told a servant, 'I hope they will not take it ill that none have access to me but my children. The best office they can do now is to pray for me.'[7] Charles then sent Parliament a request to see the thirteen-year-old Princess Elizabeth and the eight-year-old Henry, Duke of Gloucester.

Charles knew he would never see his other children again.

James, Duke of York, now fifteen, had joined his mother in Paris, having arrived from The Hague a few days earlier. His creditors had seized his baggage and the Dutch government had had to intervene to get it released. James found his mother's situation not much better. The high taxes Anne of Austria had raised to pay for the wars in Europe had prompted months of violence in Paris. It marked the beginning of civil wars in France known as the 'Fronde', after the slings carried by the mobs. Anne had fled Paris with the ten-year-old Louis XIV, but Henrietta Maria remained at the Louvre along with the youngest of the Stuart children, the four-year-old Henrietta. It was bitterly cold, they had no fuel, and the merchants of Paris were refusing Henrietta Maria any further credit.

The Prince of Wales, meanwhile, who remained in The Hague as the guest of his sister Mary and her husband, also had 'nothing to live on'. He had been obliged to dismiss many of his followers, and was living 'a private life while awaiting a wind more favourable to [his] affairs'.[8] The prince had written to his father, and the bearer arrived at St James's Palace that evening. The messenger kissed the king's hand and, weeping, embraced his knees. Charles consoled him and gave him two letters, one for the prince and another for Henrietta Maria. The prince's letter asked for his blessing and promised to do all he could to earn it.[9] 'I had rather you be Charles le Bon, than Charles le Grand, Good than Great', he wanted his son to know, but 'I hope God has designed you to be both.' 'Farewell till we meet, if not on earth, yet in heaven.'[10]

Charles spent much of the rest of the day praying with the sixty-six-year-old Bishop of London, William Juxon. The old man, who loved his hunting almost as much as he loved his God, had attended on Charles during the trial, and had performed the miracle of attracting little antipathy, even amongst those MPs 'whose ears' it was said 'were ever opened, nay itching after such complaints'.[11] Charles broke from his prayers only briefly that night. He had considered what final gifts he had for his children. Surrounded by Parliament's spies he asked the most ingratiating of them, his bedchamber servant Thomas Herbert, for his assistance. He wanted Herbert to visit one of his couriers, Lady Elizabeth Wheeler. She had kept in her protection a few things that remained precious to him. Charles offered Herbert a testimonial in exchange for his help.* Parliament would learn of every detail of what their spy was now sent to collect.

---

* One day it would come in very useful.

It was dark as Herbert left St James's Palace and security was tight. Guards were posted at 'the house, garden, park, gates near Whitehall, King Street, and other where'.[12] Herbert, however, was free to go where he wished. He found Lady Wheeler in her house behind the narrow road of King Street, with its notorious taverns. She had kept Charles's possessions in a little cabinet, which she now handed over.

When Charles opened the cabinet the following morning several jewels tumbled out, including more than one Garter with its George. Several of them appeared to be broken. 'You see', Charles said sadly, 'all the wealth now in my power to give my two children.'[13]

In the royal chapel that morning Hugh Peter gave a 'funeral' sermon on Charles. He chose as his text 'the terrible denunciation to the King of Babylon': 'All the kings of the nations, even all of them, lie in glory, every one in his own house. But thou art cast out of thy grave like an abominable branch, and as the raiment of those that are slain, thrust through with a sword, that go down to the stones of the pit, as a carcass trodden under feet.'[14]

Frantic efforts were, however, still being made to save Charles's life. The ambassador from the Venetian Republic reported great hopes of the Scots. They were insisting that the Edinburgh Parliament needed to be consulted on the fate of their king before sentence was carried out. 'It may be they repent, though tardily, of the abominable example they afforded two years ago by selling their king to the English for a few pounds sterling,' the Venetian observed.[15] The Dutch ambassadors also had an audience with Fairfax and on 29 January he duly urged his Council of War to postpone the execution – but without success.

Charles spent the rest of the day burning his papers and ciphers before preparing himself with prayer for his children's arrival at his rooms. Eventually Elizabeth was brought in, sobbing inconsolably. She would write down that night all she remembered: how he had blessed her and told her that 'he was glad as I was come ... and although he had not time to say much, yet somewhat he had to say to me'. He asked her to remind James to obey his elder brother as his sovereign, told her they should love each other and forgive their enemies – but never to trust them. He then paused and said to his weeping daughter, 'Sweetheart, you'll forget this.' She promised, 'I shall never forget this while I live.' He tried to comfort her, saying 'not to grieve and torment myself for him, for that should be a glorious death that he should die, it being for the laws and liberties of this land and for the Protestant religion'. He foresaw God settling the throne upon the Prince of Wales. They would all be happy then, he told her. Knowing Elizabeth's love of study, Charles suggested some reading from the books he still had. They included Laud's book against the Catholic martyr John Fisher, 'to ground me against popery'. He asked her also to send his blessing to her other siblings, and to tell her mother that 'his thoughts had never strayed from her, and that his love should be the same to the last'. Charles then took the eight-year-old Henry onto his knee.

With Charles's two eldest sons condemned as traitors by Parliament it was still possible Henry would be made a puppet ruler. The boy had been crying like his sister, but Charles spoke to him as plainly and directly as he could. 'Sweetheart,' he said, 'now they will cut off your father's head.' At this Henry looked steadfastly at him. 'They will cut off my head, and perhaps make thee a king; but mark what I say. You must not be a king so long as your brothers Charles and James do live; for they will cut off your brothers' heads (when they do catch them) and cut off your head too, at the last, and therefore I charge you, do not be made a king by them.' Henry replied, 'I will be torn in pieces first.' The vehemence of the little boy made the king smile. But he then had to say his last goodbyes. Charles gave Elizabeth and Henry all his jewels save his onyx George with its portrait of their mother. Then he kissed his children, with tears 'of joy and love'.

As they were taken to the bedchamber door Elizabeth cried so hard it 'moved others to pity that were formerly hard-hearted'. Charles, standing by a window, couldn't bear it and dashed to his children for a last embrace, kissed them and blessed them.[16] When they had gone, he collapsed and had to retire to bed.[17]

Bishop Juxon stayed with Charles until late that night and promised to return early for the day of his execution. Charles managed to rest for around four hours, getting up a couple of hours before dawn. His room was lit as usual by a cake of wax in a silver basin. He opened the curtains and announced to Herbert, who slept on a pallet by his bed, that he had 'great work to do this day'. It was freezing outside and he asked Herbert for an extra shirt. 'The season is so cold,' he said, and it will 'make me shake which some observers will imagine proceeds from fear. I would have no such impression. I fear not death!'[18]

Juxon arrived soon after Charles had dressed. Fairfax had gone to Whitehall in an attempt to get the execution postponed. His efforts failed. The king got together his last possessions. He wanted to give the Prince of Wales – soon to be Charles II – his Bible, which had his own annotations in the margins. For his second son, the future James II, he had something practical – a circular silver slide rule. Charles had been good at mathematics as a child. There were more religious books for Elizabeth and a catechism for Henry. There were also two gifts for friends: a romance for the Earl of Lindsey, who had commanded the scarlet-clad Life Guards of Foot at Edgehill, and a gold pocket watch which had belonged to King James and which Charles asked to be given to the Duchess of Richmond, a daughter of his murdered friend and mentor, the Duke of Buckingham. He remembered her playing with it when she was a small child.

Charles then took Communion and prepared to leave. He had been allowed to choose the hour of his death.[19] When the call came he smiled at Juxon. 'Come let us go,' he said, and took his hand.

With the bishop on his right, Charles walked through the frosted garden and into St James's Park, where two regiments of foot were drawn up on either side, their colours flying. A guard of halberdiers went before him and others behind. They were bare-headed, a mark of contempt. The drums were beating so loudly no one could hear anyone speak, although Charles tried to say some words to the colonel walking on his left. As they reached Whitehall Charles walked up the stairs and along the Privy Gallery. From the windows he would have been able to see the scaffold that awaited him outside the Banqueting House. It was draped in black. Charles was taken to one of the smaller rooms on the south side of the gallery. From here there was a different view: of the abbey where he had been crowned, and Westminster, the seat of his parliaments and the place of his trial. He had a last meal of bread and wine. It would help prevent him feeling faint.

It was just after two o'clock when Charles was brought back through the Privy Gallery and into the Banqueting House. He walked below the Rubens ceiling celebrating a peace long gone and the Stuart dynasty that was soon also to pass. Parliament had declared it illegal to proclaim a new king on Charles's death. A line of soldiers stretched the length of the room, holding back a crush of people. As Charles walked between the guard the crowd behind them prayed loudly. Charles smiled at his people, but it was noticed that, at the age of only forty-eight, his beard was 'long and grey, his hair white and he seemed greatly aged'.[20] At the north end of the room the transom and mullions of one of the windows had been removed to create a door. From here he stepped down onto the black floor of the scaffold. At his left knee, a garter band flashed with 412 diamonds. Juxon remained at his side. To one witness, watching from a nearby rooftop, it seemed Charles showed 'the same concernedness and motion as he usually did' when he had arrived at the Banqueting House 'on a masque night'.[21]

Whatever anxiety Charles felt he was keeping it hidden behind his performance. The scaffold was his stage in this theatre of death: every gesture he made, every detail of what followed, would be remembered and would impact on his heir's chances of being crowned. Standing in the bright light of that cold day he sought out his audience.

Few of those responsible for his being there would see his end. Fairfax was at a prayer meeting. Hugh Peter was ill in bed. Where Cromwell was is unrecorded. Charles could see rows of infantry and, behind them, cavalry. The crowd had been pushed far back so they would not hear anything Charles said. The confined space had also ensured their numbers had been kept low. Elsewhere the shops were open – Londoners had been encouraged to go about their normal business. On the scaffold itself there were more soldiers, but it was the executioner and his assistant who stood out. They were dressed in wigs and sailors' costumes, their faces masked with fishnet. The executioner had even added a false beard. He was taking no chances in ever being recognised.

It was said the common hangman of London had refused the task of beheading his king, swearing 'he would be shot ... rather than do it'.[22] Known as 'Young Gregory', after his father and namesake who had held the post before him, he had already beheaded Strafford and Laud and was extremely skilled at a difficult job. The type of axe used for English executions was designed to chop and shape logs, as the French doctor who had attended the execution of Mary, Queen of Scots, had noted with dismay. It had a slant in the blade, to shave wood. If you didn't know what you were doing with such an axe the blow would not strike where it was intended, but fall askew, landing on the skull or the back. The king's life could easily end in crude butchery.

Charles walked to the middle of the scaffold and looked 'very earnestly' at the block. There were ropes and chains in case he struggled. The block itself was scarcely more than a hewn log on the ground, eighteen inches long by six in height.[23] He would have to lie flat. Charles balked at that and asked 'if there was no higher'.[24] It was explained that this was what an efficient block looked like. Mollified, he took out the notes for his speech. 'I shall be very little heard of anybody here, I shall therefore speak a word unto you,' he said to those on the scaffold. He still wished to make the final defence he had been denied in court. He was innocent, he said, of starting the war and before God he had never wished to take Parliament's privileges. On the contrary, Parliament had taken his privileges, beginning with the militia. God was punishing him, not for the war, but for his role in another unjust sentence, 'that I suffered to take effect'. He did not mention Strafford's name. He did not need to.

For his own death he forgave those who were 'the chief causers ... Who they are God knows. I do not desire to know.' He hoped, however, that they would repent, 'for indeed they have committed a great sin': not only rebellion against a divinely ordained ruler, but regicide.

As Charles talked on, a soldier restlessly shifted his position and brushed against the axe. Charles paused and turned, rebuking him, 'Hurt not the axe that may hurt me.' A blunt blade, even in the hand of an expert, would end with the executioner hacking and hewing. Such had been the fate of Mary, Queen of Scots, whose ladies-in-waiting had witnessed the axe being used to saw at the last sinews that secured her head to her shoulders.

As Charles continued, his speech recalled the words on the standard he had raised at Nottingham in 1642 at the outbreak of civil war: give Caesar his due. 'God will never prosper you, until you give him his due, the king his due (that is my successors) and the people their due ... I desire their liberty and freedom as much as anybody whomsoever', but, 'I must tell you' that true liberty and freedom lay in the rule of law, 'by which their life and good may be their own. It is not for having a share of government, sirs, that is nothing pertaining to them. A subject and a sovereign are clean different things.' Yet it was for his subjects that he would die: 'I am a martyr of the people.'

Charles stopped, but Juxon now reminded him that he had yet to say something on the Church of England. 'I had almost forgotten it!' Charles exclaimed, with the relief of a schoolboy whose recital was almost over. 'I declare before you all that I die a Christian according to the profession of the Church of England as I found it left me by my father.' Turning to the officer in charge of the execution Charles asked, 'Take care that they do not put me to pain.'

He then turned to a second soldier, who again was clumsily pushing against the axe, and this time a febrile concern was more evident. 'Take heed of the axe, pray, take heed of the axe,' he repeated. Then he instructed the executioner. 'I shall say but a very short prayer and then thrust out my hands.' Having called Juxon for his nightcap he put it on. 'Does my hair trouble you?' he asked the executioner. It did, and the man helped tuck his hair away. Charles did not seem to mind his killer's touch. 'There is but one stage more,' Juxon reassured his king. 'I go from a corruptible to an incorruptible crown where no disturbance can be,' Charles observed. 'It is a good exchange,' Juxon confirmed. Charles was prepared. His last words would be for Juxon alone.

Charles took off his cloak and handed his onyx George to the bishop. Every new knight was admonished, at his installation, 'in all just Battles and War ... strongly to fight, valiantly to stand, and honourably to have the victory'. Seeking that victory was now to be the burden of his heir. 'Remember,' he said to Juxon. The king's George depicting the slaying of the dragon of rebellion was for the new sovereign of the Order.

Charles lay down flat and put his head on the low block. A doctor, who had a good view, said he caught the king's eye, which was 'quick and lively'.[25] After a short moment Charles thrust out his hands. The fishnet only minimally obscured the executioner's view. The axe fell clean. His assistant picked up the rolling head and held it high, 'the usual words uttered: behold the head of a traitor'.[26]

A Royalist, writing much later, said the crowd then gave up a 'groan as I have never heard before and I desire I may never hear again'. In truth not everyone was saddened. The soldiers showed delight, taking their plunder, and 'round the armed bands / Did clap their bloody hands'.[27] An officer cut the diamond garter from Charles's left leg. 'His hair was cut off. Soldiers dipped their swords in his blood' and swore at his body.[28] After Charles's corpse was taken to a room at the back of Whitehall to be embalmed, the soldiers continued to hack at the wood on the scaffold, hoping to sell the bloodstained chips, along with the locks of Charles's hair, either as items of curiosity or as holy relics – they did not much care which.[29]

Their brothers in arms broke up the crowd and the executioner was whisked off to be smuggled away on a barge. The waterman remembered the man seemed terrified and that 'he shook every joint of him'. His name remains a mystery, but the professional efficiency with which Charles was dispatched suggests it was, after all, Young Gregory himself.

Princess Elizabeth and little Henry were at the Earl of Northumberland's Syon House when their father was beheaded. It must have been a comfort for the grieving children when the Dutch envoys of their elder sister Mary, Princess of Orange, visited them. The envoys found no signs of a household in mourning. Only the children were in black. The countess greeted the envoys dressed as for any other day.[30] The information the spy Thomas Herbert had passed to his political masters ensured that anything of value that Charles had given Elizabeth and Henry had been confiscated and would be up for sale, along with the onyx George that Charles had bequeathed to the new Charles II.* Larger goods destined for auction, such as Charles's paintings, furniture and tapestries, were stacked up at Denmark House where, for the first time, soldiers, clergymen, lawyers and other ordinary folk could now see great European art.

It was possible also to see the corpse of the king who had collected this art. Parliament and the army had to ensure there was no doubt that Charles was dead. There had been uncertainty in the past over the fate of overthrown monarchs. Had Richard II survived

---

* The seals Charles had left Elizabeth and Henry were amongst the things listed for sale. The George, purchased for £70, would be sold on to Charles II by one of the officers who had attended the king's execution – a Colonel Thomlinson. A brother of Cromwell's son-in-law, Ireton, would purchase the garter Charles wore on his knee on the scaffold for £205, well above its valuation of £160. Its 412 diamonds were broken up for profit and resale.

imprisonment at Pontefract Castle in 1400? Had the Princes in the Tower escaped in 1483? Such questions had fuelled revolt against the rule of their successors. A surgeon had therefore been employed to embalm the king's corpse and sew his head back in place. He described the task as like stitching the head back on a goose. People paid a ha'penny to view his work and Charles's body at Whitehall.[31] In the days that followed others then queued to see it at St James's Palace.[32]

A contemporary image has a sheet pulled up to Charles's chin, as if he were lying in bed. A fanciful story emerged in the eighteenth century that even Cromwell came to see the body one night, and was heard muttering 'Cruel necessity.' A contemporary witness later span another legend, claiming the dead king was smiling as 'perfectly as if he were alive.'[33] In fact, far from smiling his face was bruised. The executioner's assistant, who had held up the decapitated head for the crowd, had dropped it heavily.[34] But the bodies of martyrs are said to defy the brutality of their end, and it was as a martyr this witness was remembering his king.

On the streets Charles's last testimony, the *Eikon Basilike*, was running off the presses. The first copies were already on sale, promoting him as a 'martyr of the people', who had died for liberties and the Protestant religion. It sold in huge numbers. There would be forty impressions and issues in 1649 in England alone, and twenty more in Latin, Dutch, French, German and Danish.

Henrietta Maria was dining in the Louvre when she learned that her 'Dear Heart' was dead. The blow left her utterly stunned. She sat 'without words, without action, without motion, like a statue', her women weeping around her until night began to fall. It was at the Louvre that they had met over quarter of a century before. Now, as Charles's widow, she was 'able to see all she had lost and what she owed to the memory of a king who had loved her much.'[35] As the candles flickered in the gloom, her sister-in-law, the Duchesse de Vendôme, at last raised her up and led her from the room.[36]

The future James II, who was in Paris with his mother, would never speak or write of what had occurred, even in his memoirs of the civil war. It was too personal and too painful. In The Hague Mary was reported to be extremely bitter. Her eldest brother, the new Charles II, had learned of his father's death only when he was addressed by his new title. He broke down and wept.

RESURRECTION

IT WAS JUDGED 'UNSAFE AND INCONVENIENT' FOR CHARLES TO BE buried in Westminster Abbey, alongside his parents King James and Anna of Denmark, and the infant children he and Henrietta Maria had lost. In such a public spot his tomb could too easily become a place of pilgrimage.[1] Instead, on 7 February 1649, Charles's body was sent out of London, 'without pomp or noise', on a simple bier drawn by six horses, each trapped in black velvet.[2] Its destination was the garrisoned castle at Windsor. Charles's plain coffin rested that night in his former bedchamber. The next day, MPs granted four of his former noble servants permission to oversee his burial in the security of St George's Chapel: the earls of Lindsey and Southampton, the Marquess of Hertford, and Charles's cousin, the Duke of Richmond.

Richmond had been made a Gentleman of the Bedchamber when he was only thirteen and had become amongst the most glamorous members of Charles's court. Van Dyck had painted Richmond many times – twice with his favourite hound, a huge, sharp-faced, elegant dog, gazing up at his master. Dogs symbolise fidelity and Richmond had certainly proved faithful to Charles through all that had brought him here. He had three younger brothers killed in action, and aged only thirty-six he was already in breaking health and destined for an early grave.

The four great peers were allowed to take three servants each and permitted to spend up to £500: a tenth of what had been spent on the funeral of the Parliamentarian general Essex in 1646.[3] They arrived at Windsor that afternoon, together with William Juxon. Richmond wore the insignia of the Order of the Garter, St George killing the dragon: that symbol of sin and of rebellion. The chivalric virtues the Order exalted – of a band of brothers bound to each other and their prince under God – had lain at the heart of Charles's view of kingship. Putting on his own George had been Charles's first action every morning, and taking it off was the last of his life.

As the men now entered the chapel where the Order was celebrated they saw that the impressive tomb of Charles's ancestor, Edward IV, lay open.[4] The vault was easily accessible and it had seemed an appropriate choice of burial spot to the military governor of the castle, Colonel Whitchcote. Parliament's latest orders were, however, that Charles be buried more anonymously, 'in H. VIII. his chapel, or the quire there'.[5]

Henry VIII had intended that a great mausoleum be built for him here, but the terror he had evoked had died with him and his orders had been ignored. The popish statues and ironwork destined for his tomb had lain abandoned in the junk room known as his 'chapel' for decades. In 1646 they had at last been sold or destroyed. Henry VIII's body lay instead in an unmarked grave beneath the stone floor between the quire stalls, and the exact spot was long forgotten. The noblemen now helped search for Henry's lost tomb in the narrow space of the quire, one tapping the ground with a staff, the others stamping with their boots. At last there was a hollow ring. The stones and earth were removed and Richmond stepped down into the gloom.

In the torchlight Richmond saw two coffins near each other, 'the one very large of antique form, the other little'. It was clear whose they were: Henry VIII and his third queen, Jane Seymour, the mother of his son. Each was covered with velvet cloth, perfectly preserved.[6]

Richmond ordered a girdle of lead be made for Charles's coffin, engraved 'KING CHARLES', along with the year of his death. The sexton was then asked to ensure the chapel was locked for the night.

The following morning, Charles's coffin was brought down into St George's Hall in readiness for the internment. There was a delay after it was discovered there had been a break-in at the vault. A soldier from the garrison was found carrying a piece of Henry VIII's skeleton. He said he had intended to whittle the bone into a handle for a knife.[7] The war had made plunder a way of life. Even Colonel Whitchcote had taken images connected with the Garter from the chapel.[8]

It was almost three o'clock in the afternoon when Charles's coffin was at last carried out of the hall. Thomas Herbert recalled a 'serene and clear day', the coffin borne by 'gentlemen that were of quality and in mourning' and the four peers carrying a black velvet pall.[9] Behind them Juxon led a short procession of their servants. As they stepped forward, however, it began to snow and the spinning flakes soon 'fell so fast, as by that time they came to the west end of the royal chapel, the black velvet pall was all white'.[10] The 'colour of innocence' was how Herbert later described it, and recalled Charles as 'the White King' who, it was said, was crowned in white. The loyal servant of Parliament surely did not believe in Charles's innocence that day and the snow may be a myth.* Yet Herbert's image fills the void where otherwise there is only the slow tramp of men walking. This was not a funeral, merely a burial. Colonel Whitchcote had refused Juxon permission to use the Church of England's Book of Common Prayer, reminding him it was 'put down' by Parliament.

No prayers were read as Charles's mourners gathered in the chapel, and it was in silence that his coffin was lowered into the blackness of the vault.

---

* The famous snowstorm described by Thomas Herbert is uncorroborated testimony recalled after the Restoration. Like the image of the smiling corpse, his tale reflects the propaganda of Charles's last testimony, the *Eikon Basilike*, that would sustain Royalists in the years ahead: the myth of Charles the martyr.

Two days after Charles was buried, the trial of Henry Rich, Earl of Holland, began. Once a client of the royal favourite George Villiers, Duke of Buckingham, Holland had become, as Groom of the Stool, Charles's closest body servant. Yet he had betrayed Charles to play a leading role in the outbreak of the first civil war. Holland had twice returned to the king's cause. His last adventure now looked set to cost Holland his life. Aging and ill, Holland stood accused of treason, but he remained as unrepentant of turning coat against Parliament as he had been about his earlier betrayal of the king.

The rebellion Holland had joined against the king in 1642 was a conservative revolt led by the political heirs of his uncle, Elizabeth I's last favourite, the 2nd Earl of Essex. He insisted his career was marked not by betrayal, but by his loyalty 'to the public and very particularly to Parliament'. He had hoped they would quickly secure Parliament's rights in a 'mixed monarchy' and the restoration of the Church of England's Calvinist credentials. It was the cause that had changed. As it became ever more radical it had 'carried them further than I thought reasonable, and, truly, there I left them', he admitted. 'But there is nothing I have said or done or professed … which has not been very constant and clear … to serve the King, Parliament, Religion.'[11]

On 6 March Holland's trial concluded in a guilty verdict. His role during the Eleven Years' Tyranny, when he had raised money for the king through Forest fines, and so aided Charles's bid to rule without Parliament, and his 'misstep' in 1643 when he had deserted Parliament's cause to join Charles at Oxford, both told against him. So did his breaking of his word not to betray Parliament again, and instead attempting to raise an army in 1648. John Bradshawe, who had pronounced the death sentence on the king, did the same on Holland.

Over the following three days Holland prepared for his death with prayer. Warwick, General Fairfax, his wife and friends pleaded with MPs to grant Holland mercy. His death sentence was, in the end, confirmed by a majority of only one: 'So his life was lost by that small part of a man's breath,' a relative recorded sadly.[12] On 9 March

1649, Holland was escorted to the scaffold outside Westminster Hall in New Palace Yard. He gave his speech explaining his actions, standing in the blood from the beheading earlier that morning of the Scottish commander, the Duke of Hamilton.

Holland, famous for his elegant dress, was ready now to 'outbrave death' in a good suit. It was a perk for an executioner to have the right to sell the clothes of the prisoner he had executed. Holland, however, had thought of this. 'Here, my friend,' he said to the executioner, handing him a bag of gold, 'let my clothes and my body alone. There is £10 for thee.[13] That is better than my clothes I am sure of it.' He was preparing to lie down on the low block, when he spoke to the executioner again: 'Friend, do you hear me, if you take up my head do not take off my cap.' He was about to lose his head. He did not want his head also to lose its hat.

Holland lay flat on the scaffold to position himself on the low block, and shuffled forward and backward on his stomach until he was lying in the exact place the executioner wanted, facing 'the hall of justice' where the king had also been convicted. Holland said a prayer and then thrust out his hands as a sign to the axeman. The executioner hesitated. 'Now! Now!' Holland cried, and before the final shout was out of his mouth his head fell.[14]

The life of Holland's friend and cousin Lucy Carlisle was, for a time, also at risk. Evidence of her leading involvement in the war of the Engagement had emerged at his trial. Less than a week after Holland's execution a guard arrived to arrest her at the house of her sister, the Countess of Leicester. She hid in her bedroom, but their commander, the regicide Colonel Thomas Harrison, knew she was in the house and demanded she appear. The arrest warrant was read to her in the hall and she was escorted out. Her sister tried to speak a few words to her but was pushed aside.

Lucy was taken away for cross-examination on suspicion of treason, and on 21 March taken to the Tower where she was kept 'close prisoner'. Lucy's many powerful near relatives eventually achieved her release on licence in the summer of 1651. She immediately continued her Royalist plotting, this time for Charles II, who was about to lead an invasion of England.

Unburdened by his father's passionate belief in the episcopal Church of England Charles II had become (in name) a Presbyterian. His reward had been a coronation in Edinburgh and a Scottish army with which to fight for his English throne. It did him little good. Charles II was defeated at the Battle of Worcester on 3 September 1651, and fled back into exile.

A batch of Lucy's letters, written to Charles II in 1648 when he was Prince of Wales, was discovered in the royal baggage captured on the battlefield near Worcester. Even more dangerously, a Royalist revealed how Lucy had continued to plot for the Royalist cause. Cromwell, the New Model Army and their allies were busy bringing their opponents to justice, be they conservative Royalists or radical Levellers. But Lucy was seen as yesterday's rebel. In March 1652 her freedom was confirmed.

A former courtier once saw Lucy during her enforced retirement sitting by herself at the top of Richmond Hill. She was gazing down at the Thames, and it seemed to him she was enjoying herself more than she had 'in all her former vanities'.[15] It is more likely that she was wistfully recalling these vanities. It was while swimming in the Thames that her friend and occasional rival, Mme de Chevreuse, had drawn crowds in the summer of 1638.[16] Now Chevreuse, like Lucy, was growing old and politically irrelevant. In Paris a satirical 'Geographical Map' of Louis XIV's court described her as 'a large, already rather ancient fortress', the exterior appearance still 'imposing but internally in a sad plight'.[17]

Meanwhile, Lucy was a mere onlooker in high politics of the English republic. The monarchy had been abolished in 1649 and the ancient coronation regalia – including the crown of Edward the Confessor, that symbol of a people's love for their king – were destroyed. Nothing would survive save for the small twelfth-century anointing spoon. But war continued. Ireland and Scotland were reduced to provinces of England under the new Commonwealth. The Scots lost their legal system for a time – and their national dignity. The Irish lost very much more: 25 per cent of the population died from famine and disease and many were sent as slaves to the colonies in the Caribbean, or as indentured labour to New England. Thus were the Catholics of Ireland 'taught liberty', as Hugh Peter put it.[18]

The long-held ambition of the Puritan and aristocratic colonisers to expand England's empire in the Americas was also not forgotten. Voyages of conquest were launched and England's Dutch rivals were defeated in the war of 1652–4. Fairfax had resigned in 1650, after refusing to lead the invasion of Scotland, but Cromwell had assumed the office of Lord Protector in 1653, and became a king in all but name. Mrs Cromwell was called 'Her Highness' and their daughters were known as 'princesses'. Warwick bore the sword of state at Cromwell's virtual coronation, a regal second inauguration as Protector, on 26 June 1657. The families even intermarried. On 14 November 1657 Cromwell's daughter, the princess Frances, married Warwick's heir, Robert Rich.

Warwick died the following spring of 1658. The war against Spain he had always pushed for had, in the end, proved less successful than he had hoped. But his own colonising activities are his legacy. Warwick, Rhode Island, Warwick County and the Warwick river, Virginia, would be just some of the places named after him in what is now the United States. He had been one of the towering figures of the civil war.

Cromwell died in September 1658. Charles I's sister, the Winter Queen, rejoiced at the death of a man she had referred to as 'the beast of Revelation' and to whom she had long wished 'the like end and speedily'.[19] In France, however, the news brought Charles I's widow, Henrietta Maria, no happiness. 'I do not as yet see any great advantage to us,' she wrote to a friend. The Royalist cause seemed quite defeated, with or without Cromwell. Cromwell's son Richard succeeded his father in an attempt to mimic the old hereditary system and secure the stability it had offered. Yet if Charles II was incapable of winning back the English crown, the Puritan Commonwealth was nevertheless to fall, leaving behind a lasting distrust in England for political radicalism.

Taxation had proved more arbitrary during the Commonwealth than it had been under Charles I, liberty was more restricted, and Parliament's privileges were ignored, while the bullying reformation of manners of Puritan piety continued to be detested. Richard had little of his father's mettle and stepped down as Protector in May 1659. In due course, a new Parliament backed by General Monck, the commander of the army of occupation in Scotland, recalled Charles II. The restored king entered London on his thirtieth birthday, 19 May 1660, to popular rejoicing.

In October 1660 ten of those associated with the regicide of Charles I were tried and executed, with another nineteen imprisoned for life. Amongst the victims was Hugh Peter, who had failed to escape back to New England as other pilgrims had done.[*] In the new year, the corpses of Oliver Cromwell and other long-dead regicides would be dug up, beheaded and dismembered like the corpses of the Ruthven brothers in Scotland on the day that Charles was born. Their shrivelled heads make a grim bookend to the king's story.

Meanwhile, on 2 November 1660, Henrietta Maria returned to London, her barge rowed up the Thames surrounded by a welcoming flotilla of boats. It was a low-key affair compared to her first entry in 1625, when the banks had been lined with cheering crowds. The Catholic queen who had fought so hard for her husband remained a controversial figure. She entered the palace without fanfare by the Privy Stairs and was installed in freshly decorated apartments. Her son also had silk taffetas and velvets in Stuart scarlet delivered from

---

[*] In due course Sir Henry Vane the younger, former governor of Massachusetts, would also go to the block.

the Great Wardrobe to upholster the carriages she would need, and for new fashionable dresses.[20]

As the queen dowager prepared to greet old courtiers, Lucy Carlisle was eager to see her former mistress once more. It was to be the first time they had met since 1642, when Henrietta Maria was preparing to flee London with the king and Lucy had failed to persuade them to stay. On 5 November Lucy enjoyed a good dinner at her rented house on the Strand, ordered her sedan chair be brought round to take her to court, and began her toilette. As she was almost ready to leave she took out a new ribbon for her audience with the queen. She never got to wear it. She suffered a massive stroke and died without being able to speak another word.[21] She was sixty-one.

Henrietta Maria made no recorded comment on the death of her former lady-in-waiting. There were other deaths to preoccupy her as she greeted curious courtiers in the palace where her husband had spent his last hours. She had often told her friends that she did not know how she had 'survived the blow' of Charles's beheading.[22] Two of their children had died since then – the watchful Elizabeth, at Carisbrooke Castle in September 1650, aged only fourteen, and Henry aged twenty, of smallpox in September 1660. Their daughter Mary – Lucy Carlisle's god-daughter – would die in England in December 1660, also of smallpox.

Henrietta Maria disappointed those who first saw her in London now. The diarist Samuel Pepys described her as 'a very little plain old woman'. She had once been an innovator in the theatre, an arms buyer, and a warrior with a conquering army, yet she had 'nothing more in her presence in any respect, nor garb than any ordinary woman'. In time, however, that view would change: the scarlet taffeta was made up into new gowns and Henrietta Maria's formidable charm would shine again. The court of the queen dowager became the most elegant in England and Henrietta Maria amused and entertained with stories of her rivalry with Buckingham, and of the favourite little dog she had once carried under shell-fire. She even declared to her sister

Christine that she was, once more, 'the most contented person in the world'.[23]

New pictures replaced some of Charles's great art collection, which had been dissipated all over Europe, as well as in Britain. Leonardo da Vinci's portrait of St John had been sold for a mere 140 livres – a little over £11 (only £1 more than Holland had given his executioner in lieu of his bloodied suit).* Cromwell had kept other pictures for himself, and had had a surprising preference for Italian artists, hanging his palaces with some of Charles's erotic nudes.[24] It was not just great men, however, who had acquired Charles's pictures and other treasures. His ordinary subjects had formed syndicates to invest in his art collection and the Commonwealth had paid debts with art. One syndicate had helped a minor official purchase two paintings by Raphael, while a plumber had ended up with a Titian in part payment of his bill for palace repairs. Indeed, there were small houses across London hanging works painted by Van Dyck, Rubens and Correggio for palaces and princes.[25] Some were now returned willingly, some less so: much remains in private collections and museums across the globe.

In September 1662, Pepys saw Henrietta Maria at court once more, sitting with Charles II and his queen as well as his current mistress, Lady Castlemaine, and his bastard son by Lucy Walter, soon to be made the Duke of Monmouth.[26] Henrietta Maria was unfazed by the sexual proclivities of kings. Her younger son, James, was also a notorious lover of women. Charles II admired the fact that James's pursuit of women surpassed even his own dedication to it. The king was ungenerous, however, to the loyal, flame-haired spy Jane Whorwood. She had returned to her violent husband after Charles's execution, and her brutish spouse had injured her several times. Believing her life was at risk, she had left him and they separated officially, but he never paid

---

* The late Duke of Buckingham's white suit that he had worn in Paris in 1625 had, by contrast, been estimated at a value of over £4,000.

her the money the courts had ordered him to, and she lived in poverty until her death in 1684 aged seventy-two.

Henrietta Maria had returned to France for good in the spring of 1665. She wished to be with her youngest child, Henrietta, who had been born while she was on the run during the civil war, and was the only one of her children who had grown up with her. Philip IV of Spain died in September 1665, bequeathing his throne to a son by his second wife and niece, Mariana of Austria. The result of generations of inbreeding, Charles II of Spain was mentally and physically disabled, and incapable of having children. In France, by contrast, Louis XIV was busy creating Europe's greatest absolute monarchy: France under the Sun King, and not Spain, was to be the great power of the new age.

Louis XIV's mother, Anne of Austria, had called Charles I's death 'a blow which ought to make all kings tremble'. Louis XIV did not forget it and he treated his aunt with great respect. When Henrietta Maria died on 10 September 1669 he paid for a state funeral. Although her reputation today remains tainted by old prejudices, she had been as remarkable as any of the consorts of Henry VIII, whose reputations have been popularly reassessed. The English ambassador sent a delegation to the Louvre to retrieve the last of her goods. They found, tucked away in a cornelian case, a miniature of Charles I. It was the only portrait of him she had kept. It had been painted in 1623, the year she had first seen him in the Louvre; it was a likeness neither of a martyr nor of a murderer, but of a 'venturous knight' who still had his dreams to fulfil, and all his great adventures before him.

POSTSCRIPT

UNLIKE HIS FATHER, CHARLES WAS NOT A WORDSMITH. HE WAS neither a keen author nor an enthusiastic public speaker. His was a cinematic imagination and his eye encompassed far more than the pictures he hung on his walls. He had used the visual – a theatre of ceremony, ritual and beauty – both at court and in church, to reform and shape a socially deferential, hierarchical society that was appropriate to divine-right monarchy and sacramental kingship.

A deferential society suggests to us a slavish fawning to snobs with an unearned and unjustified sense of superiority. Today we strive to create a 'meritocracy' in which people are able to achieve their potential through their own efforts. There is, however, another perspective. A meritocracy also suggests that those who are not successful have less merit than those who excel; and that those who have success owe nothing to luck, or the help of the less successful, but only to their own efforts and brilliance. Ours is a self-congratulatory system that also fosters a sense of entitlement.

The hierarchical society Charles imagined was underpinned by Christ's example of self-sacrifice. Everyone owed service, both to those above them (commoner to noble, noble to king, king to God) and to those beneath them, to whom they owed a duty of care. This included protecting the weak, and promoting the talented and the brave. That was the theory. Charles wanted to make it a reality. It was not a contemptible ambition. It was, however, an ambition that he failed spectacularly to achieve, and therein lies his tragedy.

Charles was, in his private life, 'the best master, the best friend, the best husband, the best father'.[1] He was both loving and loved. Yet Charles distrusted appeals to the emotions, in part because he had absorbed his father's lessons concerning the dangers of 'populism' (by which he meant demagogy), but also because he had no instinct for it. He was unable to act spontaneously: to let his spirit and passions pour out to the wonder and terror of his subjects. He found people difficult to read and his inability to interpret their actions and feelings often left him angry and frustrated. Form and order mediated relationships in a way he was comfortable with. Equally, any challenge to form and order felt extremely threatening.

Charles accepted that there were great benefits to working with Parliament, but, like his father, he never really appreciated its significance to the English people. Nor was he able to overcome his instincts, trust more to his MPs, and to his own power to control and intimidate them, accepting the compromises and slights to his regal authority that the messy business of politics sometimes required. He was always self-righteous – but rarely ruthless.

The fallen king was remembered as having had a 'compassion of nature which restrained him from ever doing a hard-hearted thing'.[2] His enemies, fearful of the reversals to Calvinism during the Thirty Years War, and believing they were fighting for its very survival, had no such compunction.

The new media of pamphlets and news-sheets, sermons and political speeches, all helped to build a narrative that would justify rebellion and foreign invasion as a necessary defence against 'popery', with godly peers and their Puritan allies whipping up ethnic and religious hatred to create a climate of fear. Targeted and organised mob violence was used to intimidate English MPs, and misogynistic attitudes to women helped demonise Henrietta Maria as the papist-in-chief. From slashing the 'popish' pictures in her chapel, it would be just a short step to slash the faces of the 'popish whores', the laundry women and wives in the Royalist baggage train at Naseby.

Not all Royalists cared, however, for the image of a saintly and merciful 'white king'. It was all very well to rely 'wholly on the innocence of a virtuous life', but, they pointed out, it had exposed Charles 'fatally to calamitous ruin'.[3] His failure to punish London for the lynching of Buckingham's astrologer Lambe in 1628 had only encouraged further violence, since it demonstrated that 'the king had rather patience enough to bear such indignities than resolution to revenge them'. Similarly the riot in St Giles's Kirk in Edinburgh against the Scottish prayer book in 1637 might not have paved the way to the Bishops' Wars, 'had the king caused the chief ringleaders of these tumults to be put to death'.[4] Archbishop Laud's description of Charles, written in the aftermath of Strafford's execution in 1641, was perhaps the most damning of all Royalist criticism: 'a mild and gracious prince who knew not how to be, or be made great'.[5]

It is worth remembering, however, that while flinching from cruel acts may be a political liability, it is not a moral weakness. Even as the fighting began Charles sought order amidst the disorder, finding time in the weeks after Edgehill to read and make suggested changes to his collection of quarto texts by Beaumont and Fletcher, controlling characters and story in a way he could not control his subjects in life.* But Charles was becoming courageous, resilient, and increasingly hard-nosed. He showed remarkable skills of leadership during the civil war and inspired great loyalty. Parliament had control of London and the majority of England's wealth and population. For

---

* Charles was more interested in plays than is commonly realised – as well as less prim. He contributed to the creation of the plot of James Shirley's racy play *The Gamester* and loved the results when it played at court in 1634. Percy Simpson, 'King Charles I as Dramatic Critic', *The Bodleian Quarterly Record*, Vol. VIII, No. 92, pp. 257–262.

a time, they also had the backing of the Scots. Despite these advantages it took four years for them to defeat Charles militarily. 'He was very fearless in his person' in battle, and had shown equal courage on the grindstone of captivity.[6]

Imprisoned from 1646, Charles never gave up the struggle to get the best terms possible for his restoration as king. In his last negotiations with Parliament before Pride's Purge, his final sticking points remained his consistent refusal to betray his God by denying episcopacy, or his brothers in arms by giving up his friends to punishment. Until the last day of his trial he hoped he could yet strike a deal. He had always underestimated the ruthlessness of his enemies.

Parliament had by then become a monster that devoured its own. The old Puritan William Prynne, who had been cropped of his ears in the 1630s and had acted as the prosecution lawyer against William Laud, was one of the MPs purged in 1648 – considered too moderate, too accommodating to Charles for the tastes of the New Model Army and their friends. Prynne even became something of a Cavalier hero in the years ahead, as the British kingdoms became subject to a virtual military dictatorship.

Today Charles's principal legacy is the Church of England, with its bishops and choral music, and which even in our secular age, and to many non-Anglicans, remains interwoven with the culture of this kingdom. At St George's Chapel, Windsor, a wreath is laid during evensong every year on the anniversary of Charles's death. The banners of the Garter knights hang above the stalls as choral music is sung in remembrance of the former sovereign of the Order. A flawed prince, but also principled and brave, Charles had been a better exemplar of a chivalric knight than he ever was a king.

APPENDIX

LUCY CARLISLE AS MILADY DE WINTER

BUCKINGHAM'S EMBASSY TO FRANCE IN 1625 AND THE TRADE WAR with France of the following year provide the complex political and diplomatic background to a number of fictional stories and gossip, often taken as fact, which helped inspire Dumas' *The Three Musketeers*.

Taken together the earlier accounts – some dating back to the late seventeenth century and other nineteenth-century forgeries of seventeenth-century memoirs – describe a plot by Richelieu to destroy the reputations of Buckingham and the queen consort of France, Anne of Austria. The origins of the story lie in Buckingham's courtly attention to Anne in 1625. Lucy Carlisle is presented as so jealous of his compliments to Anne that she agrees to work for Richelieu. Lucy is to steal some diamond pendants Anne had given to Buckingham, and which Anne had taken from a necklace that had been a gift from her husband, Louis XIII. Lucy seizes her opportunity during a ball at Windsor. Buckingham is wearing his Garter sash pinned with Anne's diamonds. Lucy, dancing with him, surreptitiously cuts off two stones. When Buckingham discovers the theft he guesses what is being plotted. As Lord High Admiral, he shuts the Channel ports. Buckingham has new stones cut in time for Anne to appear at a ball wearing the full necklace, and Richelieu's plans are thwarted.[1]

In Dumas, this story is repeated with Lucy's part reinvented in the character of the fictional Milady de Winter. In reality the only diamonds we know were given to Buckingham in France came from Louis XIII.[2] And far from being deadly enemies, Buckingham remained on good terms with Lucy 'Milady' Carlisle, although the same cannot be said of his relations, who detested her.

ACKNOWLEDGEMENTS

WRITING A ONE-VOLUME BIOGRAPHY OF CHARLES WAS A DAUNTING prospect and I couldn't have managed it without help. I am particularly grateful to Dr David Scott for reading a messy draft and commenting on it with patience and generosity. Since I didn't feel I could force him to read it a hundred times, and I work by a process of writing and rewriting, I may have swapped old errors for new ones, for which, of course, I am alone responsible. I am also grateful for conversations and email contacts I have had with other historians. John Adamson (who drew my attention to Lucy Carlisle), Sarah Poynting (with whom I have swapped transcripts, and who is editing a book on Charles I's writings), John Guy, Peter Marshall, Desmond Seward and Erin Griffey have shown much kindness and support.

Thank you also to archivist Peter Foden for his invaluable help with transcriptions and some translations, and to my friend Dominic Pearce for his crucial help with other translations, and also to my father-in-law, Gerard de Lisle. The staff at the British Library and London Library are always extremely helpful, and I would particularly like to mention those at the London Library's Country Orders Department who post me books or email me scanned pages, and make a huge difference to my working life. I would further like to thank my supportive and very patient editors Becky Hardie, Penny Hoare, Clive Priddle and David Milner, as well as my ever wonderful and incredibly efficient agent, Georgina Capel.

I am extremely grateful also for the generosity of the Duke of Rutland, who granted me permission to research from his incredible archives, to Sir William Dugdale and others who also granted me access to previously unrecorded royal letters and to the Earl and Countess of Denbigh for allowing me to photograph some of their remarkable Stuart relics. To Philip Mould for the images he freely lent me, to Florence Evans of the Weiss Gallery, to Dominic Gwynn of Goetze and Gwynn, to Simon Wright and the Sealed Knot Society, and also to the owner of Charles I's saddle, who rarely allows the publication of any images of this royal relic from the battlefield of Naseby. Finally, I would like to thank Tracey Doyle and Janette Herbert for their huge support during times of family illness, as well as Flick Rohde and Nicola Vann.

NOTES

Abbreviations

BL	British Library
CSPD	Calendar of State Papers, Domestic
CSPV	Calendar of State Papers relating to Venice
HLRO	House of Lords Record Office
HMC	Historical Manuscripts Commission
MHS	Massachusetts Historical Society
ODNB	*Oxford Dictionary of National Biography*
PRO	Public Records Office
TNA	The National Archives

Author's Note

1. Sir Simonds d'Ewes quoted in Alastair Bellany and Thomas Cogswell, *The Murder of King James I* (2015), p. 9; David Nichol Smith, *Characters from the Histories and Memoirs of the Seventeenth Century* (1918), p. 9.

Preface: Venturous Knight

1. For the best introduction to the Reformation and the Wars of Religion, see Peter Marshall's *The Reformation, A Very Short*

Introduction (2009), and for the full story of the English Reformation see his *Heretics and Believers* (2017).

2. The Reform churches had followed the beliefs of Huldrych Zwingli and later of John Calvin.

3. The origins of the term Huguenot is uncertain. They had been behind a generation of civil wars that had culminated in Louis XIII's Huguenot father, Henri de Bourbon, becoming heir to the French throne. Since Parisians were prepared to fight to the death rather than accept a Protestant king, Henri had converted to Catholicism before he was crowned as Henri IV. 'Paris is worth a Mass' were his apocryphal words.

4. In England the Reform Protestantism introduced by Henry VIII's son, Edward VI, had been swept away on his death by his Catholic half-sister Mary Tudor. If she had had children, rather than the Protestant Elizabeth as her heir, it was highly likely England would have remained Catholic under them.

5. James also feared Jesuit claims made in 'A Conference on the Next Succession' (1594/5) that monarchy was essentially elective and that the Tudor monarchy was a clear example of this.

6. Godfrey Goodman's history of James's court describes a Privy Council meeting that took place only hours after Elizabeth's death in 1603. There was a discussion on the wording of the letter the council was to write to James. Cecil produced a note composed by the 2nd Earl of Essex, 'written to some private friends, that when the time came the King of Scots might be accepted with some conditions'. Those at the meeting who supported a motion to limit the king's powers were outvoted. For more on this see Leanda de Lisle, *After Elizabeth* (2005), p. 131.

7. CSPD 12 addenda (407).

8. Julia Pardoe, *Life and Memoirs of Marie de' Medici* (1852), Vol. III, p. 218.

9. With around 20 million people, the population of France was almost three times larger than that of England, Scotland and Ireland put together.

10. In 1610 Henri IV had been poised to intervene in a dispute over the succession in two territories within the Holy Roman Empire. Although a Catholic, Henri had been supporting two Protestant candidates against the choices of the Bourbon dynasty's European rivals, the Habsburgs. His carriage had come to a halt in a narrow Paris street when a tall, red-haired man leapt onto the wheel by his window. The heavy leather curtain had been pulled back and the man reached in and stabbed Henri twice in the chest. The king was dashed back to the Louvre, but was already dead by the time he arrived. 'What we saw beggars description,' witnesses reported. 'The whole court shocked and stunned with grief, standing silent and motionless as statues.' Henri IV's widow, Marie de' Medici, was with Louis, weeping, and nearby his corpse was lying on a bed. The torture and the details of execution of the murderer, François Ravaillac, are too horrible to describe, even in this book, in which there are many horrible deaths. Bibliothèque nationale, Charles de la Roncière, *Catalogue des manuscrits de la collection des Cinq-Cents de Colbert* (1908), pp. 12ff, 64–96; *Oeuvres d'Etienne Pasquier* (1723), Vol. II, col. 1063–4.

11. Baron Edward Herbert of Cherbury, *The Life of Edward, Lord Herbert of Cherbury* (2012), p. 37.

12. *Letters of King Charles I*, ed. Sir Charles Petrie (1935), p. 8.

13. As Queen of England Henriette-Marie would be known for a short time as Henry, and thereafter as Mary.

14. *Letters of King Charles I*, ed. Petrie, p. 9.

15. Ibid.

16. They had taken rooms at an inn on the rue Saint-Jacques. Today it is a backstreet in the Latin Quarter. Then it was one of the main roads out of Paris. Cherbury, p. 45.

17. CSPV 1619–21 (576).

18. By the end of the century Protestantism would be reduced to a mere fifth of Europe's land area.

Chapter 1: 'Dearest Son'

1. Bishop Hackett quoted in Philippe Erlanger, *George Villiers, Duke of Buckingham* (1951), p. 49.
2. Edward Hyde, Earl of Clarendon quoted in David Nichol Smith, *Characters from the Histories and Memoirs of the Seventeenth Century* (1918), pp. 12, 13–14, 15.
3. Come the New Year, James rewarded Anna (only he called her Annie) with a fabulous jewel worth 1,333 Scottish pounds; Leanda de Lisle, *After Elizabeth* (2005), p. 71 and notes.
4. Thanks to Erin Griffey for this reference: Frederick Devon (ed.), *Issues of the Exchequer* (extracts of the Pell Records, Order Books of James) (1837), p. 10.
5. CSPD 1603–10 (264).
6. Sir Philip Warwick, quoted in Smith, p. 53.
7. Pauline Gregg, *Charles I* (2000), p. 295.
8. Thanks to Erin Griffey for this reference and information: Devon (ed.), *Issues of the Exchequer*, p. 48.
9. Carola Oman, *The Winter Queen* (1938, revd edn 2000), p. 36.
10. Mark Kishlansky, *Charles I* (2014), p. 12.
11. Nearly thirty years later Charles still had a small bronze pacing horse that Henry had admired and which he had brought him on his deathbed to cheer him up.
12. Oman, p. 63. The ship, the *Prince Royal*, had been named after Henry, and may be the ship that inspired Shakespeare's *The Tempest*.
13. 'A pattern for a King's Inaugeration' in *James VI and I: Political Works*, ed. J. P. Sommerville (2006), p. 229.
14. Gondomar quoted in Gregg, p. 33.
15. Francis Bacon, *Of the Advancement and Proficience of Learning* (BL, Humanities, C.46.i.1.), annotation by Charles I; thanks to Sarah Poynting for this reference and transcription.

16. 'Si vis omnia subicere, te subice rationi' (a misquotation from Seneca – it should have 'tibi' after 'omnia'). Thanks to Sarah Poynting for this information.

17. Edward Hyde, Earl of Clarendon observed that Charles had 'a nature inclined to adventures'. Glyn Redworth, *The Prince and the Infanta: The Cultural Politics of the Spanish Match* (2003), p. 75; for 'extreme resolutions' see Dorset to Salisbury [York], 27 June 1642, HMC Hatfield, xxii, 372.

18. William Benchley Rye, *England as seen by Foreigners* (1865, revd edn 2000), p. 133; Andrew Thrush, http://www.historyof-parliamentonline.org/periods/stuarts/death-prince-henry-and-succession-crisis-1612–1614.

19. Ronald Lightbown, 'Charles I and the Art of the Goldsmith' in Arthur MacGregor (ed.), *The Late King's Goods* (1989), pp. 233–55.

20. It is often asserted that Charles spoke with a Scottish accent, although no contemporary comments on it. I discussed this with Sarah Poynting, who is editing a comprehensive book on Charles's writings. She has found no real evidence that he did, beyond a few traces of Scottish spelling – such as 'hes' for 'has'. I do think, however, that this suggests an occasional and slight Scottish inflection.

21. The first reference to Murray being a whipping boy that I can find dates from long after Charles's death, in Gilbert Burnet, *History of My Own Times* (1724/1833), Vol. I, p. 436. Earlier, Thomas Fuller's *Church History* (1655) had claimed Barnaby Fitzpatrick was whipping boy to Edward VI. This in turn (it seems to me) was probably influenced by Samuel Rowley's 1605 play *To See Me is to Know Me* in which Henry VIII mentions having had a whipping boy. The play was written shortly after James's tracts on divine right were published in England. I am not aware of any earlier such stories.

22. James dedicated a collection of his writings to Charles in 1616.

23. *Eikon Basilike*, p. 167; Richard Cust, *Charles I: A Political Life* (2007), p. 13.

24. John Jewel, quoted in Leanda de Lisle, *The Sisters Who Would be Queen* (2008), p. 196; Ronald G. Asch, *Sacral Kingship Between Disenchantment and Re-Enchantment* (2014), p. 65.

25. *Mémoires de Madame de Motteville*, tr. Katherine Wormeley, Vol. II (1902), p. 84.

26. For the first decade of her reign Elizabeth felt not much less threatened by Protestants than by Catholics, and with good reason. Edward VI's Privy Councils – who had imposed the first Protestant Prayer Book on England when he was eleven – had treated her poorly. On his death in 1553 his councillors had then backed her exclusion from the succession, along with that of her Catholic half-sister Mary, in favour of her married cousin, Lady Jane Grey/Dudley. Fearful that even now they would prefer a married queen she kept her married Protestant heir, Jane's sister Katherine Grey/Seymour, imprisoned, and bastardised her children. It was only after Katherine's death in 1568 that Mary, Queen of Scots, became the greater threat. See de Lisle, *Sisters*, or relevant chapters in Leanda de Lisle, *Tudor: The Family Story* (2013).

27. De Lisle, *Tudor*, p. 356.

28. De Lisle, *After Elizabeth*, p. 29.

29. It was also key to England's victory against the papal Antichrist in the war on evil.

30. As Elizabeth had never trusted the nobility, Protestant or Catholic, she had worked hard to nurture the affections of the common sort. Unfortunately her great subjects had learned that they too could appeal to public opinion – a dangerous legacy for her Stuart successors. Essex had been loved as a hero of the war with Spain, and was expert at self-promotion. By contrast his leading rival Robert Cecil, Elizabeth's Secretary of State, was detested. Elizabeth had always ensured her officials bore the blame for unpopular

decisions. The result was that the people blamed Cecil for the failings of her government – and not the queen.

31. The ballads being sung about Essex at court was reported in a contemporary journal; see de Lisle, *After Elizabeth*, p. 8.

32. Traditionally an English king was expected to live off his own resources. Only in exceptional circumstances would Parliament raise the taxes known as subsidies that the Crown needed to pay their extraordinary expenses. It was a system designed in the Middle Ages and was no longer fit for purpose. Inflation and corruption in both assessment and collection meant Parliament's subsidies were worth a fraction of what they had been under the Tudors. One had plunged in value from £130,000 at the end of Elizabeth's reign to £55,000 in the early 1620s, and that is without counting the effects of inflation. Robert Brenner, *Merchants and Revolution* (2003), p. 200.

33. Katie Whitaker, *A Royal Passion* (2010), p. 28.

34. Clarendon quoted in Smith, pp. 13–14.

35. BL, Add. MS 19368, f. 112.

36. *James VI and I: Political Works*, ed. Sommerville, p. 230.

37. 'A pattern for a King's Inauguration' in ibid., p. 249.

38. Jonathan Scott, *England's Troubles* (2000), p. 151.

Chapter 2: Becoming King

1. *The Letters of Elizabeth, Queen of Bohemia*, ed. L. M. Baker (1953), p. 54.

2. John Rushworth, *Historical Collections of Private Passages of State*, Vol. I (1721), p. 40.

3. Specifically there were efforts to prove the legitimacy of William Seymour, Earl of Hertford, the senior grandson of the Tudor princess Lady Katherine Grey. Henry VIII had demoted the Stuart line of his elder sister Margaret in line of succession in order to protect his children from a potentially powerful Stuart rival. In their place he had promoted descendants of his younger

sister. In 1554, Mary I executed the senior of these, the so-called nine days' queen, Lady Jane Grey, for treason. Jane was regarded as a virtual Protestant martyr. The second sister, Katherine, was Elizabeth I's heir, but Elizabeth saw her as a threat and had refused to recognise her marriage to Hertford's father. This had made his father a bastard and had ensured the accession of the Stuarts. Early in James's reign Hertford had attempted to restore his tainted royal blood by marrying James's cousin, Arbella Stuart, and so uniting the lines of Henry VIII's two sisters. He was sent to the Tower from where he escaped, while Arbella starved herself to death there in 1615. Hertford had subsequently married the 3rd Earl of Essex's favourite sister, Frances. The attempts to prove his legitimacy were being made in June 1621 by the 2nd Earl of Essex's close friend Henry Wriothesley, Earl of Southampton; Henry Ellis (ed.), *Original Letters Illustrative of English History*, Vol. III (1824), p. 239. In the same year Hertford began building a vast tomb for his grandparents at Salisbury Cathedral, one which advertised Elizabeth I's unfair treatment of the couple. Hertford also commissioned several large-scale copies of a miniature of Katherine with his father as a baby in the Tower. He kept a picture of his great-aunt, Lady Jane Grey, and of his first wife, Arbella Stuart. (Longleat House, Seymour Papers, Vol. 6, f. 241, will of Frances Seymour, 1674: 'I do also give and bequeath to my s[ai]d grandaughter [*sic*] the lady Frances Thynne ... my picture of the Lady Arabella my dear Lord's first wife now hanging in the dining roome, and the picture of the Queen Jane Grey, now hanging in my chamber with another the picture of my Lady Katherine.' Thanks to Dr Stephan Edwards for this reference.)

4. Francis Bacon, *Of the Advancement and Proficience of Learning* (BL, Humanities, C.46.i.1.); Loquacity, XXXI, p. 315, Rr2r. Contra. Thanks to Sarah Poynting for this reference and transcription.

5. Sir Simonds d'Ewes quoted in Alastair Bellany and Thomas Cogswell, *The Murder of King James I* (2015), p. 9.

6. Michael C. Questier (ed.), *Stuart Dynastic Policy and Religious Politics, 1621–1625* (2009), p. 41.

7. Zahira Veliz, 'Signs of Identity in *Lady with a Fan* by Diego Velázquez: Costume and Likeness Reconsidered', *Art Bulletin*, Vol. 86, No. 1 (March 2004), p. 87.

8. The University of Santiago de Compostela in Spain has calculated what is called the inbreeding coefficient for each individual across sixteen generations of the Habsburgs, using genealogical information for Philip IV's son Carlos II and 3,000 of his relatives and ancestors. The inbreeding coefficient indicates the likelihood that an individual would receive two identical genes at a given position on a chromosome because of the relatedness of their parents. By the time Philip's eventual heir, Carlos II, was born (mentally and physically disabled), the inbreeding coefficient had increased considerably down through the generations, from 0.025 for Philip I to 0.254 for Carlos II – almost as high as would be expected for the offspring of a marriage between a parent and child or brother and sister.

9. Jonathan Brown and J. H. Elliott, *A Palace for a King* (1980), pp. 31, 32.

10. Ibid., p. 41.

11. Rubens to Palamede de Fabri sieur de Valavez, 10 January 1625: Fiona Donovan, *Rubens and England* (2004), p. 61. I have altered the translation here from 'the greatest amateur of paintings' to make more sense to the modern ear; also see Donovan on James and art, p. 86.

12. Bellany and Cogswell, p. 11.

13. John Colin Dunlop (ed.), *Memoirs of Spain during the Reign of Philip IV and Charles II*, Vol. I, p. 30 (print on demand).

14. Although Buckingham promises having once 'got hold of your bedpost never to quit it' he may not have been referring to a

sexual relationship, but of his desire to regain physical proximity to the king as the fount of honour, patronage and power. It was not unusual to greet a king by embracing his legs. Nevertheless it is difficult to imagine such letters being written to, say, Henry VIII. Bellany and Cogswell, pp. 12, 13.

15. Jonathan Scott, *England's Troubles* (2000), p. 84.

16. Ibid., p. 104.

17. Mark Charles Fissel (ed.), *War and Government in Britain, 1598–1650* (1991), pp. 111, 112; Geoffrey Parker, *Global Crisis: War, Climate Change and Catastrophe in the Seventeenth Century* (2013), p. 32

18. The war policy had its opponents. There were MPs and peers who regretted the failure of the Spanish alliance. They saw Spain as a means of containing the growing maritime power of the Dutch and the threat this posed to English commercial interests. Meanwhile the advocates of war differed on how best to achieve their aims. Some wanted to employ a mercenary force to attack Spanish Flanders, so forcing the Habsburgs to divert troops from the Palatinate. Others hoped to see royal support for their privateering and colonising efforts in the Americas.

19. Bellany and Cogswell, p. xxiv.

20. Ibid., p. 219.

21. Ibid., p. 84.

22. CSPD 27 March 1625 (2).

23. Ellis (ed.), Vol. III, p. 244.

Chapter 3: A Marriage Alliance

1. Hackneys were licensed to ply for trade from 1625, with charges regulated by Parliament.

2. CSPV April 1625 (17).

3. Charles's late mother, Anna, was reputed to have been a Catholic convert. But Anna's brother was the Lutheran Christian IV of Denmark, not the King of France, and she had also had the tact to die while the Thirty Years War was still in its infancy.

4. Quoted in Mark Kishlansky, *Charles I* (2014), p. 18.
5. Charles Cotolendi, *La Vie de très-haute et très-puissante princesse, Henriette-Marie de France, reyne de la Grande-Bretagne* (1690), pp. 10ff; Gesa Stedman, *Cultural Exchange in Seventeenth Century France and England* (2013), p. 30 and note.
6. Cotolendi, pp. 10ff; Stedman, p. 30 and note; CSPV 1625–6 (61).
7. CSPV 16 May (61); Erin Griffey, *On Display* (2015), p. 36.
8. *A True Discourse of all the Royal Passages, Tryumphs and Ceremonies, observed at the Contract and Mariage of the High and flighty CHARLES, King of Great Britain, and the most Excellentest of Ladies, the Lady HENRIETTA MARIA of Burbon, sister to the most Christian King of FRANCE* (1625), p. 8.
9. CSPV 9 May (47).
10. Griffey, p. 52.
11. CSPD 14 May 1625: Charles borrowed money off the Fielding family, for example, and they have kept the receipts for the funeral expenses they paid for.
12. Yet more diamonds glittered at his spurs, his sword, his girdle, his hatband, and he wore with a feather that was all of diamonds. *Mémoires de Madame de Motteville*, tr. Katherine Wormeley, Vol. I (1886), pp. 31–7; *Collection des Mémoires Relatifs a l'histoire de France*, ed. A. Petitot (1824), Vol. XXXVI, pp. 342–9; Richelieu, *Mémoires*, ed. A. Petitot (1823), Vol. V, p. 89.
13. *Mémoires de P. de la Porte*, eds. Petitot and Monmarque, Series II, Vol. LIX (1817), pp. 297–9.
14. Laura Knoppers, *Politicizing Domesticity from Henrietta Maria to Milton's Eve* (2011), pp. 29, 30.
15. Sir Philip Warwick, *Memories of the Reigne of Charles I* (1701), p. 14; Charles had shown loyalty to many of his father's former office holders, confirming them in their former places. This was disappointing for all those who hoped for a shake-up and new preferment.

16. Full name: Armand Jean du Plessis, Cardinal-Duc de Richelieu et de Fronsac. On the garden, see *Diary of John Evelyn*, 27 February 1644.

17. The gardens were reputed to be amongst the finest in the kingdom.

18. The title Earl of Warwick, first held by their father, had previously been held by the Dudley family. It thus linked the Rich family to the Dudley family's history: the anti-Spanish stance of the Puritan leader Robert Dudley, Earl of Leicester, who was the 2nd Earl of Essex's stepfather, and to those Edwardian Protestant reforms spearheaded by Leicester's father, and which culminated in the radical 1552 prayer book. Most famously, it was previously a Plantagenet title, held by the fifteenth-century Warwick the Kingmaker.

19. Warwick had joined the recently defunct Virginia Company in 1612 and was one of its largest stockholders. He was also a founder member and largest stockholder in the 1614 Somers Island (Bermuda) Company. Further colonial enterprises would follow.

20. Equivalent to a King of England's Groom of the Stool.

21. For contemporary descriptions of her, see note 36 in Zahira Veliz, 'Signs of Identity in *Lady with a Fan* by Diego Velázquez: Costume and Likeness Reconsidered', *Art Bulletin*, Vol. 86, No. 1 (March 2004), pp. 75–95; Richelieu, Vol. IV, p. 74.

22. A. Lloyd Moote, *Louis XIII* (1989), p. 193.

23. Some observers believed that Buckingham's attentions exceeded what was decent, and, it is said, infuriated Louis when he heard about them.

24. Convents and monasteries were as popular as, and often performed a similar function to, modern 'mindfulness' and other therapy retreats for such things as anxiety.

25. CSPV 1625–6 (92).

26. See Griffey, Appendix I, pp. 40–1.

27. Katie Whitaker, *A Royal Passion* (2010), p. 51, note 36.

28. CSPV 1625–6 (153).
29. Griffey, pp. 40–1.
30. *Letters of Queen Henrietta Maria*, ed. Mary Anne Everett Green (1857), p. 9.
31. Griffey, p. 40.
32. CSPV 1625–6 (117); Gordon Albion, *Charles I and the Court of Rome* (1935), p. 77 and note 2.
33. *Letters of King Charles I*, ed. Sir Charles Petrie (1935), p. 239. Shorter and longer versions of this letter exist – and may have been given to the queen at the same time. The shorter, with minor variations, survives in two manuscripts in the Parisian Archives nationales under the title 'Instruction de la Reine Marie de Medicis'. The longer version of the letter, which may contain additions by Cardinal de Bérulle, is in the Bibliothèque nationale de France under the title 'Instructions données par Marie de Medicis ä sa fille Henriette de France, Reyne d'Angleterre'. I have quoted from the longer version. For the further details on these letters (and more), see Karen Britland's brilliant PhD thesis for the University of Leeds, 'Neoplatonic identities: Literary Representation and the politics of Henrietta Maria's Court Circle' (2000), esp. pp. 41, 42.
34. *Mémoires de Madame de Motteville*, Vol. II (1902), p. 86.
35. CSPD 9 June 1625.

Chapter 4: 'Under the Eyes of Christendom'

1. Karen Britland, 'Neoplatonic identities: Literary Representation and the politics of Henrietta Maria's Court Circle', PhD thesis, University of Leeds (2000), pp. 43, 44. This is my own loose translation of an anonymous tract purporting to have been written by the queen on her leaving France, dated 1625.
2. Celia Fiennes, http://digital.library.upenn.edu/women/fiennes/saddle/saddle.html.

3. Henrietta Maria suffered from scoliosis – a curvature of the spine that reduced her height; Dominic Pearce, *Henrietta Maria* (2015), p. 40.

4. Thomas Birch, *The Court and Times of Charles I* (1849), Vol. I, p. 30.

5. *Basilikon Doron* in *James VI and I: Political Works*, ed. J. P. Sommerville (2006), p. 42.

6. Mme de Chevreuse was heavily pregnant and when she gave birth to a daughter in July, before her return to France, Charles would play godfather to her baby girl.

7. BL, Add. MS 72331, No. 174, Wooley (17 June 1625); Alastair Bellany and Thomas Cogswell, *The Murder of King James I* (2015), p. 198.

8. CSPD 25 June (91); Birch, p. 35.

9. Originally a Spanish three-metre dance, and considered quite erotic. The French court developed a slow version.

10. Thoinot Arbeau in 1599.

11. Karen Britland, *Drama at the Courts of Queen Henrietta Maria* (2006), p. 15; in fact Henrietta Maria would not conceive for several years, and aged fifteen she may still have lacked the physical maturity to do so.

12. David Scott, *Leviathan: The Rise of Britain as a World Power* (2013), p. 108.

13. James Larkin, *Stuart Royal Proclamations* (1983), p. 34.

14. Birch, p. 31.

15. Ibid., p. 30.

16. The Duc de Saint-Simon is the Frenchman in question, date 1698. Although many biographies of Henrietta Maria state that she spent the night at Denmark House I can find no contemporary reference for this. Several mention Whitehall; see Birch, pp. 31, 33; 'Whitehall Palace: Buildings' in Montagu H. Cox and Philip Norman (eds.), *Survey of London: Volume 13, St Margaret, Westminster, Part II: Whitehall I* (1930), pp. 41–115, http://www. british-history.ac.uk/survey-london/vol13/pt2/pp41.

17. Leanda de Lisle, *After Elizabeth* (2005), p. 265.
18. Kevin Sharpe, 'The Image of Virtue: The Court and Household of Charles I, 1625–42' in Kevin Sharpe and Peter Lake (eds.), *Culture and Politics in Early Stuart England* (1994), p. 244; John Adamson, 'The Tudor and Stuart Courts' in John Adamson (ed.), *The Princely Courts of Europe* (1999), p. 112.
19. CSPV 1625–6 (25).
20. *The Speeches of the Lord Digby in the High Court of Parliament* (1641), p. 24 (BL, E196/6, 7).
21. Tim Harris, *Rebellion: Britain's First Stuart Kings* (2014), p. 25, quoting Derek Hirst, *The Representative of the People?* (2005), pp. 104–5.
22. Jonathan Scott, *England's Troubles* (2000), p. 105.
23. Chris Kyle, *Theatre of State* (2012), pp. 109–10; tapestries purchased by Henry VIII celebrated the peace Romulus and Remus brought to Rome after civil war; quotations from *Journal of the House of Lords*, Vol. III.
24. Edward Hyde, Earl of Clarendon quoted in David Nichol Smith, *Characters from the Histories and Memoirs of the Seventeenth Century* (1918), p. 161.
25. Scott, *Leviathan*, p. 157.
26. This land edged into the neighbouring counties of Suffolk and Cambridgeshire. Robert Brenner, *Merchants and Revolution* (2003), p. 262.
27. The old merchants also included the Merchant Adventurers who had traditionally controlled the cloth trade to Germany and the Low Countries. The Levant and East India Companies traded with southern Europe, the Mediterranean and the Near and Far East. These companies were used to working hand in glove with the king. They paid taxes, negotiated with the Crown directly to the monarch, outside Parliament's control, and in exchange were granted privileged access to trade and a limited membership.
28. The Americas required risky investments in production that the great merchant companies did not wish to make. The new

merchants were involved in tobacco and later sugar, pioneering the Africa, West Indies, Virginia and New England trades in slaves, crops and provisions. Brenner, pp. 685–6; by 'godly' they meant the elect, predestined by God to enter heaven.

29. It was said that as a schoolboy at Eton, Robin had fallen out of bed just as the axe fell on his father's head, crying out 'his father was killed ... his father was dead'. The Devereux titles and estates had reverted to the Crown until James's accession in 1603. Then, as the heir to James's 'martyr', he went from zero – having neither titles nor estates – to hero of the new Stuart age. Unfortunately James later arranged a disastrous marriage for Essex with the wicked Frances Howard, daughter of a favoured councillor. Essex had been scarred by smallpox and his bride found him repulsive, cuckolded him, then tried to poison him. When that failed, she had their marriage annulled on grounds of his impotence. She later successfully poisoned a knight who had threatened her plans to marry her lover, Robert Carr, Buckingham's predecessor as royal favourite. For more on this amazing case see Anne Somerset, *Unnatural Murder: Poison in the Court of James I* (1998).

30. Scott, *Leviathan*, p. 129.

31. CSPV 1625–6 (138).

32. Charles Creighton, *A History of Epidemics in Britain*, Vol. I (1891), p. 513.

33. Malcolm Smuts, 'Political Thought in Early Stuart Britain' in Barry Coward (ed.), *A Companion to Stuart Britain* (2003), p. 283.

34. Scott, *England's Troubles*, p. 108.

35. Even those who supported the war often had different priorities from Charles. For the king it was a dynastic imperative: his sister was his heir, and the Palatinate the inheritance of her eldest son, who could one day be King of England and Scotland. Others saw the restoration of the Palatinate in terms of a Protestant crusade, and Charles could not appeal to this sentiment without alienating potential Catholic allies in Europe.

36. Scott, *England's Troubles*, p. 97.

37. Birch, p. 33.

38. A diamond signet made for her in 1628 that was a gift from Charles bears the monogram HM (an M scored through with an H). She certainly never viewed herself as Mary!

39. The poet John Donne.

40. Sir Simonds d'Ewes, *Autobiography and Correspondence*, Vol. I (1845), p. 272.

41. Birch, p. 40.

42. *Walter Devereux: Letters of the Earl of Essex*, Vol. III (1853), p. 296.

43. Taylor, the water poet, commented in verse that 'to be thought a Londoner is worse, than one that breaks [into] a house, or steals a purse'. Creighton, p. 518.

44. Christian IV avowed religious motives, but he also hoped to expand his territories at Habsburg expense.

45. *Letters of King Charles I*, ed. Sir Charles Petrie (1935), p. 43; Henrietta Maria's almoner, the Bishop of Mende, the head of her religious household, had heard that Buckingham hoped to improve his reputation by having her household expelled and renewing Catholic persecution.

46. Edward, Earl of Clarendon, *The History of the Rebellion and Civil Wars in England*, ed. W. D. Macray (1888), Vol. I, p. 48. This would have seemed no idle threat. Of the four queens executed under the Tudors, three had enjoyed strong French connections. Anne Boleyn had been a lady-in-waiting at the French court, before she went on to marry, and then fatally to anger, Henry VIII. Lady Jane Grey, who was executed when she was only a year older than Henrietta Maria, had been allied to France against the pro-Spanish Mary Tudor. Mary, Queen of Scots, was half French and a widow of a King of France, where she was remembered as little short of a martyr, hounded to her death by Elizabeth's Protestant servants.

47. *The Correspondence of Elizabeth Stuart, Queen of Bohemia, Volume I: 1603–1631*, ed. Nadine Akkerman (2015), p. 574, note 6.
48. Fiona Donovan, *Rubens and England* (2004), p. 17, Rubens to Palamede de Fabri sieur de Valavez, 26 December 1625.
49. Quoted in Bellany and Cogswell, p. 198.
50. Clarendon, Vol. I, p. 49.
51. Malcolm Smuts, 'Force, Love and Authority in Caroline Political Culture' in Ian Atherton and Julie Sanders (eds.), *The 1630s: Interdisciplinary Essays on Culture and Politics in the Caroline Era* (2006), p. 39.
52. Donovan, p. 17, Rubens to Valavez, 26 December 1625.

Chapter 5: Enter Lucy Carlisle

1. Just as Charles had been absent for the Mass following their proxy wedding so, once again, their religious differences were being emphasised. She had also refused to attend the Garter and Bath ceremonies. Also see Louis XIII's view in CSPV 1625–6 (454).
2. William Lilly, *A Prophecy of the White King and Dreadful Dead Man Explained*, quoted in Jerome Friedman, *The Battle of the Frogs and Fairford's Flies: Miracles and the Pulp Press During the English Revolution* (1993), p. 73.
3. *The Autobiography and Correspondence of Sir Simonds d'Ewes*, openlibrary.org, p. 176, https://archive.org/stream/autobiographyan01hallgoog#page/n192/mode/2up
4. For a detailed discussion and description of James's coronation see Leanda de Lisle, *After Elizabeth* (2005), pp. 261–8.
5. Calvinists believed that Christ had died only for elect souls predestined to heaven before the beginning of time. Arminius had argued against this that it was possible to fall from God's grace by committing sins. This infuriated Calvinists, who thought it too close to the Catholic belief in free will – that what we choose to do in this life (good or evil) affects where you go in the next (heaven or hell).

6. Psalm 96.
7. Their pamphlet had a ring of truth. Buckingham had motive and means to kill James. Furthermore, it would not have been the first poisoning to have taken place at James's court. Another of James's favourites, a man called Robert Carr, had been convicted, along with his wife, Essex's former spouse Frances Howard, of killing a man with poison. See Anne Somerset, *Unnatural Murder: Poison in the Court of James I* (1998).
8. Alastair Bellany and Thomas Cogswell, *The Murder of King James I* (2015), p. 225.
9. Edward Hyde, Earl of Clarendon quoted in David Nichol Smith, *Characters from the Histories and Memoirs of the Seventeenth Century* (1918), p. 1323.
10. Pym was to act as one of Warwick's trustees when he mortgaged his estate in September. He had also supported a proposal in the Commons by Warwick's kinsman Nathaniel Rich that the war be privatised, with a private navy based in Bermuda, paid for by private subscribers, which would deny Spain the wealth of the West Indies by attacking their shipping. This fleet would not have been liable to the usual taxes and the Council of War would, in effect, have run Charles's foreign policy in the interests of a group of political gentry and nobles. It proved too radical to go further, however, and the more important matter of Buckingham's impeachment now took priority; Christopher Thompson, 'The Origins of the Politics of the Parliamentary Middle Group, 1625–1629', *Transactions of the Royal Historical Society*, Vol. 22 (1972), p 80.
11. William Cobbett, *Cobbett's Complete Collection of State Trials* (1809–26), eds. Thomas Bayly Howell et al., Vol. II, p. 1324 (Impeachment of Buckingham, 1626).
12. Bellany and Cogswell, p. 238.
13. *Letters of King Charles I*, ed. Sir Charles Petrie (1935), pp. 42–5.
14. Bishop of Mende to Cardinal Richelieu, 24 July, quoted in Sara J. Wolfson, 'The Female Bedchamber of Queen Henrietta Maria'

in Nadine Akkerman and Birgit Houben (eds.), *The Politics of Female Households: 4 (Rulers & Elites)* (2013), p. 318.

15. Anne Boleyn's eyes, it was said, 'could read the secrets of a man's heart'; Leanda de Lisle, *The Sisters Who Would be Queen* (2008), p. 9 and note 16; Raymond A. Anselment, 'The Countess of Carlisle and Caroline Praise: Convention and Reality', *Studies in Philology*, Vol. 82, No. 2 (Spring 1985), p. 215.

16. Julie Sanders, 'Caroline Salon Culture and Female Agency: The Countess of Carlisle, Henrietta Maria, and Public Theatre', *Theatre Journal*, Vol. 52, No. 4 (Women/History, December 2000), pp. 449–64.

17. Wolfson, p. 317.

18. CSPV 1626 (680).

19. *Letters of King Charles I*, ed. Petrie, p. 45.

20. CSPV 1626 (712).

21. I have included these transcripts in the hope they may be useful to scholars who do not have access to the originals and I have left them untranslated to avoid passing on errors, as far as I can. Belvoir MSS QZ/6/12/1626 (date added in a different hand): 'Monsieur demande je de robe se tant que je peu pour vous escrire sen me tant come prisonniere que je ne peut pas parle a personne ny se tans descrire mes malheurs ny de me p[re]taundre seullement au non de dieu ay espetie dune pauure prinssese audessos poir et faite quelque chose a mon mal je suis la plus affligee du monde parles a ta Royne mamere de moy et lyuy montres mes maleurs je vous Aisa dieu et a tous mes pauures offisiers et a mon amie st gorge a la contesse de tilare [?] et tous fammes et filles qui ne mou blie pas je ne les oublieres pas aussy il sontes quelque remede a mon mal ou je me noeurs je ne puis je adieu cruel adieu qui me fera morir si dieu na pitie de moy au pere sauues [?] qui prie dieu pour moy et ammie que je tenus tousjours.'

   My translation is modernised and altered for sense. There is a transcript of this letter in the rare Alfred Morrison, *Catalogue of the Collection of Autograph Letters* etc., (1885), Vol. II.

22. Comte de Tillierès, *Mémoires* (1863), p. 135.

23. James was given five camels by the King of Spain in 1623. Perhaps they had been described to Elizabeth as looking like Carlisle, or perhaps she had seen a camel in the royal menagerie before 1613, or somewhere elsewhere in Europe since.

24. Victor Tapie, *France in the Age of Louis XIII and Richelieu* (1984), p. 180.

25. *ODNB*, Charles I.

26. See Appendix, 'Lucy Carlisle as Milady de Winter'.

27. Clarendon quoted in David Nichol Smith, *Characters from the Histories and Memoirs of the Seventeenth Century* (1918), p. 165.

28. Michael P. Winship, 'Godly Republicanism and the Origins of the Massachusetts Polity', *William and Mary Quarterly*, Third Series, Vol. 63, No. 3 (July 2006), p. 440.

29. Robert Brenner, *Merchants and Revolution* (2003), p. 226.

30. TNA SP 16/75; Wolfson, p. 321.

31. Smith, p. 14.

32. Henry VIII sent his friend Henry Norris to the scaffold simply to help him get rid of an inconvenient wife and in a manner that appealed to his narcissism (Norris was cast as Lancelot to his King Arthur). Elizabeth I was a master at passing the blame for her unpopular decisions on to her servants. The case of William Davidson, who she claimed (untruthfully) had delivered the warrant for the execution of Mary, Queen of Scots, without her permission, is the most notorious example.

33. CSPV 1626–8 (542).

Chapter 6: Exit Buckingham

1. *Proceedings in Parliament 1628*, Vol. 2, p. 58.

2. Ibid., p. 8.

3. Indeed, it would not be until 1789.

4. Quoted in Blair Worden, *The English Civil Wars* (2009), p. 19. Five per cent of the members of the Commons had refused the loan; Robert Brenner, *Merchants and Revolution* (2003), p. 226.

5. Jonathan Scott, *England's Troubles* (2000), p. 111, quoting Sir Robert Phelips; R. C. Johnson and M. J. Cole (eds.), *Commons Debates 1628* (1977), p. 40.

6. Robert Lockyer (ed.), *The Trial of Charles I: A Contemporary Account Taken from the Memoirs of Sir Thomas Herbert and John Rushworth* (1974), p. 439.

7. Alastair Bellany and Thomas Cogswell, *The Murder of King James I* (2015), p. 326.

8. *Acts of the Privy Council*, Vol. 43 (1617–28), pp. 492, 505.

9. CSPV 1628 (738).

10. Three versions of the portrait were dispatched in May, June and October to recipients who were probably determined by the queen: Madame Nourrice (or 'nurse', Françoise de Monbodiac, the first of the queen's original French Catholic chamberers), the Duchess of Saxony, and Charles's sister Elizabeth, the 'Winter Queen' of Bohemia. Thank you to Erin Griffey for this information.

11. Erin Griffey, *On Display* (2015), pp. 80, 81.

12. Unbound letter, Belvoir: 'La Reine dAngleterre a la Reine sa mere 53 1628 [number and date added in a different hand] Madame je nay voulu lesser partir garnier desy sans assurer vostre Maieste de mon tres humble seruise lors que mr de beaulieu estoit ysy yl me dit que vostre maiest [?] desiroit auoir mon pourtraict mes yl ne foit pas fait asses tost pour qui lenportasse maintenant que sette aucation sest presantee je dit a garnier qui le danit a mr de beaulieu pour le presantir a uostre Majeste je null jamais puisse [?] entreprandre a luy envoyer sans le commandemant que jaue reseu de sa part estant sy tard que jay honte que lon le voye mis vostre Majeste ny pranderapas parte ny a labillemantque le pentre asy malfait que jesupliray vostre Majeste de le fere la beler elle le regarde seullemant commes tres humble seruante qui nauiltre pasy on aumon de que salle que vous lastentes toute sa vie comme elle est Madame Vostre tres humble et tres obeisante fille et seruante Henriette Marie'. Garnier was her lady-in-waiting

Françoise de Monbodiac, who was an ally of Buckingham, while Mr Beaulieu was an English courtier. This letter has a partial translation (which I have not used) in Alfred Morrison, *Catalogue of the Collection of Autograph Letters* etc. (1885), Vol II. Another possible example of Henrietta Maria's dissatisfaction with an artist who had not done justice to her clothes comes ten years later. Cornelius Johnson corroborated with the artist Gerard Hoockgeest on a full-length miniature of Henrietta Maria, depicted strumming a mandolin with a spaniel playing at her feet (displayed at the Weiss Gallery, London, in 2016). Johnson was particularly talented at painting clothes but even the wonderful movement he gives her dress in this miniature, and the shine of the silk, did not impress the queen. A catalogue compiled by the surveyor of the king's pictures in 1639 describes the dress as unfinished, and it was dumped in store.

13. CSPD 1628–9 (267–81). The knife that killed Buckingham is today in the keeping of his sister's senior heir, Alexander Fielding, 12th Earl of Denbigh.

14. Unbound letter, Belvoir, dated 23 August 1628 by reference to the death of Buckingham: 'je nay peu rettenir du four je suplie vostre Majeste de croyre que je fait tout se qui esttoit en mon pouuoir a cause que vostre Majeste me lauoit commande et que je desire de luy obeir en tout de puis ma lettre escrite mr le duc de Bukingham et mort je croy que vostre Majeste le saura aues non pas comme yl a estte tue avec un couteau aumilieu de lieux sans hommes et est tumbe otit mort sans dire rien du tout que je suis mort et lhomme qui la fait dit toujours quil a fort bien fait yl est ariue ysy vn abe quy est fransois sest le plus mechant homme de la terre des choses quil dit et des aranques quil escrit yl serante de auoir fait les aferes sous mr le cardinal mes yl en est malcontant a ce mis est amuse de seu il est venu ysy. A la Royne Madame ma mere.' There is a transcript/description in Alfred Morrison, *Catalogue of the Collection of Autograph Letters* etc. (1885), Vol. II.

15. Unbound letter, Belvoir, from Queen Marie of France: '30 aoust 1628 Mon cousin Je uous en uoye una lettre que ma fille la Rayne d'anglesttere ma escreite pour mo[n]strer au Roy uous uerres en que estat ella est et en que missez' ella c'troue [?] digne de compassion Roxane uous dire des nouelles plus particvlieres estant le derniere quil a [?], e c'que l'on croine' a c'bien desebellas [?] Vous bai seres les mains au Roy de ma pearle et que ce le prie de ne concerne c'bones graces, et a uous mon cousin ie uous prie de croyre que uous n'aues persone qui soit plus que moy Vostre affectionne cousina Marie de Tours le trentieme aoust [in left-hand margin, written sideways] La contess' de la Hoye et morte La Rayne desire Madame de Leuen' pour dame d'Honor et pour dame d atour la Mony a luy ay dict que pour la mony le Roy nonli accuselera iamais.'

16. Edward, Earl of Clarendon, *The History of the Rebellion and Civil Wars in England*, ed. W. D. Macray (1888), Vol. I, p. 37.

17. Edward Hyde, Earl of Clarendon quoted in David Nichol Smith, *Characters from the Histories and Memoirs of the Seventeenth Century* (1918), pp. 14, 15, 16.

18. TNA: PRO SP 16/116 f. 4.

19. CSPD 22 November (34); CSPV 21 (603).

20. On 24 August he asked for the constableship of Windsor or the keepership of Hampton Court; CSPD 1628–9 (267).

21. Scott, pp. 110, 111.

22. Malcolm Smuts, 'Force, Love and Authority in Caroline Political Culture' in Ian Atherton and Julie Sanders (eds.), *The 1630s: Interdisciplinary Essays on Culture and Politics in the Caroline Era* (2006), p. 37.

23. Communion tables had stood altar-wise in the royal chapels since the beginning of Elizabeth's reign, and at Whitehall the table had also been railed in by the end of James's reign. This was not done, however, in the parishes. The Communion-table issue was significant because altars are what Jews – and Romans – used for a

sacrifice. They were central to the Catholic worship because, in the Mass, at the moment of consecration Christ's death – his sacrifice – becomes present. The bread and wine are adored as Christ's body and blood, a belief Calvinists judge idolatrous.

24. The Puritan in question was Peter Smart, who would be fined for his comments.
25. They included other great nobles such as the Earl of Warwick, Viscount Saye and Sele, his son-in-law, the Earl of Lincoln, and the twenty-one-year-old Robert Greville, Lord Brooke, but also lesser gentry from East Anglia and the West Country, lowly London citizens and radical ministers; Brenner, pp. 169, 272.
26. Diane Purkiss, *The English Civil War: A People's History* (2006), p. 92.
27. TNA: PRO, SP 16/106/55 quoted in *ODNB*.
28. Richard Cust, *Charles I: A Political Life* (2007), pp. 117, 118.
29. *Letters of King Charles I*, ed. Sir Charles Petrie (1935), pp. 76, 78.

Chapter 7: 'Happy in the Lap of Peace'

1. Thomas Birch, *The Court and Times of Charles I* (1849), Vol. I, p. 356.
2. This letter was found in a folder at Belvoir, marked by the 9th Duke of Rutland 'Sell'. Henrietta Maria, 1629, to Cardinal Richelieu: 'Mon cousin je reseus si viuement les obligations que je vous et toujours vne et selle que je sois maintenent de la part que vous prenes en laffliction qui mest ariuee que je croyois esttre ingrate sy je ne vous ren Remersiois par le sieur danery vous assurant que vous nobligeres jamais personne qui en toutes amations vous temoygnera avec plus daffection que moy quelle est Vostre affectionee cousine Henriette Marie'. NB in this rushed letter she omits the 'R' to her signature.
3. Belvoir MSS QZ/6 f. 7.
4. CSPV 1630 (366); Carolyn Harris, *Queenship and Revolution* (2016), pp. 128–9.

5. Belvoir MSS QZ/6/8. King Charles I and Queen Henrietta Maria to the Queen of France on the birth of Prince Charles, 29 May 1630: 'Madame La joye que j'ay, joint avec le haste de vous mander bien promtement de l'heureuxe acouchement de ma famme, ne me permett, que de vous dire, que Dieu mercie, la Mere & le fils se portent fort bien, remettant le reste a ce Porteur Mr Montague j'espere que vostre joye pour ces nouvelles ne serest plus indubitable, que vostre confience en moy que je suis Madame Vostre tresaffectionne fils et serviteur Charles R Ma femme pour vous monstré qu'elle se port bien a voulu que je escrive ce ci au son nom, affin que sa main vous tesmoinge cest verite V[ost]re tres humble et tres obeisante fille et servante Henriette Marie'. The translation in the text is modernised. A facsimile of this letter is reproduced in Alfred Morrison, *Catalogue of the Collection of Autograph Letters* etc. (1885), Vol. I.

6. Thomas Dekker, *Seven Deadly Sins of London* (1606), pp. 24–9; Charles's brother-in-law, Frederick, and Louis XIII were named as godparents, as was Marie de' Medici.

7. Letter to Madame St George: *Letters of Queen Henrietta Maria*, ed. Mary Anne Everett Green (1857), pp. 14, 15.

8. John Adamson, 'Policy and Pomegranates: Art, Iconography, and Counsel in Rubens' Anglo-Spanish Diplomacy of 1629–30' in Luc Duerloo and Malcolm Smuts (eds.), *The Age of Rubens: Diplomacy, Dynastic Politics and the Visual Arts in Seventeenth-Century Europe* (2016), p. 2.

9. Sara J. Wolfson, 'The Female Bedchamber of Queen Henrietta Maria' in Nadine Akkerman and Birgit Houben (eds.), *The Politics of Female Households: 4 (Rulers & Elites)* (2013), p. 323.

10. Fiona Donovan, *Rubens and England* (2004), p. 1.

11. Jonathan Brown and J. H. Elliott, *A Palace for a King* (1980), p. 49.

12. Donovan, p. 1.

13. Adamson, p. 37.

14. In the vulnerable – the old, or teenage boys – a woman's sexual needs could even lead to death for their male victims. The fifteen-year-old Arthur Tudor, the first husband of England's last Catholic queen consort, Katherine of Aragon, was supposed to have died of exhaustion responding to his wife's sexual demands. Henry VIII's sister, Mary Tudor, was also said to have inadvertently killed the aged Louis XII of France by the same means.

15. Raymond A. Anselment, 'The Countess of Carlisle and Caroline Praise: Convention and Reality', *Studies in Philology*, Vol. 82, No. 2 (Spring 1985), p. 218.

16. CSPV 1629–32 (209), (337); Sara J. Wolfson, 'The Female Bedchamber of Queen Henrietta Maria' in Nadine Akkerman and Birgit Houben (eds.), *The Politics of Female Households: 4 (Rulers & Elites)* (2013), p. 327.

17. HMC 45: Buccleuch Vol. III, p. 347.

18. This was enough to fund the Dutch army in its war with Spain for much of the following year, 1629; Adamson, p. 45.

19. Ibid., p. 57.

20. 'A golden lion on a red field', the Latin text of the grant to Rubens proclaimed, 'taken from our own royal armorial bearings'; ibid., p. 58.

21. In 1631.

22. Jonathan Scott, *England's Troubles* (2000), p. 100.

23. BL, Add. MS 4181.

24. This is from a chronicle composed by Magdeburg mayor Otto Guericke (1602–86). A census in February 1632 found only 449 citizens left in the rubble of the destroyed city.

25. A sixteenth-century alchemist's text had predicted a lion – or hero – would 'proceed from midnight' – that is the north – to 'pursue the eagle', the symbol of the Habsburgs, 'and after some time overcome it'. For this text see Theophrastus Paracelsus (1493–1541), *Magischer Propheceyung vnnd Beschreibung, von Entdeckung der 3. Schätzen Theophrasti Paracelsi* (1549), printed

as a supplement by Johan Nordström, *Lejonet från Norden. Samlaren. Tidskrift för svensk litteraturhistorisk forskning N. F. 15* (1934), pp. 37–9.

26. Carola Oman, *The Winter Queen* (1938, revd edn 2000), p. 82; Birch, pp. 225–8.

27. *The Letters of Elizabeth, Queen of Bohemia*, ed. L. M. Baker (1953), pp. 86–8; *Letters of Queen Henrietta Maria*, ed. Green, pp. 301, 302.

28. Letter to Sir Thomas Roe, quoted in Oman, p. 329.

29. *The Correspondence of Elizabeth Stuart, Queen of Bohemia, Volume II: 1632–1642*, ed. Nadine Akkerman (2011), p. 3.

30. Quoted in David Scott, *Leviathan: The Rise of Britain as a World Power* (2013), p. 146; in October 1633 Charles had all references to his sister and her children deleted from the Book of Common Prayer's 'collect' or prayer for the royal family.

31. John Adamson, 'Chivalry and Political Culture in Caroline England' in Kevin Sharpe and Peter Lake (eds.), *Culture and Politics in Early Stuart England* (1994), pp. 170–1.

Chapter 8: The Return of Madame de Chevreuse

1. Diane Purkiss, *The English Civil War: A People's History* (2006), p. 67.

2. HMC, Lord de L'Isle and Dudley MSS, Vol. VI, p. 94.

3. Julie Sanders, 'Caroline Salon Culture and Female Agency: The Countess of Carlisle, Henrietta Maria, and Public Theatre', *Theatre Journal*, Vol. 52, No. 4, Women/History (December 2000), pp. 454, 456, 463.

4. HMC, Lord de L'Isle and Dudley MSS, Vol. VI, p. 94.

5. Barbara Donagan, 'A Courtier's Progress: Greed and Consistency in the Life of the Earl of Holland', *Historical Journal*, Vol. 19, No. 2 (June 1976), p. 328.

6. Wentworth would later be made the Earl of Strafford by Charles.

7. HMC, Lord de L'Isle and Dudley MSS, Vol. VI, pp. 67, 94.

8. Sanders, p. 455.

9. William Prynne, *On the Unloveliness of Lovelocks* (1628).

10. Quoted in John Adamson, 'Chivalry and Political Culture in Caroline England' in Kevin Sharpe and Peter Lake (eds.), *Culture and Politics in Early Stuart England* (1994), p. 174; see also Richard Cust, 'Charles I and the Order of the Garter', *Journal of British Studies*, Vol. 52, No. 2 (2013), p. 353.

11. CSPV October 1637 (329).

12. *Letters of Queen Henrietta Maria*, ed. Mary Anne Everett Green (1857), pp. 15, 16.

13. TNA PRO 31/9/7B.

14. Cust, 'Charles I and the Order of the Garter', p. 343.

15. James Callow, *The Making of James II* (2000), pp. 33, 34.

16. Quoted in Richard Cust, *Charles I: A Political Life* (2007), p. 149.

17. Robin Blake, *Anthony Van Dyck* (1999), p. 325; one such apron, which survives in private ownership, is embroidered with blackwork figures of men gardening. It belongs to the heirs of a former Master of the Royal Wardrobe.

18. Eleanor, Countess of Sussex, quoted in ibid., p. 331.

19. The physician and naturalist Martin Lister complained how the ladies of the court 'were mighty fond of being painted in dishabille', and this 'cut out of business the best English painter of his time, Cornelius Johnson'.

20. Gregorio Panzini quoted in Fiona Donovan, *Rubens and England* (2004), p. 53.

21. PRO C82/2096 f. 28.

22. Not until the nineteenth century did it appear as it does today, clad in dull grey-white Portland stone.

23. In 1638 Van Dyck was also preparing an oil sketch for a series of tapestries depicting the history and ceremonial of the Order of the Garter, that would hang on the walls of the Banqueting House.

24. The customs duties known as 'impositions', the collection of which the Crown had long claimed as a prerogative right, had

netted £70,000 a year in the first decade of the century. Now impositions raised £218,000; Robert Brenner, *Merchants and Revolution* (2003), pp. 282, 241.

25. He was a member of the Saybrook Company that was establishing a settlement in what is now Connecticut. The origins of this company lay in a grant of land made by Warwick in 1632 to Viscount Saye and Sele, and Lord Brooke, as well as to John Hampden, John Pym and others. Brooke's brother-in-law Sir Arthur Hesilrige, who was also later involved in the Connecticut settlement, would be a key figure in the later opposition of Charles.

26. Geoffrey Parker, *Global Crisis: War, Climate Change and Catastrophe in the Seventeenth Century* (2013), p. 331.

27. CSPV October 1637 (329).

28. Ibid.

29. Edward, Earl of Clarendon, *The History of the Rebellion and Civil Wars in England*, ed. W. D. Macray (1888), Vol. I, pp. 129–32, 196; Sir Philip Warwick, *Memories of the Reigne of Charles I* (1701), pp. 78–82; Sir Bulstrode Whitelocke, *Memorials of the English Affairs* etc. (1853), Vol. I, p. 99.

30. John Winthrop first used the phrase in a sermon in 1630.

31. Laura Knoppers, *Politicizing Domesticity from Henrietta Maria to Milton's Eve* (2011), p. 37.

32. Sir Philip Warwick quoted in David Nichol Smith, *Characters from the Histories and Memoirs of the Seventeenth Century* (1918), p. 56.

33. CSPV October 1637 (329).

34. David Scott, *Politics and War in the Three Stuart Kingdoms, 1637–49* (2004), p. 16.

35. As far as Richelieu was concerned fighting the Habsburgs in alliance with Protestants abroad and tolerating the heretic Huguenots at home, were entirely compatible with his master being 'the first born son of the [Catholic] Church'. For Richelieu, Louis' status as an anointed king meant that his enemies were God's enemies.

He also suppressed any Catholic movement whose objective was spiritual renewal independent of royal authority. King James would have approved. Ronald G. Asch, *Sacral Kingship Between Disenchantment and Re-Enchantment* (2014), pp. 76, 79.

36. Charles had seemingly come close to a French alliance, but that had faded by the summer of 1637, with the king fearful of Dunkirk falling into French hands if the Spanish Netherlands were fatally weakened; Caroline M. Hibbard, *Charles I and the Popish Plot* (1983), p. 75.

37. Zahira Veliz, 'Signs of Identity in *Lady with a Fan* by Diego Velázquez: Costume and Likeness Reconsidered', *Art Bulletin*, Vol. 86, No. 1 (March 2004), p. 91, figure 19 and note 101.

38. CSPV 1636–9 (432).

39. CSPV 1636–9 (438).

40. 'Upon Madam Chevereuze swimming over the Thames'

> I was calm, and yet the Thames touch'd heaven to day,
> The water did find out the Milky way,
> When Madam Chevereuze by swimming down,
> Did the faire Thames the Queen of Rivers crown.
> The humble Willows on the shore grew proud
> To see her in their shade her body shroud;
> And meeting her the Swan (wont to presume)
> Bow'd to her whiter neck his sullyed Plume …
> Bright Chevereuze the whole difference ends,
> Adding so great a treasure to the waves,
> As the whole earth seemes useless, but for graves.

(*Musarum Delicice: OR The MUSES RECREATION*, 1656).

41. Ben Jonson's *Expostulation with Inigo Jones*.

42. Earl of Strafford, *Letters and Dispatches* (1739), Vol. II, p. 194; this is dated May 1638.

43. Jonathan Scott, *England's Troubles* (2000), p. 117.

44. CSPV 1636–9 (447).
45. William Laud, *Works* (1847–60), Vol. VII, pp. 452–3, Vol. VI, pp. 379–80, Vol. IV, p. 114.

Chapter 9: 'A Thing Most Horrible'

1. CSPV 1636–9 (528).
2. A. Lloyd Moote, *Louis XIII, The Just* (1989), p. 27; her accent is indicated by her spelling.
3. Thomas Birch, *The Court and Times of Charles I* (1849), Vol. II, p. 343.
4. CSPV 1636–9 (534).
5. TNA SO 3/12 November 1638.
6. Charles observed in the *Eikon Basilike* that the 'greatest fault' men later found with the English prayer book was that 'it taught them to pray so oft for me'.
7. The dukes of Venice (doges) could not even open foreign dispatches without officials standing over them; John Rushworth, *Historical Collections of Private Passages of State*, Vol. II (1721), p. 83; Geoffrey Parker, *Global Crisis: War, Climate Change and Catastrophe in the Seventeenth Century* (2013), p. 335; David Scott, *Politics and War in the Three Stuart Kingdoms, 1637–49* (2004), pp. 15–19.
8. *An Allegory of Marriage, in Honour of Alfonso d'Avalos, Marchese del Vasto*. Van Dyck had used the same symbol in a portrait of the Countess of Southampton. For more on this picture see Michael Jaffé, 'Van Dyck Studies II: La belle & vertueuse Huguenotte', *Burlington Magazine*, Vol. 126, No. 979 (October 1984), pp. 602–9, 611.
9. Interestingly the current Earl of Denbigh, whose family had a large collection of Van Dycks commissioned from the artist, still owns one of these 'studio' paintings of Charles in armour with his hand on a transparent sphere.
10. Sir Henry Slingsby, *Diary* (1836), p. 10.

11. Gilbert Burnet, *The memoires of the lives and actions of James and William, dukes of Hamilton and Castleherald* (1677), p. 55.

12. Christopher Thompson, 'Centre, Colony and Country: The Second Earl of Warwick and the "Double Crisis" of Politics in Early Stuart England', unpublished thesis, pp. 47, 48; BL, Egerton MS 2648, ff.1r–2r. See *The Winthrop Papers*, 7 vols (1928–47), Vol. III, ed. Stewart Mitchell (1943), p. 230. Cf. Francis J. Bremer, *John Winthrop: America's Forgotten Founding Father* (2003), pp. 232–8.

13. Malcolm Smuts, 'Religion, European Politics and Henrietta Maria's Circle 1625–41' in Erin Griffey (ed.), *Henrietta Maria: Piety, Politics, Patronage* (2008), p. 31.

14. Charles and Henrietta Maria commissioned a commemorative volume of elegies and verse; Carolyn Harris, *Queenship and Revolution* (2016), p. 128.

15. Slingsby, p. 11.

16. Ibid., p. 30.

17. Diane Purkiss, *The English Civil War: A People's History* (2006), p. 84; Parker, p. 336.

18. Sarah Poynting, 'The King's Correspondence during the Personal Rule in the 1630s' in Ian Atherton and Julie Sanders (eds.), *The 1630s: Interdisciplinary Essays on Culture and Politics in the Caroline Era* (2006), p. 87.

19. Had he beaten the Scots in 1639 Charles's future and that of his kingdoms would have been looking very different. There would have been no second Bishops' War to fight, and no pressing need to recall Parliament. The Thirty Years War had reached its climax. In 1640 Spain would be undermined by rebellion and, as the future of Protestantism in Europe looked brighter, so Puritan zeal might have withered. No wonder Warwick and other oppositionists had been preparing the ground for emigration to Massachusetts. For more on this see John Adamson, 'England Without Cromwell' in Niall Ferguson (ed.), *Virtual History* (1997).

20. Karen Britland, *Drama at the Courts of Queen Henrietta Maria* (2006), pp. 178–86; Purkiss, pp. 163–4.

21. Wentworth was also made Lord Lieutenant of Ireland to enable to him to govern the country through a deputy while he was absent; *ODNB*.

22. David Nichol Smith, *Characters from the Histories and Memoirs of the Seventeenth Century* (1918), quoting Sir Philip Warwick, p. 66; Edward, Earl of Clarendon, *The History of the Rebellion and Civil Wars in England*, ed. W. D. Macray (1888), Vol. I, pp. 197, 341–2. A stooped neck is caused by trapezius muscles being in constant tension.

23. Malcolm Smuts, 'Force, Love and Authority in Caroline Political Culture' in Ian Atherton and Julie Sanders (eds.), *The 1630s: Interdisciplinary Essays on Culture and Politics in the Caroline Era* (2006), p. 31.

24. Ibid., p. 32.

25. Warwick quoted in Smith, p. 66; Clarendon, Vol. I, pp. 197, 341–2.

26. John Forster, *Eminent British Statesmen* (1836), Vol. II, p. 352.

27. Her late husband had bequeathed her a wine customs grant in Ireland.

28. HMC, Lord de L'Isle and Dudley MSS, Vol. VI, p. 157; John Adamson, 'Policy and Pomegranates: Art, Iconography, and Counsel in Rubens' Anglo-Spanish Diplomacy of 1629–30' in Luc Duerloo and Malcolm Smuts (eds.), *The Age of Rubens: Diplomacy, Dynastic Politics and the Visual Arts in Seventeenth-Century Europe* (2016), p. 18.

29. Chevreuse was also busy at this time plotting another Huguenot revolt in La Rochelle; J. H. Elliott, 'The Year of the Three Ambassadors' in Hugh Lloyd Jones, Valerie Pearl and Blair Worden (eds.), *History and Imagination* (1981), p. 169; R. M. Smuts, 'The Puritan Followers of Henrietta Maria in the 1630s', *English Historical Review*, Vol. 93, No. 366 (January 1978), p. 42.

30. Edward Hyde, Earl of Clarendon quoted in Smith, p. 133.

31. Brian Manning, 'The Aristocracy and the Downfall of Charles I' in Brian Manning (ed.), *Politics, Religion and the English Civil War* (1973), p. 40. Northumberland was born at Essex House and was currently acting Lord Admiral.

32. John Adamson, *The Noble Revolt: The Overthrow of Charles I* (2007), p. 18.

33. D. Gardiner (ed.), *The Oxinden Letters 1607–42* (1933), p. 173; the bishops effectively linked his sacral kingship to their own claims to holding a divinely ordained office.

34. CSPV 1640–2 (64). A crown was worth five shillings, and was equivalent to a Venetian ducat.

35. CSPV 1640–2 (69).

36. Ibid.

37. CSPV 10 January 1642 (318). The term 'mob' from the Latin *'mobile vulgus'* would be invented to describe scenes that became all too familiar in London.

38. CSPD XVI (152–6).

39. Warwick quoted in Smith, p. 61.

40. Adamson, p. 31.

41. There is an MS held by the Surrey history centre listing seventeen, LM/1331/50. Those mentioned in CSPD have twelve different names, though Warwick etc. are in both CSPD August 1640 (16) and (19).

42. His wife Frances – Essex's favourite sister – had just had herself painted by Van Dyck wearing the lock of her father's hair cut off at his execution in 1601 – a symbol of royal injustice.

Chapter 10: 'A Broken Glass'

1. John Adamson, *The Noble Revolt: The Overthrow of Charles I* (2007), pp. 89–90.

2. Robert Brenner, *Merchants and Revolution* (2003), p. 369.

3. Adamson, p. 82.

4. Caroline M. Hibbard, *Charles I and the Popish Plot* (1983), p. 166; CSPV 1640–2 (126).

5. David Scott, *Leviathan: The Rise of Britain as a World Power* (2013), p. 156; BL, Add. MS 70002, f. 313.

6. Adamson, p. 62 and notes.

7. Sarah Poynting, 'The King's Correspondence During the Personal Rule in the 1630s' in Ian Atherton and Julie Sanders (eds.), *The 1630s: Interdisciplinary Essays on Culture and Politics in the Caroline Era* (2006), p. 81.

8. Edward Hyde, Earl of Clarendon quoted in David Nichol Smith, *Characters from the Histories and Memoirs of the Seventeenth Century* (1918), p. 133.

9. Hibbard, p. 174.

10. Diane Purkiss, *The English Civil War: A People's History* (2006), pp. 106, 107. The Puritan colonies in New England would similarly use branding to mark out those who had committed particular kinds of sin. The use of the scarlet letter 'A' branded on adulterers was immortalised in the nineteenth-century novel by Nathaniel Hawthorne.

11. Samuel Rawson Gardiner, *History of England* (1863), Vol. IX, p. 199.

12. CSPD Charles I, XVI (278).

13. *Mémoires de Madame de Motteville*, tr. Katherine Wormeley, Vol. I (1886), pp. 196, 197; Adamson, pp. 110, 113.

14. HMC, Lord de L'Isle and Dudley MSS, Vol. VI, p. 343: Strafford was placed in the Tower on 25 November.

15. CSPV 1640–2 (131).

16. CSPV 1640–2 (140).

17. CSPV 1640–2 (138).

18. Belvoir MSS QZ/22/1: 'La Reine d Angleterre Feur. 1641 Monsieur de chauigny ayant envoye fester a mon cousin le cardinal de richelieu pour luy faire entan dre lestat presant ou je suis et luy demander son assistance: jay cru que mayant temoygne

toujours beaucoup daffection comme vous aues fait en tout ce qui me conserne: que maintenant vous massisteries dans me afaires ou il y va de [xxx] [xxx] ma ruine entierre ou de mon bien etre comme les affaires iront maintenant quy je natans que … quasy sans resource et fautre je lespere par lassistance du Roy mon frere: je ne vous ay pas escrit quant sorter est alle car jay me suis misse entierremant a suiure les ordres que mon dit Cousin ordonneroit quoy que … ordonne forter de [xxx] desirer de luy que vous pensies estre de sette affaire: vous ayant toujours recongnu sy [xxx] prompt a mobliger que jay eru que dans sette afaire [xxx] vous ne me refuseries pas vostre asistance et que vous garderies le secret qui est tres necesaire je vous prie donc de le faire et de croyre que je [xxx] suis sy recongnoisante dessangs que vous mains despe temoynges de vostre affection que je chercheray les moyens de vous faire paroistre que je suis Vostre bien bonne amie Henriette Marie R.' It was tempting to date this letter to February 1642 – the year beginning 24 March – especially as she was then about to flee England, but as other letters of hers date the year from January I have placed it in 1641. She is writing to Léon Bouthillier, Comte de Chavigny.

19. Leanda de Lisle, *After Elizabeth* (2005), p. 264.
20. David Scott, *Politics and War in the Three Stuart Kingdoms, 1637–49* (2004), pp. 25–9; Brenner, p. 319.
21. The best book on this year – and which is a very exciting read – is John Adamson's *The Noble Revolt*. For more of the divisions at this time see pp. 158–63.
22. Re-establishing an Elizabethan-style mixed monarchy and church was all very well for the landed classes. The aristocracy and gentry dominated church patronage, access to Parliament, the county commissions and militias. For the ordinary Londoner it was a different matter. They had had no such access to power and they wanted to have it.
23. Brenner, pp. 324, 329, 331.

24. *The Correspondence of Elizabeth Stuart, Queen of Bohemia, Volume II: 1632–1642*, ed. Nadine Akkerman (2011), p. 946.

Chapter 11: Strafford on Trial

1. CSPV 1640–2 (168).
2. John Adamson, *The Noble Revolt: The Overthrow of Charles I* (2007), pp. 216, 223, 224.
3. John H. Timmis, *Thine is the Kingdom* (1974), pp. 64, 65; Adamson, pp. 221, 222, 225.
4. Adamson, pp. 224–5.
5. HMC, Lord de L'Isle and Dudley MSS, Vol. VI, p. 374.
6. Edward Hyde, Earl of Clarendon quoted in David Nichol Smith, *Characters from the Histories and Memoirs of the Seventeenth Century* (1918), p. 134.
7. John Rushworth, *The Trial of Thomas, Earl of Strafford* (1680), pp. 658–9.
8. HMC Various, Vol. II, p. 261; C. V. Wedgwood, *Thomas Wentworth* (1961), p. 153.
9. Clarendon quoted in Smith, p. 134.
10. The English officers in the north had complained bitterly of being forced to live off the people, 'contrary to our dispositions, and the quality of our former lives'. They sent notice that 'we are very sensible the honour of our nation was unfortunately foiled' in their action against the Scots and warned, 'we hope so to manage what is left that, if the perverse endeavours of some do not cross us, our future proceedings shall neither deserve the world's blame nor reproach'. HLRO Main Papers 20/3/41 ff. 78–82.
11. Timmis, pp. 126, 127.
12. A Leicestershire MP and a member of the Saybrook Company; Christopher Thompson, 'Centre, Colony and Country: The Second Earl of Warwick and the "Double Crisis" of Politics in Early Stuart England', unpublished thesis, p. 47.

13. Surprisingly Stapilton had a Catholic wife. He would fight for Parliament in the civil war, but was a moderate.

14. Richard Cust, *Charles I: A Political Life* (2007), pp. 282, 283.

15. Viscount Kells to Sir Thomas Aston, 20 March 1641; BL, Add. MS 36914, f. 199.

16. *Letters of King Charles I*, ed. Sir Charles Petrie (1935), p. 115.

17. She also asks for the cardinal's good offices in caring for one of Charles's Catholic servants who had fled to France. Holland claimed there were only two court Catholics she wished to protect – and specifically excluded a man called Wat Montagu, a son of the Earl of Manchester who had been working on expanding a list of exemptions to the order that all priests leave England by 7 April, on pain of arrest; Caroline M. Hibbard, *Charles I and the Popish Plot* (1983), p. 191. One of the lost letters from the Belvoir archives reveals her true opinion, however. In her letter to Richelieu, she recommends the bearer for his 'merit and his loyalty … in his service to my Lord the King'. He had 'been in France at the time of my marriage' (as Montagu had) and was now 'forced to leave to flee the storm that is falling upon the poor Catholics of this land'. Belvoir MSS QZ/6 f. 16 1641: 'Mon cousin seluy que vous randra sette lettre estant constraint de sen aler pour fuir lorage qui tombe sur les pauures catoliques de se peis je ne luy ay peu refuser de le vous recomman der car son merite et sa fidellite quil a fait paroistre au seruise du Roy monseigneur me ont conuiee sest pour je vous prie de le vouloir fauoriser et reseuoir de bon oeill comme une personne qui veritablemant se merite: je croy quil vous ait sy bien congnu ayant estte en france au tamps de mon mariage et fort affectione a la france qui sela ne nuira pas a ma recomman- dation: puis que vous obligeres une personne en le ferant qui est et sera toujours veritablemant Mon cousin Vostre bien affec- tionnee cousine Henriette Marie R.' Endorsed: 'A Mon Cousin Monsieur le Cardinal de Richelieu'.

18. *Mémoires de Madame de Motteville*, tr. Katherine Wormeley, Vol. I (1886), pp. 196, 197.

19. Edward, Earl of Clarendon, *The History of the Rebellion and Civil Wars in England*, ed. W. D. Macray (1888), Vol. I, p. 320.

20. Adamson, pp. 249–52.

21. For this and other comments see Brian Manning, *The English People and the English Revolution* (1976), pp. 91–2.

22. Gilbert Burnet, *The memoires of the lives and actions of James and William, dukes of Hamilton and Castleherald* (1677), pp. 232–3.

23. CSPV 1640–2 (181).

24. John Rushworth, *Historical Collections of Private Passages of State*, Vol. 8 (1721), p. 166; Vernon F. Snow, *Essex the Rebel* (1970), p. 263.

25. Dorset to Salisbury, [York] 27 June 1642, HMC Hatfield, XXII, 372.

Chapter 12: Given Up

1. John Adamson, *The Noble Revolt: The Overthrow of Charles I* (2007), p. 283.

2. Under one of Suckling's officers, a former man of affairs to Wentworth, called Captain William Billingsley.

3. John Aubrey, *Brief Lives* (1999), p. 289. He invented cribbage.

4. 'There was not among our princes a greater courtier of the people than Richard III, not so much out of fear as out of wisdom. And shall the worst of our kings have strive for that and shall not the best?' he observed; *The Works of Sir John Suckling*, ed. A. Hamilton Thompson (1910), pp. 322–4; Brian Manning, 'The Aristocracy and the Downfall of Charles I' in Brian Manning (ed.), *Politics, Religion and the English Civil War* (1973), p. 54.

5. The countess also had the care of the five-year-old Princess Elizabeth, and their baby brother, Henry.

6. CSPV 1640–2, 17 January 1641.

7. *Journal of the House of Commons*, Vol. II, p. 143.

8. CSPV 1640–2 (181).

9. Diane Purkiss, *The English Civil War: A People's History* (2006), p. 197; *Lettres de Henriette-Marie de France, reine d'Angleterre, à sa soeur Christine, duchesse de Savoie, Vol. V*, ed. Hermann Ferrero (1881), p. 57.

10. *Ceremonies of Charles I: The Notebooks of John Finet, 1628–1641*, ed. Albert J. Loomie (1988), pp. 311–13.

11. It was not his first visit. He had been to England twice previously: the first time in 1635, aged almost eighteen, when he had lived a life of idle fun at court, even siring an illegitimate child.

12. One of Charles's unpublished letters at Belvoir dating from 8 May 1638 to his sister Elizabeth concerns a possible Swedish match for Charles Louis, and another, unnamed bride for the younger brother 'Robert' – better known as Rupert of the Rhine. Belvoir MSS reference QZ/6/9: 'Charles the First to the Queen of Bohemia, 8 May 1638. My onlie deare Sister I shall onlie name those things that I haue intrusted this bearer with (his haste requyring shortnes, & his fidelitie meriting trust) First concerning the liquidation of accounts betweene me & the King of Denmarke: then concerning a Mache with Swed[en], but of this littell hope: lastlie, of a Mache for your Sone Robert: If he say anie thing else in my name; I shall desyer you to trust, to his honnestie, & not to my memorie: & so I rest Your louing Brother to serue you Charles R. Whythall the 8 of May 1638.'

13. CSPV 1640–2 (188).

14. HMC, Lord de L'Isle and Dudley MSS, Vol. VI, p. 403.

15. Purkiss, p. 193; Guillaume Groen van Prinsterer, *Archives ou Correspondance Inédite de la Maison d'Orange Nassau* (1857), Vol. III, pp. 460, 463.

16. Behind this measure lay the power of London's radical citizen opposition – a group very closely associated with the Warwick circle. They had persuaded moderate MPs that Parliament's

financial creditors had to have a guarantee Charles could not dissolve Parliament before its debts were paid; Robert Brenner, *Merchants and Revolution* (2003), p. 341.

17. The opposition were 'far too nimble for the king in printing', loyalists admitted, as he failed to respond in kind, leaving 'the common people [to] believe the first story which makes impression in their mind'; David Scott, *Leviathan: The Rise of Britain as a World Power* (2013), p. 158.

18. Edward, Earl of Clarendon, *The History of the Rebellion and Civil Wars in England*, ed. W. D. Macray (1888), Vol. I, p. 337.

19. Ibid.

20. CSPV 1640–2 (188).

21. Clarendon, Vol. I, p. 338.

22. *The Correspondence of Elizabeth Stuart, Queen of Bohemia, Volume II: 1632–1642*, ed. Nadine Akkerman (2011), p. 957.

23. Ibid.

24. Peter Heylyn quoted in John Milton, *Observations Upon the Articles of Peace* (1649), p. 95.

25. *Journal of the House of Lords*, Vol. IV, p. 245.

26. *Eikon Basilike*, p. 9.

Chapter 13: 'That Sea of Blood'

1. Fynes Moryson quoted in Leanda de Lisle, *After Elizabeth* (2005), p. 45.

2. The Treaty of London.

3. Robert Brenner, *Merchants and Revolution* (2003), p. 354.

4. *Eikon Basilike*, p. 48.

5. Caroline M. Hibbard, *Charles I and the Popish Plot* (1983), p. 198.

6. Having fallen 'from the highest degree of happiness', she said, 'into unimaginable misery'; Diane Purkiss, *The English Civil War: A People's History* (2006), p. 198; *Lettres de Henriette-Marie de France, reine d'Angleterre, à sa soeur Christine, duchesse de Savoie, Vol. V*, ed. Hermann Ferrero (1881), p. 57.

7. *Letters of Queen Henrietta Maria*, ed. Mary Anne Everett Green (1857), p. 40.
8. Ibid., p. 32.
9. Charles Carlton, *Charles I: The Personal Monarch* (1995), p. 223.
10. Thomas Carte, *The Life of James, Duke of Ormonde* (6 vols., 1851), Vol. V, p. 281.
11. Geoffrey Parker, *Global Crisis: War, Climate Change and Catastrophe in the Seventeenth Century* (2013), pp. 349–51.
12. Diane Purkiss, *The English Civil War: A People's History* (2006), p. 138.
13. Mark Charles Fissel (ed.), *War and Government in Britain, 1598–1650* (1991), p. 243.
14. Sir Philip Warwick, *Memories of the Reigne of Charles I* (1701), p. 225.
15. Malcolm Smuts, 'Force, Love and Authority in Caroline Political Culture' in Ian Atherton and Julie Sanders (eds.), *The 1630s: Interdisciplinary Essays on Culture and Politics in the Caroline Era* (2006), p. 42; Alnwick MS 15 28v, 29.
16. Samuel Rawson Gardiner, *The Constitutional Documents of the Puritan Revolution, 1628–1660* (1889/1979), pp. 206–7; Jonathan Scott, *England's Troubles* (2000), p. 147.
17. CSPV 1640–2 (279) (284).
18. CSPV 1640–2 (279).
19. In 1554, facing the Wyatt revolt, Mary had given a speech in London assuring her subjects she was a mother to them. It had helped her defeat the rebel army. In 1601, Elizabeth's many similar speeches had helped ensure the people's loyalty to her during the Essex revolt.
20. Charles had by now reached Ware in Hertfordshire where he did a walkabout amongst the people in the market square and the gentry kissed his hand.
21. Edward Hyde, Earl of Clarendon quoted in Tim Harris, *Rebellion: Britain's First Stuart Kings* (2014), p. 440.
22. Speech by Sir Edward Dering, 22 November 1641.

23. CSPV 1640–1 (296).

24. John Adamson, *The Noble Revolt: The Overthrow of Charles I* (2007), p. 445 and notes.

25. Twenty-two per cent of England's printed output at this time was dedicated to such atrocity stories.

26. Harris, p. 439.

27. Belvoir MSS QZ/22/5. Another letter, written by a Royalist, complains that papers from Ireland brought by the Irish councillor Thomas, Lord Dillon, for the king, were confiscated in Ware before Charles's arrival there, and handed to the Junto; Belvoir MSS QZ/22/6. Back in London, meanwhile, the Junto propaganda paid off on 21 December when the Common Council elections to the lower house of the governing body of the City saw a swing towards the Puritan interest. This gained the Junto the City's 8,000-strong militia.

28. CSPD 1641–3 (185–221).

29. The remaining two were placed in the custody of Black Rod; Adamson, p. 484.

30. Richard Cust, *Charles I: A Political Life* (2007), p. 320.

31. *Letters of Queen Henrietta Maria*, ed. Green, p. 71.

32. *Mémoires de Madame de Motteville*, tr. Katherine Wormeley, Vol. I (1886), p. 207.

33. Samuel Rawson Gardiner, *History of England* (1863), Vol. X, p. 136.

34. It is assumed that Lucy sent her message to Pym, but the MP's name is not certain. William Cobbett, *Cobbett's Complete Collection of State Trials* (1809–26), eds. Thomas Bayly Howell et al., Vol. IV, pp. 89–90.

35. Edward, Earl of Clarendon, *The History of the Rebellion and Civil Wars in England*, ed. W. D. Macray (1888), Vol. I, p. 483.

36. Adamson, pp. 495–7.

37. Clarendon, Vol. I, pp. 496–7; Scott, p. 148.

38. Clarendon, Vol. I, p. 434.

39. *Eikon Basilike*, p. 26.
40. Ibid., pp. 15, 21.
41. Clarendon, Vol. I, p. 507.

Chapter 14: 'Give Caesar His Due'

1. CSPV 1642–3 (8); Thomas Birch, *The Court and Times of Charles I* (1849), Vol. II, p. 349.
2. CSPV 1642–3 (8); Birch, p. 349.
3. *Letters of Queen Henrietta Maria*, ed. Mary Anne Everett Green (1857), p. 72.
4. CSPV 1642–3 (8); Birch, p. 349.
5. CSPV 1640–2 (344).
6. Henry Ellis (ed.), *Original Letters Illustrative of English History*, Vol. IV (1825), p. 2.
7. Peter Heylyn, *The Works of Charles I* etc. (2010), p. 58.
8. Ellis (ed.), Vol. IV, p. 2.
9. *The Correspondence of Elizabeth Stuart, Queen of Bohemia, Volume II: 1632–1642*, ed. Nadine Akkerman (2011), p. 1033.
10. Edward Hyde, Earl of Clarendon quoted in David Nichol Smith, *Characters from the Histories and Memoirs of the Seventeenth Century* (1918), p. 51.
11. *Eikon Basilike*.
12. Heylyn, p. 60. The word used to describe his tone of voice here is 'asseveration'.
13. From the so-called prophecy of the 'Dreadful Dead Man': a prince in white who becomes 'lost in the eye of the world ... and in the love and affections of his people': William Lilly, *A Prophecy of the White King and Dreadful Dead Man Explained*, quoted in Jerome Friedman, *The Battle of the Frogs and Fairford's Flies: Miracles and the Pulp Press During the English Revolution* (1993), p. 73.
14. Thomas Knyvett quoted in David Cressy, *Charles I and the People of England* (2015), p. 292.

15. A silk dress belonging to one of the queen's ladies-in-waiting (probably the Countess of Roxburghe) was one of the most notable items recovered recently from the rediscovered wreck.

16. Diane Purkiss, *The English Civil War: A People's History* (2006), p. 213.

17. *Correspondence of Elizabeth Stuart, Vol. II*, ed. Akkerman, p. 1032.

18. Ibid., p. 1031.

19. *Journal of the House of Commons*, Vol. II, p. 619.

20. Many of the queen's letters in the Belvoir archives from this period appear in *Letters of Queen Henrietta Maria*, ed. Green, but this one does not. Belvoir MSS QZ/22/8A: 'Ma cher coeur jestois sy hastee a vous en voyer heron pour vous dire de ne pas demeurer a aler a hull et de vous donner quelque raisons de la nessesite quil y auat pour cela que je nus pas loysire de vous proposer quel que chose en cas que vous le manquasies ayant de puis releu vostre lettre sur ce subject ray veu que vous en estties en doute et donnies iassy vostre magazin comme perdu: ce que en passant yl fault que je vous dire a estte une tres grande faulte de auoir ofert a la voir et et ne pas poursuiure car vous aues donne tamps au parlement de envoyer leurs ordres et de faire ce quils voudront pour enpecher que vous ne layes yl ne fault jamais faire les choses a demi et sest ce que vous aues toujours fait bien commance et mal ailane [?] mais lafaire est faite yl nia plus rien a dire la desus mais en cas que uostre magasin soit perd u yl fault sonner [very faint, uncertain reading] a ce que tout a afayre et se resou dre a un chemin recourir et le suiure mais mieux que bien nafait son dernier car sy vous lusies suiui esex oroit la gabiolle asette heure voysy la sec onde foy u manquee garde la troy si esme: je crois quil est a propos de enuoyer a vostre oncle pour dusecours car sy vos mu nitions sont parties vous naues plus de quoy faire la guere et yl est tres euidant que sans cela vous nores pas ce que bien doit auoir sest pour quoy yl fault songer aux moyens pour recouuri de toute ses choses et

pour sette effect yl fault sasister de nos amis vostre oncle est le plus propre ayant une armee et point de guerre sest pour quoy sil vous plaist de manuoyer une le tre pour luy yl seullemant decroyance a celuy qui luy donnera carlile trouuera quelcun ou elle est a enuoyer et aussy je acheteray de la poudre et munotions et canons ysy et je ne fais nul doute que vous ores de abandant et nauires pour transport er et ofisiers pour seruir sy vous voules: yl nia que a ce mestre entra in: sy esex a ses munitions de la gabiolle son affaire est faite sy vous naues pas yl fault pouruoir car abulament yl fault uenir a un coup et puis que vous trouues les peuples en prenes shier afection nes yl ne faut point perdre de tamps et toujours vous assurer de la gabi olle pour vostre retrayte en cas de nes esite et auoir un regimant des gar des aupres de tout et deux conpagnies de caualerie autremant bien nest pas en seurete ny personne de seux qui sont au pres de tout car quant paris voudra yl les ost era ou par force ou par craint yl nia que a commances assurement esex trouuera beaucoup de personnes affectionnes: touchant vostre onc le je croy que ce que celuy qui yra doit dire est de sauoir sy yl veut assi ster tout de caualeriee et des nau ires pour les transporter cela est tout comme je crois sur sette affaire sy yl vous plaist aussy de manuoyer un warrant soubs vostre main ou vous me donnies un plain pouuoir de engager mes pierreries a cause que les march-ants disent que une famme ne peut uandre ses pierre ries durant la uie de son mary despeches de man voyer ses deux choses la que je vous demande jatans de vos nouuelles auec grande impa-siance afin de voir ce quil fault faire je escris a holand me longe lettre vous la veres adieu mon cher coeur je suis sylasse que je naie puis plus ce 4/14 may.' Addressed: 'Au Roy Monseigneur'; endorsed in the king's hand: 'My Wyfe 4 May 1642', in another hand: 'From the Queene. 4 May 1642'.

21. BL, Harl. MSS 7379, f. 86; this one is published in *Letters of Queen Henrietta Maria*, ed. Green, p. 64.

22. Belvoir MSS QZ/22/30: 'The Queen of England La Hage. 8 Sept. 1642 Monsieur de chauigny ayant seu par le jantilhomme que jay envoye au Roy monsieur mon frere: les temoy gnages que vous luy aues donnees de vostre affection en vers moy jay voulu vous en remercier et en mesme tamps vous demander en demander en core des preuues sur une affaire la quelle est sy importante pour le Roy monseigneur et par consequant pour moy [xxx] et sy juste que je ne doute point de reseuoir la satisfaction que je y puis desirer sest que les rebelles dangletaire soubs le nom de seux du parlement ont en voye ysy un agent de leur part et au nom du Royaume dengletaire pour desirer ses estats de se joindre auec eux pour la conseruation de la religion protestante comme yl pretande et pour la ruine de la q catolique disant que le Roy monseigneur et moy sauons voulu restablir et mesme se sont seruis du nom de mon cousin le cardinal de richelieu pour leur temoynge comme monteque vous fera en tandre plus au long qui est me ... que je tiens tres faulce et alaquelle je na porte nul croyance: jantans que yls ont dispeche aussy en france assurement unitera pas sur le mesme pretexte de religion: mais sur quel quil soit jespere que yl ne sera pas escouste nil reseu venant de la part du personnes rebelles a dieu et a leur roy : et qui ont estte desilarees telle: je ne laise pourtant de demander vostre assistance la dedans afin que sette personne resoiue le traitement quil merite en estant pas escouste: se servit [xxx] coupre les trets entre les deux couronnes: [xxx] que de faire autrement quant yl nioroit pour de mon particulier estant se que je suis alafrance je me fu tant au bon naturel du Roy monsieur mon frere et a la generosite de mon cousin le cardinal de richelieu que dans sette consideration la jan atans des effets selon mes desirs: je ne diray donc? dauantage sur ce subject que vous prier de prandre lafaire dans vostre protection et de croyre que se nest pas seullemant moy qui vous obliges la dedans: mais la juste cause de dieu par la religion et que je seray toujours, Vostre bien bonne

amie Henriette Marie R. Monsieur de chauigny La Hage ce 8 sept'. Endorsed: 'Monsieur de Chauigny The Queen of England 8th Septr'. An abbreviated translation appears in Alfred Morrison, *Catalogue of the Collection of Autograph Letters* etc. (1885), Vol. II.

23. Belvoir MSS QZ/22/14: 'The Queen of England La Hage. 8 Juill. 1642 Monsieur de chauigny en voyant ce jantil homme trouuer le Roy monsieur mon frere pour le remersier de lhonneur quil ma fait par mr de qressy je saie lobligation que je vous ay dans le soing que vous aues pris de mobliger en toutes occations: sest pour quoy jay com mande a arpe de vous voir de ma part et vous en remersier: ce que je fais encore par sette lettre moy mesme vous conjura ac de vouloir continuer [xxx] [xxx] dans les occa-tions et de croyre que vous me trouue res tres sensible des seruices que vous me randres quoy que tres incapable de le vous faire paroistre mes se ne sera pas la volonte qui fallira mes le manque de [xxx] pour lexeniter et sy jan ramonore jamais les occations vous veres que se que je vous dis est veritable et combien je suis Vostre bien bonne amie Henriette Marie R. La Hage ce 8 juillett'. Endorsed: 'The Queen of England'. A brief description of this letter appears in Morrison, Vol II.

24. Belvoir MSS QZ/22/30: 'The Queen of England La Hage. 26 Oct. 1642 Monsieur de chauigny parmy toute les preuues que jay reseues de vostre affection selles que leuesque dangoulesme ma randue me sont sy sensible que je nay pas voulu tarder auons en remersier particulierement dans linsertitu de que lestat presant de nos affaires me tient ne pouuant en core resoudre de quil reste le bien des affaires du Roy monseigneur mapelle ra la conjoncture presante samble deman der fort mon retour en engletaire se que ja prehanderois plus que tout les autres haza rds sy je ne croyois conseruer la mesme part dans laffection du Roy monsieur mon frere et de mon cousin le cardinal de richelieu qui me temoygnent par lesuesque dangoules me mais quant les

aduantages du Roy monseigneur seront uses euidantes pour justi-
fier mes paines je ne dois pas craindre que sela puire diminuer
lestime des personnes sy affection nees et sy prudantes aussy
tost que joray pris ma resolution se que respere dans peu de
jours je la seray sauoir par une expres du Roy monsieur mon
frere et a mon cousin le cardinal de richelieu je ne dois pas douter
de la continuation de vos offises dans tout les besoings que jan
pour rois auoir je en ay ases dassurances par ce que vous aues
fait touchant la reseption dangier et la rest des armes preparees
pour les rebelles dont je vous remersie extrememant vous priant
de continuer vos soings en ce particulier car yls se font fort de
tirer grand aduantages par la jespere un jour de vous pouuoir
temoygner plus selon mes souest combien je suis / Monsieur de
chauigny / Vostre bien bonne amie Henriette Marie R'. This
appears in transcription in Morrison, Vol. II.

25. The vertebra of eighty-seven-year-old priest John Lockwood,
    which was cut through by the executioner, is still preserved at
    the Tyburn convent in London.
26. Richard Cust, 'Charles I and the Order of the Garter', *Journal of
    British Studies*, Vol. 52, No. 2 (2013), p. 366.
27. CSPD 1641–3, 20 April 1642.
28. The lost munitions included 7,238 muskets, 3,729 swords, 906
    barrels of powder, over 2,000 pistols and thousands of cannon
    shot; PRO SP16/490/77.
29. Belvoir MSS QZ/22/8A (see transcript above).
30. Belvoir MSS QZ/22 f. 7, 30 April 1642.
31. 'His Majesty's Speech to the Gentry of York 12 May 1642' in
    Heylyn, p. 62.
32. *Eikon Basilike*, p. 43. He also had to give Parliament the right to
    raise soldiers as it saw fit, and give up his own right to consent
    to legislation, or to choose his own officers.
33. TNA SP 16/491/21; Richard Cust, *Charles I and the Aristocracy
    1625–1642* (2013), p. 282.

34. Geoffrey Parker, *Global Crisis: War, Climate Change and Catastrophe in the Seventeenth Century* (2013), p. 363.
35. The money was being raised through the Committee of Safety.
36. At least ten from Massachusetts rose to the rank of major or above in Parliament's armies.
37. The constitutional revolution in London's City government saw the Court of Aldermen lose its power of veto over the decisions of the lower house, the Common Council, and the lord mayor lost his power to call and dissolve their meetings. Reforms ensured City freemen could also more freely exercise their right to vote in Council elections. The Royalist lord mayor was then dismissed, sent for trial and replaced with the radical City MP Isaac Pennington; Robert Brenner, *Merchants and Revolution* (2003), p. 372.
38. Diane Purkiss, *The English Civil War: A People's History* (2006), p. 138.
39. William Lily, *Several Observations on the Life and Death of Charles I* (1651), p. 239.
40. *Journal of the House of Lords*, Vol. V, p. 185.
41. Roger Hudson (ed.), *The Grand Quarrel: Women's Memoirs of the English Civil War* (2000), p. 53.
42. Ibid.
43. For example, Calvinist Royalists had disagreements with Laudian Royalists, Parliamentarian Presbyterians had disagreements with the Parliamentarian Independents who supported self-governing congregations. Some were prepared to allow Charles this power, some that, some would allow him no power at all.
44. Sir Edward Nicholas to Sir Thomas Roe, 15 June; CSPD 1641–3 (340). His council was divided between advocates for war and those who wanted yet another appeal for peace.
45. David Scott, *Politics and War in the Three Stuart Kingdoms, 1637–49* (2004), p. 38.

46. In October Charles Louis would issue a joint declaration with his mother, Elizabeth the Winter Queen, deploring his brothers' actions, and calling on Charles to reconcile with Parliament.

47. Edward, Earl of Clarendon, *The History of the Rebellion and Civil Wars in England*, ed. W. D. Macray (1888), Vol. II, p. 290.

48. Marquess of Hertford to Henrietta Maria, 11 July 1642, *Journal of the House of Lords*, Vol. V, pp. 264b–265a.

49. *Letters of Queen Henrietta Maria*, ed. Green, p. 101.

50. Slingsby, pp. 13, 14.

Chapter 15: Edgehill

1. CSPD 1641–3, 30 September 1642 (28).

2. Cumbria RO, Sir Philip Musgrave Corr D/Mus/Corr/4/28 (Sir Robert Strickland to 'Madam', 5 October 1642).

3. Carola Oman, *The Winter Queen* (1938, revd edn 2000), p. 354.

4. Mark Stoyle, *The Black Legend of Prince Rupert's Dog: Witchcraft and Propaganda During the English Civil War* (2011), pp. 22, 23.

5. CSPD 1641–3, 30 September 1642 (28); *Memoirs of Prince Rupert* (1849), Vol. I, p. 401. Angry letters were addressed to the pro-Parliament Charles Louis, who pleaded with his allies, 'It is impossible for either me, or the queen my mother, to bridle my brother's youth and fieryness at so great a distance ... and an injustice to blame us for things beyond our help'; CSPD 1641–3, 6 October (31).

6. Edward, Earl of Clarendon, *The History of the Rebellion and Civil Wars in England*, ed. W. D. Macray (1888), Vol. II, p. 356.

7. Charles Carlton, 'The Face of Battle in the English Civil Wars' in Mark Charles Fissel (ed.), *War and Government in Britain, 1598–1650* (1991), p. 236.

8. Adrian Tinniswood, *The Verneys* (2007), p. 177; *Memoirs of Prince Rupert*, Vol. II, p. 12.

9. Clarendon, Vol. II, p. 353.

10. Ibid., p. 352.
11. Mark Kishlansky, *Charles I* (2014), p. 83.
12. BL, TT, E 200 (67), 'Three Speeches'.
13. Henry Ellis (ed.), *Original Letters Illustrative of English History*, Vol. III (1824), p. 303.
14. George Lauder, 'The Scottish Soldier'.
15. Carlton, 'The Face of Battle in the English Civil Wars' in Fissel (ed.), p. 238.
16. Captain Edward Knightley, *A full and true relation of the great battle fought between the King's army, and his Excellency, the Earl of Essex, upon the 23 October last past* (1642).
17. Official Parliamentary Account, *The Account of the Battle at Edgehill* (1642).
18. Diane Purkiss, *The English Civil War: A People's History* (2006), p. 178.
19. Clarendon, Vol. II, p. 353.
20. Ibid.
21. Clarendon, Vol. II, p. 353.
22. John Vicars, *Jehovah Jireh* (1644), p. 200.
23. Purkiss, p. 180.
24. Clarendon, Vol. II, p. 353.
25. G. Davies and Bernard Stuart, 'The Battle of Edgehill', *English Historical Review*, Vol. 36, No. 141 (January 1921), pp. 36, 37.
26. John Aubrey, *Brief Lives* (1999), pp. 128, 129.
27. Clarendon, Vol. II, pp. 368, 355.
28. Ellis (ed.), Vol. III, p. 304.
29. This was Denzil Holles, the MP who had orchestrated the closing scenes in the parliament of 1629, before the Eleven Years' Tyranny; Charles Carlton, *Going to the Wars: The Experience of the British Civil Wars, 1638–1651* (1992), pp. 118, 146.
30. Clarendon, Vol. II, p. 365.
31. Quoted in Jonathan Scott, *England's Troubles* (2000), p. 149.
32. CSPV 1642–3 (171).

Chapter 16: 'Tiger's Heart'

1. CSPV 1642–3 (239).

2. *Letters of Queen Henrietta Maria*, ed. Mary Anne Everett Green (1857), p. 163.

3. James F. Larkin, *Royal Proclamations of Charles I* (1983), p. 867.

4. Sir Henry Slingsby, *Diary* (1836), pp. 89, 90; *Letters of Queen Henrietta Maria*, ed. Green, p. 163.

5. CSPV 1642–3 (244).

6. On 1 February 1643.

7. For such comments see BL, Harl. MS 164, ff. 295, 296v, 300, 301v, 302, 308; Harl. MS 1901, f. 58v; Add. MS 18777, ff. 65, 67, 148, 151–3, 158, 158v; *Mercurius Aulicus*, No. 7 (12–18 February 1643), pp. 85–7; No. 8 (19–25 February 1643), p. 95; Laurence Womock, *Sober Sadnes, Or, Hiroticall Observations Upon the Proceedings, Protences, & Designs of a Prevailing Party in both Houses of Parliament* (1643), pp. 16–17; CSPV 1642–3 (215); David Scott, 'Politics in the Long Parliament' in George Southcombe and Grant Tapsell (eds.), *Revolutionary England, c.1630–c.1660: Essays for Clive Holmes* (2016), pp. 32–55.

8. Albert Loomie, 'The Destruction of Rubens's "Crucifixion" in the Queen's Chapel, Somerset House', *Burlington Magazine*, Vol. 140, No. 1147, pp. 680–1.

9. *Letters of Queen Henrietta Maria*, ed. Green, p. 182; *The Works of Charles I*, Vol. I (1766), p. 294.

10. Belvoir MSS QZ/23 f. 16.II. The letter from Charles to Henrietta Maria concludes movingly (out of cipher), 'It is just a Fortnight since I had a letter from thee, wch I attribute to the difficulty of the passage, the same reason may hinder thee to heare frome mee; but to show thee, both my ill lucke, & diligence, I send thee this enclosed from my Agent Boswell, & lykewais asseure thee that this is the sixt letter I witten [*sic*] this Month one of wch I know has beene intercepted: At this tyme I haue no more to wryte, but

to desyre thee, to send to mee, as oft as thou canst; & to giue credit, & satisfie the desyrs of this inclosed letter from 82: the best thou may: So, longing to here from thee, & infinitly desyring to see thee, I rest eternally Thyne'. 24 March 1642–3, Oxford. Thanks to Sarah Poynting for this transcription.

11. CSPV 1642–3 (268). Some Parliamentarians insisted the impeachment was not aimed against the queen's life. Yet treason was a capital offence. She had been right that, at the very least, while the 'perpetual parliament' still sat, things were not likely to 'go well' for her in England.

12. *Mercurius Aulicus* (22–26 May 1643), p. 280.

13. *Eikon Basilike*, p. 25.

14. CSPV 1642–3 (274).

15. HLRO, Naseby Letters, No. 6.

16. HL/PO/JO/10/1/183 Letter 6; Laura Knoppers, *Politicizing Domesticity from Henrietta Maria to Milton's Eve* (2011), p. 59.

17. Belvoir MSS QZ/23 f. 16.II.

18. The more famous medal struck that year was the Forlorn Hope – depicting Charles and his heir – which was cast for all the men who fought for him. The name referred to the courage and sacrifice of soldiers who faced death in leading an assault.

19. *Mercurius Civicus*, No. 7 (6–13 July 1643), p. 53 (E60/9); *Mercurius Britanicus*, No. 23 (12–19 February 1644), pp. 175, 177 (E33/21).

20. *Mercurius Britanicus*, No. 23 (12–19 February 1644), pp. 175, 177 (E33/21).

21. Margaret Toynbee and Peter Young, *Strangers in Oxford* (1973), p. 32.

22. Charles Carlton, *Going to the Wars: The Experience of the British Civil Wars, 1638–1651* (1992), p. 93.

23. This took place in March 1643. Bodl. MS Carte 5, ff. 40r–v. Endymion Porter served as Ashburnham's second.

24. BL, Add. MS 18980, ff. 59v–60.

25. Toynbee and Young, p. 10; Ann, Lady Fanshawe, *Memoirs* (1907), p. 56.

26. John Rushworth, *Historical Collections of Private Passages of State*, Vol. 5 (1721), p. 334 (20 June 1643).

27. Behind the scenes Charles was subject to the contradictory pressures of Royalists' own war and peace parties. The war party, which was associated with the queen, wanted an outright military victory that would see their enemies punished, and not rewarded as part of a peace process. Their names included those of leading Catholics, but the men at its head were Protestants: amongst them the thoroughly Calvinist Prince Rupert. The Royalist peace party wanted Charles to offer enough concessions to strengthen the hand of the peace party in Parliament, and empower them to overthrow the 'fiery spirits' of the war party and their radical backers. They argued that Charles could then come in 'honour and safety' to London where he would be 'repossessed ... of his power'. With the war going well for the Royalists the war party had the upper hand in Charles's councils. There is, however, fragmentary evidence of a plot between Royalist and Parliamentarian moderates that summer. Under new softer peace terms both armies would be disbanded, Parliament would keep all its privileges, but expelled members would be readmitted. The hope was that Essex would back this plan. It collapsed on the rock of inter-Royalist quarrels and jealousies. Rupert had persuaded Charles to sack another of his generals – Essex's brother-in-law the Marquess of Hertford, who was a leading member of the Royalist peace party. It made Essex realise that there would be no future for him with the king restored to power. For all the details on this see David Scott, 'Rethinking Royalist Politics' in John Adamson (ed.), *The English Civil War: Conflict and Contexts, 1640–49* (1973), pp. 46–7.

28. Sir Simonds d'Ewes, *Diary*, BL, Harl. MSS 165, 146b.

29. The soldier responsible claimed it was an accidental discharge; Samuel Rawson Gardiner, *History of the Great Civil War* (1886/1987), Vol. I, pp. 186, 187.

30. Edward, Earl of Clarendon, *The History of the Rebellion and Civil Wars in England*, ed. W. D. Macray (1888), Vol. III, pp. 194, 195.

31. Sir Edward Nicholas to William Hamilton, Earl of Lanark, NAS GD 406/1/1904.

32. Clarendon, Vol. III, p. 174.

33. Carlton, p. 139.

34. *Journal of Sir Samuel Luke*, ed. I. G. Philip (1950), p. 155.

35. Carlton, p. 227.

36. Clarendon, Vol. III, pp. 194, 195.

37. In November 1643 the first contingents of the king's army in Ireland were already being shipped to England.

38. Michelle Anne White, *Henrietta Maria and the English Civil Wars* (2006), p. 131.

39. Ibid., p. 133, note 61.

40. *Memoirs of Prince Rupert* (1849), Vol. II, letter of 22 June, p. 101.

41. CSPD 1644 (46i, ii).

42. Henrietta Maria had never been close to Louis but she wrote of her 'affliction' at his loss. Belvoir MSS QZ/23/31: 'La Reyne d'Angleterre sur la mort du Roy. Juillet 1643. Mon cousin lafliction que jay eu de la perte que jay faite du Roy Monsieur mon frere vous sera ditte par le sieur de gressy: comme aussy les resentimants que jay des temoygnages que je resois tout les jours de vostre affection: que je vous prie de continuer vous assurant que vous nobligeres jamais personne qui en soit plus recongnoisante que moy: je me remest au sieur de gressy auous dire beaucoup de choses de ma part sest pour je finiray en disant que je suis Mon cousin. Vostre bien affectionee cousine Henriette Marie R'. There is a brief description (but no transcription) of this letter in Alfred Morrison, *Catalogue of the Collection of Autograph Letters* etc. (1885), Vol. II.

43. In October Anne had sent a diplomat to help negotiate an honourable peace with Parliament. In February 1644 the diplomat had returned to France in despair of success.

44. *Letters of Queen Henrietta Maria*, ed. Green, p. 149.

45. Ibid., pp. 249–50.

46. https://archive.org/stream/ ReportTransactionsOfTheDevonshireAssociationVol81876/ TDA1876vol8#page/n489/mode/2up.

47. Anne of Austria dispatched a doctor as soon as she learned of her sister queen's condition and he recommended the spa. The 'ancient and rugged castle' from which the house of Bourbon took its name dominated the spa town, standing 'on a flinty rock'. 'In the midst of the streets are some baths of medicinal waters, some of them excessive hot,' the arriving diarist John Evelyn noted. You drank the waters rather than bathed, 'our Queen being then lodged there for that purpose'. *Diary of John Evelyn*, Vol. I, 24 September 1644.

48. Victor Cousin, *Secret History of the French Court Under Richelieu and Mazarin* (1859), p.165.

49. Erin Griffey, *On Display* (2015), p. 154.

50. *Letters of Queen Henrietta Maria*, ed. Green, p. 262.

51. Ibid., p. 258.

52. White, p. 133, note 61.

Chapter 17: Enter Oliver Cromwell

1. BL, Add. MS 70499, f. 198v. He had been the Prince of Wales's governor until Parliament had him replaced. He had diverted the boy's energy into horsemanship and dance and his natural intelligence to literature and music, science and mechanics – but not so much to theology.

2. Edward, Earl of Clarendon, *The History of the Rebellion and Civil Wars in England*, ed. W. D. Macray (1888), Vol. III, p. 383.

3. Charles Carlton, *Going to the Wars: The Experience of the British Civil Wars, 1638–1651* (1992), p. 119.

4. Ibid., p. 120, quoting the scoutmaster Lion Watson.

5. *ODNB*.

6. In 1644 Prynne had his revenge, acting as chief prosecutor in Laud's long-delayed impeachment trial.

7. Sir Philip Warwick, *Memories of the Reigne of Charles I* (1701), pp. 247–8.

8. Ibid., also John Maidston quoted in David Nichol Smith, *Characters from the Histories and Memoirs of the Seventeenth Century* (1918), p. 142.

9. Edward Hyde, Earl of Clarendon quoted in Smith, p. 140.

10. Richard Baxter, http://archive.org/stream/englishpuritanis-00tull/englishpuritanis00tull_djvu.txt.

11. Tristram Hunt, *The English Civil War at First Hand* (2002), p. 151.

12. Ibid., pp. 120–39.

13. Thomas Carte, *The Life of James, Duke of Ormonde* (6 vols., 1851), Vol. I, pp. 55–8.

14. Malcolm Wanklyn, *The Warrior Generals* (2010), p. 106.

15. Margaret, Duchess of Newcastle, *The Life of William Cavendish* (1872), p. 154; Hunt, pp. 120–39.

16. Simeon Ashe, *A Continuation of True Intelligence* (1644), p. 7; around 4,000 Royalists perished, twice the number of Roundheads.

17. Belvoir MSS QZ/24 f. 55, Lord Ferdinando Fairfax to the Committee of Both Kingdoms, 6 July 1644: 'Right Honorable Wee wrote to your Lordships of the cullors Wee had taken from the enemey And have sent this gent who was an actor in the bussines of purpose to cary so many of them as upon a sudden wee could as yet receaue from the sowers who esteeme it a credite to keepe them. The victorie which God hath given us is very great And wee shall omitt nothing within our power to improve it to the advantage of the Comonn cause & the good of both Kingdomes Wee rest Your Lordships affectionat freinds &

servants Leuen Fer:fairfax Manchester from the league befor York 6th July 1644 Wee haue ressaved your letter of the 3d.'

18. For the Newbury witch reports see http://roy25booth.blogspot. co.uk/2011/09/witch-at-newbury-1643.html; for more on Boy and his legend see Mark Stoyle, *The Black Legend of Prince Rupert's Dog: Witchcraft and Propaganda During the English Civil War* (2011).

19. *The Life, Diary, and Correspondence of Sir William Dugdale*, ed. William Hamper (1827), p. 70.

20. Vernon F. Snow, *Essex the Rebel* (1970), p. 451.

21. Carlton, p. 244.

22. Ibid.

23. They won two victories that September.

24. BL, Add. MS 4106, ff. 205r–v., 6 May 1643.

25. Of 7,740 soldiers estimated to have come from Ireland between October 1643 and March 1644 only about 1,200 were Irish; see Mark Stoyle, *Soldiers and Strangers* (2005), pp. 53–62 and 209–10.

26. Charles I, *The King's Cabinet Opened: or, Certain Packets of Secret Letters & Papers* (1645), letter 9.

27. CSPD 1644–5 (159).

28. Robert Brenner, *Merchants and Revolution* (2003), p. 506.

29. The Junto, which had dominated the first year of the Long Parliament, had split into war and peace parties in the winter of 1642–3. The peace party had included men like Holland and Northumberland, who were anxious to make a moderate peace with Charles as soon as possible. The old war party had included those who had invited the Scots into England for the Bishops' War of 1640, and who wanted to ensure that Charles was stripped of all meaningful power: Warwick, Essex, Saye and Sele, Pym (who had since died of cancer), Lord Brooke (killed in 1643), and others.

30. In the House of Lords they included such former war-party stalwarts as Viscount Saye and Sele, but also that former peace-party grandee Northumberland.

31. Equally the Spanish had close ties to a number of Independents who saw Louis XIV's France as the great Catholic power and threat of the future, and men like Warwick as stuck in a fantasy of the Elizabethan past.

32. There were many MPs with a reverence for Presbyterianism who nevertheless backed Cromwell and his allies as the men who would defeat the king. Equally, many of the Presbyterian grandees disliked the notion of a Scottish-style system of church government with councils of elders, but were glad of Scottish military support against their rivals. Neither establishing Presbyterianism nor any other form of church government was the overriding concern. Most on both sides of Parliament were Erastian. They were prepared to accept a national Presbyterian church managed by Parliament, rather than Scottish-style councils of elders. London too was divided between a radical minority who supported the Independents, and the moderates who had dominated the City's Common Council since the radical-led constitutional changes to the municipality in 1642. These wanted a restored monarchy that would back their magistracy and believed Presbyterian church courts and Scottish-style supervisory assemblies of elders would transfer local church government into their hands for the enforcement of discipline and order. They differed, therefore, from Parliament's 'political Presbyterians' who wanted the state ruling the church. David Scott, *Politics and War in the Three Stuart Kingdoms, 1637–49* (2004), p. 86; Brenner, p. 462.

33. The Self-Denying Ordinance was passed the following day.

34. *The King's Cabinet Opened*, p. 7.

Chapter 18: Evil Women

1. *ODNB.*

2. CSPV 1643–7 (194).

3. Charles I, *The King's Cabinet Opened: or, Certain Packets of Secret Letters & Papers* (1645), p. 24.

4. Ibid., Charles to Henrietta Maria, 9 January 1645.

5. Edward, Earl of Clarendon, *The History of the Rebellion and Civil Wars in England*, ed. W. D. Macray (1888), Vol. III, p. 502. The fate of his three younger children, all in Parliament's hands, was also on Charles's mind. Elizabeth and Henry had been placed by Parliament in the care of Lucy Carlisle's eldest brother, the Earl of Northumberland. Lucy, like Holland, was a member of the Presbyterian party that wanted a negotiated peace. Northumberland was allied to the Independents who wanted Charles's utter defeat and Charles distrusted him as 'one in whom Parliament confided so much'; Clarendon, Vol. III, p. 449.

6. Jonathan Wilshire and Susan Green, *The Siege of Leicester 1645* (1970), with images of MS letters, pp. 12, 18.

7. Richard Simmonds, *The Complete Military Diary* (1989), p. 51.

8. Clarendon, Vol. IV, p. 39; *Letters of Queen Henrietta Maria*, ed. Mary Anne Everett Green (1857), p. 304.

9. Simmonds, p. 52.

10. Ibid.

11. Clarendon, Vol. IV, p. 39.

12. Samuel Rawson Gardiner, *History of the Great Civil War, 1642–1649* (1886/1987), Vol. II, p. 233.

13. Charles Carlton, *Going to the Wars: The Experience of the British Civil Wars, 1638–1651* (1992), p. 177.

14. *Letters of Queen Henrietta Maria*, ed. Green, p. 304.

15. *The King's Cabinet Opened*, p. 14.

16. H. C. B. Rogers, *Battles and Generals of the Civil Wars* (1968), pp. 208, 209.

17. Malcolm Wanklyn, *The Warrior Generals* (2010), p. 162.

18. Sir Henry Slingsby, *Diary* (1836), p. 152.

19. Ibid.

20. Clarendon, Vol. IV, p. 45.

21. Wanklyn, p. 165.
22. Ibid.
23. Gardiner, Vol. II, p. 250.
24. 'A Most Perfect Relation' quoted in Glenn Ford, *Naseby* (2004), p. 285.
25. Fewer than 1,000 Royalist soldiers were killed in the battle and its aftermath. Four times as many were simply taken prisoner.
26. BL, E.127 (39), 'A True Declaration of Kingstons Entertainment of the Cavaliers' (22 November 1642); Mark Stoyle, 'The Road to Farndon Field: Explaining the Massacre of the Royalist Women at Naseby', *English Historical Review*, Vol. 123, No. 503 (August 2008), p. 907; Diane Purkiss, *The English Civil War: A People's History* (2006), p. 138.
27. *Parliament's Post*, 14 July 1645.
28. He had even shielded her from knowledge of his own mental suffering, deleting words and phrases where he thought he was revealing too much. Sarah Poynting, 'Rhetorical Strategies in the Letters of Charles I' in Jason McElligott and David Smith (eds.), *Royalists and Royalism* (2007), p. 145. Also see Derek Hirst, 'Reading the Royal Romance: Or, Intimacy in a King's Cabinet', *The Seventeenth Century*, Vol. 18, No. 2 (Autumn 2003), pp. 211–29.
29. Marchamont Nedham, in his newspaper *Mercurius Britanicus*.
30. *Eikon Basilike*.
31. Laura Knoppers, *Politicizing Domesticity from Henrietta Maria to Milton's Eve* (2011), pp. 44–66.
32. Clarendon, Vol. IV, p. 74.
33. Ibid., p. 78.
34. Gardiner, Vol. II, p. 363.
35. *Mercurius Rusticus* quoted in G. N. Godwin, *The Civil War in Hampshire 1642–45 and the Story of Basing House* (2010), p. 241.
36. *The Kingdom's Weekly Post*, BL, E.304.28.
37. Godwin, p. 142.

38. Francis Bacon, *Of the Advancement and Proficience of Learning* (BL, Humanities, C.46.i.1.), annotation by Charles I. Cromwell would move into a house in Drury Lane the following year. Perhaps it was this death that opened the vacancy. Thanks to Sarah Poynting for this reference and transcription.

39. Hugh Peter, *The Fall and Last Relation of Basing House* (1645), pp. 2, 6.

40. New tax-raising powers had been instituted and an Independent-dominated executive committee created – the Army Committee, which oversaw army funding and recruitment.

41. Robert Brenner, *Merchants and Revolution* (2003), pp. 475, 476. London was a very different place from 1642. Then a radical campaign had ousted the rich, Royalist City elite represented in the Upper Chamber of the Court of Aldermen and handed power to the hosiers, fishmongers, goldsmiths and woolen drapers elected to the Common Council. Now these same councillors sought to crush political and religious radicalisation in order to maintain the status quo they had come to control. Their allies in Parliament did not, however, share their enthusiasm for Scottish-style Presbyterianism, with church government controlled by councils of elders. The 'political Presbyterians' led by the Earl of Essex simply wanted government of the Church of England by king and bishops to be replaced by government by Parliament, so extending the control landowners maintained over parish livings to oversight by MPs (most of whom came from the same classes). See note 32, Chapter 17.

Chapter 19: 'The Golden Ball'

1. *Desiderata Curiosa* ii Lib. IX, p. 20.

2. *Letters of King Charles I*, ed. Sir Charles Petrie (1935), p. 176.

3. There remained a substantial body of Royalist opinion that opposed any dealings with the Scots and their French allies.

These so-called 'patriot' Royalists wanted the king restored at English hands and were keen for him to return to his capital as soon as possible. The queen's party differed. Indeed, the split between the Royalists was almost a mirror image of the Parliamentarian splits. The Parliamentarians were split between the pro-Scots Presbyterian party and the anti-Scots Independents. The Royalists were split between the pro-Scots queen's party and the patriots who wanted no outside intervention (but did not, of course, share the Independents' religious agenda). The French had their own agenda. Cardinal Mazarin wanted a weak but restored king, ruling with their friends amongst the queen's Royalist party, the Westminster Presbyterians – who included old Francophiles like Holland – the Scots and also the Royalist Irish (but not the Catholic Confederalists, who had too many friends in Spain). David Scott, *Politics and War in the Three Stuart Kingdoms, 1637–49* (2004), pp. 111, 113.

4. Lord Lothian, CSPD 5 May 1646 (13).
5. Scott, pp. 118–19.
6. 1635, http://www.localhistories.org/newcastle.html.
7. F. J. Varley, *The Siege of Oxford* (1932), pp. 142, 143.
8. Ibid., p. 142.
9. Belvoir MSS QZ/26: Original Manuscripts 1646 f. 11AA, June 1646.
10. Thomas Birch, *The Court and Times of Charles I* (1849), Vol. II, p. 410.
11. Ibid., pp. 409, 410.
12. Scott, p. 123.
13. Also present was his favourite sister, Frances, Marchioness of Hertford, who had been painted by Van Dyck wearing the relic of their father's hair, and whose husband was a Royalist.
14. David Nichol Smith, *Characters from the Histories and Memoirs of the Seventeenth Century* (1918), pp. 218–19.

15. Samuel Rawson Gardiner, *History of the Great Civil War* (1886/1987), Vol. III, p. 186; *Moderate Intelligencer*, 24 December 1646.

16. Patrick Maule, Earl of Panmure to Sir Archibald Johnston, Earl Wariston, 23 January 1647, in Sir David Dalrymple (ed.), *Memorials and Letters Relating to the History of Britain in the Reign of Charles the First* (1766), pp. 190–1.

17. *Eikon Basilike*, p. 56.

18. The Earl of Lauderdale quoted in David Scott, *Politics and War in the Three Stuart Kingdoms, 1637–49* (2004), p 129.

19. 'Vox Militaris: Or an Apologetical Declaration Concerning the Officers and Souldiers of the Armie, under the Command of his Excellency Sr. Thomas Fairfax', 11 August 1647, p. 2.

20. Described by Parliamentary Commissioners, 1651; http://www.british-history.ac.uk/rchme/northants/vol3/pp103–109.

21. Gardiner, Vol. III, pp. 271, 272.

22. BL, E.391 (8); Robert Ashton, *Counter Revolution* (1994), p. 19.

Chapter 20: 'A Clouded Majesty'

1. Fairfax had been in Bury St Edmunds when Joyce had visited Cromwell in London. Cromwell may have assumed that Fairfax would concur later with his decision – as Fairfax had. It was later suggested, however, that Fairfax had not been given any pre-warning of the seizure of the king as Cromwell had decided Fairfax should know no more than he was 'pleased to carve and chew for him'. Andrew Hopper, *Black Tom: Sir Thomas Fairfax and the English Revolution* (2007), pp. 212–13.

2. 'A Declaration or Representation from his Excellency Sir Thomas Fairfax and the Army under his Command' (14 June), in the *Army Book of Declarations* (1647), pp. 37–44.

3. It was not his first meeting. That had been with Fairfax on 7 June.

4. *The Memoirs of Sir John Berkeley* (1699), p. 34.

5. Charles's visible reaction was recorded by a witness; R. Huntington (ed.), *Sundry reasons inducing Major Robert Huntingdon to lay down his commission* (1648), repr. in Francis Maseres (ed.), *Select tracts relating to the civil wars in England* etc. (1815), Vol. 2, p. 400.

6. *Letters of King Charles I*, ed. Sir Charles Petrie (1935), p. 231.

7. Maseres (ed.), Vol. I, p. 365; Robert Ashton, *Counter Revolution* (1994), p. 208.

8. Mary Anne Everett Green, *Lives of the Princesses of England* (1850), Vol. 6, p. 355.

9. Hopper, pp. 174–6.

10. *Moderate Intelligencer*, 22 July 1647.

11. David Scott, 'Politics in the Long Parliament' in George Southcombe and Grant Tapsell (eds.), *Revolutionary England, c.1630–c.1660: Essays for Clive Holmes* (2016), pp. 32–55.

12. Not least one that excluded the Scots and would permit the return of the Church of England of the old prayer book.

13. Huntington (ed.) in Maseres (ed.), Vol. II, p. 399.

14. They included Denzil Holles and Sir Philip Stapilton.

15. *Memoirs of Sir John Berkeley*; Maseres (ed.), Vol. II, p. 368.

16. That is excluding women, servants or other dependents. The Levellers had grown out of a group of militants who had come together in opposition to the London Presbyterians, who were particularly powerful in the City's municipal and church government. In that respect they had been on the militant wing of the Independents. They were now, however, challenging the power of the grandees of both parties.

17. *Journal of the House of Lords*, 23 July 1647.

18. *Weekly Intelligencer*, 16 September 1647; Green, Vol. 6, p. 359.

19. Richard Lovelace, 'To my worthy friend Master Peter Lely on that excellent picture of his Majesty and the Duke of York, Drawn by Him at Hampton Court'.

20. For a full explanation of Ireton's thinking see Sarah Mortimer, 'Henry Ireton and the Limits of Radicalism' in George Southcombe

and Grant Tapsell (eds.), *Revolutionary England, c.1630–c.1660: Essays for Clive Holmes* (2016), pp. 55–73.

21. *The Agreement of the People for a Firm and Present Peace upon Grounds of Common Right.*

22. C. H. Firth (ed.), *The Clarke Papers*, Vol. I (1891), p. 307.

23. Ibid., p. 322.

24. Samuel Rawson Gardiner, *History of the Great Civil War* (1886/1987), Vol. IV, p. 11; Clarendon MSS 2645.

25. Maseres (ed.), Vol. II, p. 375.

26. Numbers 35:33.

27. Raymond Phineas Stearns, *Strenuous Puritan: Hugh Peter, 1598–1660* (1954), p. 316.

28. John Fox, *The King's Smuggler* (2011) p. 118.

29. Maseres (ed.), Vol. II, p. 373.

30. CSPV 10 December 1647 (60).

Chapter 21: Royalist Rising

1. Southampton had attended on the king in the last few days before his escape; E. Whalley, *A More Full Relation of the Manner and Circumstances of his Majesty's Departure from Hampton Court*, 22 November 1647 (BL, E416/23).

2. John Rushworth, *Historical Collections of Private Passages of State*, Vol. 7 (1721), pp. 871–2.

3. Edward, Earl of Clarendon, *The History of the Rebellion and Civil Wars in England*, ed. W. D. Macray (1888), Vol. IV, p. 264.

4. The royal chaplain in question was Dr Henry Hammond, who would have been made a bishop had he not died on the eve of the Restoration.

5. Charles had, at first, the freedom of the Isle of Wight and he intended to make good use of it. On 17 December a ship sent by Henrietta Maria for his escape anchored in the waters off Carisbrooke. Charles pulled on his riding boots and 'with great

joy, ran to the window to see how the wind stood'. It was against them. The ship was trapped in the harbour for six days and his opportunity was lost. His hopes of escape had been noticed, however, so he lost his freedom and his friends. John Ashburnham, *A Narrative by John Ashburnham* etc. (1830), Vol. II, p. 120.

6. Robert Lockyer (ed.), *The Trial of Charles I: A Contemporary Account Taken from the Memoirs of Sir Thomas Herbert and John Rushworth* (1974), p. 36.

7. He scribbled the names of characters and preferred titles alongside his favourite plays – comedies for the most part. Thanks to Sarah Poynting for this information.

8. David Scott, *Politics and War in the Three Stuart Kingdoms, 1637–49* (2004), p. 159.

9. CSPD 2 February 1648.

10. *Journal of the House of Lords*, Vol. X, 24 February 1648.

11. *Journal of the House of Commons*, Vol. V, 16 March 1648.

12. Ashburnham, Vol. II, p. 124.

13. CSPV 1648 (131), (133); *ODNB* Joseph Bampfield and Anne Halkett; Linda Porter, *Royal Renegades* (2016), pp. 184–5.

14. J. S. Clarke (ed.), *The Life of James the Second* (1816), Vol. I, pp. 32–3; James had been reassured that he wasn't bound to his promise to Parliament not to escape. He was underage, and since this was a matter of state, he had needed the king's consent to take such an oath.

15. He had also been under suspicion with the Independents after the Essex petition (the county where he had his land base).

16. On Anne of Austria and her court, see *Mémoires de Madame de Motteville*, tr. Katherine Wormeley, Vol. I (1886), pp. 286, 122.

17. Ibid., p. 123.

18. Karen Britland, 'Exile or Homecoming? Henrietta Maria in France, 1644–69' in Philip Mansel and Torsten Riotte (eds.), *Monarchy and Exile* (2011), p. 127.

19. *Mémoires de Madame de Motteville*, Vol. I, p. 286.

20. Clarendon, Vol. IV, p. 414.

21. David Lloyd, *Memoirs of the Lives, Actions, Sufferings and Deaths of Those Noble Personages, that Suffered by Death, Sequestration, Decimation, Or Otherwise, for the Protestant Religion from 1637 to 1660. Continued to 1666. With the Life and Martyrdom of King Charles I* (1668), p. 678; Andrew Marvell, 'An Elegy Upon the Death of My Lord Francis Villiers'.

22. Clarendon, Vol. IV, p. 318. When the army had ridden into London in the summer of 1647, Fairfax had, in effect, conquered England for the Independents. Conquest carried with it the right by the victors to make or break laws as they pleased – to rule as tyrants. This was the slavery Holland referred to.

23. Sir Bulstrode Whitelocke, *Memorials of the English Affairs* etc. (1853), Vol. I, p. 328. Distrusted since his brief defection to Oxford in 1643, he was not even to be allowed his seat in the House of Lords.

24. Several Surrey men had been killed in May when they had delivered a county petition to Parliament demanding a treaty with the king.

25. He is buried in Westminster Abbey.

26. Holland joined 150 other prisoners at St Neots. His George with its blue ribbon – the Order of the Garter – was taken along with other personal goods.

27. *A Great victory obtained by Collonell Scroope against the Duke of Buckingham, at Saint Needs in Huntingtonshire. On Munday July the 10th* (1648), p. 5.

28. This is in a letter preserved at Yale. https://beta.worldcat.org/archivegrid/collection/data/702172379.

29. Scott, *Politics and War*, p. 175.

30. Samuel Rawson Gardiner, *History of the Great Civil War* (1886/1987), Vol. IV, p. 162.

Chapter 22: The Red-Haired Mistress

1. Lita Rose Betcherman, *Court Lady & Country Wife* (2006), p. 299.
2. *ODNB*.
3. BL, Add. MS 19368, f. 112.
4. Sarah Poynting, 'Deciphering the King: Charles I's Letters to Jane Whorwood', *The Seventeenth Century*, Vol. 21, No. 1 (2006), pp. 128–40.
5. Edward, Earl of Clarendon, *The History of the Rebellion and Civil Wars in England*, ed. W. D. Macray (1888), Vol. IV, p. 388.
6. David Scott, *Politics and War in the Three Stuart Kingdoms, 1637–49* (2004), p. 177.
7. Clarendon, Vol. IV, p. 430.
8. Robert Wilcher, 'What Was the King's Book for?: The Evolution of "Eikon Basilike"', *Yearbook of English Studies*, Vol. 21, Politics, Patronage and Literature in England 1558–1658 Special Number (1991), pp. 218–28.
9. Clarendon, Vol. IV, p. 463.
10. *A Remonstrance of his Excellency Lord Thomas Fairfax* (1648), p. 64.
11. Richard Royston, *The Works of Charles I* (1661), p. 137; C. V. Wedgwood, *The Trial of Charles I* (1964), p. 33.
12. *Letters of King Charles I*, ed. Sir Charles Petrie (1935), p. 241.
13. Ibid., p. 239. Petrie is mistaken in placing Charles at Newport.
14. Robert Lockyer (ed.), *The Trial of Charles I: A Contemporary Account Taken from the Memoirs of Sir Thomas Herbert and John Rushworth* (1974), pp. 53, 57, 58.
15. David Underdown, *Pride's Purge* (1971), p. 143.
16. Ibid., p. 144.
17. Raymond Phineas Stearns, *Strenuous Puritan: Hugh Peter, 1598–1660* (1954), p. 326.
18. Also missing was the diamond-studded great George that Charles had bestowed on the Midnight Lion, Gustavus

Adolphus, and the coat of mail that Charles's ancestor Edward IV had worn during the battles of the Wars of the Roses and which had hung over his tomb since 1483. The bronze angels and other statuary that Henry VIII had hoped would be used to make up his tomb had been sold or defaced, although some of it still survives. See Leanda de Lisle, *Tudor: The Family Story* (2013), p. 487, note 11.

19. Stearns, p. 330.
20. The French agent in London the Sieur de Grignon reported that the Parliamentarian Basil Feilding, Earl of Denbigh, had arrived at Windsor with a 'final' deal for the king backed by Cromwell. According to the rumours Denbigh hoped Charles would agree to becoming a puppet ruler in exchange for his life. Denbigh was the 1st Duke of Buckingham's nephew. His father had been Keeper of the Great Wardrobe and the family preserved some of the clothes worn by the royal children: there was a little apron with gardening figures embroidered in blackwork, a pair of black satin and crepe breeches stamped with a paisley design, as well as purses and gloves, some dating back to the Tudors.
21. Sir Bulstrode Whitelocke, *Memorials of the English Affairs* etc. (1853), Vol. I, p. 365.
22. Wilcher, p. 223.
23. 'A Winter Dream' quoted in Jonathan Scott, *England's Troubles* (2000), p. 157.
24. Samuel Rawson Gardiner, *History of the Great Civil War* (1886/1987), Vol. IV, p. 289.
25. 'And do also Declare, that the Commons of England, in Parliament assembled, being chosen by, and representing the People, have the Supreme Power in this Nation: And do also Declare, That whatsoever is enacted, or declared for Law, by the Commons, in Parliament assembled, hath the Force of Law; and all the People of this Nation are concluded thereby, although the Consent and Concurrence of King, or House of Peers, be not had thereunto.'

Chapter 23: The King's Trial

1. On 18 December 1648.
2. Boxing Day, 1648: Geoffrey Robertson, *The Tyrannicide Brief* (2005), p. 135.
3. Samuel Rawson Gardiner, *History of the Great Civil War* (1886/1987), Vol. IV, p. 290.
4. Quoted in Sean Kelsey, 'The Trial of Charles I', *English Historical Review*, Vol. 118, No. 477 (June 2003), p. 592.
5. The purged Presbyterian MP was called Edward Stephens.
6. The first proofs were ready by 14 January.
7. The house of Sir Thomas Cotton, a former MP for Huntingdon.
8. Edward, Earl of Clarendon, *The History of the Rebellion and Civil Wars in England*, ed. W. D. Macray (1888), Vol. IV, p. 483.
9. His own barber, Tom Davies, had been described as an enemy of the state in 1642; CSPD 1641–3 (274).
10. Such a hat, said to be his, is now in the Ashmolean Museum.
11. 'This is conceived will be very ominous', a news report recorded; Sir Philip Warwick, *Memories of the Reigne of Charles I* (1701), pp. 339–40.
12. *King Charles, His Tryall &c* (1649), pp. 5, 6.
13. Ibid.
14. Ibid., p. 8.
15. Ibid., pp. 9–15.
16. Gilbert Burnet, *History of My Own Times* (1724/1833), Vol. I, p. 85.
17. Mrs Nelson, sister of Sir Purbeck Temple.
18. For Charles's hopes and attitude to the trial, see Kelsey, pp. 583–616.
19. *King Charles, His Tryall &c*, pp. 39, 47.

Chapter 24: Execution

1. Sir Purbeck Temple in William Cobbett, *Cobbett's Complete Collection of State Trials* (1809–26), eds. Thomas Bayly Howell et al., Vol. V, p. 1151.

2. Sir Philip Warwick quoted in David Nichol Smith, *Characters from the Histories and Memoirs of the Seventeenth Century* (1918), p. 54.

3. An organ from this period survives today in the small church of St Nicholas at Stanford-on-Avon in the Midlands.

4. Ronald Lightbown, 'Charles I and the Art of the Goldsmith' in Arthur MacGregor (ed.), *The Late King's Goods* (1989), pp. 251, 252.

5. Sir Thomas Herbert's account in Robert Lockyer (ed.), *The Trial of Charles I: A Contemporary Account Taken from the Memoirs of Sir Thomas Herbert and John Rushworth* (1974), p. 119.

6. By the artist Gerard van Honthorst; *The Correspondence of Elizabeth Stuart, Queen of Bohemia, Volume I: 1603–1631*, ed. Nadine Akkerman (2015), p. 507.

7. Herbert in Lockyer (ed.), p. 120.

8. CSPV 1649 (224).

9. Sent on 13 January and brought by Henry Seymour, see W. Sanderson, *Life and Raigne of King Charles* (1658), p. 1135.

10. *Eikon Basilike.*

11. Sir Philip Warwick, quoted in Smith, p. 112.

12. Herbert in Lockyer (ed.), p. 123.

13. Ibid.

14. Roger Williams to John Winthrop Jr, 26 May 1649, 3, MHS Collection IX, 286; Cobbett, Vol. V, p. 1132; Isaiah 14:19.

15. CSPV 1647–52 (236).

16. Herbert in Lockyer (ed.), p. 124.

17. CSPV 1647–52 (246).

18. Herbert in Lockyer (ed.), p. 126.

19. CSPV 1647–52 (246).

20. Ibid.

21. This witness was a friend of Sir Philip Warwick, who recorded his story.

22. HMC, Lord de L'Isle and Dudley MSS, Vol. VI, p. 583.

23. Samuel Rawson Gardiner, *History of the Great Civil War* (1886/1987), Vol. IV, p. 323.

24. HMC, Lord de L'Isle and Dudley MSS, Vol. VI, p. 583.

25. Sir Ralph Payne-Gallwey, *A history of the George worn on the scaffold by Charles I* (1908), p. 28.

26. In the contemporary mica images of the execution kept at Carisbrooke Castle, the next image is of a blue sky, with wheeling birds; George Evelyn to John Evelyn, 30 January 1648, BL, Add. MS 78303, Evelyn Papers: George Evelyn Corr, f. 34.

27. Andrew Marvell, 'An Horatian Ode Upon Cromwell's Return from Ireland'.

28. William Dugdale quoted in Robert B. Partridge, '*O Horrable Murder*': *The Trial, Execution and Burial of King Charles I* (1998), p. 97.

29. Ibid., p. 96. When Charles's corpse was exhumed in the nineteenth century it was found that his hair was cut short at the back.

30. CSPV 1647–52 (246).

31. Sir Purbeck Temple in Cobbett, Vol. V, p. 1151.

32. Edward, Earl of Clarendon, *The History of the Rebellion and Civil Wars in England*, ed. W. D. Macray (1888), Vol. IV, p. 492.

33. Mica miniature at Carisbrooke Castle; Sir Purbeck Temple in Cobbett, Vol. V, p. 1151.

34. A contemporary diary notes that 'the man who had held the head up then threw it down', so that it 'bruised the face'; *The Life, Diary, and Correspondence of Sir William Dugdale*, ed. William Hamper (1827), p. 96.

35. *Mémoires de Madame de Motteville*, tr. Katherine Wormeley, Vol. II (1902), pp. 84, 86.

36. Thomas Birch, *The Court and Times of Charles I* (1849), Vol. II, pp. 381, 382.

Chapter 25: Resurrection

1. Sir Thomas Herbert, *Memoirs of the Last Two Years of the Reign of Charles I* (1815), p. 198.

2. Edward, Earl of Clarendon, *The History of the Rebellion and Civil Wars in England*, ed. W. D. Macray (1888), Vol. IV, p. 493; Herbert, p. 199.

3. *Journal of the House of Commons*, 8 February 1649: what the Commons resolution referred to as Henry VIII's 'chapel' was just the room in which the statuary etc. for his tomb (sold and broken up in 1646) had been stored, along with the marble sarcophagus that yet remained. See Leanda de Lisle, *Tudor: The Family Story* (2013), p. 487, note 11.

4. The Canon of Windsor, David Stokes, later claimed Charles planned to build a mausoleum for himself and future kings there.

5. *Journal of the House of Commons*, 8 February 1649.

6. Herbert, p. 203.

7. Allan Fea, *Memoirs of the Martyr King* (1904), pp. 149–50, and note pp. 151–2. He had also taken some velvet.

8. Ronald Lightbown, 'Charles I and the Art of the Goldsmith' in Arthur MacGregor (ed.), *The Late King's Goods* (1989), pp. 252–4.

9. Fea, p. 150.

10. Herbert, pp. 205–6.

11. Barbara Donagan, 'A Courtier's Progress: Greed and Consistency in the Life of the Earl of Holland', *Historical Journal*, Vol. 19, No. 2 (June 1976), p. 352, quoting the scaffold speech.

12. HMC, Lord de L'Isle and Dudley MSS, Vol. VI, p. 587.

13. Approximately £1,400 today.

14. *The Several Speeches of Duke Hamilton Earl of Cambridge, Henry Earl of Holland, and Arthur Lord Capel, Upon the Scaffold Immediately before their Execution, On Friday the 9. of March. Also the several Exhortations, and Conferences with them, upon the Scaffold, by Dr Sibbald, Mr Bolton, & Mr Hodges* (1649).

15. *The Correspondence of Bishop Brian Duppa and Sir Justinian Isham 1650–1660*, ed. Sir Gyles Isham (1955), p. 75.

16. Chevreuse had returned to England only once since the civil war and most unwillingly. In 1645 she had been forced, yet again, into exile from France, and was captured in the Channel by the Parliamentarian navy. They took her to the Isle of Wight and offered her back to Cardinal Mazarin who didn't want her and so Chevreuse had journeyed on to Flanders. Victor Cousin, *Secret History of the French Court Under Richelieu and Mazarin* (1859), p. 165.

17. Michael Prawdin, *Marie de Rohan* (1971), p. 190.

18. Apologists for these events insist it has to be seen in the context of the Thirty Years War. But the Thirty Years War had ended several years previously. It has to be seen in the context of British history, not that of Germany.

19. Carola Oman, *The Winter Queen* (1938, revd edn 2000), p. 157.

20. Erin Griffey, *On Display* (2015), p. 186.

21. These details are all given in a contemporary letter. HMC, Lord de L'Isle and Dudley MSS, Vol. VI, p. 623.

22. *Mémoires de Madame de Motteville*, tr. Katherine Wormeley, Vol. II (1902), p. 86.

23. *Lettres de Henriette-Marie de France, reine d'Angleterre, à sa soeur Christine, duchesse de Savoie, Vol. V*, ed. Hermann Ferrero (1881), p. 126.

24. The 'Assumption' section of a painting of the Assumption of the Virgin was, however, cut off while in his care.

25. Francis Haskell, *The King's Pictures* (2003), pp. 146–50.

26. James had been set up with his own court, and was an active Lord High Admiral: a title first given to him by his father aged five.

Postscript

1. Edward Hyde, Earl of Clarendon quoted in David Nichol Smith, *Characters from the Histories and Memoirs of the Seventeenth Century* (1918), p. 53.

2. Clarendon quoted in ibid., p. 49.

3. Peter Heylyn quoted in John Milton, *Observations Upon the Articles of Peace* (1649), p. 96.
4. Ibid.
5. William Laud, *Works* (1847–60), Vol. III, p. 443.
6. Clarendon quoted in Smith, p. 51.

Appendix

1. *Mémoires de M. de La Rochefoucauld, etc. Together with the Memoirs of A. P. de La Rochefoucauld, Duke de Doudeauville, written by himself,* ed. François Claude (1861), Vol. II, pp. 12–13. See also *Mémoires de Louis-Henri de Loménie, Comte de Brienne, secrétaire d'état sous Louis XIV* (1828), Vol. I, pp. 331–45.
2. The only gift of diamonds mentioned in 1625, when Buckingham had last seen Anne, was a collar Buckingham had been given by Louis. Besides the French memoirs Sir Roger Coke also claimed the queen had sent Buckingham, if not a necklace, then her garter 'and an exceedingly rich jewel'; Roger Coke, *A detection of the court and state of England during the four last reigns* ... (1696), p. 234. On the diamonds mentioned in 1625 see CSPV 1625–6 (153). On real plots against Richelieu and the key role of Chevreuse, possibly the originator of the necklace legend, see http://journal.xmera.org/volume-2–no-1–summer-2010/articles/dobbie.pdf.

INDEX

Index

penguin.co.uk/vintage